U0165048

"一带一路"倡议下
城市与产业国际合作论坛对话集

Dialogue on International Cooperation Forum for Cities and
Industries under the Belt and Road Initiative

智库纽带·城市伙伴·产业合作

THINK TANK LINK · CITY PARTNERSHIP · INDUSTRIAL COOPERATION

中英双语版

本书编写组 | 编

中央编译出版社
CCTP Central Compilation & Translation Press

图书在版编目（CIP）数据

"一带一路"倡议下城市与产业国际合作论坛对话集：
智库纽带·城市伙伴·产业合作：汉文、英文／《"一带
一路"倡议下城市与产业国际合作论坛对话集》编写组
编．—北京：中央编译出版社，2020.9
ISBN 978-7-5117-3690-1

Ⅰ．①一… Ⅱ．①一… Ⅲ．①"一带一路"–国际合
作–中国–文集–汉、英 Ⅳ．①F125-53

中国版本图书馆 CIP 数据核字（2018）第 300338 号

"一带一路"倡议下城市与产业国际合作论坛对话集：智库纽带·城市伙伴·
产业合作：中英双语版

责任编辑	李南男　赵　灿	
责任印制	刘　慧	
出版发行	中央编译出版社	
地　　址	北京西城区车公庄大街乙 5 号鸿儒大厦 B 座（100044）	
电　　话	（010）52612345（总编室）	（010）52612341（编辑室）
	（010）52612316（发行）	（010）52612369（网站）
传　　真	（010）66515838	
经　　销	全国新华书店	
印　　刷	北京紫瑞利印刷有限公司	
开　　本	710 毫米×1000 毫米　1/16	
字　　数	422 千字	
印　　张	26.75	
版　　次	2020 年 9 月第 1 版	
印　　次	2020 年 9 月第 1 次印刷	
定　　价	158.00 元	

新浪微博：@中央编译出版社　　　**微　　信**：中央编译出版社(ID: cctphome)
淘宝店铺：中央编译出版社直销店(http://shop108367160.taobao.com)　　（010）52612322

本社常年法律顾问：北京市吴栾赵阎律师事务所律师　闫军　梁勤
凡有印装质量问题，本社负责调换，电话：(010) 52612322

前　言

本书是由国内高端智库深圳市发展研究中心与中国工业经济联合会共同举办的"一带一路"倡议下城市与产业国际合作论坛（深圳）嘉宾讨论与发言的汇辑。该论坛是改革开放 40 周年深圳第一场国际论坛，更是 2018 年"一带一路"框架下深圳所举办的一场高规格国际活动。

深圳作为我国对外开放的重要窗口，在推进中央提出的"一带一路"倡议方面同样发挥着极为重要的作用。本次论坛的举办正是对贯彻落实"一带一路"倡议的积极响应，其目的也是充分利用深圳这一重要对外开放平台的优势，进一步促进国内外政商学界对"一带一路"倡议的深入理解，同时通过对话，加深交流、凝聚共识、寻求合作，是习近平主席所提出"五通"中"民心相通"的重要体现。

本书依照论坛的设置和安排，分为主旨演讲、主题论坛、智库纽带、城市伙伴、产业合作、中医药国际化等部分。其中主旨演讲与主题论坛环节延请我国多位省部级领导，就"一带一路"倡议的重要意义、深远影响，以及如何更好实现"一带一路"倡议等主题进行阐释。同时在这个环节也有多位国外政商学界高端人士就如何让"一带一路"倡议更好地在其所在国落地，如何实现"一带一路"倡议落实与本国发展双赢等问题进行了论述。在智库纽带、城市伙伴、产业合作等环节，重点围绕城市、产业与智库三大要素在"一带一路"建设中所能起到的巨大助力作用，邀请了各个有关领域的国内外高端智库学者、大型跨国企业高管就具体问题进行了阐述与讨论。

本书编写坚持以习近平新时代中国特色社会主义思想为指导，是一部"宣传中央精神和重大决策部署"以及"着眼提高中华文化国际话语权和感召力，服务'一带一路'国际合作"的应时之作。

本书翔实记录了论坛举办过程中，各位领导、中外学者及嘉宾紧紧围绕"一带一路"主题所进行的精彩演讲与深入对话。书中内容体现出当前外方多国政界人士，以及中外学界、商界对于我国"一带一路"倡议的认识正在不断加深，共识也在不断增多。此外，本书为中英双语版，更有益于促进外方理解支持"一带一路"倡议。

目　录

Content

中文版

开幕致辞

2018 年 1 月 17 日

熊梦（主持人）：尊敬的各位领导，各位嘉宾，女士们、先生们！

"志合者，不以山海为远"，今天，中国工业经济联合会和深圳市人民政府发展研究中心，在这里共同举办"一带一路"倡议下城市与产业国际合作论坛。来自23个国家和地区的100多位官员、专家及智库、企业代表汇聚一堂，围绕"智库纽带·城市伙伴·产业合作"主题开展研讨，这对于推动沿线城市间实现更加紧密的合作，加强不同文明交流互鉴，共同推进"一带一路"建设，携手实现和平、发展、合作的美好愿望，具有重要现实意义。

首先，我谨代表会议主办方，向出席论坛的各位嘉宾、各位朋友，表示热烈的欢迎和衷心的感谢！

首先有请：

全国政协常委、经济委员会副主任、工业和信息化部部长、中国工业经济联合会会长李毅中先生；

中国公共外交协会会长、外交部原部长李肇星先生；

中国人民争取和平与裁军协会副会长、中共中央对外联络部原副部长于洪君先生；

中国工业经济联合会执行副会长路耀华先生；

中华中医药学会临床药理分会名誉会长、国家食品药品监督管理总局原副局长任德权先生；

国家中医药管理局国际合作司（港澳台办公室）司长、主任王笑频女士；

深圳市委常委、常务副市长刘庆生先生；

深圳市政府发展研究中心主任吴思康先生。

有请各位上台参与启动仪式。

出席今天论坛的外方嘉宾有：

克罗地亚国家商会总顾问、萨格勒布城市特别代表斯捷潘·梅西奇先生；

斯洛伐克共和国驻华使馆特命全权大使杜桑·贝拉先生；

突尼斯共和国驻华使馆大使迪亚·哈立德先生；

摩尔多瓦共和国驻华使馆临时代办马佳娜女士；

罗马尼亚巴克乌市市长科斯明·尼古拉先生；

希腊雅典副市长亚历山大·莫迪亚诺先生。

出席今天论坛的中方嘉宾有：

全国政协常委、经济委员会副主任、工业和信息化部部长、中国工业经济联合会李毅中先生；

中国公共外交协会会长、外交部原部长李肇星先生；

亚洲基础设施投资银行行长、财政部原副部长金立群先生；

中国人民争取和平与裁军协会副会长、中共中央对外联络部原副部长于洪君先生；

中国工业经济联合会执行副会长路耀华先生；

中华中医药学会临床药理分会名誉会长、国家食品药品监督管理总局原副局长任德权先生；

国务院参事王京生先生；

国务院参事室业务二司司长孙维佳先生；

国家中医药管理局国际合作司（港澳台办公室）司长、主任王笑频女士；

海南省人民政府副秘书长、研究室主任朱华友先生；

广东省卫生和计划生育委员会副主任、广东省中医药管理局局长徐庆锋先生；

深圳市委常委、常务副市长刘庆生先生；

汕尾市委常委、常务副市长邹广先生。

参加今天论坛的还有来自"一带一路"沿线国家和地区智库的专家学者、企业代表以及新闻媒体界的朋友们。

让我们再次以热烈的掌声对各位领导和嘉宾的到来表示欢迎！

现在，有请深圳市委常委、常务副市长刘庆生先生致辞并宣布大会开幕。

刘庆生：尊敬的李毅中先生、李肇星先生，各位来宾，女士们、先生们、朋友们，大家早上好！在这美好的时节我们相聚深圳，举办"一带一路"倡议下城市与产业国际合作论坛，共商创新合作大计，在此，我受王伟中书记、陈如桂市长的委托，谨代表深圳市委、市人民政府向各位来宾表示热烈的欢迎和衷心的感谢。

当今世界，和平与发展是时代的主题，开放与合作是时代的潮流，习近平主席高瞻远瞩地提出"推动构建人类命运共同体"，为共创人类美好未来指明了方向，为中国引领时代潮流和人类文明进步方向树立了鲜明旗帜，在这一背景下我们坚持把推动构建人类命运共同体和共建"一带一路"紧密结合起来，打造国际合作新平台，增添共同发展新动力，积极弘扬和平合作、开放包容、互学互建、互利共赢的丝路精神，为沿线各国的开放合作打开新的机会之窗。

深圳是中国第一个经济特区，也是中国对外开放的重要窗口，因改革开放而生，因改革开放而兴，因改革开放而强。过去的一年，深圳在严峻复杂的外部条件下，以习近平新时代中国特色社会主义思想为指导，推动经济社会实现更高质量、更有效益和更可持续的发展，预计 2017 年全市 GDP 突破 2.2 万亿元，人均 GDP 超过 18 万元，继续稳居全国各大城市前列，进出口总额达到 2.8 万亿元，连续 25 年位居全国第一，新增世界 500 强企业两家，累计达到 7 家，全市产业结构进一步优化，创新发展优势不断增强，全方位对外开放格局加快。深圳历史上就是海上丝绸之路的重要节点之一，经过 30 多年的改革与发展，与世界各国、各地区的经贸往来、科技合作、人文交流日益密切。

2017 年"一带一路"沿线有 41 个国家和地区在深圳投资，新设企业 302 个，增长 39.8%，开通了深圳至明思特、杜伊斯堡中欧班列，连接集装箱班轮达到 205 条，举办"一带一路"文化发展论坛、"一带一路"大型国际音乐节等人文交流活动。深圳愿意与"一带一路"沿线各国、各地区共同坚持开放合作、共赢未来，携手把"一带一路"建设成为和平之路、繁荣之路、创新之路、开放之路、文明之路。

本次论坛汇聚了众多来自"一带一路"国家的杰出代表，希望大家集思广益、增进友谊、广泛合作，在深圳率先开花结果，深圳也将极力为推进"一带一路"各项建设，为构筑人类命运共同体贡献更多智慧和力量，最后祝尊敬的各位来宾、各位朋友 2018 年健康、快乐、幸福，预祝论坛取得圆满成功，谢谢各位！

熊梦（主持人）：谢谢刘庆生先生热情洋溢的致辞。有请中国工业经济联合会执行副会长路耀华先生致辞。

路耀华：尊敬的刘庆生市长，李肇星部长，女士们、先生们，各位来宾朋友，非常高兴与各位相聚在美丽的深圳，共商"一带一路"倡议下的合作与发展，我谨代表本次论坛的主办方之一——中国工业经济联合会，也代表李毅中会长向在座的中外嘉宾表示热烈的欢迎和诚挚的问候。

本次论坛在全国上下贯彻党的十九大精神热潮中举办，聚焦"一带一路"倡议下的城市与产业国际合作，围绕"智库纽带·城市伙伴·产业合作"这一主题展开讨论，具有重要的现实意义。

城市与产业是推进"一带一路"建设的两个重要载体，一方面，"一带一路"倡议为沿线城市重新界定自身功能和发展目标提供了千载难逢的机遇，在新的开放格局下，一些节点与枢纽城市的要素体系、产业体系将面临新的变革与重构，应深入挖掘各自的比较优势，加强城市间合作，以探寻新的经济增长点，力争在全球化过程中创造新的发展机遇。

另一方面"一带一路"建设也为沿线各国产业注入了新的活力，深入挖掘各国的产业比较优势，加大技术创新，实现资源的最优配置，特别是加强在新一代信息技术、生物、新能源、新材料等新兴产业领域的深入合作，推动建立创业投资合作机制，将有效开辟"一带一路"国际合作的新局面。

城市和产业相辅相成密不可分，作为改革开放的前沿城市，作为年轻的一线城市，深圳在"一带一路"建设中积极作为，努力发挥了节点城市的示范和引领作用，中国工业经济联合会致力于推动"一带一路"产业协同发展，本次会议由中国工业经济联合会和深圳市人民政府发展研究中心共同主办，希望与会嘉宾在今天的会议上广开言路、充分交流、凝聚共识、深化合作，为"一带一路"倡议下的城市与产业国际合作贡献智慧和力量，为全球的合作、创新、发展、进步，为建设人类命运共同体尽忠言、献良策。谢谢大家。

熊梦（主持人）：有请国务院参事室二司司长孙维佳先生致辞。

孙维佳：尊敬的李毅中会长、李肇星会长，各位来宾，女士们、先生们，大家上午好。非常荣幸参加本次论坛，首先我谨代表国务院参事室向论坛的举办表示热烈的祝贺！

当今世界各国政府在国家施政和全球治理的过程中均面临着前所未有的复杂问题和严峻挑战，为了有效应对挑战，政府越来越重视汲取专家学者的智慧，倾听来自民间的声音，不断提升决策的科学化、民主化水平，智库的作用日益凸显，已成为全球治理中不可或缺的思想源泉。

"一带一路"倡议提出四年多来，从理念转化为行动，从愿景变为现实，已成为迄今最受欢迎的国际公共产品。构建起了发展战略对接、各自优势互补、彼此互联互通、包容开放发展的国际合作平台。为应对当前世界经济难题提供了中国方案。

"一带一路"倡议是中国的，更是世界的，"一带一路"倡议的推进落实离不开沿线国家城市和产业的合作，这既为智库的一展所长创造了条件，也为智库间的交流合作提供了机遇。概括地讲，"一带一路"倡议将致力于四个方面的目标：

第一，通过各国发展战略的对接和政策的对接形成优势互补和协同发展，解决各国发展不平衡、国际合作碎片化问题。

第二，通过集中突破基础设施不足这一发展瓶颈，从供给侧挖掘经济增长的潜力，推动跨境互联互通产生辐射带动效应，实现各国联动的发展。

第三，通过加强金融合作，打造世界经济持久增长的支撑体系，完善区域产业布局。

第四，通过深化各国人民的友好往来形成经济合作和文化融合的良性循环，营造和平、安宁的发展环境。

在实现上述目标进程中，各国智库和智库间的交流、合作至少可以在以下四个领域发挥积极而重要的建设性作用。

一是阐释中国政策、解读中国方案，以专业的态度、全球的视野对"一带一路"倡议进行科学的论证和评价，为"一带一路"的决策咨询提供扎实的学理支撑和方法论的支持，进而形成广泛的学术共识、政策共识、国际共识，引领科学的发展。

二是促进战略沟通，深化战略对接，发挥智库的支撑引领作用，深化"一带一路"的路径开放研究，本着共商、共建、共享的原则，在深入把握沿线国家的发展条件、核心利益、战略安排的基础上，着重在规划对接、政策对接、机制对接方面提出有利于各方广泛、深入开展合作的政策建议。

三是深化务实合作，推进"一带一路"不仅在谋划上需要智库的真知灼见，在项目的选择和论证上更需要各国智库的深入研究和献计献策。在这方面各国智库可以通过合作着力就"一带一路"倡议实施的重点领域和目标达成共识，着力在进一步推动互联互通建设、产能务实合作、人文交流合作等方面提供智力支持，着力推动更多务实合作项目落地，为提升地区经济增长、增进各国人民福祉贡献智慧。

四是推动人文交流合作，文明的交流互鉴是古代丝绸之路留给我们的共同精神财富，民心相通是"一带一路"国际合作的重要组成部分，沿线国家智库应致力于共同推进多层次、宽领域的人文合作，深化教育、科技、文化、卫生、旅游、体育等方面的交流，搭建更多的合作平台，开辟更多的合作渠道。智库作为沟通民间与政府的桥梁，应努力通过专业化的传播手段发挥作用，缩小不同国家民众对"一带一路"倡议的认知差距，因地制宜地为"一带一路"建设营造积极的舆论环境，增进沿线国家民众对"一带一路"倡议的了解和认同，并让他们从中获得真正的利益。

国务院参事室是国务院直属的政府咨询机构，其主要职能是参政议政、建言献策、咨询国事、民主监督。国务院参事为总理直接聘任，包括来自经济、社会各领域的知名专家、学者和官员等有识之士。国务院参事的意见和建议可以直接送达国务院领导同志的案头，我们形象地称之为"直通车"，开展公共外交、拓展国际视野，深化同国内外政府、咨询机构和智库的交流合作，是国务院参事室的一项重要的职能，我们希望借此论坛的契机，同到会的各国智库和专家学者深化合作，共同推动"一带一路"倡议下的城市与产业国际合作取得更加丰硕的成果。

最后预祝本次论坛圆满成功，谢谢大家！

熊梦（主持人）：谢谢孙维佳先生。女士们、先生们，开幕式致辞环节到此结束。接下来进入嘉宾主旨演讲环节，有请海南省政府副秘书长、省政府研究室主任朱华友先生主持，大家欢迎！

主旨演讲：打造国际合作新平台，推动经贸人文合作，构建新型城市伙伴关系

朱华友（主持人）： 谢谢熊会长！尊敬的各位领导，各位来宾，我作为广东的"邻居"——海南的代表应邀参会，今年是中国改革开放 40 周年，深圳经济特区成立 38 周年，海南经济特区成立 30 周年，这个时点上召开这次论坛非常重要。和平与发展是时代的主题，交流和合作是发展的基础。今天中国工业经济联合会和深圳市人民政府发展研究中心在这里共同举办"一带一路"倡议下城市与产业国际合作论坛，来自 20 多个国家和地区的 90 多位知名政要、学者汇聚一堂，围绕"智库纽带·城市伙伴·产业合作"主题进行交流。演讲环节邀请到 8 位重量级演讲嘉宾出席，分别是：李毅中先生、斯捷潘·梅西奇先生、李肇星先生、金立群先生、于洪君先生、杜桑·贝拉先生、王京生先生、李惠武先生。他们将围绕推动经贸、人文创新的合作，构建新型的城市伙伴关系进行交流，与大家共同分享他们的真知灼见。

首先有请全国政协经济委员会副主任、中国工业经济联合会会长、工业和信息化部原部长李毅中先生发言。

李毅中： 尊敬的李肇星部长，各位领导、各位专家、各位企业家、各位朋友，祝贺深圳论坛的成功举办，我准备了两个问题与大家共同交流。一是说说工业制造业在"一带一路"中发挥什么作用。二是说说粤港澳大湾区和珠三角制造业是什么关系。

第一，习近平主席号召我们把"一带一路"建设成为和平、繁荣、开放、文明之路，那么工业制造业如何发挥作用？总结这几年的经验，我认为要依托项目驱动，深化产业的务实合作。我总结为五个方面：

1. 交通运输、电信、管网基础设施建设。互联互通是发展经贸和人文交流的前提。到目前为止，我们已和"一带一路"沿线 15 个国家开通了上百条公路运输线，开通了 51 列中欧铁路班车，已经与 36 个国家签订了海运协议，参与了 20 多个港口的建设、管理、运营，与 43 个国家建立了民航的直飞，海陆空共同组成了交通的立体大通道，尤其是铁路建设成效卓著，例如印度尼西亚的亚曼高铁、中国到老挝的铁路已经开通了。另外，我们在俄罗斯、泰国、马来西亚、匈牙利、吉尔吉斯斯坦等国家的高铁项目正在做前期准备。

信息网方面，我们和东盟的邻国共同建立信息网。前两天我看报道，尼泊尔使用了我们给他们建设的光缆和通信网相连。中国移动、华为、中兴等在境外建立了 20 多个 4G 网络。我国和哈萨克斯坦、俄罗斯、缅甸的油气管道已经建成。入冬以来天然气紧缺，我们把俄罗斯北冰洋附近的气田运到中国来的项目正在紧张地施工。我国的基础设施、工程运营效率不客气地讲在国际上是先进水平，得到了大家的赞誉。

2. 投资工业项目，推进产业合作。我们自主研发的核电第三代技术在英国、阿根廷落户。中核集团和阿根廷合作建设了两座核电站。中车集团已经在美国的芝加哥、波士顿和洛杉矶建立了机车制造基地，不仅是出口机车，而且在美国制造。近几年我们在境外的投资，原来是单个项目，现在已经发展到工业园区了，我们的一些优势企业抓住机遇开展并购，比如吉利并购了沃尔沃，2010 年吉利公司也收购了福特的股份，这两年发展很好。近来海尔并购通用电气公司的家电，海信收购东芝的影像，特别是中国化工收购了瑞士先正达集团——世界著名的头号农业种子公司。通过并购我们提高了工业水平，投资是经贸合作的高级形式，我们对外投资应该保证技术先进、可靠，而且我们要帮助东道主做好营销服务，尽量做到员工本土化，我们要警惕出现的风险，如社会风险、法律风险、市场风险等。

3. 工程承包和劳务合作。我国的铁路、公路、桥梁承建工程实力雄厚、装备精良，中铁建、中交建、中国路桥、中国建筑，具有良好的信誉。斯里兰卡科隆坡港口第一期工程已经竣工，以著名的三一重工、徐工集团、中联重科为代表的工程机械伴随着工程走出国门，展示了质量、性能，创出了品牌。工程项目是百年大计，质量第一，同时我了解到它们更重视在所在国的生态环境保护。

4. 制造业为外贸提供了有力支撑。我们是世界出口第一大国，出口额中工业品占 95%，其中机械设备、电子信息产品已占 57%。年产 20 亿部手机，其中三分之二用于出口，74%是智能手机，OPPO、vivo 在国际上很知名。我们的轻纺产品是传统出口产品，注入先进技术、现代文化，高端、时尚。我们的食品工业、深加工，绿色、安全。我们是第二大进口国，进口额中工业占了 72%，其中一部分是国内制造业现在还生产不出来、急需的零部件、元器件和关键原材料，还有铁矿、石油，这是制造业需要的能源和原材料。我们出口产品以质取胜，我们还要防范贸易保护主义，要维护我们自身的合法权益。

5. 发挥我们的优势，开展资源的合作。比如五矿集团到澳大利亚办铁矿，有色矿业集团到赞比亚合作开发铜矿。刚才我听闫总介绍，刚果铜矿、镍矿更丰富。中海油收购加拿大的尼斯森公司，使中海油探明原油储量增长 30%。中石油境外的份额油占原油当量的三分之一，中石油帮助沙特建设 2000 万吨的炼油厂。资源的合作要着眼长远，而且要互利双赢，要带动东道国的经济发展。

以上就是我的简要总结。我举的这些例子可以说明，在"一带一路"的产业务实合作上，工业和制造业是主要领域。

第二，粤港澳大湾区是海上丝绸之路的重要基地，珠三角制造业是经济支柱。世界上著名的大湾区都有发达的工业，都占据世界的制高点。纽约湾有大型跨国公司落户于此，信息产业、电子制造、生物医药、高端装备制造、纳米材料、光学制造高度发达。旧金山湾位居创新前沿，高科技企业云集，宇航、电子制造业领先。日本的东京湾的京滨工业区，钢铁、船舶、电子、石化工业发达，是日本最大的制造业中心。著名的三大湾区，工业制造业都是它们的经济基础，为制造业的发展创造了条件。反过来发达的制造业构筑了这些大湾区的经济支柱。

珠三角在粤港澳大湾区中具有独特的产业优势，粤港澳大湾区是海上丝绸之路的重要基地，香港是著名的金融、海运、商贸中心，澳门是著名的旅游休闲胜地。香港的制造业都转移出去了，我得到的数据显示，香港的制造业产值占香港 GDP 不到 1%。珠三角制造业实力雄厚，广东的 GDP 占全国的九分之一，工业增加值占全国的八分之一。

珠三角制造业主要集中在列入粤港澳大湾区的 9 座城市中,下面有一个表,我给大家分析一下。

深圳市制造业主要指标 2017 年 1—10 月数据

项目	GDP增幅(%)	工业增加值增幅(%)	工业占GDP(%)	高技术产业占工业增加值(%)	规上工业企业增加值率(%)	规上工业企业主营利润率(%)	进出口总量增幅(%)	外贸依存度(%)	利用外资增幅(%)	2016年万人有效发明专利拥有量(件)
深圳	8.8	9.4	36.3	69.2	27.8	6.4	6.8	143.2	18.4	80.8
全国	6.9	6.7	约33.1	12.5	约22	6.24	16.6	34.2	-2.7	8

深圳市 2017 年 1—10 月,制造业的主要指标明显领先于全国水平,全年的数据还没出来,目前只有 1—10 月的,从左往右,GDP 的增幅、工业增加值的增幅领先于全国,优势明显。去年不少省市扭转了前几年的状况,深圳工业占 GDP 的比例高于全国,规模以上工业企业的运转状况好于全国。特别是工业增加值率全国是 21%、22%,深圳一直保持在 27%、28%,全国最高。

进出口增幅,全国增加是出乎意料的,深圳是比较平稳的,关键是外贸依存度 143.2%,全国是 34.2%,什么意思?这两个数不是一回事,不能比。人们往往用这个数说明这个国家和地区经济的外向型,深圳达到 143.2%,全国第一。利用外资到 10 月止,深圳是增加 18.4%,全国到 10 月是负值,11 月转正。最后一个数是每万人具有的发明性专利的件数,全国是 8,深圳是 80.8,是全国的 10 倍还多,高技术产业占工业增加值全国是 12.5%,深圳是 69.2%。深圳建设国际制造中心,要注意有效投资的关键作用。

前面说了深圳的好,再说说深圳的不足,我去年来的时候也说过,请看下面这个表。

深圳市近两年投资主要指标

项目		固定资产投资与GDP之比%	投资增幅%	工业投资占总投资%	工业投资增幅%	房地产投资占总投资%	房地产投资增幅%	银行存贷比%
深圳	2016年	20.9	23.6	17	17.1	51.4	26	62.9
	2017年1—10月	23.9	28.4	17.3	40	43.1	25.8	55
全国	2016年	80.2	7.9	38.2	3.6	22.7	6.8	72.1
	2017年1—10月	约79	7.2	36.8	3.1	17.5	7.5	73.5

深圳到2025年要初步形成创新活跃、结构优化、规模领先、配套完善、服务发达、世界一流的产业体系，远景非常鼓舞人心，要成为国内智能制造、绿色制造、高端制造排头兵。深圳带动珠三角经济，珠三角的制造业夯实了粤港澳大湾区的经济基石，香港、澳门基本没有制造业，制造业在珠江三角洲，而一个大湾区如果没有制造业不堪设想，所以珠三角是"一带一路"的重要支点，有效投资是拉动经济发展、社会进步的关键措施。投资不能过分，不能过分依靠投资拉动，有效投资是关键作用，这在党的十九大报告里也论述了。

深圳为此做了不懈努力，分析一下情况也应该看到问题，扬长避短。这里我列举了深圳市和全国2016年全年的状况和去年1—10月的情况。固定资产投资最好用全年的数，往往第四季度固定资产投资的量比较大，所以我列了两组数。固定资产投资和GDP的比例，深圳的投资强度远低于全国，全国80.2%，深圳20%多一点，这个太低了，不客气地讲在沿海城市里是最低的一个。深圳投资总量低但它的增幅上来了，这就是一个好的苗头。全国投资增幅2016年是7.9%、2017年1—10月是7.2%，深圳2016年是23.6%，去年1—10月是28.2%。因为一下子调不过来，结构上还有问题，深圳工业投资占总投资的比例比较低，只有17%左右，全国不是这个状况，相比之下深圳工业投资更少，结构上有问题。但深圳工业投资的增幅上来了，2016年是17.1%，去年1—10月是40%，说明深圳认识到这个问题了。

当然，后面两个指标不是太好，房地产占总投资的比例，深圳是一半左右，说明很多资金投入房地产。房地产投资的增幅也还不算低，说明结构在调整，但是调整的力度还不够大。

银行存贷比，全国是 73.5%，这个是合理的，深圳 55%，低于全国，说明资金积压了、沉淀了。但是反过来说，资金多有较大的潜力，建议深圳市为今后的发展测算一下投资需求，适度加大投资力度，调整结构，尤其是要建设国际知名制造业强市。

希望深圳为粤港澳大湾区的建设和"一带一路"的建设做出更大的贡献，谢谢大家。

朱华友（主持人）：李部长曾经讲过一句话，"不做具体工作了，真话还要讲"，感谢李部长，讲了很多真话，列举了很多翔实的数据、资料，阐述了工业制造业在"一带一路"倡议中的作用以及工业制造对大湾区的作用，也指出了深圳发展中需要着力解决的问题，对于我们很富有启发，谢谢李毅中部长的精彩演讲。

这次会议还邀请了来自克罗地亚国家商会的总顾问、首都萨格勒布市的代表斯捷潘·梅西奇，他非常重视发展对华关系，致力于推动与中国的交流合作，有请斯捷潘·梅西奇先生演讲。

斯捷潘·梅西奇：尊敬的女士们、先生们、贵宾们，首先我向各位致以诚挚的问候，并衷心感谢主办方对我的盛情邀请，我认为，和平是国际关系的最高价值，中国国家主席习近平先生提出的"一带一路"倡议，以促进所有国家的和平与经济发展为目标，所以这个倡议一经提出，我就非常赞同。我个人认为，"一带一路"倡议在实质上是指导欧亚与非洲经济共存，维护和平，发展合作。

作为中国 21 世纪的全球倡议，"一带一路"倡议本身也秉持了中国外交的传统原则，即目标长远、逐步实施，并以经济发展为手段，建设更稳定的多极化世界。"一带一路"倡议连接三大洲，重点在于发展未来海陆经济走廊沿线国家的新经济能力。今天对于我们来说，更为重要的就是落实这一倡议。换句话说，由于中东、北非、乌克兰问题和大批难民涌入欧洲，国际政治、经济的稳定性已严重恶化。这种局势具有破坏性趋势，会把国与国之间的关系裹挟到武力强权、民族沙文主义和经济保护主义，所以必须建立新的、稳定的世界基础结构和经济、金融结构来遏制它，因此我认为应始终同时重视并强调"一带一路"倡议的经济和非经济价值。这既是该倡议的立足点，也是我们当今维护世界稳定的重要方向。

2011年，我应邀到中国扬州，为扬州马可波罗纪念馆开馆剪彩。13世纪马可波罗在威尼斯出版了自己在中亚和中国的游记，并强调书中所写、所闻不及所见的一半。

马可波罗连接欧洲和中国，无论中欧外交或中克外交，马可波罗的话题都不可缺少，提到马可波罗，我想他并不只属于克罗地亚，我认为他是属于全世界的旅行者，当然中国朋友们也都知道关于马可波罗到底是克罗地亚人还是意大利人的争议，而让我高兴的是，你们对双方的论证都有足够的耐心。提到马可波罗，我想说"一带一路"不能只是简单的经贸交易，而忽略了历史、文化、科技、互换留学生、旅游等领域的交流与合作。

今天的大会正是为了增进我们彼此的了解，当然如果没有人民的互相了解，不了解现在的关系，不尊重文化差异，没有和平、友谊、稳定的价值观，就不可能发展贸易，更不能建设新的公路、港口、铁路、物流中心，这是我对"一带一路"的理解，如果没有中国推进打造人类命运共同体的努力，也就不可能有"一带一路"倡议，"一带一路"倡议既是中国也是亚洲和欧洲经济发展战略的重要组成部分。

亚洲已成为对世界经济有决定性影响的地区，就如同欧洲常在历史上表现的那样，从2000多年前古老的丝绸之路形成到欧洲工业革命和殖民地化，有许多特点，都可以被定义为今天全球化的前身。经济全球化给中国带来了许多优势，当中国从一个人口大国转型为经济平衡发展并保护环境的人力资源大国时，世界为之震惊，中国通过全体人民的努力和改革开放取得了长足的发展。

当今时代，世界经济相互依赖，不是仅仅依赖西方，我们现在所看到的经济一体化进程，多项并进，欧洲内部、跨大西洋、跨太平洋、欧洲和中国，这意味着中欧国家可以同时参与不同方向的经济一体化进程，中国把对中欧国家的新政策称为中国中东欧国家合作即"16＋1"。中国中东欧国家在"16＋1"机制下呈现出积极特性，因为通过增进中国投资和优惠贷款，可以增强欧洲经济的稳定性。

发展对华关系能助力东欧、南欧国家减缓经济危机。2013 年我在北京呼吁布鲁塞尔要像支持德中、英中关系一样支持 16 个中东欧国家发展同中国的关系。因为发展这些关系的目标是一致的，即发展经济，特别要指出的是中东欧 16 国总共有 1.23 亿人口，相比中国同欧盟发达成员国家的关系，在贸易投资领域中国中东欧关系还有很大差距。对我来说"16＋1"机制所取得的成果尤为重要，因为我认为这一机制是实现"一带一路"目标的现实支柱。

中国国家领导人将中国和东南欧的关系纳入"一带一路"更广泛的外交政策理念中，丝绸之路经济带的港口、铁路、公路也将穿越中东欧国家，并将与亚洲相连，中国对中东欧国家的新外交政策推动了政治关系的发展，更多的高层互访使合作机制化，带来了投资、贸易和新基础设施项目的增长，并促进了教育和旅游合作。中国支持金融合作，推动本地跨境贸易，从而使人民币代替美元成为另外一种选择。

最后我想强调的是，要增进中东欧国家相互了解，我们应共同保持并继续发展这一趋势，支持并落实从华沙到布加勒斯特、贝尔格莱德到萨格勒布的所有措施，这些措施也实现了"一带一路"倡议的重要因素，所以"一带一路"不仅有巨大的经济效益，更有巩固三大洲和平与合作的非经济效益，谢谢大家聆听我的发言，谢谢。

朱华友（主持人）：谢谢斯捷潘·梅西奇先生热情洋溢的演讲，作为国际友人充分肯定了"一带一路"的价值，不仅有经济价值还有非经济价值，强调它对于世界的繁荣、稳定可以发挥重要的作用，特别强调不仅是经贸的合作，更多要加强文化、科技、教育等领域的合作，谢谢斯捷潘·梅西奇先生。特别感谢马可波罗作为友谊的使者去过我的家乡扬州。

下面有请中国公共外交协会会长、外交部原部长李肇星先生发言。

李肇星：亲爱的各位朋友，我想讲的话刚才我的老同事、老战友李毅中同志已经讲过了。

我退休之前应克罗地亚邀请，曾经见过斯捷潘·梅西奇阁下，我向他们表示感谢，并祝贺他们演讲的成功。我最近运气好，觉得自己又年轻了一点，因为我这几个月看到了世界上最年轻的两个国家的代表，看到了最年轻的一家大企业的领导，看到了最年轻的现代化城市。两个国家一个是斯洛伐克共和国，今天杜桑·贝拉大使也在场，另一个是克罗地亚前领导人斯捷潘·梅西奇代表的克罗地亚，也是一个年轻的国家。年轻的国际知名大企业就是刚刚成立不久的，和"一带一路"有紧密关系的亚洲基础设施投资银行，今天它年轻的第一任行长立群老朋友也在这儿，我也感到特别高兴。两个月前我见到了法国最年轻的总统，才39岁，不久前他访问中国取得了成功。我们国家特别有名的城市比这个法国新总统还年轻1岁，它就是刚满38周岁的深圳。我曾在广东省劳动锻炼三年多，我也把广东省看作第二故乡，在纪念深圳建市38周年的时候我们参加这次论坛，真是一件幸事。

我讲讲我参加外交、外事工作半个多世纪以来的一点小体会和小故事。

第一，祖国唯一。和我们每个人都有一个母亲一样，我们只有一个祖国。我最近就感到，不管你走了多远的路，在祖国面前，你还是一个长不大的孩子，在知识面前自己还是一个毕不了业的小学生。要永远记住爱祖国、爱家乡，我在美国待过六年多，到过美国所有的州，但是我现在最难忘的是在两个州受到的欢迎特别热烈，我自己当时有点飘飘然，觉得自己像是国王，像是英雄一样。后来才知道，人家可能连我的名字也记不住，他们欢迎我是因为我的家乡，因为我的祖国。

我到了美国一个工业不太发达但是农业比较发达的一个州，叫蒙大拿州。他们把我赞扬得让我觉得非常奇怪，我都快忘记自己是谁了。后来才知道那个州的州长、参议员看了我的内部材料，知道我是中国人，是中国山东青岛市郊区的乡下长大的孩子，他们说特别感谢中国，感谢我的家乡，要是没有中国，特别是我家乡的啤酒厂进口他们的大麦和大麦芽——这个州的主要出口产品之一，这里老百姓的生活不能这么富裕、不能这么好，所以特别欢迎我。不是因为我自己怎么样，是因为我的祖国对那个州人民的生活改善、经济发展有贡献。还有一次我到南卡罗来纳州，州长派飞机接我和夫人去，后来他说因为我来自中国山东青岛，海尔一次性在他们州投资了许多项目。十多年前美国移民政策要求外来企业一次性投入 50 万美元，一次性解决美国 12 个以上公民的就业，海尔公司一次性投资超过 50 万美元，一次雇用了超过 200 位美国工人，州长感谢得要命。我们要感谢祖国、依靠祖国。

还有一个小故事。我曾应利比里亚邀请正式访问，会谈之后，女总统说她原来走路不太方便，经过中国医疗队的治疗，特别是中医的针灸、按摩，她不仅走路快如轻风，而且乒乓球打得也挺不错，感谢中国和中国人民，不仅是在教育上和中国友好互利，也感谢对她个人的帮助。所以我还是感谢祖国，我的体会是祖国是我们的根，祖国是我们力量的源泉，我们参加"一带一路"建设也要怀着热爱祖国的心。

第二，永远记住"老百姓是我们的衣食父母"。想到人民我就想到下面的三个字、四个字、五个字、六个字。

三个字，民为贵。我的"老乡"两千多年前的孟子说过，"民为贵"。

四个字，人民万岁。

五个字，为人民服务。这一定会使我们有信心、有决心把"一带一路"建设好。

六个字，以人民为中心，习近平总书记多次强调一切工作都要以人民为中心。

这三、四、五、六个字会成为我工作、生活的座右铭和风向标，大家要一起以人民为中心好好学习、好好劳动，参加"一带一路"的建设。

第三，永远听党的话。牢记习近平总书记最经常讲的一句话，也是在党的十八大时第一次作为总书记接见外国记者和中国记者时所讲的："人民对美好生活的向往就是我们的奋斗目标"。

我 20 年前写过歌颂深圳的诗歌，深圳是中国改革开放的"少年先锋队的队员"。深圳进步这么快、发展这么快要感谢中国共产党，我们要好好学习习近平新时代中国特色社会主义思想。

第四，团结就是力量。我学过中国历史、世界历史，所以我们也要记住列宁那句话，"忘记历史就意味着背叛"，奋力前进的同时也要接受历史的教训，这样才有前瞻性，不能忘了历史。我们要坚定地加强团结，要抱团取暖，团结就是力量。"一带一路"建设中和"一带一路"沿线各国人民应该紧密团结，相互学习，争取合作共赢，构建人类命运共同体。

我有幸参加了2014年在上海召开的亚洲相互协作与信任措施会议第四次峰会，在会上习近平主席发表了重要讲话，他强调"中国坚定不移走和平发展道路，始终不渝奉行互利共赢的开放战略"。

昨天我去参观了两个大公司，我觉得它们有很多东西值得学习，我也会向将来我能见到的企业家推荐，一个是腾讯公司，一个是海能达公司，它们做了很多好事。首先是在精准扶贫方面，它们和大西北、大西南一些欠发达的地区都有合作，提供了慷慨的赞助，值得学习；还有它们的创新，在智能高科技产品方面，在全国走在前列，甚至在全世界走在前列，我觉得值得其他公司、其他企业来学习。

我很感谢有这次学习的机会，借这个机会我祝大家都高兴、快乐，中国的新春佳节即将到来，祝大家在新的一年快乐、成功，谢谢。

朱华友（主持人）：谢谢李部长精彩的演讲，李部长的脱稿演讲可以用两个词概括一下，一就是"根"。李部长告诉我们，我们的根是祖国，根源于人民、祖国，我们要为人民服务，为人民谋福利。二是合作共赢，我们要抱团取暖、加强团结，还要借鉴各种文明和文化，在这个过程中实现合作和共赢。谢谢李部长。

下面演讲的是亚投行行长金立群先生。

金立群：女士们、先生们，我非常高兴参加本次论坛。深圳今年是"38周岁"，马上是"不惑之年"，今天是亚投行进入第三年的第一天，昨天是亚投行两周年纪念日。亚投行是体现了中国发展理念和经验，闪烁着中国时代精神的新型的国际多边发展机构。亚投行是中国领导人习近平主席倡导发起成立的，亚投行仅仅用了两年时间就完成了跟57个国家谈判达成一致意见，通过了《亚投行章程》和其他一些主要的政策文件。在筹建的过程中，中国本着民主协商的精神，团结广大亚洲和其他地区加入亚投行的所有成员，中国发挥了引领作用，得到了广泛的认可。中国政府遵守诺言，言必行、行必果，以国际标准来指导、运营这个机构，中国政府通过董事会作为最大的股东行使它的权力，中国发挥的建设性作用得到了国际社会广泛的认可和肯定，体现了中国的影响力、塑造力。

亚洲在世界范围内是非常重要的区域，亚投行进一步致力于促进可持续发展的项目，为人类创造更好的未来。今天是亚投行进入第三个年头的第一天，我们期待未来有更多的新发展。

在两年内我们出台了很多的项目，涉及 48 亿美元，涵盖了很多基础设施的建设，在 2018 年以及未来，我们亚投行会带来更多的价值，我们会进一步与各国政府进行合作，以及与不同的机构进行合作，同时也会进一步投资不同的项目，去帮助大家实现可持续发展，我们希望借此机会为城市提供更好的基础设施、创造更好的生活，我们希望在全世界范围内能实现共赢。

亚投行与"一带一路"是两个不同的倡议，我们既有不同的使命，又是相互关联的。我们会在"一带一路"的沿线国家中进一步支持基础设施的项目，"一带一路"和亚投行像两个驱动器，会进一步促进相互之间的发展。我们也可以相互合作，进一步促进不同国家的经济发展，我们非常骄傲我们能成立这样的银行，非常感谢中国政府以及银行其他的股东。我也要感谢我们 48 个合作伙伴，我们也非常期待亚投行与深圳有更加紧密的合作。

朱华友（主持人）：谢谢金立群先生独到的见解，让我们耳目一新，如果说会议上的讨论是务虚的，那么亚投行则是一个务实的推动者，谢谢金立群先生。有请中国人民争取和平与裁军协会副会长、中共中央对外联络部原副部长于洪君先生发言。

于洪君：尊敬的克罗地亚前总统斯捷潘·梅西奇先生，尊敬的李毅中部长、李肇星部长和各位领导、朋友、专家，大家上午好！非常感谢会议主办单位邀请我参加这次论坛，现在关于"一带一路"的论坛应该说非常密集，参加论坛的专家、学者云集。

"一带一路"倡议作为国家意志，作为 13 亿中国人民的共同行动，它的意义重大而深远，习近平总书记是"一带一路"的倡导者，高度重视推动"一带一路"，在党的十九大报告中他就提到"一带一路"，在论述党的十八大以来经济建设成就时特别提到"'一带一路'建设，京津冀协同发展，长江经济带发展成效显著"，将"一带一路"摆在三大发展战略之中。谈到新的发展理念，建设现代化经济体系，阐述坚持和平发展，推动构建人类命运共同体新理念的时候，习近平总书记讲，"中国坚持对外开放的基本国策，坚持打开国门搞建设，积极促进'一带一路'国际合作，努力实现政策沟通、设施连通、贸易畅通、资金融通和民心相通，打造国际合作新平台，增添共同发展的新动力"。

在认识思考、理解推进的过程中，我觉得应该遵循这样的思路，去理解、把握和认识。要认识到"一带一路"倡议是习近平总书记代表中国共产党、代表中国政府、代表中国人民向全世界发出的庄严承诺，它是我们给国际社会提供的公共产品，是在全球发展阴晴不定，反全球化倾向翻腾的背景下我们提供的中国智慧、中国方案、中国道路，是一个中国引领的全球行动，是合作发展、互利发展、共赢发展的全球行动。

推进"一带一路"建设，重点要把握好三项原则，这就是共商、共建、共享，不能急于求成，不能一蹴而就，不能强人所难，要稳中求进，不能因为自己的意愿而不顾合作伙伴的感受，不顾他们的利益和诉求，共商、共建、共享是"一带一路"持续推进最基本的保障。

"一带一路"建设要实现四个突破，这就是要突破意识形态分歧，突破社会制度差异，突破发展水平的鸿沟，突破新冷战思维，实现这四个突破，"一带一路"推进才能顺风顺水，才能排除干扰、战胜阻力、一往无前。这不仅是我们要做到，我们的合作伙伴也要做到，把握好"一带一路"所要完成的主要任务是我们反复讲的"五通"。

现在"一带一路"重点把握的是六大经济走廊，中国—中亚—西亚经济走廊、中巴经济走廊、中国—中南半岛经济走廊、中蒙俄经济走廊、新亚欧大陆桥走廊、孟中印缅经济走廊，围绕六大经济走廊我们做了大量的前期准备，做了大量的投入，打造了更高水平的区域合作平台，创造了更新的区域合作模式，引领区域合作共同发展，通过区域合作引领全球经济合作，引领经济全球化的新浪潮，引领全球经济治理的新阶段。

"一带一路"正在成为全球行动，"一带一路"建设也存在几个风险：政府更迭、领导人思维改变给我们造成的冲击；经济方面、金融方面、技术方面，我们的技术标准和对方的技术标准是否对接，是否被外方认同；社会文化心理方面、环境方面，有些国家经济不发达，技术不完备，急需升级换代，但是环境高于一切，我们必须有充分的准备；安全方面的威胁、困难和挑战，恐怖主义的威胁，不用多讲，很多企业在外面遭遇过重创；最后还有由于新冷战思维，第三方势力对我们的干扰和冲击。

最后想说的是，昨天上午，中央召开了"一带一路"工作会议，这是今年我们的一个非常重要的工作会议。"一带一路"工作会议由王沪宁主持，张高丽作为"一带一路"工作领导小组的组长做了重要讲话。他的讲话媒体做了报道，主要讲下一步我们要认真贯彻党的十九大精神和中央经济工作会议精神，以习近平新时代中国特色社会主义思想为指导，坚持稳中求进的工作总基调，推进"一带一路"建设取得新的更大发展，他的讲话内容非常丰富。主要归结起来是以下几点：一是要凝聚更加广泛的合作共识，加强战略对接、规划对接、机制平台对话，增强"一带一路"的国际感召力。二是要加强互联互通合作，大力推进基础设施的硬连通和规划标准的软连通，互联互通是硬连通、软连通两个方面，软连通同样重要，没有软连通就实现不了硬连通，要继续实施好标志性的示范项目。三是要提升经贸投资的合作水平，深化国际产能合作，增添沿线国家共同发展的新动力。四是要创新金融产品和服务，发挥好各类金融机构的作用，提高金融服务"一带一路"建设的水平。金行长提供了很好的范例，我们这方面已经做了很多的工作，还会继续加大力度。五是要拓展人文交流合作，夯实"一带一路"建设的民意基础。六是积极履行社会责任，加强生态环境保护，共同建设绿色丝绸之路，过去有些企业在这方面重视不够，这次强调在"一带一路"建设过程中要重视环保理念，建设绿色丝绸之路。七是要继续做好风险评估和应急处置工作，强化"一带一路"建设的安全保障。现在党中央高度重视应对风险、应对挑战，保障"一带一路"顺利推进。

深圳是改革开放的排头兵，是改革开放的示范区，相信在"一带一路"的推动中深圳能发挥自己的巨大优势和潜力，为城市伙伴关系的发展，为我们同相关国家的产业合作，包括智库之间的交往与合作提供新鲜的经验，作出更大的贡献，最后祝愿论坛取得圆满成功，谢谢大家。

朱华友（主持人）： 谢谢于部长精彩的演讲，对"一带一路"如何进一步推进，如何真正建成共商、共建、共享的"一带一路"发表了很好的见解，给我们很多启发，谢谢于部长。接下来演讲的是杜桑·贝拉先生，他曾任斯洛伐克驻华大使，为在"一带一路"倡议下促进两个国家的互联互通、造福民众做了很多事情，欢迎杜桑·贝拉先生。

杜桑·贝拉： 尊敬的朱华友先生，亲爱的嘉宾，女士们，先生们！首先，我想感谢组委会邀请我参加此次论坛，并与大家分享我的观点。对我来说，在这样一个特别的城市进行演讲，是个非常难得的机会。

今天的论坛体现了丝路精神，是在习近平主席于2013年提出的"一带一路"倡议背景下召开的。千百年来，丝路精神象征着东西方交流与合作，推动了人类文明的进步，为丝路沿线国家的繁荣发展作出了巨大贡献。

"一带一路"倡议旨在推动亚欧非大陆间互联互通，加深了沿线国家之间的友谊。相较于其他城市，深圳最有潜力成为连接世界的纽带，使丝路精神在21世纪的现实中得以实现。

众所周知，深圳拥有大量知名高新技术企业，如华为、腾讯等，都是在这里发展起来的。高新技术是深圳的支柱产业，因此这里被称为"创新之都"。深圳的研发投资总额在世界上名列前茅（占GDP的4.1%），深圳国际专利申请量已连续13年占全国的一半，2016年同比增长约50%。

此次会议的主题是适时的。创新已成为21世纪经济增长的驱动力和竞争力。它不仅加深了我们的知识，满足了我们的好奇心，并且促进了社会的发展，提高了人们的生活水平。创新并不是孤立存在的，只有进行充分的思想交流，加深对大局的理解并不断实践，才能产生新的解决办法和科技创新。我想，最好的方法就是"走出去"。

为此我想强调，智库是一个非常重要的角色，为合作交流提出新想法，搭建新平台。几千年的人类文明证明，城市是创新发展的载体，特别是那些拥有大量贸易和游客量的城市，成功地吸引了来自世界各地的人才。例如雅典和长安，就如同现在的硅谷和深圳。

借此之机，我想谈谈斯洛伐克共和国的创新政策和成为中国合作伙伴的潜力。尽管斯洛伐克是个小国家，但我们的汽车制造业全球领先，平均每千人生产191辆，我们拥有开放的经济体制，发达的传统工业，近年来在对外贸易方面成果不俗（2016年贸易顺差为3.67亿欧元）。关注全球经济变化、注重科学、创新、科技等方面的合作，一直是斯洛伐克共和国明确的目标。

我们目前正在实施国家智能专业化研究和创新战略（RIS3），侧重于先进材料、纳米技术、信息技术、生物医学和生物技术、农业、环境和可持续能源。智能工业（工业4.0）和智能城市同样受到重视，个别项目已经开始实施。

我想提请大家关注我们的成果——斯洛伐克是许多初创公司和创新型公司的发源地，它们已成为各自领域的领导者。斯洛伐克的斯皮尼亚公司是欧洲唯一一家为机器人生产高精度减速变速箱的制造商；第一辆飞行汽车 AeroMobil 的目标是在21世纪末彻底改变交通运输现状；C2i 公司为汽车和航空航天工业提供优质碳纤维复合材料；SYGIC 公司是离线 GPS 导航应用中的全球领导者；ESET 公司的防病毒解决方案在网络安全防护中扮演了举足轻重的角色。

我想强调与中国的创新合作，因为在中国—中东欧国家合作，即"16+1"合作中，我们选择了创新和技术作为专业领域。在首都布拉迪斯拉发主办了第二届中欧经济共同体与中国创新专题讨论会，会上成立了虚拟技术转让中心，推动了中国与中东欧16国之间的进一步合作。此外，2017年11月中下旬在布拉迪斯拉发举办了中欧经济共同体与中国创新问题第二次部长级会议。此次会议强调了生物技术、绿色能源清洁技术、信通技术和材料工程，另外举行了公司展示会及 B2B 对接论坛。

说到创新，我还应该提到斯洛伐克首都布拉迪斯拉发，在2017年欧盟区域创新记分牌（EU Regional Innovation Scoreboard）上获得了高分，成为欧盟新成员国中最具创新力的地区之一。

最后，我想强调，今年是中国与中东欧 16 国开展区域合作的一年。在我看来，这是一个能利用斯洛伐克创新优势的好机会，如果能在斯洛伐克的创新集群和中国创新领导者——本次论坛主办方深圳之间建立起高效的合作模式，我相信，双方都将获益良多，我愿为双方国家、城市间的创新合作贡献一份绵薄之力。

感谢大家的聆听。

朱华友（主持人）： 谢谢杜桑·贝拉先生带给我们独到的观点，有请国务院参事王京生先生发言。

王京生： 尊敬的各位朋友，刚才听了以上嘉宾的演讲，确实大开眼界，我主要想简单阐述一下，"一带一路"在中国开放中的地位和作用，题目就是"'一带一路'：中国对外开放的新阶段、新境界与新格局"。

首先，为什么说"一带一路"是中国对外开放的新阶段？我觉得有三个方面：第一，从梯度开放向全方位开放转变。从开放初期的先沿海后内陆，到现在陆上、海上、天上、网上四位一体的连通，中国境内各区域有特色的经济板块，通过发达的交通、信息，直接对应"一带一路"沿线国家和地区，各尽其能、各具优势，又相互配合地与世界经济相连接。

第二，是从短缺经济到外溢经济的转变。"一带一路"既是中国经济发展逻辑的内在延伸，也契合了中国经济发展的外在需求，充裕的资金、产业凝聚力、产品、强大的基础设施建设能力，使中国"走出去"具有得天独厚的优势，同样重要的是我国拥有庞大的人口数量和广大的国土，以及迅速壮大的中产阶级需求，中国将成为世界最大的市场，我们的市场也会随之更加活跃。

第三，是从全球化的参与者到积极推动者的转变。

其次，为什么说"一带一路"是中国对外开放的新境界？

第一，"一带一路"倡议是中国走和平之路的行动宣誓，当中国宣布要和平崛起时，无论是国际政治界、外交界还是学术界质疑的声音都很大，为什么？因为国强必霸，国强必武，似乎是大国崛起的普遍逻辑。过去兴起的列国无疑都走过这条路，而我们之所以提出"一带一路"倡议，就是要让大家知道，一直以来中国提倡和平通商、互利共赢、共享贸易繁荣，使世界人民得到好处。中国丝绸之路是这样，中国传统文化的取向是这样，21世纪的"一带一路"更是如此。

第二，"一带一路"倡议是中国推进全球化和自由贸易的责任宣誓。

第三，"一带一路"倡议是中国致力于构建人类命运共同体的情怀宣誓。

再次，为什么说"一带一路"是中国对外开放的新格局？

第一，"一带一路"建设植根于历史的土壤，重点面向亚欧非大陆及沿海岛屿，但同时向所有愿意加入的国家和地区开放。

第二，内容博大，"一带一路"不但涵盖贸易、投资、交通等经济领域，还涵盖政治、社会、文化等方方面面。这一点越来越凸显，如政治上的求同存异、社会的稳定和文化上的多元共存。共建"一带一路"顺应了世界多极化、经济全球化、文化多样化、社会信息化的时代潮流。

第三，共同利益博大。习近平总书记说："'一带一路'追求的是百花齐放的大利，不是一枝独秀的小利。"孔子也曾说过"己所不欲，勿施于人"，这句话在世界上影响很大。其实比这更能代表我国"一带一路"态度的是他的另外一句话，"己欲立而立人，己欲达而达人"，现在我们恰恰是在这样做。

第四，视野博大。随着陆路交通工具的发展，欧亚大陆的心脏地带成为最重要的战略地区，并出现了著名的世界岛理论。时至今日，如何发挥心脏地带的作用，"一带一路"给出了答案，它是一个战略大迂回，因此"一带一路"既重新开辟欧亚大陆这一传统的贸易通道，规避可能出现的海上风险，同时通过加强与沿线发展中国家的投资、贸易往来，有效回避与发达国家和地区的贸易摩擦。老子说过，"天之道，利而不害，圣人之道，为而不争"。这样我们既占领主动、保证安全，也谋求了共赢。

必须保持战略定力，注重经济效益，必须按经济规律办事，不能一哄而上，拍脑袋决策，要投资与效益并重，既然是做生意，就不能乱花钱，要有科学的效率评估。必须确保战略重点，"一带一路"区域广阔，道路漫长，不可能同时下令。孙子说："知己知彼，胜乃不殆；知天知地，胜乃可全。"针对不同的地理和国家状况，要采取不同措施，确保战略重点。

"一带一路"兴于贸易、成于文化，要打好文化流动这张牌，丝绸之路的贡献是巨大的。相对于经济的贡献，以历史的眼光看，它对文化的贡献更加伟大，促进东西方和世界的文化交流，使人类相互沟通和了解，并在交流碰撞中产生出奇异而丰硕的成果。文化的空前流动造就伟大的文明，文化自信是包容而不是孤芳自赏，文化因多样性而可爱，不因为单一性而高贵。

中国历史上开辟了丝绸之路，为什么受到世界的重视和欢迎？是因为我们的东西好，因为我们的瓷器、丝绸等产品的质量过硬，因为四大发明的先进。当时认为中华文明伟大的更多的是觉得我们的东西精美，器物先进，因此要反复强调，一国产品之质量乃一国国民之素质，一国产品之信誉乃一国国民之尊严。解决质量问题是推进"一带一路"有效实施的关键，商品质量好买卖才长久，"一带一路"才越走越兴旺，中国才有信誉，中国人才有尊严。所以我们必须全力以赴生产高质量产品，谢谢大家。

朱华友（主持人）：谢谢王京生先生的精彩发言，有请广东省政府发展研究中心副主任李惠武先生发言。

李惠武：尊敬的各位嘉宾，各位朋友，女士们、先生们，大家好！首先我要非常感谢这次论坛的主办单位邀请我出席这次论坛，并且给我提供了在大会上做发言的机会。

我想给大家分享一下近几年广东在参与"一带一路"合作过程中主要做的一些事情，以及对地方智库如何发挥作用提出几个期望。

习近平主席在 2013 年出访中亚和东南亚的时候提出推进建设"一带一路"的倡议，这是共同建设互信包容、合作共赢伙伴关系，促进亚太大繁荣的重要平台，也是构建人类命运共同体的重要组成部分。四年来这一倡议已成为相关各方积极参与和共同推进的伟大事业，并且朝着开放、繁荣的目标有序迈进，为增进各国人民的福祉提供了新的发展机遇。

广东是"一带一路"的起点和重要的节点，改革开放以来，我们广东更是充分利用地理、历史、人文和政策的便利，迅速与世界各国建立起密切的经贸关系。广东的经济总量已经达到1.3亿美元,进出口总量达到1万亿美元。广东是连续29年中国第一大经济省区,去年我们的经济总量占全国的1/9,进出口总量占全国的1/4,近几年来广东积极响应国家的号召,积极参与"一带一路"的合作,2015年6月出台的《广东省参与建设"一带一路"的建设方案》,提出三个目标,即把广东建设成"一带一路"合作中的重要引擎、经贸合作中心和物流枢纽。同时我们也提出了参与"一带一路"合作的重点:促进基础设施的互联互通、加快产业投资的步伐、推进海洋领域合作、推动能源合作发展、拓展金融业务合作、提高合作水平和密切人文的交流合作,有力推动沿线国家的经贸合作。目前我们广东的广州港和深圳港的枢纽港口已经开通了国际集装箱的班轮航线300多条,覆盖了世界各大洲的主要港口,我们的航空口岸也已经开通了国际客货运航线120多条,直达的航线覆盖全球的五大洲30多个国家和80多个城市。

我们广东对接"一带一路"的合作已经开通了"粤新欧"国际快运班列,就是广东经过新疆到欧洲的线路;及"粤满俄",就是广东经过满洲里到俄罗斯的国际铁路联运专列,目前运行非常稳定;东莞的石龙到深圳盐田开通了集装箱班列,也开通了中韩快线集装箱班列。现在我们的水铁和陆铁的多式联运也取得了快速发展。随着广东陆上丝绸之路快速发展和周边各省区高速铁路的相继贯通,我们粤港澳—西南省份—东盟国家的国际综合物流大通道将陆上的丝绸之路大通道全部融合衔接。广东充分利用产能优势,在境外参与沿线国家的16个园区建设,其中广东独立组织和推进的境外产业合作园区有6个。广东先后和东盟国家签署了旅游合作协议备忘录,我们向东盟国家提供文博援助等,正在积极开展文化交流,广东省内的很多高校和沿线国家的高校开展一系列的交流合作。

本人因为工作的性质,每个月要接待两批以上来自"一带一路"沿线国家的政府、议会和政党的代表团。在这些交流合作过程中,我感觉到智库的作用是非常重要的,在这里对"一带一路"合作过程中如何充分发挥智库的作用提三点建议:

第一,加强智库合作,密切沟通交流。沿线国家智库间要汇聚众力、探索新途径、开辟新动力,助推沿线国家共同繁荣。通过举办多种形式的论坛活动，比如说今天在深圳举办的论坛，开展学术研讨，围绕政策性、前瞻性和务实性的问题展开合作研究，努力实现资源共享、信息共享、成果共享。

第二，搭建交流平台，促进务实合作，加强"一带一路"国家的经济合作和交流衔接，共同探讨合作的思路，打造政府、智库、业界、媒体等多方参与的正式交流合作平台，深化沿线国家资源更好地融合。

第三，注重差异化研究，寻求利益的契合点。智库要积极了解和深入研究沿线国家的经济发展状况、互补的优势、文化的传统、消费的习惯以及合作的意愿等各种信息，为参与合作的企业提供更有实际价值的意见和建议，使他们充分了解和尊重各国的社会、经济、文化、就业、习俗等特殊性，以互利共赢为宗旨，兼顾双边多边就业、双边多边利益，寻找利益的契合点和合作的最大公约数。

各位来宾、各位代表，2000 多年前航海的技术不发达，剩余的物品不多，语言的交流不便，我们的祖先经历了许多艰险，闯出了东西方友好交流、互通有无的丝绸之路，成为人类经贸、交流史上的奇迹，2000 多年后的今天，我们有了应对自然的技术装备，也形成了足可交换的文化盈余，理应在平等互惠、共同发展的原则下加强合作。

广东是丝绸之路的重要节点，也是中国对外开放程度最高的省区，我们将通过积极参与"一带一路"的建设分享红利，实现共同发展。

我们广东省政府发展研究中心也愿意积极为推进"一带一路"合作作出我们应有的贡献，发挥我们应有的作用，谢谢大家。

朱华友（主持人）：谢谢李惠武先生分享了广东在对外开放方面的一些经验和做法，也讲到我们如何发挥好智库的作用，谢谢李惠武先生。作为主持人衷心感谢各位嘉宾的配合以及所作的精彩演讲，你有一个苹果，我有一个苹果，我们交换一下还是每个人一个苹果；如果你有一个思想，我有一个思想，咱们交流一下就有两个思想，今天各位嘉宾分享了精彩的思想、精彩的观点，让我们享受了一次思想的盛宴，感谢各位嘉宾贡献的智慧，衷心谢谢大家。

主题论坛：发挥区域及产业优势，推进"一带一路"沿线城市间合作交流

吴亮（主持人）：有请讨论嘉宾上场：

希腊雅典副市长亚历山大·莫迪亚诺先生；

中国综合开发研究院（深圳）常务副院长郭万达先生；

中欧文化教育协会主席、欧盟亚洲研究所首席执行官顾爱乐先生；

中国人民大学重阳金融研究院执行院长、教授王文先生；

克罗地亚地缘经济论坛研究所所长贾思娜女士；

正泰集团副总裁陈建克先生。

深圳是一个创新的城市，是一个活力之城，也是国家现代化的示范城市，对于"一带一路"主题下，如何务实强化城市合作、产业合作、智库纽带，如何更高效地推进"一带一路"倡议下的合作，今天各位嘉宾每个人将分享一个观点、一个解决方案。

在座几位嘉宾有来自智库的、研究机构的，还有代表城市的、产业界的，我们先请外国朋友第一个发言，国内智库嘉宾后发言。首先有请希腊雅典副市长亚历山大·莫迪亚诺先生讲一讲，贵市对"一带一路"最大的合作期待或者合作点是什么？

亚历山大·莫迪亚诺：非常感谢主办方邀请我来参加此次论坛，关于城市与城市之间的合作，今天的论坛发言，改变了我很多观点。就我们的城市来说，历史上有很多的起起伏伏。在很久以前，那时我们有很多城市国家，它们在重塑世界格局，在悠久的历史中，经历了很多起伏。现在我们有了新的国际关系，秉持双赢的愿景，同时也获取了更好的机会促进城市的发展。

雅典是个非常古老的城市，是欧洲甚至整个世界最古老的城市之一，深圳是个新兴的城市。我们一个在西方、一个在东方、一个是古老的、一个是新兴的，但我们的人民是没有区别的。城市的居民有着同样的动力，他们需要繁荣、健康、良好的环境和教育。无论什么样的政治体系，人们都有这样的动力，这也就是说如果你的目标会使你受益，那么你所有的愿望都将实现。在这里，我们意识到一切都可能发生，你可以有无限期待，我们所有的想法都有可能实现。深圳就是一个生动的例子，我们不会擦拭城市的历史，我们更多期待城市有更好的未来。非常感谢中国发起的"一带一路"倡议，将重点放在务实的项目上，并促成它的实现。

吴亮（主持人）： 如果想与深圳合作，雅典最想和深圳在哪个方面开展合作？有没有这样的规划？

亚历山大·莫迪亚诺： 我希望更多地开展智力、技术以及其他方面的合作，期望有更多的创新投资，在一些基础领域方面的合作我们是非常期待的。

吴亮（主持人）： 今天讨论的是城市和产业，我们再请产业界的代表——正泰集团副总裁陈建克先生，谈一谈正泰集团在"一带一路"方面有哪些想法和计划。

陈建克： 谢谢主持人，正泰集团来自浙江，我们致力于高端制造业，在李部长的关心下，三十多年来发展得比较快，除了在国内的市场进行创新发展之外，我们的触角更多地"走出去"，伸向"一带一路"沿线国家。今天的论坛正好涉及城市伙伴和产业合作，我想一个产业"走出去"，在一个城市里发展和当地融为一体，进行融合创新是很有意义的。正泰集团从 2014 年起，就开始与德国法兰克福当地的企业合作，德国生产太阳能光伏的企业不是很景气，我们去了以后，把我们的市场优势和我们的品牌、资金、力量同它们融合发展。现在，企业的情况变得非常好，当地的市议会和州议会对我们高度认可，把当地的大道改为"正泰大道"，还把一个火车站更名为"正泰火车站"，在文化方面互相借鉴，效果很好。现在，正泰集团 500 多亿元的销售额中，国际销售占了 25% 左右。

吴亮（主持人）： 我和陈建克先生 18 年没见了，我还保留着我做记者时您送给我的剃须刀，是日本产的，现在国产的已经很好了，包括正泰集团的智能电器已经更多地走了出去，"一带一路"带来了很多的机遇。

下面引入一个问题的讨论：请问来自智库界的专家，在"一带一路"整个推进过程中，不管是城市间的合作、产业的合作，还是文化的交流，目前面临最大的障碍是什么？我们怎么解决这些障碍，让"一带一路"倡议真正成为越来越广泛的共同行动？有请克罗地亚地缘经济论坛研究所副所长贾思娜女士发言。

贾思娜：谢谢，很高兴能参加这个论坛！我很高兴能和今天在座的人分享价值观和目标，能够讨论在国家间如何开展自由贸易、投资、工作、文化交流等。

我认为，所有这些讨论都可以使经济全球化更加公平、平衡，使欧亚成为一个更加强大的一体化大陆。

我还要强调，两年前，李克强总理支持并提出了一个非常重要的倡议，这一倡议与城市的发展也有着非常密切的联系。这个倡议的名字是"三海合作"，它是关于亚得里亚海、波罗的海和黑海之间的合作。而非常重要也是必不可少的一点是产业合作。通过这些举措和项目，我们可以看到"一带一路"在本地区取得了很好的进展。

另一方面，我也要强调，这一城市合作也非常重要，因为我认为这是一个很好的机会，可以作为一个工具应用于加深发展政策之间的协调。这是发展地区、国家和城市之间合作的最佳途径。在欧洲的政治层面上，这是一种被广泛接受的做法。现在的城市合作、区域合作和次区域合作等各种合作都面临着几乎相同的机遇和挑战。而欧洲作为一个地区面临的最大挑战，就是所有这些层面的合作都聚焦于如何遵守欧洲的标准和法律上。我认为这是一个重要的敦促，也是必要的条件，谢谢。

吴亮（主持人）：谢谢贾思娜女士，克罗地亚是一个年轻的国家，也是一个非常伟大的国家，希望您能常来中国。下面有请智库界的王文教授讲讲他的观点。

王文：谢谢，有关我们要克服的问题：一是现阶段"一带一路"建设要进入真拼实干期，我赞同您讲的，要来点实的东西，越多实的东西越好，不仅中国方面，其他国家也是一样。二是精耕细作，投入的项目，有很多做得很不错的港口、大的基础设施建设如水电站等，下一步还得做精、做细，不能建一个铁路和水电站，运行一两年，就运营不下去了，这个时期很关键。三是真拼实干、精耕细作、综合发力，外国很多部门同样如此。"一带一路"是一个非常复杂、非常综合的、难度很大的重大的全球性构想，是一个重大项目，未来要发展下去还有很多的工作要做。就像人体一样，既涉及表面上整体的健康，也涉及每个毛细血管里的每个细胞健康，这个是挺难的，这恰恰需要更多综合性地发力。谢谢！

吴亮（主持人）：谢谢王文教授。我们再请中欧文化交流协会主席，欧盟亚洲研究所首席执行官顾爱乐先生。

顾爱乐：非常感谢你们给我机会让我再次来到深圳，今天能够来这里非常开心，我第一次来的时候是 20 世纪 80 年代，那时中国刚把深圳作为特区。现在我又来深圳，看到了深圳的发展以及取得的成就，现在这里有将近 2000 万人口，在这么短的时间内，深圳就从一个小渔村变成国际大都市，这真的令人非常吃惊。在深圳，极少数是本地人，全国各地乃至世界各地的人离开家乡，来到深圳开始自己的生活、自己的事业，所以深圳相对来说是比较具有吸引力的，这里的人口流动性比较强，这里的人口也很多样化，我觉得这可能也是深圳发展比较快的原因。"一带一路"倡议刚开始发展会遇到这样或那样的问题。欧洲对"一带一路"也有评论，认为"一带一路"是非常大胆的设想。同时我们还要看到，它的发展也遇到很多问题，这些问题会使我们对"一带一路"产生怀疑。

综合来看，"一带一路"确实是一个大胆的设想，而且具有巨大的潜力，它是一个新的概念、一个新的战略、一个新的理念。我觉得最重要的一点，"一带一路"是一个开放性的平台，相对于其他倡议来说，真的能带来更多的机遇，有很大的潜力。

我们来看一下深圳的发展，这么短的时间内，深圳经济特区成立还不到四十年，它的发展就已经举世瞩目，在深圳的发展过程中肯定也会遇到这样或那样的问题。"一带一路"也不例外，所以在"一带一路"向欧洲进行开拓的时候，也会遇到问题，这不是一个个例，而是所有新兴事物都会遇到的问题。很多欧洲人根本不知道"一带一路"是什么，他们对"一带一路"的观念很多很刻板，对中国的理解可能停留在五到十年前，五到十年前的中国和深圳与今天的中国和深圳比是非常不一样的，所以有一些欧洲人不了解中国，他们根本不知道中国正在发生什么，现在的中国是什么样，很多对中国的认识可能会有一些误解。

"一带一路"一定要注重交流，互联互通。在座各位也有人提到，中国注重并正在提高品牌质量，让自己品牌产品"走出去"，这一点是非常重要的。

我们要采取有效途径来提高产品的质量，我觉得"一带一路"不仅仅只是一个硬件，我们不仅要注重硬件，还要注重软件，所谓的软件就是信息、文化、教育这些方面。

我觉得文化和信息的交流是非常重要的，希望以后能更加注重信息的交换，让欧洲人更加了解中国的政策，包括一些新的战略。举个例子，欧洲很多人在谈论"一带一路"，但很多可能是假消息。我觉得这方面问题还是存在的，希望未来我们能加强交流，包括信息交流、文化沟通。欧洲有些人在批评"一带一路"，因为欧洲离中国比较远，了解不多，就很容易什么都去批评，如果这个东西很具体地出现在他们眼前，就会有非常直观的了解。

欧洲现在遇到的情况大体是这样的，所以我们更应该去改变这样的现状，中国一定要在交流、信息更新方面加大力度，加强欧洲对中国现状包括一些战略和政策的了解。相信深圳也有自己的问题，我们国家也派遣了很多代表团来北京、上海、深圳。中国政府也派了代表团到欧洲，我们经常去北京、上海，来深圳的机会比较少，之前在卢森堡也开过一些会议，我当时也去了，去年11月我去了北京、上海，就是没有来深圳，很遗憾。2015年到2016年，为了促进交流，卢森堡也派遣了一些人员到深圳来学习，看深圳在发生什么。我觉得深圳的金融地位不比其他城市轻，除了金融方面，在高科技、创新领域的发展地位也是举足轻重的。

吴亮（主持人）：谢谢来自欧洲智库的专家代表，讲得非常好。下面有请郭万达院长做总结性发言。

郭万达：谢谢吴先生，大家提了很多"一带一路"怎么落地的问题，也讲了怎么加强城市之间的合作，合作有很多障碍，以我的观察，智库在这方面做了很多研究,我认为城市之间的合作最重要的是对接城市的发展战略,国家层面可以对接国家的战略,但国家的战略往往最后要落到很多城市的节点中,如果不对接城市的发展战略,国家的战略在有些方面会显得落空。举个例子,深圳对接一些城市的战略,有几个方面我觉得做得还是很好的,我去年访问希腊的时候,希腊就提出来深圳对他们的机场是不是有兴趣,希望他们的机场和深圳有些合作。另外他们的温泉旅游,希望和深圳对接。高铁等大型基础设施不是某个城市能做的,但机场、港口、地铁往往都是城市的战略中应该去对接的,深圳的地铁公司已经"走出去",和一些"一带一路"沿线国家进行地铁的合作,帮助他们运营,这是第一种合作方式,我认为这个非常好。

欧盟的顾爱乐先生也讲到,很多"一带一路"的城市都在讲智慧城市、互联网发展,深圳也在做这方面,现在我有一个正在做的项目,我们帮助印度的城市进行智慧城市之间的对接,深圳有很多很好的公司,它们在支付方面是非常领先的,在 B2B、B2C 的平台上做得非常好,当然包括华为的基础通道建设,我觉得很多的智慧城市建设,深圳可以提供一揽子的解决方案。

还有一个对接的方案是园区,深圳有各种各样的园区,有工业制造业、物流的园区,还有一些自由贸易园区,总而言之我们称为特殊经济区。我没有去克罗地亚,我去过黑山,黑山是一个比较小的国家,他们说你们来帮我们做一个港口园区,像深圳那样。他们说我们没你们那么大,但能不能经过 10 年或 20 年发展得像深圳的蛇口一样?我说这个很好。如果要做园区我们给他们提建议,首先要立法,深圳当初是全国人大给它地方立法权,如果没有这个权力做起来很难。有了法律以后再有一个规划,吸引深圳的投资者过来。

我感觉就是一句话,城市之间的合作某种程度上是基于国家战略层面对接,但要落在城市战略对接上。城市一定有它的战略,怎么样和中国的城市去进行对接?刚才讲的基础设施也好、智慧城市也好、园区也好,我提的这三个只是我作为智库纽带去做的,我觉得还有很多方面可以对接。谢谢大家。

吴亮(主持人):谢谢郭院长。刚才大家讲的可以总结为一点,交流、合作都要有具体的载体,围绕城市之间的合作,围绕具体产业链间的合作,要在具体载体的基础上加强沟通、加强交流、加强互惠互利，加强文化的融合、感情的融通。刚才大家讲了心里想说的话，讲了大家最想做的事情，希望大家将来做得越来越好。今天的讨论到此结束，谢谢各位。

平行分论坛（一）：智库纽带

加强政策沟通，构建城市智库伙伴网络

第一节

王义桅（主持人）：我们先有请第一个发言代表，韩国欧亚研究院院长金锡焕先生，大家欢迎。

金锡焕：谢谢主持人。首先，关于智库间的交流合作，我个人有很多经验和体会。最近我在主编一本政策性刊物，我们韩国外国语大学和俄罗斯的一个机构共同出版这个刊物，我们想通过这个合作刊物表达一些观点，我觉得这是两个智库之间的合作，非常有意义。在我本人所在的机构，也就是韩国欧亚研究院，我们也发起了一些论坛，这是韩国和俄罗斯之间非常重要的交流平台，我们邀请在欧亚大陆知名的专家发言，两年前在莫斯科举办了第一届，第二届在韩国，今年可能会在哈萨克斯坦举办。像这样一个为欧亚学者搭建的平台是本人和机构的同事共同提出的，我觉得这是非常好的智库合作模式，值得借鉴。

当然，在智库合作经验方面，我们和俄罗斯的智库——瓦尔代俱乐部有合作，在此背景下，我们与挪威、新加坡、日本、中国以及俄罗斯等多方智库共同开展了一个为期三年的研究项目，该项目主要由挪威方出资，但他们并不会对我们直接进行管理，管理是由新加坡的智库进行的，所以我们与出资方之间是平等的合作伙伴关系，我们智库之间的合作共赢会一直持续下去，我们在如何增进双方的理解，如何获得共同目标等方面获得了很好的进展，最后的成果由俄罗斯合作的智库出版，所以说在过去的三年中，这个智库合作研究项目非常成功。虽然这个项目已经结束了，但从今年开始，韩国方面、俄罗斯方面和日本方面决定继续扩大合作，吸纳更多的欧洲智库、私人智库进来，目前我们也正在商谈之中。

第二个主题讨论点是关于合作中的难点和问题，在上午的讨论中，我们讨论了智库的角色和其难点，我觉得智库需要有一些新的常态、新的形态，传统的角色应该说消失了，所以我们需要在这方面进行一些革新。智库的角色是很多年前定义的，当时从传统上来说，智库就是写备忘录、做研究，然后把我们的观点分享给政府或议会，同时追踪这些观点在现实世界中的实施情况。但是这样一个模式现在已经是非常滞后或者过时的，例如美国的布鲁金斯学会，以及其他一些西方领先智库，包括我们韩国的一些同行都深有感触的一点是，智库需要有一个新的发展模式，为什么会出现这样的现象？首先，政策的焦点已经开始从中央政府转移到城市及大都市、跨大陆、跨大洲的层面，所以在华盛顿、北京、东京、首尔这些传统的中央政府驻地之外，我们有更多的话语权和声音，资源的分布也有很大的变化，比如有些民间投资者所起到的作用比一些小国的公共投资更加重要。其次，政策已从国家层面转到地方层面，我们的公共机构也扮演更多的角色，相应智库的角色也要做一些调整，之前智库在撰写一些研究报告后可以通过网络把经验和观点表达出去，随着技术的创新和进步，我们的受众也发生了变化，我们发现现在有越来越多的"个体智库"，一个人就是一个智库，这种现象在很多国家也屡见不鲜，所以 20 世纪的传统智库模式已经过时，我相信一个新型的智库模式是亟待出现的，我们新型模式的智库可以对新型资源的转移做出响应。

我觉得"一带一路"倡议是非常成功和有意义的创举，我觉得中国之前从未在世界上获得如此大的影响力，"一带一路"倡议实现了这一点，从这个角度来说它是成功的，当然它也面临一些大的问题，例如中国将如何在实际中落实"一带一路"倡议，如何在实际中落实这些概念和计划？当然现在中国有一些宣传，这种宣传是针对全球的，融合和互联互通是非常重要的，只有相互融合和联通才能给世界带来繁荣和和平。这个基于相互理解而产生的规则，本身是符合逻辑的。但同时我们也需要知道，缺乏交流或者缺乏共识，会成为我们的障碍，当然，如果对新技术、新进展漠视的话，也会是一个非常重要的问题。现在科技发生了翻天覆地的变化，对我们的劳动力等各个方面都造成重大的影响，所以我们在彼此的联通和融合过程中更需要从思想上深入广泛地了解当前的问题。

互联互通和相互融合给了我们发展的机会，它也会带来一些很大的风险，包括我们社会方面的风险，比如越南现在就很缺乏这种互联互通，缺乏一些传播、自动化及数字的管理等方面的经验，越南面临的困难其实比中国和韩国更严重，对于劳动力来说，75% 的工人就面临着这些压力。如果我们可以促进彼此间的连通性，建立一些基础设施和交通设施项目，那么对于我们未来的劳动力就不会是一个问题，因此，需要更多地关注一些原则问题，以及这些策略最终在什么地方发挥作用。谢谢大家。

王义桅（主持人）：谢谢，之后的讨论过程中可以进一步交流您的观点，您刚刚介绍了自己所在的智库欧亚研究院，也对我们面临的风险、危机进行了分析，我觉得我们确实要引起重视，我也非常喜欢您提到的新类型的智库。中国现在提出国际关系的新形态，我觉得智库也需要有一个新形态，这不仅仅是关于亚洲和"一带一路"。下面邀请下一位演讲者，盘古智库的理事长易鹏。

易鹏：我们是一个民间智库，我简单浓缩三个观点。第一个观点，我们机构基本上参加智库之间的频率是每年 150 场以上，智库之间要多交流，只有多交流彼此之间才能消除误解，多交流才能达成共识，坦诚的交流是基础，如果不坦诚，不真诚，不坦率，可能我们最后无法达成共识。

经验给我的体会是，目前不同国家、不同的形态的智库组织，都有各自文化的差异、价值观的差异、国家利益的差异，彼此之间往往从自己的角度去思考，换位思考不够，这点可能不利于问题的解决，我们一致认为换位思考有利于智库的交流，这中间可能有些叫作坚持，有些也叫作固执，但我认为有必要通过更多的换位思考来提高智库之间的交流质量。

第二个观点，因为后面说要构建"一带一路"倡议下的城市智库伙伴网络，我们也非常愿意参与其中。

第三个观点，智库的核心在于推动项目的落地，目前智库中有时聊宏伟蓝图比较多，谈方向比较多，但智库更应立足于解决具体问题，比如落实"一带一路"除了提倡文化、人心等各种相通，我认为还有一点——项目要连通，举个例子，当前而言，"一带一路"国家之间完全可以推动以城市为主题的各种产城合一的项目合作。例如深圳就是全国改革开放的缩影，是中国产业和城市互动非常良好的榜样，像印度、印度尼西亚等"一带一路"沿线国家可以通过一系列"一带一路"的合作，通过智库的谋划、策划、规划，推动更多像深圳一样的产城联动比较成功的项目落地，这些项目的落地既有利于"一带一路"产城合作，同时也有利于这个国家经济的发展，有利于老百姓的就业和收入的提高，能够实现双赢和多赢。

因此，我提出两个建议，第一个建议是，我们进行智库之间的交流，一个方面是我们想面对面沟通和交流，但事实上互联网的技术发展很快，我们一直倡议建立互联网视频技术为基础的网上智库连线，所以我们前年在北京成立了一个盘古智库连线，一直主张采用新的技术，像华为公司远程视频的技术手段非常发达，这种技术的进步使得我们完全可以在网上进行24小时不间断的智库沟通和交流，城市与城市沟通和交流，讨论话题可以很宽、很广。

第二个建议是，当前参与智库的是国家，另外一个维度是，一些跨国公司的影响力可能已经超过了一个国家的力量，所以现在就整体而言，国际组织的力量在发生改变，我们既要谈国与国，也完全可以进行跨国企业和城市、跨国企业与国家、跨国企业与智库等各种层次的路径探索，因为"一带一路"的建设也需要在不同组织的理念上落地。

我代表盘古智库邀请大家到北京香山进行沟通和交流，也祝愿这个会议取得圆满成功，谢谢大家。

王义桅（主持人）：谢谢易鹏，您刚才谈到了未来要加强不同层面的沟通来解决项目合作中的问题，也许未来我们可以实现这种理想化的建构，能够使我们每个人都成为一个具有智慧的人。下一位演讲者是来自于克罗地亚地缘经济论坛研究所的副所长贾思娜。

贾思娜：正如同刚才主持人介绍的一样，我是克罗地亚地缘经济论坛研究所的副所长，我们与中国政府开展了很多高效合作，涉及很多方面，我们也与来自北京的相关高层机构在近2个月进行了高层经济对话，这些对话都有效促进了我们之间的高层对话和经济的往来，我们都非常高兴地达成共识，就是我们急切需要"一带一路"倡议下国际城市合作的进一步发展，需要各国之间更具有透明性和交流性的"一带一路"的沟通和合作。

我想要说的是，今天在"一带一路"的倡议下，我们有这样一个非常好的架构和网络，在我们了解新的智库之前，我们需要了解智库的多面性。从我自己的经验来说，"一带一路"的智库有着多层面的含义，过去我们很多时候过多地关注于介绍一些项目、一些情况，能够使我们不断地拓展影响力，不断地促进在中小型企业和各个层面间进行更具透明度的交流，有效地提升"一带一路"的影响力，我认为这一点是至关重要的。

另一方面我想要建议的是，可以说每个智库都有各自擅长的领域，我们也需要每个智库有自己专攻的项目，而不是所有的东西都是能做的。中国的智库可以说处在非常领先的地位，我们希望能够看到更加公开透明的合作，这就要求我们共同努力，彼此分享和承担压力，这样才能共同进步。

另一个目标是要增强我们的影响力，使智库的工作不断本地化，让当地的企业从中受益。在"一带一路"建设中，我有一个新的想法，那就是智库也应该更多关注金融还有商业方面的领域，并且连接各个国家、各个区域、各个城市，使之能够更好地融合。希望未来在这方面能够更加透明一些，能够看到它是如何运作的。

与此同时，对我们来说非常重要的是，促进和推广"一带一路"倡议下的项目。例如有些自给自足的项目能够给更多的沿线国家而不是仅仅一个国家带来实际的好处，我们必须有这样区域之间的合作。当然我们谈到高层次的合作的时候，也要有一些高层的发展策略，更多的时候我们需要进一步把它化为更加现实具体的策略，这些合作可以说是至关重要的，特别是对"一带一路"倡议实实在在地在我们的体制下实施。

从我们的机构来说，我们也希望"一带一路"倡议成为一个非常好的领导性项目，能够让我们与中国更好地开展合作，通过这个项目，我们希望不仅与中国，也和亚洲各国有更好的互动。我认为我们需要在"一带一路"倡议下发展出新形式，探索出更多新的东西，从而能够从这个倡议中获益。当然我们也要注意负面的影响，欧盟包括其他国家似乎都有一种并不是基于数据和事实的偏见或说法，如果说有这样一种偏见或说法，我本人不会有任何评论。但我觉得这样一种情况在欧洲东南部很常见，这个区域的很多国家有些是欧盟的成员国，有三个已经是欧盟的候选国，这些国家有一种氛围，觉得"一带一路"倡议和欧盟的规则是相对立的，我觉得事实并不是如此，只是说我们需要采取一些措施来解决现在的问题，这方面我相信智库是大有可为的，我们可以去影响现在的思潮。

我们应该强调"一带一路"倡议对欧盟是一个很大的促进和支持，这并不仅仅是中国想通过"一带一路"在欧洲交更多的朋友，比如说在去年"一带一路"的论坛上，欧盟就派出观察员，有很多文件、政策向我们证明"一带一路"倡议是非常有价值的，我觉得这与我们彼此融合和一体化有关，所以需要求同存异，在"一带一路"的倡议下发现更多的共性，从而进一步实现合作。

最后，"一带一路"所有的参与国都应该得到相关智库研究的一些支持，来了解"一带一路"区域层面、次区域层面、城市层面以及其他层面的优势、劣势和存在的风险。首先我们要对"一带一路"有一个本地的见解，让当地社区真正从中获益，这是一个起点，谢谢大家的聆听，谢谢大家。

王义桅（主持人）：谢谢贾思娜的分享，克罗地亚是欧盟最年轻的成员国，也是"16＋1"这样一个合作项目的参与国，我觉得克罗地亚是其他欧盟国家的榜样，它们可以借鉴你们的方式，我也非常同意刚才说到"16＋1"的合作可以与"一带一路"倡议形成协同作用，可以让倡议更好被欧盟接受，当然我也希望东南欧可以尽快获得欧盟成员国的身份。不管是国家层面、城市层面还是洲际层面上，我们都需要有一种合作，需要有这种互动和联系，欧洲的智库经常把"一带一路"视为中国新兴的丝绸之路项目，因为其实有很多的丝绸之路项目被日本、韩国、土耳其发起，其实并不是这样，丝绸之路是关于文化的，"一带一路"超越了文化，更多的是政策的协同、金融等各个方面，所以我觉得"新丝绸之路"并不能全面概括"一带一路"，它是一个有丝绸之路内涵的全新项目，但这不是全部。下一位演讲人是北京大学产业技术研究院院长陈东敏。

陈东敏：女士们、先生们，下午好！我是北京大学的陈东敏，我们的智库研究所关注的是了解国家的创新机制和生态系统如何协同发展，以及了解如何能够在国家和国际层面上通过创新给予更多的支持，从今天上午的会议和刚刚的交流中，我也收益很多。我自己也有一些见解，"一带一路"是一个新的模式，我也非常同意刚刚几位发言人的观点。

"一带一路"是一个非常宏大的视野或者宏大的愿景，智库需要更多地了解这中间的一些问题来考虑我们如何能够使这样一个宏大的愿景得以实现，刚刚主持人也提到现在"一带一路"其实是一个非常包容的概念，并不仅仅是文化贸易，它也有经济、创新、科技、技术、政策各个方面的合作，所以我想单——一个智库并不能涵盖这样一个宏大的项目。作为一个工程师，我们总是想要一个路线图，知道不同的时间节点、不同的里程碑、不同的目标，但是我觉得智库会稍稍有点不同，我们有一个模型了解我们要解决哪些问题，从创新的角度来说，我们先是发现问题，然后再建立一个模型来解决问题，但这个模型我觉得应该更多的是一个路线图，但它不是通用的路线图，而是各个区域特殊化的路线图，我非常相信我们的智库在促进交流、融合、解决问题方面大有可为，包括促进多边合作。

我想再举一些具体的例子，就是我刚刚提到的模型，我觉得应该"先找马，再建马车"，我想提到的就是创业和创新，我觉得其中一个非常重要的观点是我们的 IP，我们的知识产权，每个国家都有各自不同的知识产权体系，我们现在是鼓励各国之间、各个产业之间有更深入的知识产权保护的交流，我相信智库在这方面可以通过促进我们的交流来解决分歧，如果我们仅仅依靠专利体系，我觉得并不会非常行之有效，不是每次出现专利纠纷我们都要走法律途径，这是费时费力的。因此，我们需要有一个更快解决问题的方式，我们可以加快技术的转让，我想中国和中国的智库以及其他国家都需要在这方面做出更多的努力。

中国在保护知识产权方面其实有很大的进步，现在我们这方面的声誉越来越好，也是让大家认识到我们的法律体系是在保护公司。最近国内有一个法律诉讼，外国公司胜诉了，中国的公司败诉了，这证明我们的立法体系在保护知识产权方面越来越健全。

我也谈一下各国之间的创新合作，我想讲的是网络问题，智库网络或者智库伙伴网络其实有不同的领域，技术是一个问题，知识产权是一个问题，人才也是重要的问题，我觉得公共的人才智库网络是我们需要进一步利用的。目前我们与"一带一路"相关国家的大学也建立了更多的合作，我们想通过教育来进一步促进我们的合作伙伴关系。现在是一个互联网的时代、技术的时代，越来越多年轻创业家崭露头角，所以在大学中我们非常感兴趣的一点是鼓励新的创业人士、鼓励大学生有创业精神，我们也是希望通过"一带一路"在沿线国家建立起这个网络来帮助大家。谢谢大家。

王义桅（主持人）：谢谢陈教授刚刚的分享，创新是一个关键词，习近平主席在 2017 年 5 月的"一带一路"国际合作高峰论坛上也提到创新，他提出"第一，我们要将'一带一路'建成和平之路"，"第二，我们要将'一带一路'建成繁荣之路"，"第三，我们要将'一带一路'建成开放之路"，"第四，我们要将'一带一路'建成创新之路"，"第五，我们要将'一带一路'建成文明之路"。其实这也是我们人类现在面临的一些问题，是我们发展上面的一些缺陷，当然习主席也提到创新是基于我们的创业和创业精神，不仅仅是技术上的创新，所以在机制层面上，我们要有更多的创新，这方面其实我们智库也是大有可为，我们要想出一些新的模型和新形式的智库。在上午的会谈中，我们的演讲人也提到"一带一路"是一种新型的工业化，工业化其实就是从英国先发起的，整个欧洲经历了工业化的浪潮，美国也经历了这样一个浪潮，现在在中国和印度的工业化发展涉及数十亿人，工业化的模式不能复制，我们要依靠更多的技术。现在我们的世界面临着前所未有的思潮，我们的经验、观点和以前都有非常不同的地方。

第五位演讲人是复旦大学国际问题研究院南亚研究中心副主任林民旺，他的演讲是关于智库网络国际合作的项目。

林民旺：我来自大学，我集中谈三点。第一，"一带一路"建设中的智库合作的必要性和高校的作用。"一带一路"是习主席在 2013 年底提出来的，在 2014 年年初习近平主席又呼吁中国国内要开始智库建设，所以"一带一路"和智库建设其实是连接得非常紧的，为什么是这样？我个人认为无论是"一带一路"还是智库建设的需求是中国对整个世界的视野扩大导致的必然结果。中国有了"一带一路"，所以更需要智库拓展中国对整个世界的认识，我们知道今天有很多欧洲的学者来这儿，我想欧洲对世界的了解很大一部分也是因为视野的范围和利益的扩大导致的，事实上"一带一路"推进到现在已经好多年了，我们也会发现其实问题很多，智库和大学可以发挥很大的作用。我主要从事南亚研究和印度研究，比如印度的 GDP 总量在世界排名第七，很快要超过英国、法国，很快会排在世界第五，但我觉得中国很少有人真正了解印度，对印度的了解很有限。

我觉得研究一个地区或一个国家需要做大量的田野调查，缺乏调查的话怎么可能有高质量的成果？所以带来的问题是一样的，现在"一带一路"建设之后，我们对印度这样的国家了解都这么少，更别说其他国家了。中国不仅缺乏对很多"一带一路"沿线国家的了解，对其他国家也是一样的。我认为现在很需要新的智库或高校提供关于地区、国家的有效、可靠的知识。

第二，我们需要整合中国大学和智库的关于地区、国家的知识以及合作的需求。每个研究者都有他的局限，每个研究机构有它的局限，就我个人来说，我的优势是我比较了解国际关系，我想也同样因为我曾经在印度当过外交官，所以我与印度的官方机构和中国的官方机构有一些联系。刚才发言的盘古智库主要集中于经济研究，易鹏理事长和中国很多的企业有非常广泛的联系，所以我们两个见面之后，易鹏理事长决定在盘古智库下面成立一个印度研究中心，把我们两个有效的知识整合一下，我觉得这是一个非常好的创意和做法，我觉得很多的智库，不论是中国国内的智库之间还是不同国家的智库之间都应该进行合作，这样能够取得大量更有效的成果，能够促进利益共享。

第三，其实"一带一路"吸引了大量的国外学者，可能很多学者包括印度的学者还有巴基斯坦的学者经常引用中国学者的话。但是有学者说，南亚的"一带一路"沿线国家为中国牺牲了，是为中国实现战略需要才加入"一带一路"的，我说这个想法是错误的，中国邻国太多了，中国可以投资的地方太多了，"一带一路"国家都是市场环境相对较差的，我认为中国没有那么多的地缘政治，中国的"一带一路"倡议主要还是出于经济的考虑，还是以市场的逻辑为主，这是我个人的看法，我就谈到这儿。

王义桅（主持人）：谢谢林教授，林教授提到很多与中国相关的"一带一路"

活动和宣传，实际上我们在思维领域方面也要进行很多的改变，我们需要更客观地看待外国，我们对有些国家可能了解得不是特别深，比如印度，这就要加强我们之间的互相学习，还有英国、德国等。实际上我们从印度那里学习了很多东西，我们也从邻近的国家学到了很多，我们还要了解不同的大陆和不同洲的情况。下一位是来自华沙经济学院亚洲研究中心的海杜克教授，他在波兰是研究相关经济政策的。

海杜克：大家下午好！我接下来给大家讲的跟其他演讲者有所不同，我希望更多给大家展示一下我们的研究成果，给大家看一下我们的数据，向大家展示"一带一路"倡议和英国脱欧的情况是怎样的。大家知道，英国脱欧前后有很多的变化，我们实际上就是希望能够更多地去根据实际情况进行分析，根据中国的"一带一路"相关政策和英国的实际情况进行调整。

首先给大家讲一下"一带一路"的情况，我主要关注一些要点，主要关注如何达成互惠，如何保持平衡的发展合作。当我们看中英之间关系时，我们首先从高层面的角度去看一下我们在政治方面的一些辞令，首先从政治层面进行合作，很多时候我们可以从新闻的首页看到中英之间的合作。另一方面是前首相大卫·卡梅伦与中国达成的协议，除此之外还有很多协议，我们需要看这些政府相关的举措是否适合于合作和发展。与此同时下面有很多具体的项目，当我们谈到中英之间关系的时候，特别在近期，致力于建立面向 21 世纪全球全面战略伙伴关系，不仅仅是中英之间，中国与其他欧盟国家之间也是以这样的基调来进行发展的。

下面，让我们关注一些经济领域的情况。我们看一下中英贸易数据，可以看到 2014 年之后贸易趋势是下滑的。中国现在是英国第七大贸易伙伴，贡献率仅仅达到 4.4%，这是非常低的。看完贸易之后再看一下投资，我们发现中国的对外投资，在整个欧洲，英国是最大的投资目的地，但与中美投资相比微不足道，而且中国对德国的投资不断增加，对英国的投资出现了下滑，且最大一部分投资是房地产，大家知道，中国从去年 8 月起出台新规定，有三类受限的投资，其中一类就是对外房地产的投资，娱乐、体育、俱乐部、房地产都是投资受限项目。再看 2015、2016 年中欧投资数据，首先是欧洲三大国，英国、法国、德国，然后是"一带一路"沿线国家，最后是整个欧盟。

我们再来看一下"一带一路"在英国脱欧前后的情况对比。我想对比四个项目，首先是义乌—伦敦的铁路项目，另外一个项目是我之前提到的核电站项目，第三个项目是一个投资计划，是中国在伦敦的金融城进行的投资，其实是一个港口项目，第四个项目是伦敦金融城，我想看一下伦敦金融城在"一带一路"中对中国起到了哪些促进作用。今天早上亚投行的行长说，亚投行从来没有否定会在伦敦建立本地的办公室，这个可能性是依然存在的，这也是亚投行相关的项目。

我想说的是，英国脱欧后，对这些在脱欧之前就已经确定的项目会有什么影响呢？首先是"义乌—伦敦"铁路，它并不是一列直接从义乌到伦敦的火车，它首先在德国停留，这些集装箱会卸载到更小型的列车上，列车通过海底隧道再进入英国，也就是说，其实这个列车的重点是到德国的城市卸载集装箱后，再出发到伦敦，当然回程也是这样的流程。脱欧之后，英国和欧盟不再是一体的，是否有更多的壁垒出现？我们发现这个铁路和之前不一样了，德国的城市并没有以前那么有吸引力了，如果英国不愿意做出一些调整，它脱欧之后的壁垒是存在的。因此，是否可以看到中国有一个项目，它不经过欧洲大陆直接到英国呢？下面是一个铁路线路的提议，我们可以将它叫作北海或者北极的线路，可以从上海或者香港、深圳出发，这样一个线路会历经22天直接到达伦敦，不用途经欧洲大陆的任何城市。这样一个线路和之前途径欧洲大陆的线路相比时间更短，前者需要37天，后者只需要22天。"但问题在于，这样一个走北极海的项目需要很多前期投入"，这里我也引用了中远集团高层对此项目的评论，毕竟这是海运项目。

接下来是一个核电站的项目，一个棘手的地方在于，这个项目一开始是与法国电力公司合作的，中国的中广核加入，根据当前欧盟的法律，它是基于欧盟关于核电站的标准，大家知道核电站的标准是非常高的，这是一个协议的安全标准，创立于1952年，因为英国脱欧后也就退出欧洲原子能共同体的公约，脱欧之后就变得非常复杂，尤其涉及安全标准问题。英国脱欧之后欧洲原子能反应堆项目被推迟了，因为脱欧后英国退出了欧洲原子能共同体，退出原子核供应链，包括设备和员工培训等。还有很多类似这样的项目被推迟，中国正在协商，因为中国也在洽谈英国的核电项目，其中一个在塞姆塞特郡，还有英国另外一个地方。中国在英国三个地方建立了核电站的项目。

第三个受影响的是在伦敦的合作项目，由中国 ADP 发展公司和中国中信银行共同出资，预计 2026 年完成。项目真正开始之前，我觉得肯定会有很复杂的磋商和谈判过程，英国政府本来是希望在脱欧之前启动这样一个项目，这样其实更简便一些。现在启动这些项目需要基于欧盟的规则，在脱欧之后英国肯定需要对这些规定和规则进行改变，这也是英国想脱欧的原因。

另一个项目是伦敦金融城，从中国的角度来说，这是非常重要的项目，因为有越来越多的"一带一路"项目，那就涉及越来越多的资金，这些项目融资应该怎么办呢？伦敦依然是全球最大的金融中心。当然了，现在有一些银行想撤出英国，但当前伦敦依然是全球最大的金融中心，从经济的角度来说，这就是"锁定效应"。关键在于如何保持它的活力，当前我得出了一些结论，想和大家简短地讨论一下。

首先是对英国方面的观点，脱欧之后的英国需要支持中国"一带一路"的项目，这是现在英国财政大臣的观点。尽管英国离开了欧盟，它依然是一个举足轻重的国家，依然会在"一带一路"倡议下扮演非常重要的角色。非常重要的一点是，在脱欧之后，中国依然会对英国保持非常大的兴趣，因为伦敦依然是世界最大的金融中心，对于人民币国际化或者作为离岸交易中心，伦敦这个地方是非常重要的，超过一半以上的人民币包括贷款等都是在伦敦实现的，而不是在亚洲或者美国。当然我也有一些政策建议，中国应该更多重视伦敦作为全球经济中心的角色，如有必要的话，中国还应该作出一些最坏情况和最好情况的假设，假如说伦敦失去了这样一个金融中心的优势，中国应该怎么应对？如果说英国脱欧之后，它的金融中心地位得到进一步巩固，中国又应该如何应对？我想强调的一点是，中国应该设想出不同的情景，如果伦敦作为金融中心它有这样或那样的变化，中国应该如何应对？

第二点依然是关于核电站的项目，我相信非常有必要的是，对于中国来说，我们应该建立起全新的商业模式来运作核电站。两个合作伙伴一个是欧盟，一个是英国，中国工业上的标准和技术应该怎么和脱欧后的英国标准进行融合，这需要新型的商业模式解决这个问题。

第三点是关于义乌—伦敦铁路的想法。我们知道有一个海陆快线，途径贝尔格莱德、布达佩斯等城市，我认为这会涉及 2021—2027 年度欧盟预算。我建议中国政府能够努力参与到这个合作框架下，并且有一些预算，因为这将使中国政府有机会参与到相关的项目中来，通过新的框架职能，结合英国和中国不同的创意，能使我们在各个国家的不同领域比如农业等领域，结合不同的情况，加快各区域协同发展，这为我们建立了一个更好的未来，并结合了中国城市和各行业的优势。

作为智库来说，我们主要是从经济的角度出发，进行分析数据，建立不同的模式，促进经济发展。希望能够与中国建立很好的网络联系，共享一些信息，能够与中国政府还有相关的智库机构整合资源，使得我们都从中受益。因为很多的智库都是基于数据或模型，有时研究不仅仅只是一个想法，需要基于很多实际的数据。以上是我的一些观点，谢谢大家。

王义桅（主持人）：非常感谢海杜克先生的分享，可以说你刚才分享了很多具体的内容，当然也分析了一些不确定性，我们需要了解我们的合作不应该双输，而应该是双赢。你刚才也提到我们需要进一步分享数据，在"一带一路"的框架下加强彼此的合作，在中国很多智库也是希望能够不断分享彼此的知识和数据，这个想法非常棒。接下来有请来自深圳大学的陶一桃教授发言。

陶一桃：女士们、先生们，大家下午好！我今天演讲的题目是"'一带一路'倡议实施的制度文化约束"，我想简单地谈两个问题，第一个问题是"一带一路"倡议实施的制度约束，第二个想谈一下包容性发展的意义和价值。

我认为从根本上，"一带一路"倡议的实施无论对中国还是沿线国家来说，都不是单纯的经济问题，而是文化大于资本、技术重于制度的非经济问题。来自技术和文化的约束，既是最柔性的约束，也是最根本的约束，实际上是共同的价值观和规律界定的社会共同体及其个人的行为。而来自一个社会和共同体发展起来的并已形成的非正式的制度习惯、价值观,不仅是制度系统的组成部分,同时也是文化系统的组成部分。所以我认为,跨越制度和文化约束,建立一个富有包容性的、可操作的制度文化这样一个认知共同体对于"一带一路"倡议的实施是有益的,无论从逻辑上还是现实意义上来讲,这都应该是优先的策略。

我认为"一带一路"推进的最重要的问题是自身观念和思维方式、行为方式,中国将近40年的改革开放的经验证明,举国体制是行之有效的,它在集中资源、办大事方面,在迅速地调动民众参与重大项目方面,在整齐划一地高效解决群体问题方面都具有其他体制无法比拟的效率与优势,但是我们不能简单以这样的思维方式和习惯处理"一带一路"项目,尤其是直接涉及当地居民利益甚至是文化信仰这样的大工程,我们要做的应该是依法行动,按国际惯例办事,用时间换共识,用了解换共赢,用法律保障利益,这是我们应该考量的事情。

这是第一个方面的问题,下面我再讲第二个方面的问题:包容性发展的意义和价值。"一带一路"概念的提出是中国向国际社会传递的信息和价值导向,也是中国与世界合作方式的新变化,在过去的近40年时间里,中国集中精力完成由计划经济向市场经济转型,探索由普遍贫穷走向共同富裕的道路,这条中国道路是成功的,是一个国家坚持独立自主、自力更生、摆脱贫困和落后艰难而曲折的过程,更是一个国家致力于改革开放,打破闭关锁国,寻求和平发展的美丽故事。价值认同是中国与周边国家及世界合作的潜在制度性成本,构建能够一致理解的价值共同体有助于共同体内在制度的演变,使其变得更加可预见,对于演变中的共同体内在制度而言,共同价值观发挥过滤器的作用,包容性发展无论对于国与国之间还是区域共同体之间都不是价值观,而是真实合作,切实谋取共同繁荣发展,缔结盟约的思想基础。

从这个意义上来讲,观念、价值、共识本身就是资源,是创造财富的财富,是能够带来繁荣的无形资本和保障。包容性发展的宗旨就是共同发展繁荣,人类共同发展繁荣的过程绝不是用观念战胜观念的过程,而是观念对观念的认同,观念能够改变人,而人能改变社会。同时我还认为,包容性发展的要旨在于对成员国自身发展的肯定与支持,是对国别差异性的接纳和尊重,而不是此消彼长的厮杀，经济全球化的实现不仅在经济运行体制内已经为共同体的成长、发展、繁荣提供了空间，也为共同体的共同繁荣发展提供了无限的可能。包容性发展更重要的前提是对于彼此核心利益的保护和尊重，市场以公平交换为前提，市场非战场，市场要培育对手，培育生意伙伴，有健康的生意伙伴关系才有健康的市场秩序。

在讲包容性发展的时候我还想强调包容性发展必须要直面矛盾、分歧甚至冲突，因为在区域合作中矛盾、分歧、冲突的存在都是在所难免的，因为各个国家都有各个国家的利益、价值观和价值判断甚至政治倾向，但关键的问题是，如何化解、减少、弱化、解决上述问题，我认为在这些方面中国的老庄哲学是值得我们借鉴的。

最后，我想说几个观点，第一个观点是，"一带一路"倡议绝不是短期工程，它将对改变世界经济政治格局产生深远影响。第二，"一带一路"倡议的实施最需要完成的任务是互信的确认，国与国之间的互信是可以通过文化与价值认同来实现的，文化与价值的认同不可能是一种文化对另一种文化的简单认同，而应该是在彼此尊重中达成共赢。我认为共同繁荣发展的最重要问题是让所有国家在"一带一路"倡议下都有所收获，这是最重要的。谢谢大家。

王义桅（主持人）：谢谢陶教授刚刚的介绍，我觉得"一带一路"是中国不仅仅从西方，也是从发展中国家和整个外部世界来学习的过程，很多国家的经济、基础设施并不是非常完善，它们的政治体系可能也受到西方的影响，因此它们可能不能直接复制中国的成功模式，当然您也提到包容发展，我觉得这是非常重要的，我曾在书中也提到了"包容全球化"的概念，我觉得跟您谈的有异曲同工之处。下一位演讲人是来自孟加拉国企业研究所的研究主任谢哈布汗先生。

谢哈布汗：谢谢大家，下午好！谢谢主持人刚刚的介绍，我觉得刚刚的讨论非常有意义，大家提到各种各样的问题，我们的不确定性、我们新的模型还有各方面，当然我们也发现我们进入了新的发展维度，因此，我们一定要确定我们到底是什么样的想法，我们的想法和别人有何不同。亚洲是"一带一路"的相关区域，当然还有其他的相关区域，我们觉得经济是发展非常重要的一个因素，之前的发言人都谈到了智库的作用和相关的经验、我们的互动方式，陶教授也提到了相关的框架模式，我想从技术方面具体地和大家谈一谈智库在"一带一路"倡议下能作出哪些贡献。金教授提到传统的智库模式已经过时了，我们要有新的模式，我完全同意这一点，之前智库给政府提供建议，现在智库要更多地与公众进行互动，我们要考虑到新的技术、社交媒体，人们有更多的工具获取信息，也就是说，传统模式已经过时了，我们需要触及更多的受众，智库不仅仅要做研究，还要传播我们的研究结果，传播我们的观点，我们要在执政者和公众之间取得非常好的连接，我觉得我们需要更多地使用社交媒体和其他新的技术。

非常有意思的一点是，我发现中国的智库发展是非常不一样的，我们发现有很多新型的智库，之前是关于贸易、经济、国际关系、外交政策等，其实我个人也是关注外交领域的，我觉得在亚洲有一个问题，更多来说可能是说东南亚有一个问题，我觉得一般会提到在东南亚有一些连接的问题，但我觉得更多是融资的问题以及政府本身兴趣不大的问题，一些项目之前的投资或融资更多考虑捐赠人的利益，这个问题在东南亚是非常明显的，这些项目会有市场的限制、融资方面的意识形态问题，这都是智库需要关注的。

智库进行能力建设也是非常重要的，我来自孟加拉国的企业研究院，我们在市区有很多合作机构，我们是如何来扩大我们的信息传播的呢？我们有一个网站，我们会公布一些信息。2016 年习近平主席访问了孟加拉国，这促进了两国的关系，我们现在也是战略性的合作伙伴，我们也是想确保孟加拉国是"一带一路"的合作伙伴之一，我希望南亚和东南亚在这个倡议中发挥更大的作用。当然我们也有一些非常根本的问题，那就是很多国家可能战略上并没有完全实现对接，作为一个国家来说，尤其是对孟加拉国这样一个小国来说，我们需要在这个过程中进行权衡，取得平衡，我们希望这些项目不仅仅是孟加拉国需要的，也是中国以及其他相关方比如说韩国需要的，是我们共同利益的代表。我们也希望我们有一个资源库可以进行共享，为了使"一带一路"更好地连接，我们需要有更多的合作方式和模式，我们现在并不是在 19 世纪或 20世纪，我们是一个新的时代，我们需要有新的解读和新的合作方式。

之前主持人也提到我们要实现经济一体化和加强合作，不仅要在货币层面也要在金融层面，我们这些合作无疑要有非常好的研究成果做佐证，之前也有发言人提到现在有很多的基建项目、能源项目都可以给双方带来益处，如果通过我们的研究能够推动更多这样的项目，"一带一路"也会建设得更好。我们现在有一个非常时髦的词，那就是"互动的研究"或者说"可解读的研究"，一旦研究成果可以解读出来，你就可以制定相关的政策进行国内的一些改革，它会是一个非常好的促进国家和地区层面上的一些变革的动力。

我现在再来说一下南亚，因为这是一个非常巨大的市场，我可以说整个南亚和东亚、东南亚比起来，我们的一体化都是做得比较差的，我觉得就是因为我们各个区域、各个群体之间并没有实现很好的互通性，我们这个体制或者系统就是一个非常大的问题，这也是我们智库需要思考的问题。在这种情况下智库可以介入进来，可以起到非常积极的作用，能够使得"一带一路"沿线国家彼此之间互融互通，在面对危机的时候可以接入这个机制解决问题，在资金方面提供一些支持，这样也能够很好地发挥我们这个机构的作用。

与此同时，智库也可以很好地连接相关的当局和公众，在他们之间建立桥梁，充分认识到分歧、共同利益和承诺，我建议在理解方面进行合作，比如说生产和供应网络，另一方面是中小企业的合作，第三是收入不平等的问题，还有技术和社会媒体的问题，推进这些合作并且促进市场协作，能够实现更多的一体化，与此同时能够满足政治和社会需要，维护安全和战略协调，也能实现粮食、能源、环境、水资源变化的协调合作。各国之间的相互信任对于经济一体化和合作是必不可少的，智库应该促进对话，帮助解决争端和分歧，使得"一带一路"在这个问题上能够了解所有利益相关者的关注点，与此同时，我们需要全面地考虑决策过程和改革，也许智库可以帮助协调区域和国家目标，因为区域利益是相辅相成的。

智库应该寻找解决地缘政治问题的方法以及连接各国的方式，并为他们提供互利互惠，比如利用基础设施加强亚洲邻国之间的联系，当然我们从经济的角度去考虑问题的时候，我们需要能够不断地加强亚洲之间的、彼此之间的利用基础设施的联系，这也是我来自的区域共同的关注。我认为不仅仅是政府，还有亚洲基础设施投资银行等机构，都可以为亚洲和其他地区进一步的智库合作提供一些基础，这不仅仅是亚洲还有其他一些国家的合作，亚洲国家将会变得与以前有所不同，我可以打个比方，从我自己的国家来说，孟加拉国已经是世界上第 32 大经济体，根据我们的预计，到 2030 年 GDP 总量将增长到 1.324 万亿美元，经济规模更大，增长和规模更加多样化，我们需要为这些变化做好准备，这些变化背后有很多的因素，比如人工智能的发展，这是我们都比较了解的一方面，还有青年人口的统计学的改变，这需要我们建立新的系统以及新形式的信息技术和媒体等，这对于我们来说都是至关重要的。

最后，对于我们的革新，"一带一路"倡议也非常有好处，我们能够不断地进行改革，有的时候我们可能在一些发展中国家对有些东西忽略，我们现在就建议各个智库之间可以更加通力合作，使我们不断地融合，使得我们成为一个平等、互惠互利的团体，并且这些方面的努力能够使得我们最终脱离贫困，最终繁荣起来，谢谢大家。

王义桅（主持人）：我想简要评论一下。第一，孟加拉国并不是一个小国家，你们的人口达到 1 亿。我们需要不断重新发现已知的国家，比如说你们的"邻居"缅甸也是非常重要的国家，还有巴基斯坦。东亚和东南亚国家在"一带一路"倡议中是非常重要的参与者，这对于我们不断地促进彼此的文明发展有很好的推动作用。

第二，刚才你提到人工智能的发展，刚才陈东敏教授也提到两个方式的革新，一个是关于能源资源，另外一个方面的创新是能够不断节约人力成本，可以说这些方面的一些能源节约和使用的确能够使我们帮助到发展中国家，能够不断地最大化地使用我们的资源，达到最好的结果，这也就是新的工业化发展。

最后，我想简单总结一下，刚才的讨论大家的确说了很多问题，对于智库来说有很多重要的工作，很多智库都是在大城市，我们的确是不断地鼓励我们之间能够互相学习，这是我们的首要工作。

第二方面的工作对于智库来说，是能够解决实际的问题，我们的策略能够发挥协同效应的时候，我们就有能力解决不同层面的问题，不管是采用中国的技术还是采用英国相关的法律法规。刚才在座的各位没有谈到一个问题，在布鲁塞尔的重要智库——CEPS（欧洲政策研究中心），它的确做了很多的工作，很多的国家都有相关的人员加入这样一个智库机构，这的确是一个新的动向，也许可以帮到很多的人，比如关于难民的问题，可以帮助他们解决，还有环境的改善等，当然这个智库的目的不仅仅是解决目前的问题，而且还要发现潜在的问题并且及时解决，这是长期的综合性解决方案，这的确是我们需要进一步了解的。

第二节

金锡焕（主持人）：首先欢迎各位来到第二个环节，正如同我们之前达成的共识，我们前面的环节的确讨论了很多有趣的问题，非常具有成效，使我们之间增进了了解，特别是关于"一带一路"倡议的问题，并且了解到问题来自哪些方面，第二个环节可以说比第一个环节更加简单，因为我们彼此互相熟悉了。接下来我想将讲台交给中山大学粤港澳发展研究院教授毛艳华。

毛艳华：感谢主办方的邀请，我来自中山大学，我们中山大学有个粤港澳发展研究院，它是高端智库，专门研究整个粤港澳区域发展的问题，我今天想和大家交流的主题是建设一流的智库来服务共建"一带一路"。

我想表达的第一个观点是，"一带一路"倡议符合一流的智库建设，我想一流智库的形成也源于对它的需求。2008年全球金融危机以来，整个全球化进程进入到一个拐点当中，从经济的数据来看，比如我们会谈到过去5年以来，全球的贸易增长速度都要低于全球经济增长的水平，这在过去20年全球化进程当中是很少见的，同时全球的投资也出现了很大的下滑。此外，过去二三十年高速的全球化，使得全球的生产网络发生了很大的变化，欧洲、美国以及以中国为首的东亚形成了全球三足鼎立的格局。同样，在全球价值链当中，其实很多发展中国家仍然处于很低端的位置，所以这就是全球化面临的新问题——不平衡。

我觉得中国经济发达的地区深度地参与了全球化，比如广东，改革开放已经 40 年了,这是一个对外开放非常快的区域。我们所在的深圳,2016 年它对外直接投资的存量达到了 852 亿美元。从整个广东来看,当然主要集中在珠江三角洲地区,它对外的投资存量达到 1250 亿美元,这占了中国整个直接对外投资存量的 23.9%,同样的像和珠三角毗邻的香港,一直是世界市场和中国内地市场在资金、物流、贸易等方面连通的渠道,中国内地的外商直接投资当中,大概有 29% 是通过中国香港进来的,同样中国内地对外直接投资当中有 60% 是从中国香港出去的,所以港澳和珠三角地区是高度参与全球经济分工的。

在新的全球化阶段,包括在中国提出"一带一路"倡议的新的发展阶段条件下,城市智库应该是很有条件来参与国际交流和政策的咨询的,深圳现在要建设智库、交流、资源要素配置的中心。

第二个我想表达的观点是,今天很多在座的智库领导也谈到了,智库在新的全球化发展条件下扮演着很重要的角色。我觉得第一个方面是在于它的一些专业性理论研究。"一带一路"作为引领全球化的方案,和我们过去的全球化的差异在哪儿?它和过去跨国公司引领的全球化本质差异在哪儿?在全球价值链的构建方面,"一带一路"怎么带动参与国家的经济发展?这些都是新的理论需要探讨和研究的。

第二个方面我觉得是咨询建言,"一带一路"倡议提出以来,不同的国家都得到益处,产业园区的建设、产能合作、基建等,原先各个国家都有或多或少的收益,但在这过程当中也面临很多的问题,比如某一个标准的不一致、投资管理体系的差异、汇率的波动以及法律的冲突,刚才讲到还有一些人文、宗教等的因素,这些都需要我们各个国家来共同解决探讨,智库可以在这里扮演很重要的角色,进行咨询和建言。

第三个方面我觉得是理论的研究和引导,我们在 2017 年 7 月曾到迪拜去考察,发现其实在迪拜这样一个全球化城市当中,"一带一路"的宣传还是不太够的,这些都需要我们一些专业的智库发挥引导作用去传播"一带一路"的理念。

另一方面我觉得要进行专业的评估和评价,比如国际组织要进行评估,我们很多专业的智库也可以参与"一带一路"合作项目的评价和评估,像我们现在试验区的建设也进行评估，对它的制度创新成效、投资环境、营商环境等方面都可以发挥智库的评估作用。

"一带一路"倡议强调的是共建共享，围绕"一带一路"建设，智库应该聚焦在哪些领域？我认为主要是这两个方面需要关注：

第一个方面智库要关注探讨开放型经济新体制的建设，习近平主席在很多场合都提出要建设开放型经济新体制，在这个过程当中如何推动开放型体制的对接，我觉得这是很多发展中国家希望参与的，比如说便利化的合作、投资的合作等。

第二个方面要关注"一带一路"过程当中的产业和创新合作，如工业4.0、互联网、人工智能等，这些领域的发展为全球价值链合作提供新的机遇和挑战，比如怎么应用新技术，如何让中小企业更好地融入全球市场并利用新经济，还有如何开展产权领域的合作，等等。我觉得还要关注青年问题，其实青年问题是全球性的问题，青年一代的发展和过去的传统高速发展时期面临的环境不太一样，每个国家、每个地区都或多或少出现青年的问题，智库应该围绕青年问题开展交流和探讨，当然还可以关心可持续发展的问题、绿色发展的问题等。

最后，我想谈谈发挥智库纽带作用的关键。第一要创新智库的运行机制，比如像中国提出来要建立新型的高端智库，这种新型高端智库应该有很好的运作模式，能够发挥第三方的作用，它又跟政府有密切的联系，还可以和社会有很好的关系。第二要加强和政府的联系，这就能够有助于解决经济发展、区域合作当中面临的一些问题，可以更好地向政府反映诉求，建言献策。第三要扩大城市智库的网络，通过"走出去"开展调研，今天我们主题谈到了构建城市智库伙伴网络，这是非常重要的，每个国家、每个城市的智库之间要加强合作，相互走动，开展调研，一起解决经济发展过程中存在的问题。第四要利用大数据技术进行分析，刚才也谈到我们的智库和传统智库不一样，我们要有新的手段和应用。第五要加强企业与社会的联系，服务好企业在"走出去"过程中面临的问题。谢谢。

金锡焕（主持人）：非常感谢毛艳华的精彩演讲，非常感谢您的真知灼见，现在我们邀请下一位演讲人，中欧文化教育协会主席、欧盟亚洲研究所首席执行官顾爱乐先生。

顾爱乐：我有个小"问题"，但不是一个真正的问题，它是我们很多的演讲嘉宾都提到的，可以说我们在同样的一条线上想法都是一样的，我们都非常关注智库之间潜在的合作和未来的机遇，我们希望能够不断地促进智库间的合作。实际上刚开始是在欧洲国家，比如英国开始采用智库，后来美国又开始采用起来，中国随着"一带一路"倡议的提出，在这方面也采取主动的机制，可以说在这方面中国也展示了主动的姿态，给我们带来很多新能量，这是非常好的一种现象，给了我们不同层面的视角。

实际上我们在这方面有很多经验，我们在布鲁塞尔建立了第一个关于欧亚之间的智库，涵盖了很多的研究机构，都是全职研究人员。早期的时候我们仅仅是关注一些比较简单的问题，对有些问题并没有深入地进行讨论，可以说当时都是泛泛而谈，和现在不能比，现在可以涵盖2000个来自世界各地的智库成员共同合作。

第二个问题，我们有时候也需要考虑资金支持的局限，比如涉及欧盟的项目，需要有资金的支持。当我们完成某个项目时，我们需要得到另外的相关资金的支持，有的时候资金非常有限，我们可能在某个项目完成之后，再进行另外的项目就非常困难了。

我刚才提到的问题不仅仅是我们这个机构面临的情况，也是其他智库机构面临的问题，经过多年的努力，我们在布鲁塞尔的智库机构，也进行了很多的工作，也建立了一些网络，更多的时候我们关注不同的项目对话，我们也有相关的高层智库成员引领整个线路的实施。当然我们也有一些正在进行的项目，非常具有灵活性和动态性，如果要做这样的项目，具有弹性的工作能力的人员是至关重要的。不管这些智库的成员持何种观点，他们都需要领先于各个领域，并且不断发掘新的潜力。对于我们来说，这些智库不仅仅关注欧洲和亚洲的关系，而且还要了解中国的情况，并且了解未来发展的潜力。与此同时，这些智库在现在5—10年的时间里能预估到未来5—10年的发展趋势是怎样的，也能够在潜力分析的情况下找出一些可行性的解决方案。在我们的机构里有些人是年长的，比如说有一些已经步入 50 岁、60 岁的年纪，他们非常了解过去五六十年的发展情况，也能提出具体的解决方案。我们现在看到中国的发展趋势非常迅猛，但是未来的 5—10 年可能涌现新的问题，那就需要更好地分析未来可能出现的情况，这就是我们的工作方向。研究如何解决在未来 5—10 年间出现问题，是我们机构的指导方针，而这个指导方针能够不断敦促我们的智库机构和成员永远站在时代的前列，对问题进行分析和整合。

对智库来说，我认为我们有三大关注点。我们关注学术的机构，我们还关注大公司的机构，对公司层面的机构主要关注短期的情况。与此同时，还有政府方面，可以说智库不是仅仅从学术角度分析问题，也关注实际出现的问题，我们也需要从政府层面了解各个机构的运作情况，需要把各个不同方面整合起来。当你处于领先地位时，有时可能会跟主流媒体的一些观点和方向不同，我认为作为智库，要想取得领先地位，需要具有不断前进的精神，想在别人之前，有时有些人不接受我们提出的最新观点，甚至认为我们的想法是不正确的，这些都是没有问题的。

我们不应该把自己定位为一个非政府组织的推动者或运动的推动者，我们需要有明确的概念和理论，能够找到解决问题的方案。有时候问题可以被进一步探讨，但不能被真正解决，作为智库我们希望用具有建设性的、积极的方式来提高我们影响施政的能力，从而为我们的社会带来好处。没有什么是十全十美的，欧盟并不完美，相反它还有很多地方有待改进。在过去 100 年间我觉得欧洲已有很大的发展，我记得我小时候在比利时生活，当时我开 2 个小时的车从比利时到别处需要经历两个国家，你需要有不同的护照才能完成这 2 小时的车程，现在欧盟国家之间不需要出示不同的护照，欧盟内部已经实现交通一体化，这就是欧盟统一的概念。

当然我们也应看到，作为智库我们需要取得一些平衡，我们要在政治正确和政治不正确之间取得一个平衡，有时候你可能需要接受一些限制让自己变得政治正确，但如果太过于政治正确，又没有办法为施政者提供很好的建议。从长期来说，主流的观点会慢慢有一些变迁和转移，主流的观点会随着时间的推移慢慢和你个人的观点进行融合，你原来觉得非常奇怪的观点慢慢也会成为非常主流的观点，所以我觉得权衡是智库需要做到的一点。

在作权衡的过程中，我们要考虑区域、社会和人民的利益，其实有些智库是政府建立的官方智库，有些是由私人资助的，有些智库是由政治团体建立的，有一些是偏学术的智库，比如说教育机构等智库，还有一些独立的智库，所以说智库本身的类型也是多种多样的，这就是为什么我们需要考虑资金的问题，我们要看到一个机构、一个智库它背后的出资方是什么人，虽然整个智库是一个群体，但是里面也有各种各样的智库，所以会提出不同的方式，我们可以求同存异，可以互相学习和借鉴，以取得进一步的发展。

现在的智库有很紧密的联系，在中国我们也有非常有意义的合作，因为现在我们有同一个方向，那就是要建立新的智库伙伴网络，这样可以把中国、欧洲和世界其他地区联系起来，通过这样的方式，我们可以实现新型的智库伙伴网络，但我觉得一个智库伙伴网络是不够的，我们需要更多的网络，因为智库涉及很多方面。通过建立智库合作伙伴网络可以更好地发挥智库作用，为社会创造更大的价值。谢谢大家。

金锡焕（主持人）： 谢谢演讲人给我们分享他的一些见地，他和我们讲述了智库的历史和未来可能的发展方向，非常感谢。接下来我想将讲台交给深圳市人民政府发展研究中心副主任邓盛华先生。

邓盛华： 非常感谢各位嘉宾的到来，我是这个活动的主办方——深圳市人民政府发展研究中心的负责人之一。

今天我说三个方面的信息，第一个是向大家介绍一下深圳的一些基本的经济情况，第二个是介绍深圳在"一带一路"倡议中的一些具体作为或者可以合作的领域，第三个是提几点相关的想法和建议。

三四十年前大家觉得深圳是小地方，经过 40 年的发展深圳已经大变样了，可能有些专家、学者不太了解，所以一些基本的信息我向大家介绍一下。今年是深圳发展历史上特别重要的一年，深圳的经济总量第一次超过香港，去年超过了广州，地方生产总值达到了 3500 亿美元，人民币是 2.24 万亿元，按照目前的发展速度，深圳在中国城市格局中的地位还会进一步变化，比如说我们和中国的第一大城市上海相比，我们的经济总量在 10 年前是它的 55%，5 年前是它的 64%，今年我们是上海经济总量的 74%，也就是说 10 年来将近提高了 20 个百分点，我们甚至有可能成为中国经济总量最大的城市之一。

深圳的地域面积是 1950 平方千米左右，但是这里居住了 2100 万人，也是世界上人口密度最大的城市之一，从地方财政和中央的关系来看，中央政府从深圳获得的中央财政的收入超过人民币 5300 亿人民币，我们地方财政收入也有 3322 亿人民币，今年实际上和香港是接近的，也就是经济总量会进一步增大，经济发展的质量也是比较好的，也是中国经济效益最大的城市之一。从产业上来看，我们现在也是中国境内以信息产业为核心的城市，还有生物技术产业、新能源产业、新材料产业等六大战略性新兴产业，都是在中国走在最前列的。从城市建设上来看，我们现在是全球 150 米以上高楼最多的城市，去年全球 20 个最高楼宇中有 4 个是在深圳，3 年以后深圳 120 米以上的高数量会超过香港，这也是与我们城市比较小、山比较多、平地不多的地理环境相关的，所以我们只能往高空发展。我们的城市发展也采用新的信息技术和新的规划方式，比如城市准备大规模建设双层快速路，上面是和城市社区相连的路，下面这一层是长途快速路，这种建设模式在全球都是比较领先的。深圳现在的国际航线不多，有 40 条，但是我们未来要规划到 200 条，深圳现在也有油轮港口，从集装箱远洋航线来看也是全球最多的，海运数量在全球前十大海港中排第三位，如果加上香港，深港两地加起来在很多领域都是全球第一。所以中国南方的这个"小地方"，正成为全球的信息、资金、货物运转的枢纽和热点地区。

作为一个新兴城市，我们希望未来能够朝几个有特色的方向发展，这也是我讲到的第二个问题，即深圳在哪些领域可以与大家有更好的合作。

第一个方面是科技创新方面，我们现在全社会研发投入占 GDP 的比重达到 4.13%，达到以色列的水准，我们瞄准硅谷这个目标，我们希望实现企业在硅谷产生创意来深圳发展，因为深圳制造业生产链是非常完善的，而且成本相对较低，和全球的合作有非常多的机会。这几年很多在欧美的留学生回来，深圳也是吸引科技人才最多的城市之一，一年达到 8 万人左右。

第二方面是基础设施建设方面，深圳一些大企业在斯里兰卡等海外的地区都有非常多的工程经验，深圳同时也在创新、金融方面有很多的合作机会，深圳有深圳证券交易所，深圳证券交易所这几年在全球排在前列，我们希望未来打造全球创新企业集聚区，如果有好的企业来这里可以与我们对接。

第三个方面是旅游领域，深圳新开的游轮也有一定的影响力，还有在远洋方面，这些领域有我们的优势，特别是贸易方面，我们以前主要关注欧美发达国家，现在转型开发新市场，在"一带一路"地区有很大的开发空间。

最后，我提两个方面关于合作的想法，第一个是我们希望和各位一起努力，也希望把这个论坛继续办下去、办好，这个论坛是第二届，也需要大家的支持。第二个是我们希望在这个过程中加强智库在合作中的作用，希望大家更多地和深圳，特别是和我们联络，欢迎介绍项目来深圳落地，我们会一如既往做好相关的支持工作，感谢大家，谢谢。

金锡焕（主持人）：非常感谢您的精彩介绍，邓盛华先生提到了很多实际的内容，带给我们很多新的信息。深圳的环境非常与众不同，和中国内陆城市相比是非常领先的，可以说深圳作为一个窗口，起到了领先的作用，帮助中国改变了一些过去的情况。刚才您也提到了中国的未来需要深圳的发展，这的确是非常具有雄心壮志的想法。下一个演讲者是来自乌克兰奥列克山大拉祖姆科夫经济政治研究中心的经济项目负责人，瓦西里·优奇施恩先生。

瓦西里·优奇施恩：我想谈论的是我们怎样互相了解和互相沟通，相互理解和沟通能够帮助我们建立好的合作机制，对各个国家来说也是至关重要的。我们的国家有所不同，我知道很多其他国家的情况，而乌克兰也非常希望参与到"一带一路"倡议中来。

但是我们也面临一些问题，我们不仅要不断推动倡议在各国的发展，还要解决一些具体的挑战，特别是在我的国家乌克兰。作为智库，我们可以说是与政府并肩合作，在现代世界中我们要面临很多的问题，我们可以从不同国家和不同情况中积累更多经验，我们希望更多地关注一些成果案例的分析，特别是来自中国的案例能够为我们未来的行动做出非常具有效率的指导。我之前也看了一些相关书籍，还有一些来自我们当局所发行的资料，我们国家也越来越关注这方面的问题，因此我们需要更多关注这些成功的项目，并且从中学习经验，我们需要了解它的发展潜力，我们在这里谈的多数项目都涉及"一带一路"，可以说"一带一路"项目可能会得到不同的反响，我们需要采取措施，使不同的国家之间彼此合作，取长补短。我想强调乌克兰与欧盟的协议仍然有效，当然还有另外的协议，但这些协议会帮助我们与中国进行合作。当然，我们和加拿大也有一些协议，这些合作项目和协议都是我们所感兴趣的领域。很多人不相信"一带一路"倡议对乌克兰是有利的，对我们来说，我们建议可以在项目中更多体现出人民的利益，并且能够及时回馈公众，这样做可以加强政府和公众之间的协调和沟通，促进智库在政府和商业方面的合作，也能加强各政府间的了解和沟通。

关于财务支持方面，实际上我不了解财政方面的东西，例如中国提出的一些项目，其中有些财务的内容我并不是非常了解，但对欧洲东南部地区的项目我有一些了解，当然有些项目是欧洲东南部的国家在乌克兰开展的，非常具有实践性，对当地也非常有帮助；也有一些非常好的智库项目，都非常有利于发展。对我们来说，为使项目发展，需要关注相关的财务机制，比如说丝路基金、亚洲基础设施投资银行，这些财务方面的支持无疑都是非常有帮助的，也希望有长期的投资机构的联合活动和项目，包括民意调查，这些都是非常有益的，谢谢各位。

金锡焕（主持人）：非常感谢您，谢谢您的真知灼见。下面我邀请王义桅，他是中国人民大学的教授，有请。

王义桅：我认为互联互通决定城市的竞争力，而不再是劳动力、技术，和平不是任何一个国家的，而是城市之下的和平，一种新型的人类文明正在产生，所以"一带一路"是人类新型的工业化，也是人类新型的城镇化，城市的基础设施赶不上要求就会存在城市问题，所以习主席在去年"一带一路"国际高峰论坛上特别讲到，"聚焦关键通道、关键城市、关键项目"，有些城市别看它GDP总量不大，但它就是一个关键的节点，而且它是智慧城市，我们要挖掘它在全球互联互通中的重要性，这就是我们讲的主题。

从历史上看，是城市让国家、地区之间互联互通。自从欧洲人走向海洋之后，很多城市主要集中在沿海地区，90%的贸易通过海上进行，今天的"一带一路"要改变内陆地区的落后状况，我觉得很大程度是改变海洋型全球化这样一个背景，今天你看晚上的灯光大部分集中在沿海地区，广大内陆地区一片漆黑，"一带一路"就是要点一盏灯，让全球化没有死角，改变原来把世界越分越细而导致世界碎片化的结果。古代的联系工具是马、骆驼，到今天是互联网、高铁，中国在高铁和互联网领域在世界上都是领先的，尤其深圳在互联网领域让全球更加互联互通起来，努力改变原来不够互联互通导致一些城市和国家被边缘化的状况。

中国在海外修高铁，让海外有更多港口连接在一起，把整个世界更加互联互通起来，还有包容性的发展，在世界层面是包容性的全球化，很大程度上消除了全球化不够持续的状况。中国现在城镇化率达到60%，离欧洲的百分之七八十还有很大的差距，广东、江苏的GDP总量已经超过了俄罗斯，这些城市群成为中国主要的人口聚集地、GDP产出地和信息的来源，内陆城市像云南、四川等省的城市通过高铁互联互通，因为高铁把内陆地区的劣势弥补上来了，信息上的互联互通如阿里巴巴、云计算让贵州由以前相对落后的省份变成了改革开放"前沿"的省份。

这是一张城市发展图，世界上15个发展最快的大都市，大部分集中在发展中国家，发展中国家普遍有城市病，现在"一带一路"能不能够帮助避免城市病？我认为要发展新型的城镇化要依赖新的技术，中国现在和欧洲合作，像中兴、华为、诺基亚在研究5G，正在帮助城市建立智慧城市、智慧医疗的合作。这是"一带一路"产业信息发展上的布局。

我们和东南亚合作，和东南亚17个城市取得港口联盟，进行信息港的建设，港口不仅是贸易，还是金融、信息、教育各种医疗的中心，所以我们讲联动式的发展是一个精髓，我们要申请世界文化遗产，发展海上贸易网络，开展海上文化交流和海上医疗、旅游、培训、教育。城市之间连接不仅是原来意义上的友好城市，"一带一路"把城市间的合作从原来的政治上的友好城市变成互联互通的节点，用网络的概念，可以说以中心城市为支点，通过重点港口连接内陆地区的网络让这个城市活起来，让城市的文化、精神也活起来，让城市之间更加连通在一起，带动国家、地区之间的连通，依托城市群的建设，通过各种各样的贸易、设施、金融的连通带动"一带一路"互联互通。

最后谈谈国际间的合作。深圳是中国改革开放的缩影，深圳已经变成了"海外"深圳了，大量的国家来深圳取经，"一带一路"确实要在深圳办一个学院，很多国家的政党在学习中国的改革开放，包括城市治理，我觉得深圳模式是全球的深圳模式，现在很多地方了解改革开放是从深圳开始的，所以我觉得非常有意思，将来深圳会成为"一带一路"合作中城市外交或者城市互联互通的一个节点、中心。中国城市人口将来也会越来越多，中国的"一带一路"倡议和精神更多体现在改革开放前沿城市中，所以我觉得应该提出"城市外交"的概念，而不光是外事，原来的外事迎来送往，现在我觉得应该发挥好城市在互联互通方面的排头兵作用、前沿性的作用，这不仅是国家间的互联互通，更多是城市的互联互通，城市是中国改革开放的展示，城市治理、城镇化都成为城市外交的重要内容，它丰富了原来外交的形式，从主体上、使命上都越来越把中国的城市变成国际化都市和外交特区，例如深圳变成外交特区以后在外交上要赋予新的职能。

深圳在"一带一路"的背景下会有更多创新。新的试点，新的特区，新的工作，所以城市让生活更美好，"一带一路"也会让生活更美好，互联互通点亮"一带一路"，超越原来旧的文明，今天中国的"一带一路"项目已经印在一些国家的货币上，还出版了很多相关的书，这些书都用的是本土语言，而不仅仅是官方语言，我已经写了四本书，第四本正准备出版。一些我书中的内容已经成为中学课本中讨论的话题。

这就是我给大家汇报的内容，更多的我以后来向大家分享，谢谢大家。

金锡焕（主持人）： 非常感谢王教授的精彩分享，也感谢您的细节介绍，介绍了很多"一带一路"的内容，您的讲解使我们了解了"一带一路"具体涵盖哪些内容。下面有请最后一个演讲者，来自俄罗斯莫斯科高等经济大学欧洲和国际综合研究中心的副主任，安娜塔西亚·丽佳契娃女士。

安娜塔西亚·丽佳契娃： 我会做一个简短的演讲，非常高兴能够被邀请来到这里。我们的确有很多类似的项目，也有很多涉及"一带一路"，下面给大家介绍一些具体情况。

我们主要分三个板块，第一是官方内容，第二是学术方面，第三是一些相关出版物的发行。我们已经建立了一个委员会，并且出版了相关刊物，我们也会把相关刊物进行整合。这些资料给了我们一个方向，使我们有了具体的工作。我们的目标是希望通过这些项目增进彼此的了解，有些项目并不是非常容易，尽管进程有一些困难，但最终都有非常好的结果。我们的目标和结果都规划得非常清晰，能够上升到非常高的层面，我们也正在着手准备出版两本书籍，涵盖的内容不仅仅是一些相关的项目研究，还有一些相关国际上的合作、介绍地区的情况等。

我们需要了解我们具体面对什么样的情况，并且如何进行改善，这些对于我们来说是跟踪的记录，使我们知道现在在做什么，以后做什么。我们还开展了很多学术讨论，我们公开了具体研究项目，希望能够推动未来的工作，能够建立非常好的、公开的平台，我们也有一个具体的行动指南，解释了我们该如何进行合作。对于远东地区的合作和发展，我们关注世界经济走廊和我们具体的情况，当然也包含了众多国家，比如中国、日本等国家。在过去3年里我们组织了很多国际合作项目，在莫斯科、东京还有新加坡举办了很多相关论坛，加强了国家间的连接和沟通，加强了双边或者多边对接，推动了各个具体项目的实施和开展。

接下来我想给大家具体讲一下未来的情况。正如金教授所提到，当我们展望未来的时候不仅仅是对现在情况的预估，更需要了解对方的需求。我们需要进一步加强与中国、日本还有欧洲国家的合作，并且关注经济及其他方面的合作。如果中国对这些方面感兴趣的话，我们也可以开展类似项目的对接。

俄罗斯也希望在这个机制中能够彼此连接，共同合作。可以说"一带一路"倡议是非常好的，能够很好地连接我们国家，也可以连接欧洲其他国家。在2016年5月，习近平主席提到了很多相关的内容，实际上我们刚才也谈论了很多正在进行的项目。俄罗斯希望加强与整个欧洲及其他国家的合作，这也是我们的一个重要机制。现在我们正在开展一些关于股票方面的研究项目，可以说已经取得了很好的进展，对欧洲进一步合作发挥了非常积极的作用。同时，我们希望能够在不断合作和竞争中良性发展，我们也非常欢迎中国的投资方来俄罗斯，大家有什么感兴趣的项目，我们可以再进行具体探讨。

金锡焕（主持人）：非常感谢您的演讲，我想所有的参与者都已经发表了自己的想法，非常遗憾来自希腊的斯塔夫罗斯·阿瑟尼迪斯先生没有到场，以及中欧文化教育协会主席、欧盟亚洲研究所首席执行官顾爱乐先生没有时间具体地讲解一些内容。

顾爱乐：非常感谢。20 世纪 80 年代时我来过深圳，可以说我有第一手的感受。深圳发生了翻天覆地的变化，如果我当时能够投资一块地的话，今天我可能就会成为亿万富翁。深圳奇迹般的变化的确是举世瞩目的，可以说深圳的产业结构非常好，还有深圳企业家的创新精神都是非常令人惊讶的，给全世界都带来了一个全新的认识。

与此同时，我认为"一带一路"倡议是一个非常好的平台，我们需要关注不同的需求，达到一个平衡，这是非常棒的，这也带来更多可能性，能够使我们不断加入新的倡议。我们所有人都希望能够在亚洲建立很好的友好网络，并开展相关工作，这是需要我们重点注意的。我相信通过倡议能够构建一个亚洲的网络，能使我们用全新的、令人感兴趣的角度看待倡议。我非常高兴和荣幸来到深圳，我感受到深圳精神，在深圳开这次会是非常棒的选择，因为这是非常棒的城市。

金锡焕（主持人）：谢谢您，您讲得非常棒，真诚地感谢所有与会发言人的参与和精彩发言，我衷心感谢你们非常棒的想法和对于倡议的理解，非常感谢诸位的莅临，非常感谢组委会充实的安排和周到的服务，感谢深圳，感谢全体中国人民，谢谢大家。

平行分论坛（二）：城市伙伴

加强城市人文经贸往来，构建城市智库与伙伴网络

斯捷潘·梅西奇 （克罗地亚国家商会总顾问、萨格勒布城市特别代表）

多少年来，我始终倡议并坚持以多边主义政策和经济合作来加强克罗地亚与欧洲及世界的联系，今天看来，如果欧盟和中国继续推动自由贸易和全球化的力量不削弱，这些观点就依然适用，我认为中国国家主席习近平先生提出的"一带一路"倡议是非常重要的经济倡议、文明倡议，因为这一倡议有能力深入中欧关系，并加深全球经济联系。

我希望欧洲各国领导人都能好好研究"一带一路"倡议，因为这项倡议将对世界发展和稳定产生重要影响，也将推动国际贸易和投资的增长，在"一带一路"的框架下，欧亚工业将通过各个创新中心进一步发展，正如中国国家主席习近平先生提倡的"一带一路"要遵循共商、共建、共享原则，我相信在实现"一带一路"的目标方面，中国和欧洲是天然的伙伴。

"一带一路"建设连接欧亚非三大洲，当前正在顺利推进，欧亚经济和文化的相互依赖性也随之增强，"一带一路"给各个国家和全球治理提供了新机制，我想在此强调，我们应该在"一带一路"框架下通力合作，共同巩固和发展多边主义合作，从而让"一带一路"像欧盟和其他一体化模式一样，增加世界经济的开放性，改善全球治理，共同应对全球性挑战，世界需要这样一种能引导多极化发展并建立互利共赢新型国际关系的力量，在尊重世贸组织国际贸易体系标准和透明的前提下，我们应该抓住"一带一路"在中欧层面带来的新机遇，并把它们扩展到区域和地方合作层面。

当今世界，比以往任何时候都更加紧密相连，例如支持"一带一路"的中国企业家——阿里巴巴集团董事长马云正在全球范围内建立电子平台，让企业家们在世界各地随时随地通过手机进行买卖交易，在这里，我想强调的是，"一带一路"也将有力推动亚洲和欧洲的数字化连接。

"一带一路"不仅是一个重要倡议，更为调动私营与公共部门等一切资源，加速全球经济发展提供了最佳时机，展望未来，我们必须加强中欧各领域合作，互联互通，不仅为东欧和亚洲经济发展提供良好机遇，也为世界和平带来巨大的空间，和平不是全部，但是没有和平是万万不能的。谢谢大家。

朱华友 （海南省人民政府副秘书长、研究室主任）

我简要讲一下我关于营商环境的观点。打造好的营商环境，是城市间推进国际合作贸易的焦点。营商环境就是生产力，抓住了营商环境就抓住了外资，抓住了发展。海南省是 1988 年邓小平提议创立的中国最大的特区，深圳市是最早的经济特区。再过三个月就是海南经济特区建立三十周年，海南是南中国海上的一个岛屿，面积有 3.5 万平方千米，昨天晚上吃饭的时候，好几个外宾都说海南岛很美，在此我也欢迎大家有机会去度假。

我们有五大港口，有全世界唯一的环岛 700 多千米的高铁，全程每一站不停的话仅需 1 个小时，每一站都停的话需 1 个半小时。有 475 条国内国际航线，其中 100 条国际航线，为什么讲这个航线呢？因为它对于投资环境很重要，我们曾经跟夏威夷有一个投资项目，他们愿意来海南岛投资，就是搞花卉的种植，这是一个效益比较高的产业，我们也很感兴趣，后来没有谈成，重要原因就是：当时我们的国际航线偏少，花卉不能够今天采摘，明天同一时间出现在伦敦、巴黎、纽约，这样花卉产业就支撑不住规模和效应。国外航线在发展经济效益的同时也能改善我们的旅游环境。2009 年底的时候，海南正式被中央确定为国际旅游岛，主要发展服务业，目前服务业的增长在 70% 左右，至 2017 年底，我们接待了国内外游客 7000 万人次。

另外，就是开放的环境。比如：我们目前对 26 个国家免签，很快就会对 59 个国家免签。换句话说，在座的外国朋友基本上都可以拿着护照直接进入海南。还有免税购物，中央政府给海南一个免费购物的政策，也就是说，所有的国内游客（不包括港澳台地区）到海南旅游可以在 1.6 万元范围内免税购物，这个对于游客还是有吸引力的。

我们还在博鳌搞了一个博鳌乐城国际医疗旅游试验区。博鳌亚洲论坛是我们很重要的国际论坛，在座的很多外国来宾应该都曾去过，今年 4 月又将召开博鳌亚洲论坛年会，规格很高，在会场旁边有 20 多平方千米土地，中央政府批准开发博鳌乐城国际旅游医疗先行区，现在很多中外的医疗机构去投资，比如说国外的医生可以在那里执业三年，外国的医疗机构可以独自在博鳌投资，这个在其他地方是不行的，外国的药品包括在欧洲、美洲、美国上市的药品可以第一时间在这个区内同步使用。外国的医疗设备可以免税进入这个区。所有这些政策是全国独一无二的，现在很多中外医疗企业在博鳌落户，以后可以为中国和亚太医疗合作提供很好的平台，可以吸引东南亚甚至其他国家的游客到我们的乐城去体检、治疗、养生、美容等。

我们海南除特别集中于以基础设施扩大开放以外，还特别注重基础电力保障，以核电、清洁能源为主，前几天大家看到马克龙总统和习近平主席在北京有签约活动，其中海南就参加了签约，我们跟法国电力公司有一个关于海南清洁能源示范区的合作项目。我们想尽可能利用海南的特点，积极参与"一带一路"建设，我们是"海上丝绸之路"的必经之地，就处在南海之中，所以我们要充分利用这个优势，发挥好作用，加强与"一带一路"沿线城市的合作，当然也包括与粤港澳大湾区的合作，我们的油轮有十几条航线一直开到东南亚。我们希望发挥我们独特的优势，参与"一带一路"的产业合作。谢谢大家。

吴思康　（深圳市政府发展研究中心主任）

我演讲的题目是"聚焦城市产业和智库"，我讲的第一个问题就是城市合作是"一带一路"建设的重要依托，为什么这么讲呢？因为我这里也收集了一些数据，可以说明城市是全球经济合作的枢纽，目前全球超过一半的人口居住在城市，70%的经济活动发生在城市，或者说来自城市。美国一研究机构发布数据：全球最大的300个城市，人口占全球总量的20%，经济占全球总量的50%。我想讲的第二句话就是有些城市富可敌国，如果把城市当成一个经济体，我们可以看到有些城市的体量已经很大，像上海市2016年GDP的总量大概是4000亿美元，相当于全世界排名第26位的泰国。深圳2016年的数据是2900多亿美元，相当于世界排名第40位的爱尔兰。2017年深圳的GDP是3400多亿美元，排名进一步靠前了，这也进一步证明了我的观点，有的城市是一个很大的经济体。结论就是，在"一带一路"的建设中，国家已经搭建好合作框架，城市要发挥好重要的枢纽和载体作用。

第二，产业合作是我们需要关注的最重要的内容。我这里也收集了一些数据，"一带一路"沿线大部分地区其实都是发展中国家，它们面临的突出问题还是发展，2016年的数据显示，在60多个沿线国家和地区中，GDP1000亿美元以上的国家大概是 40 个，也就是说，三分之一是在 1000 亿美元之下，它们的总量只相当于深圳市的三分之一。从人均 GDP 也可以看到，人均收入 5000 美元以下的大概是 32 个，也就是说，有一半还处于不发达或者中等发达以下的程度，这就说明一个问题，产业合作是我们要关注的最主要的方面。

我们国家把推动产能合作也摆在重要的位置，截至 2017 年 3 月，我们已经在沿线国家建立了 56 个产业园区，投资超过 180 亿美元，目前只能拿到 2016 年的数据，2016 年我们为东道国创造超过 10 亿美元的税收，16 万个就业岗位。

第三，智库合作是"一带一路"的重要支撑。为什么这么说呢？因为沿线国家的宗教、文化、语言、法律、习俗差异很大，所以我们很需要智库的研究，来加深彼此的了解，增进共识。沿线地区的宗教有佛教、基督教、伊斯兰教等，实际上还有很多其他宗教。文化也是差异很大，在东方更强调的是儒家文化，西方、中东主要是西方文化、阿拉伯文化等。习俗差异就更大了，最简单的就是用餐方式差异，我们是用筷子，西方是用刀叉，也有的直接用手抓，这就说明地区差异很大，需要研究。

智库不仅在制度规划、方案设计、政策咨询等方面发挥作用，在释疑解惑、凝聚共识、政策沟通等方面也具有独特的作用，我们认为智库合作有利于分享发展经验、促进凝聚共识、加强政策沟通，推动战略对接、提出解决方案。

深圳的实践和一些关于未来的想法有独特的优势，首先深圳毗邻国际中心香港，地处国际贸易的要冲，大家可以看到从太平洋到印度洋的航线，深圳距离主航线近，也是中国与"海上丝绸之路"沿线国家距离最近的发达城市。我们也有非常发达的港口，去年集装箱吞吐量达到 2520 万标箱，在全世界排第三位。

还有经贸的优势，2017 年深圳 GDP 预计 2.2 万亿元（约 3400 亿美元），跻身全球城市 25 强。进出口总量是 2.8 万亿元（约 4300 亿美元），出口总量 1.67 万亿元（约 2600 亿美元），连续 25 年居中国城市（不含港澳台地区）首位。

还有产业和金融的优势，深圳是全球重要的电子信息产业基地，这一大产业去年的产值就达到了 1.6 万亿元，相当于 2500 亿美元左右。其中新兴产业占到了41%左右。深圳也是中国的三大金融中心之一，作为金融中心，在全球大概可以排到20位左右。

我们还有企业的优势。企业的优势是我们的总量很大，昨天跟一位市长谈到，我们一共有300万家商事单位，有180万家注册企业，这个总量很大；在深圳产生了本土成长的七家世界500强企业；在深圳投资的其他世界500强企业，有280家；境内外上市企业有382家；国家级高新技术企业11200家。

我们具有创新优势。深圳是国家创新型城市和国家自主创新示范区，被《经济学人》杂志誉为"硅洲"。2017年深圳全社会研发投入占GDP比重4.13%，比肩以色列和韩国。超材料基因测序、新能源汽车、无人机、太赫兹技术领域跻身世界前列，通信技术产业也是全球领先的。

深圳未来的发展目标是要建设创新引领型全球城市，要实现这个目标需要进一步发挥"一带一路"倡议的平台作用，加强与沿线国家和城市、地区的经济、文化合作。深圳过去一直是开放包容的城市，我们与全球83个城市建立了友好伙伴关系，我这里列了深圳的"朋友圈"，像釜山、加德满都、阿尔梅勒、雅典等。我们未来还是要加强与沿线城市的合作，完善多层次的沟通交流机制，以智库为纽带，构建城市伙伴关系网络，开展更密切的交流与合作。

第四，我们会大力推进与沿线国家的产业合作。深圳企业在全球投资或设立分支机构的接近5689家，其中有137个项目布局于"一带一路"。

大家都知道的华为，在"一带一路"的沿线国家实施了26个产业项目，总投资达125亿美元，我们还有很多这样的企业。未来，我们要发挥这种产业和金融优势。深圳是一个资金富裕的城市，也是一个金融中心城市。我们要继续发挥产业和金融优势，鼓励企业到沿线国家投资设厂、建保税仓、建产业园区等，输出产品、技术、资本和管理。也欢迎沿线国家、地区企业在深圳设立机构，共同开拓中国市场。我们国家的政策也是鼓励消费，大家都知道最近中国实行了一个特别大的利好政策，就是降低了进口产品的关税，所以我们也很乐意，也很鼓励深圳的企业和国外的企业合作，建立共同的市场开拓机构来开拓中国市场。

第五，加强与沿线智库的合作。2016年2月，我们在这里举办了"一带一路"国际智库合作研讨会，沿线50个国家的7位前政要、120多位智库领域专家参加，成立了"一带一路"的智库联盟。

作为地方政府的政策咨询机构，我们希望加大人员互访的力度。希望跟各个城市共同开展课题研究，就我们合作中存在的一些问题，开展专题研究，来找到一些方案，提出一些建议。

杜桑·贝拉 （斯洛伐克共和国驻华使馆特命全权大使）

非常感谢，让我在这里跟大家分享我的想法。我相信这是很好的，这个倡议也是很好的，特别是在经济合作方面，斯洛伐克跟中国合作密切，在"一带一路"倡议之下，我们的交流合作也在不断扩大。"一带一路"倡议的目标是在交通、基础设施、人员等方面进行合作。下面我来谈一下如何去推进"一带一路"在斯洛伐克的商业项目。在2017年11月就已经连通了斯洛伐克到中国北部的交通线路，现在我们实现了火车运输，并且我们也打算连接中国五个城市来推广我们之间的交往以及合作。

另外，我还想说一下在数字化的合作领域，我们是如何在"一带一路"的倡议下开展城市之间的合作的。

例如ICT（信息通信技术），我们在斯洛伐克跟东欧合作的机制下，也去配合相应的技术合作和技术创新合作方面的工作，并且研究如何让这种技术能够提高健康、公共卫生安全方面的行业，我们的市民也非常感激我们在技术领域、商业开发、公共卫生方面的成就，所有的这些技术能够帮助我们解决很多问题，能够构建交通智能城市和实现智能管理。我们需要了解一下智慧城市，这有助于我们管理城市，以及改善城市卫生。深圳的华为能够在智慧城市方面提供更多的城市解决方案，能够推广到111个国家，现在华为公司仍然不遗余力地去构建更加便捷的城市设施概念。智慧城市的意思是能够让我们传播信息，并且能够跟我们联结在一起，能够让我们分享到生活的便捷性，智能设施的运用都有很大的贡献，能够推动卫生、健康事业的发展。这些解决方案能够帮助我们解决很多问题，能够推动我们更好地管理城市，并且让我们的市政府扮演好管理者的角色。

构建智慧城市之后，我们能够构建智慧国家，能够给人类带来福祉，目前已经有一些城市合作项目，利用创新智慧的概念，来应对气候变化，解决水污染等各种各样的问题。

我的观点是要运用"一带一路"倡议，构建这种城市合作伙伴关系，进行多边合作，使用、运用智慧城市的解决方案，把解决方案用到城市的方方面面，谢谢。

邹广　（汕尾市委常委、常务副市长）

谢谢吴思康先生的邀请，我来自中国广东省汕尾市，国内的朋友可能会问我汕尾在广东处于什么位置，和另外一个经济特区汕头是什么关系？国外的朋友可能会问我，你那有什么让我感兴趣的事或感兴趣的食物或其他东西？这两个问题我下面进行回答。

我们的位置是深圳向东 150 千米，我们和另外一个经济特区汕头是兄弟城市，我们的交通非常方便，如果从广东深圳到汕头来，要先路过汕尾，如果大家有兴趣的话，可以在午后从深圳出发，一个小时后我就可以在汕尾请大家喝下午茶。

第二个问题，杜桑·贝拉问我，汕尾是否有着像杜克雷先生所在的南加州一样的山脉，我曾经有一个朋友在汕尾的山上、山下、海边、海上走了一圈，他拿出照片跟我讲，这里和他的家乡很像，如果杜克雷先生去过汕尾的话，可以鉴定一下是否一样，所以在此请大家到汕尾去享受杜克雷"家乡"的风光。

我们毗邻深圳，毗邻粤港澳大湾区，粤港澳是一个世界级的大湾区，有6000 万人口，有最完整的产业链条，有最充沛的资金，有发展最完善的市场机制，还有最有活力的全球的人才，包括在座的各位。

珠三角的九市包括广、佛、肇、深、莞、惠、珠等，也在加速融合，我们看到了港珠澳大桥、广深合作、广深港高速铁路，看到了一系列交通、人才、产业之间的密切合作。

广东省除掉珠三角九市之外的 12 座城市，分别在东、西、北，所以俗称为"粤东西北"，面积占到广东省的 69.5%，人口占 49.5%，GDP 只占 20%，固定资产投资和财政收入只占 12% 左右，也就是说是非常不平衡、不均衡的发展阶段和状态，去年党的十九大召开，在这次大会上提出了重点解决我们国家发展不平衡的问题，我们 12 个城市肩负着重要的使命。如何跟粤港澳、珠三角城市伙伴加强联系？我们现在提倡用一个词"凝聚"，在此之前，我们提到更多的是"辐射"。

之前我们讲的是辐射外溢，现在是凝聚，这两个词的变化是被动到主动的关系，从城市发展角色来讲，我们做了几件事。

我们很高兴加入了圆桌会议，就是原来的深莞惠经济圈，包括深圳、东莞和惠州，原来的"3"变成了"3＋2"，加上了汕尾和河源，两个东西北的城市，就像今天在会议上交流，我们可以得到更多的深莞惠的信息，可以得到很多的共鸣，很多的愿望可以共同实现。

2013年开始，汕尾已经建成和广州、深圳相通的铁路，正在建设的铁路有3条，2013年12月28日厦汕铁路开通，去年广州到汕尾的铁路开通，从广州一个小时可以到汕尾，晒"南加州"的阳光。

为了充分发挥这几条铁路的功能，去年1月5日开通了深圳到汕尾的捷运化交通，点对点地开通了深圳北到汕尾的列车，每天5对共10列，目前运营一周年，效果非常好，之前铁路公司担心客源问题，但去年主动将5节车厢加到8节，而且我也问了广铁的老总，问他是否会停运，他说绝对不会停，运行的效果非常好，交通上有了同城化的联系。

我们汕尾有468平方千米土地交给深圳来管理、运营、发展、整合资源，也就是说通过这一轮的变化，我们从这儿到汕尾市区原来有150千米的距离，从此以后，我们是"零距离"，也就是说，汕尾的土地有着深圳的新区，所以从这个角度来讲城市伙伴关系越来越密切。我们也不能浪费这样的资源，从2016年10月开始到现在，我们每天会在高铁站问卷调查100位旅客，志愿者会问三个问题，"你从哪里来，在这里待几天，来这里做什么？"我们每个月都会对调查问卷进行分析，我们很高兴地看到来自珠三角的客人越来越多，愿意在汕尾待一个月以上、一年以上的客人越来越多，来汕尾从事公务的客人越来越多。我们希望这样的问卷会一直问下去，看10年、20年会发生什么样的变化，也希望各位参与到这个问卷调查之中。

今天这次论坛的主题是"'一带一路'倡议下的城市伙伴关系"，通过我们跟粤港澳大湾区的合作关系我有几点心得：一是城市和城市之间同行才有力量。二是碰撞产生火花，也就是说，我们有交流才有更多的机会和新意。三是独特方显魅力，每一个城市即使是在同一片土地上，也是不同的城市，有不同的魅力，所以希望跟在座的"一带一路"沿线的各国家的朋友一起同行，多做交流，以我们各自独特的魅力散发出更强的光辉。谢谢。

亚历山大·莫迪亚诺　（希腊雅典副市长）

尊敬的各位领导，非常欢迎你们来到这里。

今天首先要问大家一个问题，为什么要来到这里？像我还有其他的一些在座的嘉宾，从很远的地方来到这里，我们为什么会坐十几个小时的飞机来这里开这个会议呢？我们只是为了享受这一个旅程或者只是为了来这里照相、发朋友圈而已吗？我们的目的是什么？

因为中国取得越来越大的成功，我们来向它学习。我们大家都是一个共同体，很多朋友来自欧洲，希腊又是欧洲到中国的必经之地，所以希腊的位置是非常独特的。中国也越来越开放，我们看到中国现在是我们的朋友，中国做任何可以做的事情，来让欧洲更加强健，中国可以做任何事情来团结欧洲，跟16个欧洲国家来进行合作，并且构成一个非常强大的力量。

我认为唯一的出路就是跟中国合作，我们能够很好地相互帮助，相互对接在一起，可以看到很多的城市状况是完全不一样的，"30年河东，30年河西"，国家和国家也是不一样的，每个国家形成体制是不一样的，有的国家中央政府能很好地管理政府，例如新加坡就是中央集权的城市国家，很多时候有决策的权力，所以说简单对比一个国家或城市能做什么事情是不公平的，它们有很多的差异。

另一方面就是中国能够表达雄心和愿景，可能长期之后，可以看到中国一直是开放的体制和贸易，"一带一路"的倡议非常有利于国家的发展，能够让我们在信息上互通有无，能够用我们各自的资源相互支持。中国能够提出这样的倡议，能够让很多的国家实现共赢的局面。

我们先了解一下，要想集中政府优势来使我们各个地区通达，并且促进经济一体化，从城市角度来看，第一要考虑的问题，就是让人跟人的关系变得更加便利，使得我们双方都能够互享互利，多边或双边发展的新模式必须要采取，并且在今天早上我也提到绿色合作以及多边合作，我希望很多国家能够包容、相互拥抱、相互合作，千万不要惧怕拥抱整个世界、拥抱整个世界的多样性，希望大家不要奉行孤立主义。

指南针有八个角度，八个角度都要拥抱，那么，"一带一路"倡议能够指引着我们，不让我们在全球化的趋势中迷失方向，就像马可·波罗一样。找到自己的方向，首先要加入相应组织，分享互利共赢的方法。

第一，要有自上而下的方法，比如斯里兰卡要开展哪些项目，要开展这些项目要从多边角度去考虑两个或多个国家，有多边的角度方案，能够解决很多的问题，能够建设得非常好。

第二，就是坚持执行我们的计划，必须要研究策略，必须专注于创新，去支持所有的服务。

第三，就是不断地推广协动的合作、协动的发展。其实，很多时候，我们看到有些地区是不平衡发展的情况，我们需要政策的支持，我们首先要了解不平衡的情况在哪里，国家都是不平衡的，发展方面是不一样的，我们能够了解很多国家的问题、很多诉求，我们要采取相应的方案，能够让我们的国家比以前更好。

第四，就是投资。中国做了很多投资，是不容易的，很多国家避免投资，其实很多时候涉及资金的投资，需要去考虑很多的风险，很多国家想要做 PPP（政府和社会资本合作），我现在想要去告诉他们，基建设施建设需要因地制宜投建，比如在我们地区进行基建投资，需要公共部门、私人部门、公共和私人部门之间的中间的部门共同参与，所以我们在进行基建的时候，为了更好地推动和落地要多方面了解需求，保持社会安全，必须要保持三方的平衡，这样才能确保我们基建投资顺利。另外就是要去落地一些关键的项目，首先要保有试点的项目，用非常容易的策略去进行投资项目。

第五，就是必须要进行财政、财务的创新，比如说对中国的支付宝或者微信支付，重建金融体制，进行多边的金融合作。

第六，就是城市的角色，就是要建立人与人之间的纽带，这是非常重要的一方面。人与人之间的纽带要有利于文化、有利于国家，这也是涉及相应的软实力的问题。我们需要去了解这个城市如何去拓展自己的软实力，可以看到历史上强大国家的文化是如何渗透和拓展的。尤其是，这些强大国家能够把文化、价值观融入年轻人的精神当中，比如中国，能够影响一代又一代的年轻人。可以举一个小的例子，在雅典有 6 到 7 个社区，大多数是中国人的居住区，他们的设施也建得非常好，他们有很好的精气神，中国小孩到我们的公共学校读书，但他们了解中国的语言、文化，学习中国的菜肴，很好地保留着中国的文化，在家里，他们要跟父母学习中国的文化，在雅典他们也能够接触到当地的历史遗址，能够学习当地的文化，这些孩子同时学习中国的文化、雅典的文化。我想说的就是，这种模式是非常适用于这些现实的，中国在这方面做得非常好。在 2018 年，雅典将会成为"一带一路"沿线地区重要的城市，能够跟中国进行大量的合作。

第七，就是必须要发挥"指南针"的作用，进行全球化合作必须要有方向感，就像指南针一样，我们需要构建城市伙伴关系，另外是智库的建设，智库就是需要用各种语言把建议传播给很多人，并且智库需要解答很多问题，需要把他们的观点以及他们先进的概念很好地传播出去。在合作的时候，也要保证主权。

第八，我想说强化安全，我们做投资，要去进行商业监控、监督机制的建设，很多国家进行合作的时候很注重国家的安全，中国跟其他国家合作的时候也非常注重国家安全，所以需要保证双边的安全，需要能够保证安全的保障体制以及排除所有的风险。谢谢。

陈有文　（中交城市与区域开发规划研究院院长）

我先介绍一下我们单位，CCCC（中国交通建设股份有限公司，简称"中国交建"）是世界 500 强企业，排名 110 位。中国交建在海外具有 110 个驻外机构，遍布全球 100 多个国家。每年有 3000 亿的营业额在海外实现，在今年，随着"一带一路"倡议的实施，中国交建在亚非拉、东欧有大量的项目投资，与沿线国家在城市新区、产业新城方面有大量的合作，并承担国家大通道、大枢纽的合作，同时帮助企业"走出去"，协助本国政府和外国政府开展大量的工作。

我们是中国交建内部的智库，在这几年参与了大家很熟悉的国际投资项目，今天我的演讲主要集中在两个点上：一是对于国内的企业来说，与"一带一路"的沿线国家合作时,如何找到切入点?二是深圳在"一带一路"国际合作中的角色是什么?

首先我们看一下切入点。根据我们这些年在国外几十个国家的深度合作的项目,我们觉得在不同发展阶段的国家里面,机会、合作领域和方向是不同的,为了简化,我们分成三种情形:发达或后工业化国家;进入工业化中后期的新兴工业化国家;工业化发展初期或中期的国家。

看一下以东非地区跟北非地区为代表的非洲国家,工业化水平较低,文盲率较高,达到80%多,对这一区域,我们要区分若干种情况,有些地方劳动力资源很丰富,对于很多地区来说,农业土地很多,而且基本上人口都是农业人口,比如东非的维多利亚大概有6000万人口,我们提出的方案就是促进农业的现代化,还有延伸农业的产业链,发展农业加工业,还有农业贸易,以这种方式来说,一方面可以释放人口,另一方面可以快速提高人们的收入。矿产资源多但没有其他的支撑的国家,总的思路是协助它们发展直接贸易,进一步发展成加工产业链,促进资源型国家的工业化发展。

"一带一路"的重要节点,起到贸易门户枢纽功能,对后方的内陆国家形成很好的支撑,这些也是枢纽功能的提升,也是未来很重要的合作方向,所以我们国家现在合作了很多点,比如沙巴就属于这样的类型。

对于很多地区来说,缺乏基础,但是有需求,在合作初期,以贸易作为驱动是一个比较容易实现的方式,像这个国家的基础设施非常落后,非常缺,所以融入城镇化要解决持续的城市基础设施,我们过去在非洲这方面的投入很多,是通过政府合作框架来改善当地基础设施的现状。

第二种情形就是中国大体上属于沿海国家,中国还是工业化后期发展阶段的国家,这跟中国利用外部市场使工业发展起来是同构的,一些国家的城市发展跟中国遇到的问题是一样的,面临产业升级、转换经济增长模式等问题,不愿意跟劳动密集型产业进行合作,希望引进高科技的产能,这个也就是在合作的选择方面,可能要考虑到这个特点。还有就是在这方面,东欧也有很大的优势,东欧的教育是非常好的。我们与东欧建立相应的研究中心,是有比较好的条件。还有这些即使到工业化后期的国家,由于各种原因基础设施还是滞后的,包括土地等方面,也面临着需要改善的问题,所以这里也存在着机会,包括我们中国交建在马来西亚投资 700 亿的铁路也是属于这个范围。

还有第三种情况，跟发达国家如何合作。可以看得出来，对于西北欧，在技术方向都有很好的优势，而中国的制造业产能有基础，市场推动能力很强，在发达地区和东欧有先进技术和先进产能合作的机会。包括这三个方面不同的国家，其实就是中国对于未来的驱动，中国市场驱动的因素可能未来会越来越大，随着中国城市化进程的提升，中国会成为全球最大的市场，过去 30 年全球市场是由欧美推动的，包括中国最初是受欧美市场的外部需求推动，未来，中国的内部需求会逐渐成为驱动全球市场的重要力量，在利用中国市场驱动方面，科技服务是未来方向。

其次，深圳市在"一带一路"国际合作中的角色和作用。

深圳市委市政府提得很清楚，从我们的角度来说，我们是与"一带一路"沿线国家交往的门户和枢纽的地位，在这样的框架中，深圳能够发挥什么作用呢？我们认为深圳的作用是独特的，深圳在我们国家，在构建"一带一路"倡议中，不能做所有的东西，但是能做的部分，很多是其他地方所不具备的。我们遇到很多发展中国家的总统、领导人，都是提出来想到深圳参观，为什么呢？因为深圳也是他们国家的梦想，一个城市从零到一，成为全球的典范城市，深圳长期发展的迭代还有各种方式的创新，这些东西都是很多发展中国家非常希望能够借鉴的内容，所以我们认为深圳能为发展中国家提供卓越的发展城市的经验。

第二点作用就是，因为深圳走在国内很多城市的前面，珠三角在改革开放前 30 年或者前 20 年是更多地依附于香港驱动的发展，现在深圳可以成为驱动发展的新的引擎，这样的转变，在中国现有的城市里面是独一无二的，这样的科技创新驱动的能力不但能够驱动深圳转型，也带动着很多城市的转型，比如深圳的制造业和研发转移到东莞，给东莞未来的转型提供了非常好的机会，同样，我们看到发展中国家的一些地区或者城市希望看到这样的局面，所以深圳科技创新方面动能的外溢可以给其他城市带来机会。

还有一点就是以深圳为中心的整个体系是很完整的，包括金融中心、国际航运中心、世界级产能在这里集聚，所以这样的能力能够使深圳为西方高科技成果转化提供快速的通道，这点可能是未来发展非常有前景的方向。

所以根据这样的理解，我们提出近期的建议就是：第一，对于工业化初期和中期的国家，深圳在劳动密集型产能合作领域没有优势，重点应放在服务于科技产品的输出贸易方面。

第二，对于进入工业化中后期的新兴工业化国家，深圳具备良好的高科技产能合作优势。

第三，对于发达或后工业化国家及地区，深圳具备吸纳西方高科技成果，并通过珠三角先进制造业进行快速产业化转换的优势。

最后再谈谈深圳模式与深圳经验分享。首先，我们认为深圳是"一带一路"非常独特的城市名片，所以可以实施"一带一路"品牌营销，促进深圳模式与深圳经验的分享。其次，可以以深圳的大学、科研机构为载体，为"一带一路"沿线国家城市提供城市治理模式制度框架构建的咨询支持。最后，通过政府合作，参与境外经济特区合作。

菲利普·麦康菲 （北京大学国际法学院）

我是北京大学国际法学院的院长，我们的法学院是独特的法学院，能够融合各个地方的法律，并且对各地方的法律进行研究，比如对欧盟法律的研究，并且也能够研究很多国家的法律体系。其实我们作为学校，进行研究的目的，就是让人们相信我们所做的事情能够参与到世界的进程当中，让中国的世界影响力与日俱增。珠三角地区的法制与其他地区是不一样的，我们跟很多的国家、地区大学进行合作、交流，我们很多的学生也研究了"一带一路"沿线国家的法制体系，并且在雅典也跟雅典大学进行交流，我们觉得实现"一带一路"必须要了解当地法制体系。

另一方面，要推动"一带一路"倡议，一定要在教育和法制方面做得更好，并且可以看到我们也关切一些基建设施的投资和建设，可以看到有两件事情是非常重要的：首先要去贯彻这种投资的原则。这些城市是独特的城市，并且珠三角地区也是人口最密集的地方；其次，可以看到经济的转型从专业化时代转型成为科技化时代，我们需要去把这种制造业的中心转移到其他地方，比如说生物体系、制药体系。所以我们能够做的、我们所关切的就是在产业升级过程中，如何通过了解法制，或者以法制的研究去推动产业升级的过程。比如说在产业提升的时候，必然涉及政府管制的问题，还有政府的法规的问题，这是我们所关心的问题。谢谢。

杜克雷　（美国南加州大学中美学院院长）

非常感谢能够参加这次会议，我非常佩服深圳，我第一次来深圳的时候，基本没有什么，那是 1982 年，从 1982 年到现在，变化很大，甚至在全世界有很大影响，所以我这次非常感谢主办方的组织，我要表达我的感谢。

首先今天非常荣幸能够在这里跟大家探讨，从你们身上学到东西，大家来自不同的行业，从不同的角度分享，特别是我身边的这位来自汕尾的领导，所以今天这个论坛实在太棒了。

我今天的任务是什么呢？对于在座的外国人来说，我们今天在这里开会的酒店是五洲宾馆，我来自美洲的南加州，大家来到"一带一路"的论坛可以学到很多东西。问题是在你们的国家中，是否会听到"一带一路"倡议，或者是否受到"一带一路"倡议的影响，在美国基本上很多美国人都没有听说过"一带一路"倡议，他们都知道中国的发展非常快，但是他们不了解中国这个非常棒的创意，确实某个程度上他们意识到中国在"走出去"，但是每一个美国人了解到这一点是因为很多中国人去到美国。所以无论是学校还是其他的层面，人才的流动越来越多，平均每天都有 6000 个美国人来到中国，平均每天有 8000 个中国人到美国去，那么美国会了解到"一带一路"倡议的什么方面呢？或者是什么时候才会了解到呢？

所以，对于不同的国家，不论是美国人还是欧洲人都了解"一带一路"倡议，是可能的吗？我想这是我想问大家的第一个问题，大家可以看到刚刚的视频，其实这个视频是在美国的中国人制作的，就是他们选取"一带一路"倡议相关的片段创作了一首歌，他们知道"一带一路"连通了很多的国家，包括美国的不同的城市，甚至是德州的一些城市。所以"一带一路"会涉及很多的语言，如西班牙语、英语等，我们相信很多外国人来到中国做生意，在有了更好的了解之后，大家都会学习到一个词语叫"关系"，所以中国人要是跟外国人讲的时候，"关系"在中国是非常重要的，如果你不能处理好关系的话，不能取得很大的成功。所以很多人跟中国人打交道的时候，就会提出在中国跟谁关系比较好，有很大的帮助，所以了解这个很有帮助的。

但是，我刚才提到"关系"的时候是中文的词语，其实是比英语中的意义更广泛的，西方人也开始思考关系的重要性，所以很多年来我都会举这一个例子。但是其实关系已经非常重要了，现在在我们的字典上已经更新出来了，就是用拼音出现在字典上，因为跟翻译出来的单词意义是不一样的，大家可以看到它的重要性。很多人都会开始思考"一带一路"，很多人都会重视"一带一路"，其实很多人都关注到我是来自于北美的，在这里我想跟大家讲一下，其实南美非常期望"一带一路"能够扩展到那边去，所以我们可以看到习近平主席去到这些国家，还有其他的一些国家也在逐渐地扩展。刚才展示了中国在这些"一带一路"沿线国家所做的投资，如果这些计划能够成功的话，那么中国将会成为非常大、非常成功的投资者。

所以，很多国家非常希望能够和中国建立外交关系，然后能够受到"一带一路"的影响，如巴拿马，其实可以看到很多的投资者，他们对于"一带一路"的创意充满好奇心，可以看到很多人去了解。

加州是美国对于中国出口的第一大州，相信中国的市场会产生十分大的经济机遇，对于美国人来说机遇也是非常大的。腾讯公司，收购了洛杉矶的游戏公司，其他公司收购了 AVP 公司或者是超市、零售公司，大家看到1800 名加州人在中资公司工作，我觉得这个趋势能够抵消我们对中国消极的看法。这是非常重要的看法。我们看到越来越多的现象，我们也了解到了，中国对于美国的投资以及很多公司对于美国公司的收购，例如华为在美国有很多员工。为什么中国要去这么做呢？中国的公司通过项目的构建，是为了让所有的项目得益。在加州有两个州长，来自民主党和自由党，都想跟中国合作，可以看到他们跟中国探讨如何建造高铁，跟中国来签约，在有关于"一带一路"倡议的方面能够看到机遇，这就是在构建中国和美国之间的合作。

两个洛杉矶的公司，希望能够参与到"一带一路"倡议中，其中一个在中国上海也建造了非常高的大厦，所以他们也希望能够在其他的城市创造更好的生活，深圳也是其中的一个。

从 20 世纪 90 年代开始，一些国家开始采用"东亚发展"模式，但很困难。所以，"一带一路"对于它们很重要，对于中国也是战略合作的重要部分。中国将变成其中非常有希望和影响力的国家。

所以最后我想总结一下：我对这一个非常勇敢的倡议，其实是印象非常深刻的，我觉得这对中国以及世界各国来说都是非常重要的，我希望美国能够参与到中国的"一带一路"倡议当中。谢谢。

迪亚·哈立德　（突尼斯驻华大使）

今天我非常荣幸地来到深圳这个美丽的城市，刚刚听到上一个发言人精彩的演讲，我非常敬佩，在他之后，我讲一讲我自己的看法。

首先我想要对这里的政府领导的支持表示感谢，因为他们能够给我这么一个机会参与到论坛当中，另外我也想要跟大家讲一下，我也非常祝贺中国共产党成功举行了十九大，这为中国未来的更好的发展奠定了基础。

今天大家一起坐在这里探讨以后会取得哪些更好的合作，特别是不同国家的经济合作。我们也知道城市之间的合作是非常重要的，我也恭喜城市合作伙伴在城市合作当中取得了非常大的成功。也希望中国之后能够有更好的前景。

今天这一个发言的主题当然也是和"一带一路"有关，大家也知道城市发挥越来越大的作用，在不同行业都有涉及，所以不同城市发展的成功经验能够被其他的城市学习。当然，我们也知道我们还面临着其他的挑战。另外我也非常高兴突尼斯政府和中国有很多的合作，特别是和中国深圳这个城市合作，我在深圳虽然待得不久，但是我在这里的体验非常好，而且我也知道突尼斯和深圳的合作是非常紧密的。

特别是我们两国之间的政策红利，联系也越来越紧密。所以，我们两国的合作潜力都非常巨大，我也希望中国能够来到我们国家进行投资，其实今天我有一个小创意，就是我们合作建立一个创业园，也是基于"一带一路"倡议的，我觉得这能够大大激发我们两国之间的合作潜力，我们可以在制造业、新能源、IT还有物联网这些领域加大合作。大家也知道我们国家是位于地中海的中间的地带，我们知道中国在推动非洲和中国之间的合作伙伴关系上也是在不断地努力，而且我们也在筹划中非的第二个论坛，所以我希望强调，突尼斯对于中国的"一带一路"是非常关键的，所以突尼斯将会成为中国非常大的投资市场，而且我们在 1995 年就和中国建立了自贸协定，这也是我们的政策红利。就像大家所知道的我们的合作网络推广，可以看到我们有很多的成就能够呈现出来。并且大家知道我们突尼斯经济相对脆弱，跟中国合作能够使我们大大提高对各种挑战的抵御能力，我们在 2000 年已经成立了经济合作中心，研究经济合作。有两个中国的公司——中兴和华为在突尼斯运营，希望有更多的公司来到突尼斯。

2000 年，我第一次来深圳，18 年后，我发现深圳变化巨大，非常漂亮，我非常高兴见证这一切。我们必须要眺望未来，我觉得要抓住这个机遇来恭喜深圳乃至广东，它们有非常大的成功，在城市规划和城市建设方面取得了很大的成功，同时也要抓住竞争的机遇，感谢主办方，我们有机会展望未来，并且以话题的方式来讨论全球问题，实现双赢，通过这种方式我们能够大大地提高城市间、国家间、内地间的连通。突尼斯是快速发展的经济体之一，我们要去寻求跟中国进行合作，成为"一带一路"倡议积极的参与国，让"一带一路"的倡议能够延续下去。谢谢。

冯坚 （新华社）

在当今现代化浪潮和全球化浪潮席卷之下，在这样一个时代，我觉得一个企业、一个城市、一个国家，媒体形象的重要性已经不容置疑，形象的必要性通常不掌握在自己的手里，随着社会的发展进步，人们对形象的意识越来越提升，对于塑造权有了前所未有的关注和重视度，要把握形象塑造的主动权提升自己软实力，增强自己的吸引力、感召力和引领力。在"一带一路"的大框架下，如何提升塑造能力，把握形象的塑造权，我觉得是许多企业面临的课题。

我觉得媒体，特别是重要的媒体，在形象塑造功能上有非常重要的作用，一个是媒体的出现或者是科技的发展，为信息的共享提供了大的平台，同时也提高了信息搜集、传播、塑造的速度，媒体有三个角色：信息汇总、友谊之桥、塑造者或者塑型者。

媒体信息汇总的作用，我就不多言了，大家都很清楚，比如说现在很多的大媒体不管是西方的路透、法新、美联等主流的媒体，还是国内也是一样的，央媒在信息汇总方面发挥了很大的作用，比如新华社就有信息用户5万多家，发行期刊600万份，也是国内发行量最大的报刊群体，新华网在全球是非常有影响力的网站。互联网将越来越多的人和设备系统联系起来，伴随着信息技术的进步，连通能力更加快，更加便利，成本越来越低。

媒体是一个沟通的纽带，是一座友谊之桥，媒体不仅仅传播信息，而且沟通文化，增进了解，我们经常讲的"一带一路"的"五通"里面，有一条是民心相通，我想媒体发挥的作用是不可替代的。

习主席也经常讲："要讲好中国故事，传播好中国声音。"就是告诉我们要打造民心相通，特别是针对发达国家的"一带一路"报道，民心方面的报道。我们都知道民心相通是国际交往的前提，增进相互了解，也是合作的基础，更是可持续发展和合作的黏合剂和助推器，在"一带一路"倡议提出后，各大媒体就进行了社会文化和民生方面的报道，宣讲和谐的文化。

媒体是影响塑造者，媒体具有信息采集和传播功能，采集什么样的信息，如何传播信息，如何传播有用的信息，都是在塑造一个形象，大到一个国家，小到一个群体、一个企业，都在向外界传播信息，媒体在这个时候具有形象塑造功能。正面信息传递得多，传播得广，就会塑造一个正面的形象，负面信息传播得多，传播得广，塑造的就是负面的形象。

媒体在价值判断上有信息选取的作用，采集什么样的信息，报道什么样的新闻，是媒体必须要做的价值判断，在这方面各个媒体也在做。媒体影响面取决于信息的传播领域，也取决于信息的传播影响力。议题设置也是信息能力，行为舆论议题的设置有人为设置和重大发生实践，行为议题设置也非常重要，表达能力也非常重要，没有让人耳目一新、引人入胜的议题，受众也不会感兴趣，影响也不会产生，形象塑造能力也不会强。

我觉得一个企业、一个城市下一步应该加强形象的自塑能力，下大功夫。以媒体为支撑，以媒体为筹码，要塑造良好形象，提高形象自塑能力，就要积极与媒体合作，共谋良策，利用媒体传播平台提升产品的形象，从而提升产品的吸引力、感召力。

城市要掌握议题形象塑造主动权，要发挥主观能动性，主动地设置议题，常言道"善谋者赢",所谓谋,我觉得就是议题的设置和策划,策划和设置议题也是一种功能,即策划什么、发布什么,现在很多国家也意识到议题的重要性,纷纷推出各自的亮点。现在很多活动例如文化周、企业展览会等,我觉得就是一些议题设置活动。

传播力决定影响力,议题设置是否具有影响力非常重要,需要根据一个国家、地区、受众、当地文化,设置不同的议题,比如说在阿拉伯世界,就要考虑阿拉伯文化特点设置议题。

政府也好、企业也罢,要增强塑造形象的意识,汇聚塑造形象的合力,现代社会人人都是信息的传播者,人人都是媒体,人人都是播种机,人人都有麦克风。加强对社会每一个人、每一个群体、每一个企业的培养,进而提升形象塑造意识,是提升形象塑造的一方面。政府可以加大这方面的培养力度,举办各种提高公民形象塑造意识的活动,组织这种培训项目,提高人们的公民和市民意识,提升他们的归属感、荣誉感、自豪感,一个城市的成就是每一个人、每一个组织的成就,突出展示成就,就会增强归属感、荣誉感和自豪感,这需要学习和培训工作。

还要提高企业的社会责任感,一个企业在发达国家投资,不仅要为利润,还要为一个国家的形象塑造承担责任,有责任在当地展示城市形象、国家形象。

马佳娜 （摩尔多瓦驻华使馆临时代办）

摩尔多瓦共和国人民对中国人民表示大力的支持,并对中国人民继往开来、坚定不移、凝聚千年智慧所取得的成就深表钦佩。今天的中国作为一个现代化国家,在建设经济、科技和文化精神方面取得了历史性的巨大成功,与中华悠久的古文明交相辉映,水乳交融。中国不仅仅是世界第二大经济强国,也是包括摩尔多瓦共和国在内的世界上所有国家的重要伙伴。摩尔多瓦共和国愿做出一切努力,继续加强与中华人民共和国的双边关系。

去年,中国和摩尔多瓦共和国庆祝建交 25 周年。虽然 25 年是很短的一段时间,但是一直以来,我们两国都保持友好和睦、互惠互利的合作关系,并不断将这种关系在各个领域进行多样化和发展加强。2013 年中国国家主席习近平阁下提出的"一带一路"倡议给摩尔多瓦共和国和中国带来了巨大的机遇并创造了新的合作领域。摩尔多瓦政府坚决支持"一带一路"倡议。我们相信，这将大大地加强我们两国政府和人民之间的友谊，并将双方的经贸合作推向一个新的阶段。

鉴于此，建立可持续的城市伙伴关系对于推进区域经济一体化、探索新的合作领域、拓展新的发展空间方面将发挥重要的作用。我要感谢深圳市政府和其下属的发展研究中心给我机会，切身了解深圳的商业环境和经济优势。深圳给我留下了深刻的印象，这座城市本身就是一个传奇，在过去不到40年的时间里发展疾如闪电，在短短数十年内，它的经济出现翻天覆地的变化，引起了国际社会的广泛关注。深圳在分销、物流、制造业等领域具有显著的优势，为加强深圳和摩尔多瓦企业之间的经济和商业合作创造了无数的可能性。

2017年5月，摩尔多瓦共和国副总理兼经济部部长屋大维·卡尔梅克阁下参加了"一带一路"国际合作高峰论坛，并和其他国家与会的代表一起签署了《推进"一带一路"贸易畅通合作倡议》。我们希望，这一具有全球重要性的文件不仅仅将促进摩尔多瓦共和国和中国之间的双边合作，也将为摩尔多瓦各大城市和深圳市的合作带来契机。摩尔多瓦与深圳之间的经贸合作将是开放的，在两国政府的扶持下，城市间的合作也将得到增强。

摩尔多瓦共和国亦希望借此机会发展本国经济，吸引更多中国投资者和游客到摩尔多瓦来。对于摩尔多瓦来说，中国是一个非常值得信赖和可靠的合作伙伴，为了摩尔多瓦和中国人民的利益，我们希望能继续发展两国优良的双边合作关系。

摩尔多瓦共和国地处欧盟和独联体之间，地理上具有接近西部和东部市场的优势，可以确保东、西之间的沟通和联系。我们能够全面利用地理上的优势变成连通欧洲和亚洲的桥梁。这将成为中国投资者打开拥有8亿消费者市场的窗口。摩尔多瓦政府提倡经济开放，签署了若干双边和多边贸易协定。摩尔多瓦共和国继续探索新的可持续发展战略以为中国投资者建立良好的商业环境并提高国家的整体竞争力。

现将吸引投资和促进出口的优先产业项目罗列如下：信息技术和通信；机械设备制造（汽车）；管理和支助事务活动；机械及零配件制造；纺织品；电

气设备；食品工业和农业，包括葡萄酒行业。

为了方便贸易交流并让两国公民互相了解以进入对方市场，我们两国政府就自由贸易协定的签署开始进行讨论。这些年来，我们两国就这一问题进行了多次筹备性讨论，目前已顺利签署了正式启动自由贸易谈判的谅解备忘录。我们希望今年年底之前能够完成谈判并签署协议。自由贸易协定的签署将成为加强两国经济关系和增加贸易额的里程碑。

作为摩尔多瓦出口到中国市场的最重要的产品，我们希望自由贸易协定也能对摩尔多瓦葡萄酒出口起到促进作用。葡萄酒产业是摩尔多瓦共和国经济重要支柱。摩尔多瓦共和国有 3000 年以上的葡萄酒酿造历史。摩尔多瓦共和国拥有世界上最大的地下酒庄——克里克瓦和米列什蒂·密茨酒庄，两个酒庄各有长度超过 120 千米的地下贮酒隧道。与此同时，我们拥有世界上最大的葡萄酒储存量，达 150 多万瓶，被吉尼斯世界纪录记录在册。

中国市场作为我们的目标市场之一，我们已为 2018 年制定了市场开拓计划，其中包括参加中国最大的葡萄酒类展会，举行葡萄酒品尝活动和针对中国消费者的葡萄酒文化培训等一系列推广活动。

深圳是中国最大的城市之一，也是十分重要的市场。我们欢迎深圳的企业和友人们到摩尔多瓦世界上最大的地下酒窖参观，去品读醇厚千年葡萄酒文化的同时挖掘在葡萄酒出口和投资领域合作的可能性。

在此，我想指出，为加强我们两国和两国人民直接的交流，摩尔多瓦共和国政府通过了一项关于简化中国公民签证材料的决定。自 2017 年 8 月 1 日起，中国公民如持有欧盟成员国任何一国或申根协定的缔约国签发的有效签证，在该签证有效期内可进入摩尔多瓦。我们希望此举能促进游客的数量和商务人士的互动，以期鼓励双方推动新的合作项目。

我想借此重申，摩尔多瓦政府特别重视发展与中国的关系，并同意与中方携手共进，落实两国官员在互访期间就两国合作所达成的共识，在"一带一路"倡议框架内促进摩中关系与合作，增进两国人民福祉，取得更丰硕的成果。与此同时，摩尔多瓦共和国大使馆将努力促进以上关系的进一步发展，并将大力支持深化地方一级和两国公司之间的合作。

最后，我想再次感谢本次论坛组织方的诚挚邀请和热情欢迎。在此我祝愿大家今天进行的讨论可收获累累硕果，并灵活机动地诠释论坛的主题，从而实现真正意义上的互利共赢。

谢谢大家。

詹玛丽　（香港东帝汶总商会执行主席）

我本人是出生在东帝汶的第三代华裔，我的祖父在100年前移居到东帝汶，我们的家族从事塑胶、檀香、咖啡产业，我们在那边有自己的生意，在20世纪70年代，东帝汶发生了政变，跟印度尼西亚发生了很大的冲突，一直持续了30年，直到2000年才脱离，脱离的时代刚好遇上我们新任的总统，让我回东帝汶，重建家园，我回去的时候，他首先要我在香港成立总商会，因为我是祖籍香港的华裔，对于祖国的语言比较熟悉，也懂得东帝汶的语言，所以在2013年成立了东帝汶总商会。我们东帝汶总商会，宗旨是有助于东帝汶开展跟香港、东盟等各地区的经贸合作，有助于中国经济"走出去"和"引进来"，我们东帝汶总商会将会带动更多的中国内地跟东盟等国家的企业家、商人、市民到东帝汶考察、投资、观光，尤其是深圳来的企业家我们见过50个，我们跟他们交流的时候，希望他们将深圳市的高科技产业带到到我们东帝汶来，到东帝汶投资合作，到我们东帝汶搞一个培训班、培训中心。东帝汶地理环境非常具有优势，李肇星部长今天跟我谈过，他也认为东帝汶有很大的优势，是天然的旅游胜地，他去过东帝汶，每天看到海滩，一定要下水去游泳。东帝汶也有很多的天然资源，我们的石油、太阳能、天然湖储备量大，集体农业、建筑业发达，现在在建飞机场、公路等。东帝汶是非常年轻的国家，商机无限，所以近一两年，很多中国的企业家到东帝汶去找商机，而且目前东帝汶是发展中国家，东帝汶一定会加强跟周边国家的合作，为中国的发展与繁荣稳定，为东盟的发展做出更大贡献，为更多文化、体育、高科技、专业人才提供交流平台作出更大的贡献。

东帝汶总商会，一直在跟进我们祖国推动的"一带一路"倡议。东帝汶跟印尼交界，是邻居。郑和下西洋的时候，曾到过我们东帝汶采摘檀香。我们东南亚很多人不知道什么叫"一带一路"，去年和前年，我已经推广到马来西亚，他们问什么叫"一带一路"，我来到深圳、香港、澳门以及中国其他城市,大家都有对"一带一路"的认识,所以我回答他们"一带一路"是扶贫之路,因为习近平主席提倡互联互通,我认为这对我们来说就是一条扶贫之路。

作为东帝汶来讲,天时地利人和,资源非常丰富,商机无限。我们一定为中国的招商引资,互惠互利,尤其是在我们深圳市带领之下,将经济合作贯彻到企业当中,积极贯彻落实习近平主席提出的"一带一路"倡议。

科斯明·尼古拉　(罗马尼亚巴克乌市市长)

首先感谢国际合作论坛,非常感谢你们的邀请,同时感谢深圳政府的盛情邀请,罗马尼亚把中国看作是兄弟之国,在1949年我们毫不犹豫地跟中国建交,虽然那个时候我们还没有相互了解,周恩来总理在1961年的时候就造访了我们国家。习近平主席所提出的"一带一路"倡议,就是要带来和平,以和平崛起为目的,从和平开始发展,我们两个国家作为兄弟之国,在经济方面是相似的情况,也贯彻相应的经济发展计划。创造对话的机会来分享经验是非常重要的,能够让更多的人了解如何发展,把成功的经验传播出去。意识形态的差异不会阻碍我们的文化和经济的交流,在罗马尼亚,其实我们也有很好的促进经济增长的措施和机制,是符合"一带一路"倡议的,合作机制对于城市是有必要的,找到方法促进商业的合作,必须像兄弟一样相互对待,拓展我们的倡议,把政策和措施实施到"一带一路"的沿线国家。我们一定要抓住经济发展,对文化教育方面也要有非常好的把握,并且需要了解我们两个城市之间的差异以及文化的共通性,要实现经济和文化上的交流,使我们的合作上升一个台阶,其实我觉得"一带一路"倡议,将会成为我们经济的推动力,能够推动智慧方面发展的方方面面,并且能够促进民生。

这是我第一次来到中国,第一次来到深圳。深圳是一个奇迹之城,对于我来说深圳是一个模范城市,我作为罗马尼亚巴克乌市的市长把深圳30多年从无到有的发展作为例子,其实就是我想把深圳的模式借鉴到、运用到我们的城市当中,在欧洲我们热衷于智慧城市、智能城市,所有的东西都需要智能、智慧,我觉得智慧城市话题,可以从深圳找到答案。举个例子:华为、中兴都来自深圳,深圳是一个智慧城市,可以在深圳借鉴相应的经验。

从合作方面来说，像我们刚才所说的需要考虑很多的问题，如经济、文化上的问题，同时跟深圳相互联结在一起是非常有必要的，我觉得我们下一个重要的步骤，是要充分利用好"一带一路"这个平台，要很好地合作，通过非常好的体系进行合作，我觉得我们可以通过这个方式、通过这个平台来进行系统的合作，我觉得就是你们开发的平台能够引领我们发展的大方向，再次感谢你们的邀请，我希望在适合的时机邀请你们去考察我们巴克乌市，并分享经验。谢谢。

钱小琴 （徐州海伦哲专用车辆股份有限公司代表）

各位领导、女士们、先生们，大家下午好！今天非常荣幸代表杨娅女士在这里给大家做演讲，杨娅女士是徐州海伦哲副董事长和深圳市连硕教育投资管理有限公司董事长。

我们公司是做新能源的，比如新材料方面的硬件，特别是母机的通讯，我所在的部门是通信定位部门，所以我也非常高兴今天能够和在座的各位坐在这里开会，特别感谢主办单位的邀请，其实我们的联系还是挺多的，我想问一个问题，就是大家所在的国家和"一带一路"倡议有什么关系呢？

在这里我想给大家做一个报告，讲讲在"一带一路"倡议下我们做了什么事情。我们有一个母公司，跟"一带一路"沿线国家合作的历史非常久远，就是为他们提供了很多设备。我们的连硕教育投资管理有限公司和中兴以及其他深圳的高科技公司也有一些国际上的合作，就是在"一带一路"倡议下的相关的国际合作，而且我们所做的这个东西是获得教育部的授权。我们作为一个先行或者试验型的单位，在去年年末得到了教育部的大力支持，以及深圳市政府的支持，我们成立了一个学校，我们这个学校现在发展得不错，输出了很多人才，我们这个机构的使命之一就是要为"一带一路"倡议作出我们的贡献，我们对于产业的整合也做出了很大的努力。

刚才我跟大家介绍了我们做了什么东西，或许有人会问，作为一个私营企业，为什么要做这样的事情，这个不是中国政府应该做的事情吗？我们虽然是私人企业，但是我们有这样一个部门叫作社会责任部门，所以我们也给他们提供信息服务以及系统，就是刚刚我们提到的中兴这些公司，我们也合作，特别是回到"一带一路"话题上来，我们在"一带一路"沿线国家也有很多的合作。

因为"一带一路"沿线的部分国家非常缺综合性的人才，我们公司就解决了这个短板。就是技术非常成熟的人才是非常缺的，我们希望那些经济不是特别发达的国家能够有更多的人才帮助他们，我相信他们会获得更好的发展。

最后，今天我们论坛的主题之一也是提到了"智库"，我们的杨娅女士也提到过，在这里我也想代表她说一下她的看法，她觉得智库的合作是趋势，其实我们公司暂时来说还是提供不了这样的服务，因为我们公司暂时还没有那个能力为政策制定者提供培训，我觉得在这个话题上需要企业的参与，有了他们的参与，我们会做得更好，而且我们也有这样的激情、热情来做，而且我们公司其实也有市场营销等各方面的经验。

罗伊·菲德尔 ［安可顾问公司（APCO）特拉维夫办事处总经理］

感谢深圳市政府，邀请我来到这次会议，感谢主办方辛勤的组织。

我非常乐意做这样的事，能够获得更多的信息，可以观察，我是作为公关公司的执行总裁，同时我要做的就是解决国际沟通的问题，我们在全球范围内有 36 个办事处，在中国有 3 个，在过去有幸为以色列政府提供顾问服务，并且支持中国跟以色列之间的贸易连接。还记得在 2010 年第一次来中国的时候，我去拜访了一些技术公司，当时有几个公司聚在一起，华为、中兴以及其他公司，我有幸看到了中国的先进技术，看到中国做得非常好，看到中国全球化的步伐，并且看到很好的发展，我觉得很多公司在过去几年中遇到了问题，我能够很好地帮助它们解决。

非常荣幸跟大家分享我的观点，对于我来说，深圳是最好的分享我观点的地方。SIGNAL（中以学校交流促进协会）是以色列唯一进入"一带一路"的智库平台，它能够推动学术合作和国家跟国家之间的网络合作关系。可以看到以色列 GDP 体量也是比较大的，以色列也有相应的绰号——全球技术产业创新中心，深圳作为中国的"硅谷"，两个地区代表了创新的中转站，看到中国因很多技术因素而腾飞，中国的企业会变得越来越强大，看到中国的企业在未来几年有数千亿美元的投资，我们将会在人工智能或者是医疗保健和教育方面有非常大的合作。

我们以色列虽然是小国，但是能够给中国带来补给。我想谈谈在"一带一路"倡议下，如何进行更好的合作。我们两个国家的合作不仅局限于技术方面，还有经济方面。下面谈一下以色列经济的推动因素，我们看一下以色列如何与中国互惠互利。

天然气是重要的推动因素。以前，大家说以色列没有任何能源，其实是有很多的能源的，2010年我们找到了1000BCM（十亿立方米）的天然气（以色列人一年的总消耗量是7BCM），可以更好地推动人类的发展。有这么大的天然气储量，可以推动经济发展，给我们创收，提供11亿美元资金到我们国家当中，也能够推动中国和以色列之间的合作，能够减少制造业成本，对于中国来说，从以色列进口天然气比中国自产天然气成本更低，对于中国是利好的产业，我们的地点是非常接近欧洲市场的，更加重要的是中国可以把生产中心转移到以色列，更加接近我们的市场。

提到港口，就是以色列北部海港成为通往约旦和其他阿拉伯地区的贸易通道，在连接以色列和约旦自由贸易区之内的约旦河上架了一座桥梁之后，我们以色列的地位大大提高了。

另外正在发生的就是，可以看到以色列边境跟贝特谢安的网络连接，我们也分享共同的经济利益，使我们跟希腊、塞浦路斯关系更加密切，我们也建立了南欧的天然气管道，能够把能源共享起来，能够相互联系起来，同意建立1000英里长的电缆，使得跟欧洲的电能够共享。

以色列大部分工人把钱存入养老金计划，去年还制订了全国养老金计划，这意味着以色列金融机构现在管理超过4000亿美元的功能储蓄，金融机构能够有机遇和优势。其实，我们国家许多金融机构因为现金比较足，想寻求投资机遇，我觉得就是对于"一带一路"倡议来说，也是非常好的。我觉得，我们面临很大的机遇，不论发生什么事情，都可以通过机遇来发展自己。

有一项研究非常有趣的，就是由EIU（经济学人智库）对以色列"一带一路"市场进行风险评估，评估结果发现风险比新加坡还低，这是非常重要的，是超越技术的，技术有不稳定的因素，我们的投资环境是非常稳定的，意味着我们是非常安全的投资体系。谢谢大家。

平行分论坛（三）：产业合作

创新合作模式，构建城市智库与产业伙伴网络

第一节　分享经验，构筑"一带一路"
倡议合作下的企业合作新模式

朱光超　（国家电网公司副总工程师）

女士们、先生们，各位来宾：

非常高兴代表国家电网公司参加此次论坛，我向大家介绍一下国家电网公司的服务和推进"一带一路"建设的成果、经验和认识。

一、对"一带一路"倡议的认识和体会

习近平总书记提出的"一带一路"倡议是我国主动参与全球治理，推动经济全球化深入发展，构建全方位对外开放新格局的重要举措。"一带一路"已经成为世界上最受欢迎的国际合作倡议，已成为有关各国实现共同发展的重要合作平台，100多个国家和国际组织积极支持参与，实现了倡议来自中国，成效惠及世界。

"一带一路"沿线大多为发展中国家，市场潜力巨大。根据多家权威机构预测，未来5年，"一带一路"沿线国家对电力投资需求达到1.5万亿美元，用电需求年均增长4%以上，高于发达国家和其他发展中国家，为我国电力企业提供了难得的市场机遇。国家电网公司作为全球最大的公用事业企业、全球财富500强排名第二位的能源电力企业，有责任、有义务、有能力在"一带一路"建设中切实发挥骨干和领军作用，与沿线国家分享我们的技术和经验，支持当地经济社会发展。

二、国家电网公司服务和推进"一带一路"建设情况

近年来，国家电网公司贯彻落实习近平主席提出的"一带一路"倡议，坚持共商、共建、共享原则，将服务和推进"一带一路"建设作为国际化发展的核心，制定了《"一带一路"建设规划》和《国际产能合作行动计划》，发挥综合优势，通过规划对接和标准联通助力政策沟通，通过基础设施投资建设推进设施联通，通过国际产能合作促进贸易畅通，通过国际资本运作推动资金融通，通过"本土化经营"和国际交流合作促进民心相通，在"一带一路"

建设中切实发挥着骨干和领军作用。

一是稳健投资运营能源电力基础设施。成功投资运营菲律宾、巴西、葡萄牙、澳大利亚、意大利、希腊等国家的骨干能源网，境外资产规模达600亿美元，所有项目运营平稳、全部盈利。这些项目均为关系经济社会发展的重要基础设施，是 "一带一路" 建设的重点。项目运营效率和安全水平稳步提升，得到当地社会和监管机构的广泛认同，建立了良好信誉，有力促进了设施联通和民心相通。

二是积极推进电力基础设施互联互通。累计建成中俄、中蒙、中吉等10条跨国输电线路，交易电量超过240亿千瓦时，促进周边国家能源优化配置。通过投资、工程总承包等方式推动并参与 "一带一路" 沿线国家间联网工程，承建埃塞俄比亚—肯尼亚、土耳其—伊朗等联网工程建设，积极推进菲律宾、希腊等国家岛屿互联项目，跟进潜在跨国跨洲电网互联项目。

三是优质高效推进国际产能合作。依据公司综合优势，建立了投资运营、规划设计、工程建设、装备制造、技术标准全产业链 "走出去" 的产能合作模式，服务 "一带一路" 沿线国家基础设施建设，参与建设了巴基斯坦、埃塞俄比亚、埃及、波兰、缅甸、老挝、巴西等国家骨干电网项目，分享我们的技术和经验，改善当地电网基础设施水平，为解决当地供电和更好地利用清洁能源做出了积极贡献。

四是大力推动中国标准 "走出去"。坚持自主创新，全面掌握一批特高压输电、智能电网等核心关键技术，在国际上率先建立了完整的特高压交直流、智能电网技术标准体系。国家电网公司负责制定的我国电动汽车充换电标准体系，与美国、德国、日本并列为世界四大标准体系，公司累计主导制定国际标准47项。一些沿线国家通过采用中国标准，进一步完善了本国技术标准体系。在菲律宾、巴西、巴基斯坦、埃及等国家的电网建设和运行中广泛使用公司标准。

五是积极推进民心相通。在服务和推进 "一带一路" 建设过程中，国家电网公司作为长期战略投资者，秉持可持续发展理念，坚持市场化运作、专业化管理、本土化运营，不断提升资产运营指标，提供安全优质服务，履行企业社会责任，注重宣传国家电网公司发展成果，展示公司发展理念，讲述中国故事，得到了当地社会各界高度评价，促进了民心相通。例如，我们建设的埃塞俄比亚复兴大坝水电站 500 千伏送出工程被当地政府确定为青少年爱国主义教育基地，世界银行和多个非洲国家对工程质量和技术水平给予了高度评价。

三、"一带一路"建设经验体会

一是坚持发挥综合优势，打造核心竞争力。国家电网公司拥有特高压、智能电网、新能源接入等领域的领先技术，以及在大电网建设和运行管理等方面的丰富经验，为服务和推进"一带一路"建设提供了坚实的基础和保障。近几年我们"走出去"不断取得突破的一个重要原因，就是充分发挥技术、资金、运营、管理、品牌综合优势，形成了服务和推进"一带一路"建设的核心竞争力。

二是坚持规范运作，实现长治久安。在国际项目推进过程中遵守国际规则和所在国法律法规，规范运作。一方面要规范审批，我们在菲律宾项目中标后形成了特许权法案，使项目保持比较平稳的运营。在葡萄牙国家能源网公司、意大利能源网公司和希腊国家电网公司收购过程中，公司规范地进行了欧盟反垄断审批沟通。另一方面科学设置治理结构。我们所有的海外投资项目，均争取了与股比相对应的董事席位，并派出高管团队参与公司管理，确保了与股本相对应的管控治理权。

三是坚持长期战略投资，保持稳健和持续发展。国家电网公司秉持可持续发展理念，坚持长期战略投资，深耕细作。在巴西，我们实现了存量资产并购、绿地项目开发和国际产能合作的不断深化，业务范围涵盖输电、配电、新能源和装备制造合作等。在巴基斯坦，我们不仅建设该国首条高压直流输电工程，还将在 25 年运营期内为巴基斯坦培训大量技术人员。在埃塞俄比亚，在把复兴大坝水电 500 千伏送出工程建成非洲最先进的输变电工程基础上，我们又获得首都轻轨配套供电工程、中低压配网升级改造项目和埃肯联网 ±500 千伏直流输电工程总承包。

四是坚持共商共建共享，实现合作共赢。在菲律宾，我们进入菲律宾国家电网公司后，帮助建立电网事故抢修指挥中心和体系，电网事故抢修时间和故障恢复送电时间大幅减少，我们也获得监管奖励。在巴西，我们进入巴西市场后，在积极运营好存量资产的基础上，积极分享国家电网公司的技术和经验，经与巴西电力主管部门和电力同行的多轮沟通交流，我们将特高压输电技术引入巴西，投资建设巴西美丽山水电特高压送出一、二期特许项目，将巴西北部亚马孙流域丰富的水电远距离大容量输送到巴西东南部负荷中心，成为贯穿巴西南北的"清洁能源高速公路"。一期项目习总书记见证签约，李克强总理奠基。2017 年 12 月，特许权提前两个月建成投入运行，创造了巴西电力建设的历史记录，实现了国家电网公司技术和标准"走出去"，体现了中国质量和中国速度，带动了中国装备"走出去"，也为巴西创造了一万多个工作岗位，并且促进了巴西清洁能源的开发利用。

夏　忠　（国家电力投资集团公司副总经理）

国家电力投资集团公司，主要涉及核电、火电、水电、新能源、铁路、港口、煤矿、电解铝产业，以及环保、资本、金融几大板块。清洁能源比例比较高，刚成立的时候大概是 26.7%，通过 15 年的努力，现在已经超过 45%，在几大集团里，清洁能源的占比是最高的，目标是到 2020 年装机容量达到 50%。

经过五年多的"一带一路"实践和学习十九大精神，央企对推进"一带一路"倡议的重要性、紧迫性和艰巨性有了更加深刻的认识和体会，五年来集团公司积极推进经济发展、国际化发展。党的十九大提出要"不忘初心，牢记使命"，"为实现中华民族伟大复兴的中国梦不懈努力"，"既要全面建成小康社会、实现第一个百年奋斗目标，又要乘势而上开启全面建设社会主义现代化国家新征程，向第二个百年奋斗目标进军"。要实现"两个一百年"的目标，主要基础还是经济，要实现经济强国，才能支撑我们科技、国防、外交强国，实现经济强国非常重要的标志就是企业要成为世界一流的企业，在党的十九大报告中习总书记明确对国有企业提出了要"培育具有全球竞争力的世界一流企业"的目标。我们觉得跟世界一流的企业比较，我们中国的企业还是任重道远，世界一流企业没有具体的量化指标。从目前来看，总体是向好，我国已经有 120 多家企业进入世界 500 强，但确切来说是 500 大，很多企业是大而不强，特别是从现在全球比较著名的世界一流企业来看，科技创新能力、持续盈利的能力、现代化的法人治理结构还有国际化的经营业绩、规模来看，我们还是有相当的差距。下面简要介绍一下我们集团发展的体会和经验。

一、坚持绿色经济发展的理念

从《京都议定书》到《巴黎协定》，全球绿色、低碳已经变成不可阻挡的趋势，比如非洲，尽管经济没我们发达，他们对环保的意识比我们还要强，因此我们在"一带一路"实践、国际化发展中一定要坚持绿色清洁发展的理念。特别是通过近几年的努力，国家风电和光伏已经非常接近平价上网。国家能源局也要求太阳能发电到 2020 年实现平价上网，在资源好的地区像北方地区，基本能够实现这样的目标，清洁发展，随着科技进步，成本优势、电价优势、长远的资源优势还是非常明显的。

二、坚持创新驱动的发展理念

"引进来、走出去"的思路。我们承担了国家的重点专项科研任务，一是核电，像从美国引进技术做高铁一样，通过引进消化吸收再"走出去"，山东核电项目正在准备装料，很快将投产发电。另外在"走出去"方面，南非、土耳其等国家核电的前期工作正在推进。二是重型燃气轮机技术，一方面是国内自主化，引入了东方电气、哈尔滨电气、上海电气，清华大学、中科院产学研结合，还有国外企业如日本三菱、GE 等。三是太阳能发电，在青海建设了国家级实证基地，也建成了最大的水光互补项目，这是国内企业在"一带一路""走出去"方面必须要加强的方面。

三、坚持合作共赢发展理念

跟国外合作的项目，无论是投资 EPC（工程总承包）项目还是电站服务业项目，都要跟当地的政府、企业密切合作，我们现在已经投产的项目和正在建设的项目，还有正在谈的一些储备项目，都是当地企业参股，我们来控股，取得了比较好的、稳健的收益，特别是对风险的控制非常有效，项目整体也取得了比较好的成效。

下面就中国企业"走出去"积极参与"一带一路"建设的协同机制问题阐述几点看法。

第一，"走出去"很重要的一点是要实现合作共赢，建构共同利益，从前期策划到整个实施过程，要兼顾地方政府和当地企业，以及当地民众的利益和诉求，这些考虑进去，共同的合作，才能推进项目的成功。

第二，要积极发展"一带一路"项目中人才的属地化，在国际化的基础上要属地化，尽可能把当地的优秀人才用起来，国际化地配置人才。目前在澳大利亚、巴西、日本的项目，大部分员工是当地人，个别是日籍华人，还有一些是从欧洲聘用职业项目经理来做这方面的工作，但最大的困难仍是人才不足，怎样补齐人才短板，是我们共同面临的问题。

第三，特别是央企，一定要与世界一流的企业合作，并与之同台竞争，从国内比赛打到国际比赛，通过这样的合作和竞争，能够锤炼和提炼央企的竞争能力，现在很多企业实际上是处于大而不强的阶段，真正做到又强又优，必须要跟最优秀的企业合作、竞争。

秦 钢 ［中国国际海运集装箱（集团）股份有限公司总裁助理］

中国国际海运集装箱（集团）（简称"中集集团"）名称含有"集装箱"三个字，但实际上集装箱业务只占集团总收入的30%左右，目前主要是面对物流和能源行业提供装备、工程和服务。中集集团成立已有35年，到现在为止集团已拥有十来个全球领先的产品，去年宣传较多的是南海试采可燃冰，半潜式钻井平台是中集集团生产制造的，基地设在烟台，试采的营运也由中集集团操作。中集集团最早是源于改革开放前沿蛇口，所以具备市场化的基因。早前做集装箱制造，注重所谓大进大出的业务，原材料进口，订单是海外的、设备是海外的，劳动力等资源是中国的，这是此前国际化业务的起点。从早期开始，集团设立了八大板块，按照全球化战略规划发展物流和能源行业。现在海外企业，包括经营实体和生产基地已超过60家，海外收入包括出口业务以及海外当地的销售，占整个集团总收入的60%，集团员工总数大概是5万人，海外员工大概7000人，这是有关中集集团的主要业务情况。

下面，我主要想汇报中集集团的全球化战略和"一带一路"的执行情况。在全球化战略过程中，集团发展变化大概是这样的过程，从市场上来说，首先是打开欧美市场销路，出口很多产品到欧美，逐步发展到新兴市场和第三世界。投资形式上，开始是并购欧洲、美国的制造型企业，再到另类投资、新设项目、新增投资。业务范围，从设备制造开始，包括能源设备、半挂车，向下延伸包括营销和产品设计，为项目提供融资，包括承接海外的 EPC 工程。

从集团自身投资营运到广泛开展国际产业合作，"一带一路"背景下，要用新的价值创造新的商机，早期我们并购东南亚沿线国家的企业，怎样让这些企业获得更好效益，这是我们面临的非常重要的问题。我们做了以下工作：

一、用人方面

调整管理者，我们自己选派的干部不多，基本上是在当地选拔、当地培养，让他们建立增长目标，我们收购的企业，原来业绩平平有钱赚，但是没增长。经过我们的努力，基本上所有企业业绩都达到增长。

二、对生产线升级改造

即使一些欧美企业，整个生产手段、能力、设施还比较陈旧，多年没有投资，中欧互动、中美互动协同起来，形成协同，能让生产能力提升。

三、提高收购企业的销售

利用市场网络包括中国市场、海外市场网络，利用金融知识，有了业务需要融资、需要担保，利用我们的金融手段，也加以激励手段，把国内实施好的激励政策应用在海外企业上，这样加大他们的国际市场开拓。激励他们、引领他们开拓国际市场，包括面对中国市场、东南亚市场，举个例子，我们在德国波恩有一家天然气的工程公司，主要是做液化天然气接收站，这十来年中国液化天然气的进口很多，需要新建 LNG（液化天然气）的接收站，我们帮助中国企业接单子，提供融资支持，基本上囊括了中国 LNG 接收站的主要订单。2013 年底我们收购了消防车企业，2012 年到 2017 年集团帮他们营销，去年成为中国进口海外消防车的第一品牌。

集团在海外投资做生意、并购，其实要为当地带去税收、增加就业，这是很重要的方面，不论是欧美的企业还是东南亚、非洲的一些企业，基本上都是通过投资、市场开拓、管理的改善，把业务、销售搞上去，让税收增加，就业增加。经过对几年的发展经验总结，集团全球化的理念可以归纳为：全球营运、地方智慧。全球运营是指在治理结构、管控体系、资金、技术、人才、原材料和共享平台方面为海外企业提供支持。地方智慧的意思是充分尊重当地管理团队，他们熟悉市场特性，给予他们更多的授权，通过一个董事会的管理架构来去管理这个团队，发挥他们的作用。

今天的会议主题是关于"一带一路"的，结合这些年全球化战略的实施

以及在"一带一路"沿线国家我们做的一些尝试,我想谈几个观点:

一是作为企业来说,要寻求"一带一路"政策与市场机会的交汇点,作为企业要根据自身的业务能力和发展方向充分调研"一带一路"沿线国家的市场需求,找到业务能力和市场需求的结合点,很多沿线国家都是产油区、产气区,我们的海洋的业务能力和天然气的业务能力可以和这些国家结合。举例来说,里海是一个内海,要打油、钻油,做了半潜式的钻井平台不能从海上开进去,我们就与俄罗斯某船厂在伏尔加河进行合作,把主要的部件在烟台做好运输过去,去当地指导他们和他们合作,在土库曼斯坦进行安装。

二是除了简单的产品销售和项目交付以外,作为企业和产业来说,"一带一路"倡议的实践应该拓宽产业链的输出,而不是简单的产品交付,也不是简单的项目交付,企业应组团出海开展合作,向营运和服务延伸。中集集团和深圳燃气合作在东南亚的一个国家计划投资液化天然气的接收站,通过投资和营运,未来向下游延伸,这样就把天然气的业务链在东南亚国家里进行延伸,在国外获得成熟的经验和能力。

三是发挥核心城市的整合作用,深圳有很多资源,在"一带一路"沿线国家,无论是能源项目、旅游项目,如果政府能起到牵线、协调、组织的作用,把有关的企业组织起来抱团出海、组团作战,其效果比企业单独做更好。

在"一带一路"的实践过程中,我们提高了自身的全球化战略以及市场开拓、商机挖掘的认知水平,丰富了实践战略,特别是在一些沿线国家加大了业务推广以及投资力度,带来很多实际业绩。例如东南亚缺乏用电等基础设施,我们利用天然气设施和发电技术,设计了方案并生产出产品帮助当地。随着"一带一路"倡议的实施,在发展中国家加大投资力度,成效显著。比如我们 2013 年底收购了一家德国消防车企业,其子公司在印尼,由于有"一带一路"的政策指导,也带来了其印尼分公司的业绩提升,带来订单量的增加。

在"一带一路"的倡议下,我们积极行动,参与投资吉布提自贸区,做模块化建筑,一年左右的时间就可以从签订单到落成,而当地传统的混凝土建筑需几年才能建好。加强与其他央企的合作,加强与政府的对接,应该是我们下一步去努力的方向。

张建卫 （中国外运长航集团有限公司副董事长）

中外运长航集团是招商局集团名下的一个子公司，早在 21 世纪初，就已经着手布局海外物流网络，这个布局也正好契合了我们现在的"一带一路"倡议。20 世纪 80 年代初的时候，我们的经济体制还处于从传统的计划经济向市场经济转型的过程中，中外运是最早的一批走向海外的企业，国内的经济结构调整促使我们认真思考总结原来海外业务发展过程中的得失，并开始铺设以客户为引领的海外综合物流服务网络。我认为现在的"一带一路"倡议实质上也是一次重要的经济全球化的结构性调整，重构既是重大的机遇，同时也是一个严峻的挑战。"一带一路"沿线国家基本上是经济发展相对落后的国家，而且政治环境、人文环境会给正常发展建设带来意想不到的问题，这些是不容回避的。

我们在发展过程中既有成功的经验也有失败的教训，即便与非常熟悉的长期合作伙伴进行股权合作，当真正深入到该国家以后，也会发现还有很多具体问题需要我们重新认识、加深认识。实践"一带一路"倡议也是我们央企的责任所在，我们必须要按照中央的战略要求加快发展，但也千万不能忽视已经存在的问题以及将来发展过程中与当地接触过程中产生的新问题。海运如此，铁路同样如此，举一个最简单的例子，我们作为欧亚班列的具体经营者发现，不管中欧的班列在国内段协作得如何顺利，口岸过境这一环节还是占用了大量的时间。这对班列的运营来说，就提出了如何缩短口岸过境时间这一十分重要的问题。

下面再就海外投资和运营的各种风险防控体系建设谈两点看法。

第一，"一带一路"沿线国家的人文环境、意识形态、宗教信仰、基础建设都各不相同。假如对这些国家缺乏认识、缺乏深入了解，就难免会遇到较难克服的问题。过去这些年里，成功走向海外的企业不少，成功的经验总结得也不少，但失败的教训总结得还远远不够，而失败的教训恰恰是我们宝贵的财富。是不是我们每个企业、每个地方都具备去"一带一路"沿线国家发展的条件？战略的选择非常重要。我们一定要搞清楚我们的企业到底出去干什么，然后才需要解决怎么干的问题。当然没有很好的人才队伍，再好的战略也落实不了。企业内部的机制也要灵活，包括用工制度、激励机制等问题。

企业尤其是央企和地方国企，长期以来在计划经济和计划经济向市场经济转型过程中，比较适应政府主导的经济发展环境，一旦离开政府由我们自己闯荡市场时，我们的市场适应能力就显得较差，因此政府在我们企业走向海外、参与"一带一路"发展的过程中需要给予指导。

第二，企业走向海外，参与"一带一路"发展，千辛万苦，也难免出现问题。市场上不可能有常胜将军，因此建立容错机制与风险管理机制都非常重要。

严弟勇 （中国有色矿业集团有限公司副总经理）

今天我的演讲主要围绕三点：一是中国有色集团国际化经营的基本情况，二是集团公司关于在国际产能合作方面的基本体会，三是路径选择。

第一，中国有色集团的主业是矿产资源开发以及建筑工程，包括相关的贸易和服务，也是有色金属行业开展国际化经营比较早的企业，十年前李毅中部长在给中国有色集团的批示上讲过，中国有色集团走得早、走得远、走得稳，中国有色集团在有色行业国际化经营方面是比较早的。同时我们是在海外投资合作比较多的企业之一，拥有境外的重金属资源，主要是有色金属2000万吨，在全球拥有七座矿山、七座冶炼厂和一个经济贸易合作区，现在集团公司业务遍布80多个国家和地区，包括"一带一路"沿线的30多个国家和地区，产品主要是以有色金属为主，有40多个有色金属品种。

第二，谈谈有色集团公司在"一带一路"倡议下开展国际产能合作的新体会。近些年来有色集团公司在项目所在国共同发展、共同成长，实践"走出去"，释放项目所在国的经济潜力，集团在1998年在赞比亚收购了一家铜矿，2007年投资建设了赞比亚中国经济贸易合作区，这也是中国在非洲成立的第一个合作区，经济贸易合作区总面积将近18平方千米，开创了中非合作的新模式。基于有色集团公司自身的优势，我们将合作区定位为以有色金属为主，延伸有色金属加工产业链，适当发展配套产业和服务业，建设具有辐射和示范效应的以有色金属为主的综合性园区，将我国的工程技术以及采选的工艺引进到蒙古，取得了良好的经济效应，也曾被胡锦涛同志誉为中蒙合作的典范。

第三，推动项目所在国工业化进程，实现国际产能合作的共享，中国有色集团在有色金属铜铅锌产业方面达到了领先水平，"一带一路"沿线的许多国家是以矿业作为支柱产业，对资源的开发有迫切的需求，这种需求的导向是我们合作的方向。我们在中东的伊朗氧化铝、东南亚地区的铜矿、在中亚地区的哈萨克斯坦的电解铝以及在南亚地区承建的印度铅锌项目等，都具有一定中国自主知识产权，成功走出了国门。到目前为止，我们集团公司承建境外工程建设合同总额超过 1000 个亿，与东道国形成了"你中有我、我中有你"的利益共同体和发展共同体。我们寻求项目所在国的支持，中国有色集团一直坚持秉承融合、融入，在积极履行社会责任、依法纳税、用工最大限度的本地化和公益事业方面努力先试先行，尤其是在有色金属工业行业中。我们集团公司首先发布了赞比亚、蒙古国、缅甸等国别的社会责任报告，通过积极推动职业教育"走出去"的试点工作，培养了大量熟悉中国传统文化、矿业文化的当地产业工人，建设绿水、蓝天下的绿色企业，此外还设立了赞比亚中赞医院以及中国企业独资的医院。

"走出去"的企业还是要牢记使命和责任，尤其作为国际化经营的企业，必须确立履行社会责任也是核心竞争力的理念。企业要"走出去"，需要不断调整、充实完善人员，要广交朋友建立互信，不仅是中国朋友，更多是外国朋友、当地的朋友，我们应该秉承合作共赢、共同发展的理念。

张　鹏（安徽江淮汽车集团股份有限公司副总经济师）

最近中国出口到"一带一路"国家的汽车产品大幅增长，应该占到中国汽车全部出口量的一半以上，江淮汽车 2017 年出口 6.5 万辆汽车，在行业中排第五位，其中中高端的轻卡和 SUV 排在中国第一，出口"一带一路"沿线的国家 30 个，出口量 4 万台，占江淮汽车总出口量的 60% 以上。总计建设了 19 家海外工厂，其中 11 家海外工厂是分布在"一带一路"沿线国家。

第一，坚持协作包容，增添发展的新动力。"一带一路"沿线国家经济发展很不平衡，汽车工业发展尤其是不平衡、不充分的。中国改革开放以来，在促进经济发展和产业转型升级方面，也是积累了大量的成功经验，同时也要在充分尊重"一带一路"沿线国家各国差异的基础上,共同探讨符合各个国家国情的发展道路,深度对接有关国家的区域发展战略,结合沿线国家的产业发展需求,考虑到合作双方的优势,以协同共赢的理念和机制整合资源,形成优势,逐步实现产业规划的协同和体系的兼容,谋求共同长远发展。通过示范项目运行的成果,不断增强参与方的获得感,充分调动各方面的积极性和创造性。我们出口到阿尔及利亚的轻卡量产第一,他们把技术标准做了升级,江淮汽车也是第一个在中国汽车厂家中达到当地标准的,比中国现行的要求更高一些。我们要在当地建组装工厂,目前建设工作已接近尾声,当地的产业政策和吸引外资政策是不断地发生变化的,所以也非常感谢商务部和外交部的协同支持,目前的对接工作进展顺利。从国家的层面来说,如何与发展中国家共商合作是非常重要的,对他们的产业规划、他们的发展道路,一定是要在坚持包容的基础上加强沟通和协同。

第二,把握"五通"机遇,打造产业合作新平台。从汽车产业层面来说,沿线国家大量基础设施的建设以及物流运输网络的形成会促进商用车的消费需求增长,经济的发展、基础设施的完善、人民生活的提高又为乘用车的进入提供了机遇,同时汽车产业对经济发展的带动效应比较强,汽车发展对汽车装备制造业有很强的拉动作用,也会带来批发、零售、金融、保险、广告、物流等服务业的发展,例如江淮在哈萨克斯坦的项目,是中哈战略合作的典范,也是哈萨克斯坦32个产业振兴项目中唯一的一个汽车项目,受到了两国领导人的高度关注。汽车组装利用当地合作伙伴的闲置产能,江淮汽车提供技术、产品和管理,另一家央企提供资金,在当地进行合作,产品不光是在哈萨克斯坦组装消费,还出口到俄罗斯和中亚其他国家,不仅生产燃油车,还生产电动车,而且这个项目为"一带一路"物流大通道的增长作出了贡献,也受到哈萨克斯坦铁道部的支持和欢迎。

产业层面上,中国有独特的优势,因为产业的门类比较齐全,发展比较均衡,无论是在制造业还是服务业,无论是在传统产业还是在新兴产业,我们都有这样的优势,跨界的合作和融合是我们在"一带一路"沿线国家发展的潜力所在,也是目前最奇缺的中长期发展动能。

第三,坚持创新驱动发展培育,加快培育竞争新优势。从企业层面来说,在发展中国家，产品竞争力是非常重要的，我们的产品主要根据我们目标国的需求做了大量适应性的改进和渐进式的创新，包括适应排放标准，从欧洲 I 号到欧洲 VI 号，针对高原、高山、高寒、高温、高湿，做了大量适应性的改进。首先把产品做得非常可靠、非常成熟，不仅仅是靠产品的性价比优势，最终是从产品输出到技术管理输出、资金输出，我们现在 19 个海外工厂已覆盖了全系列的商用车和乘用车产品。

企业的发展如果只是在制造环节，是没办法获得中长期发展的，在国外不仅要做制造，还要做营销和服务，包括做一些适应性研发的考量，还有提供汽车金融服务，推动汽车全价值链"走出去"。企业的层面上，通过创新驱动、通过转型升级，提供全产品生命周期和全价值链系统的解决方案来提高我们的核心竞争力。

回到今天的创新合作模式，从国家层面、产业层面、企业层面来看，在"一带一路"国家中的发展大有可为。下面就打造国际品牌、提升质量形象给予一些自身建议。

企业的竞争力分为产品的竞争力、营销的竞争力和品牌的竞争力，其中产品竞争力有三性：一是可靠性，在国际市场上的可靠性要比国内更高，发展中国家和备件工艺远远落后于中国现有的体系，所以产品要做得比国内更加可靠，这是针对发展中国家讲的。针对发达国家，由于劳动力成本较高，所以产品高可靠性是第一位的，避免在国外出现问题。二是产品的适应性，当地使用的环境和使用的情况和中国有很大的不一样，包括燃油的标准、路况气温、地形的条件都有很多的不一样，要做很多改进。三是产品的复合性，要符合产业的标准、技术的标准，还要符合消费的文化。

童来明 （中国诚通控股集团有限公司副总裁）

诚通集团是国务院国资委确定的两家国有资本运营公司之一，我们在参与"一带一路"建设中一直在思考和探索，作为国有资本运营公司该以何种形式来参与合作，更好地发挥自身的独特作用。

近年来，我们与"走出去"的中国企业以及"一带一路"沿线国家和地区企业在合作模式上做了一些探索。总的思路是坚持服务国有资本全球布局和国有企业海外发展，归纳起来主要是三种形式，结合一些具体的做法，跟大家分享讨论：

一是赋能式的合作，依托中国国有企业结构调整基金（简称"国调基金"）等资本力量，利用专业的投资能力，发挥资本在引导、支持投资以及促进经营管理等方面积极的赋能作用，服务国有企业参与"一带一路"建设和"走出去"战略。2017年，国调基金参与中国电建（SH601669）非公开发行，募集资金的主要投向就是老挝南欧江二期水电站等"一带一路"重要基础设施建设项目。此外，我们还投资了洛阳钼业（SH603993），支持其海外项目发展。国有资本运营公司还协助其他央企和地方国企"走出去"，探索海外并购的新模式，受到国际资本市场的关注。

二是平台式的合作。主要通过投资建设海外经贸交流平台，深耕当地市场，促进我国与所在国经贸关系的合作发展，同时为中国企业"走出去"提供公共服务。诚通集团在俄罗斯投资建设莫斯科格林伍德国际贸易中心（简称"格林伍德中心"），这是迄今为止我国在境外最大的商贸类投资项目，格林伍德中心集商务办公、商品展示交易、会议会展、酒店餐饮、法律金融服务、清关物流等综合服务为一体，是中国品牌企业的境外展示营销中心和中国企业"走出去"公共服务平台，以及"一带一路"和"欧亚经济同盟"对接倡议的实践平台。目前，已经有14个国家和地区的300多家企业在此经营，中国工商银行、华为、海尔、柳工、华晨汽车、中国重汽、京东方等品牌企业在内的中资企业占到三分之一，给当地带去1.2万个就业岗位，新增贸易额20亿美元，成为中俄贸易与投资的压舱石和"一带一路"的重要节点项目。未来，这个模式有望在"一带一路"沿线复制、推广。

三是服务式的合作。这一模式主要是侧重发挥诚通集团在仓储物流、大宗商品贸易等产业方面的传统优势，以"一带一路"沿线为主，延伸全球布局，通过商业模式创新来打通国际国内的业务环节，为中国企业"走出去"提供专业的供应链服务，2015年，诚通集团旗下的上市公司中储股份（SH600787）收购了国际知名大宗商品交割库运营商 Henry Bath & Son Limited（HB集团）51%的控股股权，成为全球唯一同时拥有国内、国际主要期货交易所交割仓库运营资质的跨国物流运营商。中储股份成为 HB 集团的股东以后，践行"一带一路"倡议，落实习近平主席访英期间达成的两国合作意向，和英国伦敦金融交易所（LME）签订《战略合作谅解备忘录》，在"一带一路"沿线地区推广 LME Shield 新库存系统，促进中亚、俄罗斯、欧洲陆地沿线以及东南亚、印度洋海上沿线的投资、贸易活动，活跃该地区的大宗商品交易，促进基础设施和产业建设。同时，中储股份和 HB 集团、上海期货交易所合作，设计探索国际、国内市场双向业务联动的模式，已经为国际客户成功实现了进口业务的全过程服务，以及国内客户境内物流供应链＋出口及国际市场交割的一体化服务，这一商业模式创新受到国际商业伙伴的广泛关注。

此外，我们在国际产能合作方面，比如在俄罗斯远东地区进行的一些探索，为增进"一带一路"倡议下的企业合作，努力发挥着自身的独特作用。

李晓强　[香港中华电力控股公司财务及行政高级总监（中国香港）]

中电控股有限公司成立于 1901 年，目前市值约 2000 亿港币。下面介绍一下我们公司在"一带一路"方面的实践以及一些思考的问题，我们在香港贡献了 80% 人口的电力，在中国改革开放的早期阶段，在"引进来"方面还起到了一定的排头兵和桥头堡的作用，1979 年向广东供电，1980 年代投资大亚湾核电，随着中国改革开放的深入和电力体制改革，我们又陆续投资了火电、水电、风电和太阳能，2002 年我们投资印度，迄今为止还是印度最大的外来电力投资商之一。在"一带一路"倡议下，我们在印度投资的电厂虽然是持有百分之百股份，但在印度两台 60 万的机组，工程设计、设备制造、施工承包都是由内地的国企承担，这也是"一带一路"成功的模式。现在我们在越南的投资也有邀请内地电力企业以及银行参与，内地电力企业以及银行表示非常乐意支持，关于未来"一带一路"合作的模式思考还在深化。

港资企业，特别是我们在"一带一路"沿线有些国家深耕多年的港资企业，基本上做到了员工本土化，像在印度我们百分之百控股，但从总裁到基层员工都是印度的员工。如果将来我们不能完全匹配投资，至少可以提供一些服务给国内"走出去"的企业，例如商务谈判、尽职调查、人力资源等。过去香港在我国改革开放早期的"引进来"方面比较好地发挥了排头兵和桥头堡的作用，将来在"一带一路"倡议下，香港的企业应该可以起到更好的桥头堡的作用。

下面分享一下作为香港企业在粤港澳大湾区建设以及"一带一路"建设中的独特优势、建议。粤港澳地区其实在粤港澳大湾区概念提出之前，已经有投资上的交流、贸易上的往来，这些年打下了很好的基础，毫无疑问对于下一步粤港澳协同效应会有很好的作用，香港跟澳门和广东相比有很好的优势，特别是在人才、制度等软环境方面有比其他伙伴更独特的地方。尤其是这些年来，我们电力行业建立了粤港澳电力高峰论坛，每年与南方电网、广东电网、澳门电力、中广核定期的有高层面上的交流，要进一步推进粤港澳大湾区的合作，其实除了投资、贸易方面的往来，交流还是不能忽视，多交流比少交流好，这是现阶段应该充分强调的。

德米特里·丘赫兰采夫 ［TONAP 集团首席执行官（俄罗斯）］

TONAP 集团是从事激光热处理、零件表面硬化设备的企业，集团下设 6 家公司，在各自的领域都是属于行业的排头兵。因为集团的产品在行业中有一些独特性，集团具有其他企业没有的技术。除了生产激光热处理的设备以外，集团还生产激光打印的原料、粉末。国际上真正掌握这个技术的公司不太多，只有大概 5 家公司掌握这种技术，因此希望在中国寻找到合作伙伴，双方投资，我方来投资技术，合作过程中可以提供专有技术和相关文件。中国在未来工业发展上会有非常大的潜力，我愿意把我们的技术带到中国再进行生产。

我公司还计划建设一家联合激光热处理工程公司，经过初步的调研，目前的计划是在中国的四个城市进行合作，包括上海、台州、深圳、东莞。经过调研，我看到中国很多的工业企业对我公司技术产品需求非常大，乘着"一带一路"倡议的东风，希望这个项目推进落实。合作的第一步是在技术上，我方提供技术相关的文件，包括专利技术，还有员工培训，下一步合作是进入批量生产阶段，建立联合的企业，我方提供技术，中方提供一些基础设施，包括当地的法律、公司创建、公司管理方面的帮助。

林锦胜 ［马来西亚中华总商会（中总）署理总会长（马来西亚）］

马来西亚中华总商会，成立于 1921 年 7 月 2 日，是马来西亚组织最庞大、规模最具代表性的华商总会，旗下有 17 个属会，人脉网络遍布全国各地，直接、间接包括 10 多万华资企业商号，中总的会员商号汇集国内很多的商贸领域，除了积极参与中马商贸交往，还协助其他周边国家的发展和建设。"一带一路"倡议提出以后，中总感受时代的大使命，不断加大力度和深度，参与响应倡议，"一带一路"倡议虽然由中国提出，然而具体动作和声音都惠及全体沿线国家，也完全符合各国的发展意愿。

事实上，过去的全球化运动声浪大，动作也很多，然而对如何消除贫富鸿沟，缩小发展不均衡，如何铺平其他各领域规则，去打造互惠互利的合作，都没有达标。"一带一路"的动作和声音已经充满创新和分享的基因，未来继续优化、细化之后可以真正带动一点突破全面，协助沿线国家实现新世纪的幸福和理想。

"一带一路"倡议立志帮助沿线国家实现各自的强国宏业，结合整个大区域的资源和力量，互补、互利，连线推动大规模的发展建设。"一带一路"确实做到了双管齐下，对准沿线国家的精准需求，提出个性化的建设纲领，也同时汇聚各国、各地的资源、力量，推动具体化的转型和改变，这已经是一个了不起的创新和改革，沿线国家参与"一带一路"的建设和发展都能够感受真正的双赢共享。通过这次会议，我们将以更大的信心和毅力为人民的幸福和理想一起奋进、努力。

自从"一带一路"经济合作框架运行以来，中总订立工作新指标，深化双边交往，扩大互动对接，引领会员商家一起走过学习和提升的日子。在马来西亚中华总商会，我本人常年负责接待中方代表团，"一带一路"倡议提出以后，我们奉行"走出去"的路线，之前中总商贸代表团常年出席和参展厦门投洽会、春秋两季广交会、南宁东盟博览会、昆明中国东盟华商论坛等。"一带一路"倡议提出之后，我们决定拉队参与东莞海事博览会，2017 年 6 月和 11 月间，我们进一步扩大范围，到上海出席国际食品饮料展览，也到过哈尔滨参加哈洽会、中蒙俄马经济合作论坛。

"一带一路"倡议提出之后，马中对接交流的动作和声音必然延续下去，过程中将配合其他新兴卖点，力求创新改良，未来越搞越精彩，也是必然的演变。过去两年来，我们的商贸代表团到过东北三省、江苏、安徽、浙江、上海和云南拜会当地的商务厅、工商联、侨办、侨联、海外交流协会等。在相关单位的安排下，代表团也沿途考察了当地的新兴开发区，近距离探索神州大地的商贸动脉。在巡回各地考察拜访的过程中，签署了双边友好协议，从此可以更系统化、制度化以及效率化地从事双边贸易对接，提升企业交流以及信息互换。过去两年多来，与中总签订企业友好协议的组织和单位包括浙江省工商联、云南省侨联会、福建省侨商会、昆明市人民政府以及吉林省商务厅等。

展望未来，中总将继续推动制度化双边对接，2018 年的目标锁定在陕西、宁夏、四川，我们深信中国地大物博，东南西北各省各区经济生产和结构、商品特征、市场特性、文化系数也不一样。因此，我们将带领商家会员多做调研探访，同时建立制度化双边关系，以后继续优化、细化，希望能做到线上即时接通。中国企业发展神速进步，经济生态繁衍茂盛，应该成为全球企业和市场人士继续考察和学习的对象，当然随着中国国力富强，商贸生态生生不息，不久之后，每一个经济热点都可以成为海外企业界追求传奇的机会，中国是它们造梦、圆梦的地方。

第二节　开拓创新，打造"一带一路"倡议下的产业合作新格局

俞曾港　（中国远洋海运集团有限公司副总经理）

中国远洋海运集团是航运物流企业，早在 20 世纪 60 年代就开始走向世界，目前在全世界的 100 多个国家都有分支机构，海外员工有 10000 多人，派驻世界各国的中国员工有 600 多人，船舶遍布世界各地。现在，我跟各位分享一下我们企业在实施"走出去"战略和近五年来在推进"一带一路"建设中的体会和思考。

一、坚持集群性的发展，实现互利共赢

"一带一路"沿线国家的投资牵涉到一些比较大规模的基础设施项目，建设周期比较长，资金需求量也比较大，所以企业间的抱团出海对降低我们单一企业的资金压力和财务的杠杆率应该是很有帮助的。比如说近两年我们企业在

国外的港口方面投资都比较大，特别是在中东、欧洲国家的一些投资，例如阿布扎比，我们在资金方面与中国的一些大型金融机构积极开展合作，在建设方面我们更多跟央企进行合作，这样对防范政治、法律、信用、汇率各个方面的风险，提升综合影响力和突发事件的应对能力都是很有帮助的。

二、坚持商业模式的创新，全力提升航运企业的国际竞争力

"一带一路"倡议为我们国家，特别是国有航运企业拓展国际市场，提升国际化经营能力带来了新的机遇，同时我们还要看到与新机遇并存的还有新的挑战。一是全球经济贸易持续处于比较弱的复苏状态，还是持续在低位振荡。二是跨界竞争打破了行业原有的竞争格局，削弱了传统行业的整体盈利能力，给我们航运企业的传统业务实现持续的盈利造成了巨大的挑战。我们要想在竞争中占据有利地位，就必须坚持商业模式创新。

三、和供给侧改革有机结合

"一带一路"项目进行转型升级，对国有的航运企业而言，要认识到做好船队结构的调整对提升企业在海上丝绸之路竞争力的重要作用，把去除老旧船过剩的运能和开发"一带一路"建设项目有机结合。我们在消除过剩运力拆解一些老旧船舶的同时，更加重视船只建设。公司的1100多条船，平均的吨位在10万吨左右，船龄在8年左右，船比较新、技术比较新，航行中跟国际上其他航运公司的竞争具有一定的优势，对提高我们海上丝绸之路的竞争非常有帮助。

四、加强文化的融合，推行海外投资项目的本土化

一个企业要走向全球成为国际化的企业，必须坚持和平合作、开放包容、互学互建、互利共赢。怎么样把我们的高级管理人才与当地的员工在文化、思想和经营上融合起来，是我们在不断思考的问题。我们收购比莱埃夫斯港的时候也遇到劳工方面的问题，在港口工作的1200名希腊劳工，在港口被收购后他们第一反应是失业。对此，我们跟他们进行了比较有效的沟通，保证他们的工作岗位，并告诉他们中国公司并购了你们的码头以后，在当地的业务会蒸蒸日上。我们通过一系列文化融合活动消除了相互之间的隔阂，取得了良好的效果。

覃伟中 （中国石油天然气集团公司副总经理）

下面我来谈谈几点看法：

一、"一带一路"沿线国家和地区的能源合作与开发会成为国际能源企业的重要选择

沿线国家的能源、资源非常丰富，探明石油剩余储量占全球55%，天然气剩余探明储量占全球3/4。20世纪以来，"一带一路"沿线国家和地区一直是全球油气合作的重点领域。1997年，中国石油签订了位于哈萨克斯坦的大型油气合作项目，迈出"一带一路"油气合作的第一步。截至目前，中国石油与"一带一路"沿线19个国家开展了超过50个项目的合作，权益油气产量占中国石油海外权益油气总产量的比例达60%，形成天然气管道输送能力670亿立方米/年，在我国天然气冬季保供过程中发挥了重要作用。

二、中国石油致力于在"一带一路"油气合作中转型升级

作为中央企业实施"走出去"战略的早期实践者，回顾二十年以来的实践，我们在国际油气合作过程中也促进了自身的转型升级。一是国际化水平大幅度提升。我们以全球视野谋划发展，以国际标准开展合作，与国际大公司同台竞争，中国石油的国际化指数从20年前的2%提升到目前的30%以上。二是市场竞争力显著增强。中国石油上下游、海内外、产炼销储贸业务链条逐步完善健全，投资业务与服务业务互相促进，提升竞争力，在全球范围内塑造了负责任大公司的良好形象。我们在中亚地区以上下游、一体化的合作模式，建设了横跨中亚三国的油气长输管道，开启了政府间和企业间的合作新模式。中国石油在海外的油气田勘探开发荣获了国家科技进步一等奖。通过"一带一路"合作，形成了高素质的海外人才团队，对中国石油自身的转型升级也起到了很好的促进作用。

三、几点建议

一是继续把能源、资源开发与基础设施建设作为"一带一路"产业合作的重点领域。秉承"资源与市场共享，通道与产业共建"的思路，加大区域能源、资源开发以及油气通道基础设施的投资合作，依托能源合作促进政策沟通，依托通道建设推动设施连通，依托能源投资引领贸易畅通，依托重大项目带动资金融通，依托社会责任履行促进民心相通。二是重视以高起点、高标准、高质量项目带动互补性合作。"一带一路"沿线国家法律、税制、市场、技术、标准等受西方国家长期影响，且国际大公司在这些地区深耕多年，中国企业在推进项目合作时应提高起点、标准和质量，以产业发展和技术创新促进互补性、互利性的合作。三是建立企业主导、政府推动的协同发展机制。"一带一路"产业合作离不开政府推动，特别是能源合作项目，但是也必须强调企业的主体地位，中央企业可以发挥引领作用，带动国内社会投资，构建全产业链联盟，形成中国企业的竞争优势。四是加强"一带一路"沿线的安全防控。建议政府建立"一带一路"风险评估和预警机制，帮助企业做好应对预案和安保措施，努力把"一带一路"国际能源合作打造成为安全可靠、繁荣稳定、美好和谐的大走廊、大动脉。

杨光耀 （远大科技集团首席运营官）

远大集团是创立于 1988 年的民营企业，现在拥有两个园区、四个主要核心业务板块，十个分、子公司，4000 名员工，产品销售到 80 多个国家和地区，其中"一带一路"国家有 30 多个。下面我汇报三点体会：

第一，远大以颠覆性的技术，严苛的安全、技术、质量标准，实现产品品质高于全球行业标准，引领全球的行业技术进步。我们用发电尾气实施制冷的技术，创造出全球最高效的冷热连产系统，在非电空调领域我们持续保持全球领先，能源的效率从传统的 35%—40% 提升到 85% 以上，并且在这个行业中持续保持市场占有率第一，这些项目在欧洲、巴基斯坦、印度、土耳其、东南亚、俄罗斯等地区和国家得到广泛的应用。土耳其的伊斯坦布尔机场、希尔顿酒店都是非常典范的冷热连产项目使用代表，在节能减排方面获得了很好的社会和经济价值。此外，我们进一步提升能源的综合利用技术创新，采用低温的技术，为韩国、丹麦、俄罗斯等国家的大型热电厂研发低温烟气回收技术。以韩国项目为例，我们在首尔热电厂回收热电厂的烟气余热达到 200 兆瓦，实现免费新增采暖用户 4 万户，将排放掉的尾气热量变废为宝；我们在哥本哈根等城市的项目中，推进绿色供暖项目，社会和经济效益也是非常显著。在建筑领域，我们 2009 年创新了钢结构的装配式建筑，并且我们的建造速度在全球领先。20 世纪 90 年代深圳创造了三天建一层楼的世界纪录，远大在 2015 年创造了一天建三层的纪录。一天三层结果是快，表现是快，但是在内核，这个快的背后更加强调的是节能环保，所有的建筑全部采用厚保温，三层、四层窗，窗外使用热回收系统，可持续的建筑比传统的建筑能耗节约80%，新建的装配式建筑的综合能耗只有传统建筑能耗的20%。

第二，业务和商务模式创新上，我们从传统制造业企业过渡转型到制造业加服务业的企业，为客户、社会提供整体的解决方案，创造出了超出政府、社会、业主实际所期待的效果。在产品和供求方面我们输出设计、制造工程技术，为我们的终端客户和当地的项目提供一揽子的整体解决方案。比如说我们在印尼的造纸企业 IKPP 的项目，为节能节碳立下汗马功劳，制造领域加上向服务端延伸，通过我们的设备和技术输出，加上节能服务，让客户享受更高品质的体验。随着运营项目不断增加，我们在技术领域，工程领域得到不断拓展，更进一步开拓我们在产品设计、工程建设、投融资风控关系上的眼界，提升了风控的能力，产品的性能进一步提升，智能化、网络化顺利推进。

第三，推进海外企业本地化的进程。在"一带一路"倡议下，我们在很多国家，如印尼、丹麦、土耳其都设立了我们的分公司，我们的总部输出核心的高管团队，招聘当地的员工，实现了很好的文化认同，提升了远大在当地国家的品牌认同度。我们通过与当地共建平台，真正实现合作共赢，在当地深耕市场，与当地国家的资本财团开展合作。我们做好服务，更加延伸和巩固了我们的价值链，增加了资本收益。

作为生态文明的推动者，我们有几点想法：

一是在基础设施特别是在能源基础设施开发的过程中，能源的开发和能源资源的节约利用应该并举，总结中国的经验，我们在"一带一路"沿线建设城市不能重走中国20世纪90年代和21世纪初期的老路，我们不想看到"一带一路"沿线国家的城市同样会发生伦敦、洛杉矶雾霾的情况。

二是进一步扩大合作，提升平台。从中国的行业内部来讲，实际上要合作而不是竞争，不论是国企还是民企，走出去的过程中，我们有很多深刻的教训，政府的引导非常重要。

三是在平台建设方面，我们内部企业和资本的结合还要快速提升，并且扩大资本和中国智造的影响力和创造力。谢谢大家。

严云福 ［上海振华重工（集团）股份有限公司总工程师］

振华重工长期以来一直致力于争当企业自主创新的排头兵，在全球港口装备行业从 1998 年以来一直排名世界第一，19 年来保持港口装备行业的全球市场领先，我们靠的就是技术。我们每年要有 8 亿元左右的研发投入，每年承担 5 到 10 项的研发项目和企业自主立项的研发项目，承接 4 个国家工程中心建设。

"一带一路"沿线国家、地区经济承受能力的差别非常大，必须通过科技创新研制出因地制宜、适销对路的技术、产品和工程，才能让这些基础设施建设得快、用得起，尽快地造福当地的民众。振华重工和控股股东中交建比较擅长的有北斗卫星导航定位和通信技术，以钢结构代替混凝土结构，装配式建筑，海上风电整体的运输、安装技术，港口码头的卸船装备，高能电池和液化天然气作为动力的装备和技术，这些技术和装备的效果都接近零排放，绿色、低耗，这些技术和产品在沿线国家都有很大的需求。

振华集团一直聚焦物流自动化领域的科技创新，促进智能发展。尽管目前我们国家有那么多的电商，但是物流领域里的货物识别、分拣、投送的调度、搬运、送达等环节大部分还是由人工完成的。我们振华建设自动化的码头，非常感谢中国远洋海运集团的支持，他们决定率先在远海建设自动化码头，并把这个重大任务交给了振华。去年我们又为青岛港建成了自动化码头，洋山四期码头正式开港，是我们与港口用户一起合作开发的。我们的不断努力得到了国家领导人的肯定。振华重工的两项工程都被习近平主席在 2017 年新年献词中提到，一个是港珠澳大桥，一个是洋山四期的自动化码头工程。

振华重工研制成功的自动化码头装备，可以实现计划的自动化、调度的自动化、搬运作业的自动化和搬运装备本身动力供应的自动化，码头与人、车、船、集装箱、货物和搬运装备信息的互联互通，为码头行业提供装备支撑。这套智能装备系统我们正在扩展研究，准备用于普通货物的智能物流，沿线国家对智能化的装备需求也是非常大的。

聚焦数字化、智能化、网络化制造业创新，推动传统制造业的转型升级，可以普遍地推广。我们离散型的行业智能制造技术还没有攻克，如果完全地达到智能制造或是达到工业4.0，一个是技术上一下子难以逾越，另一个是成本承受不起，也没有必要。我们应该选择其中某些环节、某些工种，比如说危、累、重、苦、差、机械性重复劳动研究适合的机器人，以机器人代替人，并且建立信息物流系统，实现人与设备、物料、工艺、环境的纵向、横向和端到端的信息互联互通，提高生产效率保证质量和管理水平。制造业的发展水平差距极大，不同的工序、不同的环节发展的层次参差不齐，有的在工业1.0、2.0、3.0，最后才逐渐需要补课到4.0。传统制造业升级的需求潜力是巨大的，合作的空间是广泛的，也是科技创新和产业合作领域又一个重要方面。

刘　辉　（中国农业发展集团有限公司副总经理）

一、"一带一路"倡议下的农业合作实践

中国农业发展集团（简称"中国农发集团"）是国务院国资委管理的唯一一家综合性中央农业企业，是我国实施农业"走出去"的排头兵，有着30多年的海外合作经验。目前我们在渔业、畜牧业、种植业领域的境外业务已经遍布亚洲、非洲、南太、拉美等"一带一路"沿线几十个国家和地区，作业区域遍布四大洋，境外业务已成为集团的一张靓丽名片。在新的发展阶段，我们根据集团的"十三五"战略规划，围绕"一带一路"的建设，在不断总结海外发展经验的基础上，继续积极推进农业领域产品、技术和资本三个方面的"走出去"合作。

中国农发集团畜牧业是我国动物重大疫病防控的"国家队"和主力军，综合市场占有率位于前列，业务一直以兽药疫苗为重点。为了优化产业结构，实现转型升级，我们选择进军乳业行业，重点推进的是在新西兰的乳业投资项目。通过投资控股两个新西兰原料工厂、加工工厂，增资控股上海纽瑞滋销售公司，共同形成婴幼儿配方奶粉全产业链，从源头到终端打造集团乳品品牌。这个项目的创新性体现在三个方面：

一是在合作模式上，构建乳业全产业链体系。项目从源头实现对优质乳业资源的掌控，在生产上对接国际一流技术，在销售上借力成熟终端网络，实现产业链上下游联动，完成乳业全产业链的布局。

二是在品牌建设上，充分利用国内外两种资源和两个市场。项目将央企的品牌影响力、新西兰优质乳业资源和国内对高端乳产品的市场需求有机结合起来，对树立中国食品的安全形象具有深远意义。

三是在战略推进上，由纯资源开发向构建产品综合服务体系转型。项目通过布局制约我国乳业发展的关键环节、薄弱环节，提升产业核心竞争力，推动中国乳制品产业的转型升级。

大家都知道在2018年1月1日，国内婴幼儿配方奶粉已施行新政，我们将依据新政的要求来推进这个项目。目前，我们是除了中粮的下属企业蒙牛以外进入乳业、奶粉行业的第二家中央企业。

我们还一直致力于打造国内一流、世界先进的高品质远洋渔业产品供应商。1985年，中国农发集团组建了我国第一支远洋捕捞船队从福建马尾启航，拉开了我国远洋渔业的序幕。从当年的航行路线初期的合作区域到现在的业务布局，都与"一带一路"沿线的重点国家有高度的契合度，从马尾到新加坡的马六甲海峡、亚丁湾、苏伊士运河再到西班牙、非洲，整个航行路线，就是海上丝绸之路的路线。在中国农发集团的带领下，我国3000多艘船只走出了国门，扩大了我国在世界渔业资源配额管理条件下的权益。如今，我们的远洋捕捞还处在产业链的前端，在终端市场还有所欠缺。我们还要继续发挥远洋渔业板块的引领作用，进一步完善区域布局，推动一批远洋渔业综合服务基地建设，如在瓦努阿图除了做金枪鱼的捕捞，我们还投资建设码头、冷库等，创新发展提升渔业综合服务能力，努力成为国际上有竞争力和影响力的渔业企业。

在种植业领域，我们下一步继续扩大对外合作。围绕"一带一路"的推进，中国农发集团已先后在非洲、东南亚、东欧、澳大利亚等区域建立了十几个海外农场，并承担了我国政府对外农业技术的合作项目。近几年来，我们不断扩大特色农业的种植规模，加大对坦桑尼亚剑麻种植加工基地、乌克兰小麦种植基地、柬埔寨水稻种植加工基地、澳大利亚畜牧养殖基地的支持力度，为推进农业供给侧结构性改革，实现对外农业技术转移发挥了中央企业的重要作用。

二、"一带一路"倡议下农业合作的机遇与挑战

今天演讲嘉宾提到工业、制造业、资源等方面的合作很多，并着眼于长远互惠互利共赢。"民以食为天"，但农业的投入大、周期长，回报率低。"一带一路"上的互联互通为农业合作奠定了坚实的基础，也为我们开展农业合作创造了良好的机遇。"一带一路"沿线国家多为发展中国家，例如我们项目所在国哈萨克斯坦、柬埔寨等国家和地区大都有良好的农业禀赋，土地平整集中，农业物种资源优良，气候条件适宜，同时也存在基础设施薄弱、农业生产技术落后、产业体系不完善、发展资金不足和内外市场尚未完全开拓等问题，这与中国企业的资金、技术、人才、市场等方面存在较强的互补性。当今世界各国日益重视农业的基础地位，更加注重全球农业资源的整合利用和农产品市场的深度开发，对开展农业国际合作的诉求也更加强烈，这就为我们中国农业对外合作提供了难得的历史机遇。

同时我们也应该看到，中国对"一带一路"沿线国家和地区的投资主要还是在租赁和商务服务业、制造业、能源、批发和零售业、采矿业、金融业、建筑业等，农业领域的合作还有很大的潜力值得挖掘。极端天气的频繁影响、国际大粮商的垄断力量、中国农业企业竞争力尚有待提升等构成了"一带一路"上农业合作面临的挑战。农业持续增长动力不足和农产品市场供求结构显著变化，已经成为世界各国需要共同面对的新问题、新挑战，需要各国加强农业合作，共同促进农业的可持续发展。

新形势下，开展国际农业合作要秉持三个理念。一是共享发展的理念。国际农业合作不是单纯对所在国农业资源的占有和控制，而应该在合作过程中，实现对双边资源的挖掘与利用、对先进技术的示范与推广、对技术和管理人才的培育与配置。二是创新发展的理念。农业开发关系国计民生，是很多不发达国家的支柱产业，但又存在投资大、周期长、风险大的问题，需要摆脱多年来单打独斗的做法，与能源、基建、制造等行业结合起来，实现跨行业合作，创新模式发展。三是绿色发展的理念。农业资源的开发不应以破坏自然环境和人文环境为代价，而应和谐发展，打造安全、环保的绿色农产品。

"一带一路"倡议是区域合作发展机制的创新和探索，其根本是合作共赢。我们可以预期，中国与"一带一路"沿线国家将继续全方位深化合作，

投资规模将继续扩大，投资领域将继续向多元化发展。作为中央农业企业，我们也愿意与国内外的合作伙伴，进一步探索"一带一路"框架下的农业合作创新之路，为推动构建人类命运共同体作出贡献！

李新华　（中国建材集团有限公司副董事长）

尊敬的路主席，诸位在座的企业家，很荣幸参加本次论坛。我是中国建材集团有限公司（简称"中国建材"）的副董事长李新华，刚才燕生秘书长介绍到了中国建材，我们的主要业务分为三大块，包括生产销售传统的水泥、玻璃等基础建材，国际工程服务，以及新材料业务。

21 世纪初，中国建材开始"走出去"从事国际产能合作，开始主要是做干法水泥和浮法玻璃的 EPC 业务，采取以技术带装备、带服务的方式在全世界建设交钥匙工程。十几年来，我们在 75 个国家和地区（北美、南美、欧洲、非洲、中东、东南亚等地区都有）建了 312 条水泥生产线，60 条玻璃生产线，全球占有率 65%，连续十年保持第一。

国家提出了"一带一路"倡议后，我们也在不断思考，总结帮别人做"交钥匙"工程的经验，我们重新提出了"走出去"、参与国际产能合作的几个原则：一是彰显我们中国企业的形象，"走出去"就不仅代表中国建材，更是代表中国。李克强总理参观我们在连云港的碳纤维工厂时，讲到央企除了肩负经济责任、政治责任、社会责任，还要承担国家责任。二是促进当地经济社会发展。三是与我们的合作伙伴、当地民众甚至是竞争对手要合作共赢。

我们提出"六个 1"的"走出去"战略，首先是要建 10 个迷你工业园，平均建设资金在 5 亿—10 亿美金，不做大型的，现在已经启动了 2 个；第二是我们要做 10 个海外仓，作为海外的仓储、中转枢纽分布在"一带一路"沿线上；第三，要做 10 个海外区域检测认证中心，中国建材旗下有一家以认证检验为主业的上市公司叫国检集团，国内所有建材、建筑，包括 G20 以及各种峰会的建筑所用的材料都是由我们做的认证；第四，要做 100 个建材连锁分销中心以及建材超市，这块业务我们做了几十年，现在已经建成了四五十个；另外是做 100 个智慧工厂管理项目，还要争取再做 100 个 EPC 交钥匙工程。

过去我们走的是技术带装备、带服务的路子，现在我们还要把资金投出去。这方面我们才刚起步，到现在为止海外投资总额在 260 亿人民币左右。我举一个赞比亚的例子，说明我们如何深入参与当地的发展。在离赞比亚首都 20 千米的小镇上，我们搞了一个迷你工业园。用当地镇长的话讲，赞比亚国家独立之后给这个小镇画了一个宏伟的蓝图，但小镇一直都没变化，是我们去了才改变了他们的生活。我们在那边的工作就是在一块白纸上作画，当地很落后，所以我们把包括修路、修清真寺、建学校、建医院等事情都做了。还有就是对当地人来说打水井是一笔巨大的花费，他们以前喝的一直都是浅地表的苦涩又不卫生的苦水，我们过去花几万美元打了几口深井，当地叫甜水井，小镇所有的民众非常感激。我们还把国内的艺术团拉过去和当地交流。曾经有一段时间，一些喝醉酒的人去闹事，每次都是警察没到村民就先到了，我们与村民关系十分融洽。这样我们花很少的钱就跟当地居民相处得非常融洽。赞比亚总统也说："你们什么时候建完，我亲自给你们剪彩！"

对于央企的形象宣传其实还有很多亮点。再比如说我们在埃及投资 5.2 亿美元建了 20 万吨的玻纤项目，是三条智能化程度非常高的生产线，招聘当地员工近 2000 人，占总人数的 98%，还送 200 多人到中国培训，生产的玻纤产品以埃及为核心辐射到非洲、欧洲、中东地区，效果非常好。再比如，我们在德国收购了一个做薄膜太阳能电池的研究所，这家研究所最早是西门子的，我们收购后给予了很大的投入。2017 年底我们在国内建成了 300MW 的生产线，生产的薄膜太阳能发电转化效率达到 16% 以上，可以挂在建筑外墙上，不占地面空间，效果比传统的多晶硅好很多。我们不光是"走出去"，在国外建一些研究和生产机构，同时也把一些可以针对中国特色产业化的技术和产品拿回来。

天　山（土耳其实业银行上海代表处首席代表）

首先对主办方表示感谢，是你们邀请我，我才有机会在这里发言。广东省 GDP 有 1 万多亿美元，占了全中国 GDP 的 1/9，可以看到这个地方的贸易占比也是比较大的。昨天我们去拜访了腾讯还有另外一家公司，我们看到中国的发展到底有多迅速，发展新技术的速度有多快，现在在开发物联网、智能加工制造，它们创造的科技可以促进其他行业的发展，同时还能减少劳动力的投入。

刚才讲到深圳和广东，现在我们看一下土耳其，现在中国常提的是工业

4.0，这一点和我们国家的战略是不谋而合的。行业重组、工业重组还需要一些时间，在这里要跟你们分享一下我们的经验。在我们国家，"一带一路"能带来更多的机遇，比方说在人力资源方面，另外是资源、资金方面的互联互通和技术方面的互联互通，也就是技术转移方面，"一带一路"可以在人力、财力以及科技等方面带来更多的便利，所以我觉得"一带一路"可以让沿线国家变得更加繁荣，可以带来更多的机遇。

我来自金融行业，我想把我们这个领域的内容跟大家进行分享。在我看来，我们的金融是非常有包容性的，我们能提供金融方面的服务，不管是我们个人的项目、大型的国际项目还是风投，我们都可以提供。中国现在金融行业的发展也是非常迅速的，我们非常尊重上海，同时上海也是中国的金融中心，我们也在上海有个分部，在"一带一路"的项目中，不仅仅可以用贷款大的银行，同时也可以用资本市场，我们可以用资本市场来吸引更多个人到某个领域进行投资。

今天早上的时候有嘉宾说，深圳有 55% 的钱在银行里，在投资方面有很大的潜力，我们可以用资本市场吸引更多的个人投资、个人存款和闲置的钱，我们可以用这笔资金投资一些项目，这是我对今天你们上午讲的一些数字的看法。

我们银行在上海是有分部的，我们也投资了很多项目，不管是政府还是企业都可以在我们银行进行贷款。人民币可以作为投资的主要货币，因为中国现在对世界作出的贡献比较大，但是相对于美元来说，人民币的国际化影响力还不够大。

至于项目的风险管理，我觉得我们可以有担保函，利率比较低，而且贷款时间比较长。中国人也可以在这边进行贷款，到其他国家进行投资，我们是土耳其的一家比较大的银行，土耳其会有更多的游客来中国，也希望更多的中国游客到土耳其进行旅游。现在有移动支付，如微信支付和支付宝发展非常快，希望在移动支付方面我们会有一些合作。

胡安德 ［德国思爱普（SAP）公司副总裁、中国事务部总经理］

非常高兴能代表德国 SAP 参加这次论坛，我们是一个德国的公司，是全球最大的企业管理和协同解决方案供应商，我们为不同行业提供解决方案，拥有很多消费者，在中国也有很多的客户。我们的一些客户想进入中国市场，想了解中国的情况，会来我们公司进行咨询。1998 年我们进入中国市场的时候，与中国本土的公司进行合作，比如说华为、阿里巴巴等中国著名的公司，取得了很好的效果。

谈到合作，在"一带一路"的框架下，我们非常期待去执行习近平主席所提出来的美好倡议，比如说"互联网＋"等好的想法，我们作为德国的一家公司，非常愿意提供这些方面的帮助。

德国的方案与"中国制造 2025"的方案是非常相似的，中德两国在制造业方面有很多可以合作和探讨的地方，希望可以为中国的议题提供解决方案。我们在宁波建立了创新中心，助力 2025 年目标的实现，期待通过更多的合作与中国企业探讨我们所面临的挑战，发现如何找到更好的解决方案，给中国政府和公司分享我们所拥有的技术来提供更好的解决方案。

我们认为"一带一路"是非常好的契机，会有很多国家的公司来到中国，很多中国的公司"走出去"。如何解决在中国遇到的一些挑战需要倾听更多国际上的经验，并将这些国际上的经验引进到中国，与中国企业进行分享。有一些问题我们在海外会遇到，在中国不会有这样的问题，也许有一些事情在中国很容易做，在德国又不是很容易做。鉴于相互的优势，可以把相互的优势点引入中国，或是从中国引出去，解决我们潜在的问题，我们愿意和你们对面临的挑战进行进一步的探讨。

平行分论坛（四）：中医药国际化

中医药国际化创新发展之路

李楚源 （广州医药集团有限公司董事长）

今天论坛的主题是"中医药国际化创新发展之路"，几十年来，在座的任德权局长、张伯礼院士、王笑频司长带领我们行业在中医药国际化方面不断探索、不断创新，也取得了很多成效，今天在座的都是专家行家，我想讲一个观点，跟大家一起分享一下。中医药的国际化，应该能够跳出中医药来看中医药的国际化。

第一，我觉得我们对中医药要有自信，这些年对中医药有不同的声音，但是在国际舞台上，我们要不断地发声，因为现在大家可能会觉得日本、韩国的中医药好像超过了中国，我并不这么想，他们觉得很多东西好像很相近，所以我参加达沃斯论坛，包括上个月我们承办 500 强财富论坛分论坛，我都大声疾呼，中医药是世界上非常棒的，大家对中医药确实要有自信。

其实现在人类对生命的期望一个是希望长寿，一个是提高生活质量，中医对这两个方面是很重要的，确实中医药在延年益寿这方面的功劳很大，早在 2000 多年前，一位叫徐福的人告诉秦始皇，我可以给你找长生不老药，秦始皇也相信了，后来他到了日本，无论怎么样，现在按照国家来说，日本人口平均寿命最长，日本喜欢中药，很可能是我们中国人教他的，所以我觉得中医药对于延年益寿确实很好。代表中国的文化符号，第一是中餐，第二是中药，第三是武术。我觉得中医药要国际化，首先我们对中医药要自信，我们自己要自信，这样世界才能信任我们。

所以我觉得从人类健康哲学的角度，我们切实有必要为世界输出中国的健康理念和方案，其实中华民族很伟大，8000 年前三皇五帝的时候，伏羲帝在《易经》中就说，"易有太极，是生两仪，两仪生四象，四象生八卦"，这就是最早的二进制。现在世界的科学再发展，计算机也是二进制，没有三进制、五进制，我觉得中国在世界上确实有这个发明，并且这个发明是几千年、上万年都不落后的，所以我们应该为世界的健康方面输出我们的健康理念和方案，这是我要谈的第二点。

第三，我有一个观点，中医药里面要提倡中药，我们是做千年企业，对中药一直都很重视，也有很多沉淀、很多想法，我觉得中药要让老百姓真正有获得感，能感受到对大家有帮助。我觉得要提倡"时尚中药"，时尚中药是什么概念呢？就是用现代的科技，用大家容易接受的市场模式，做出大家喜欢的健康产品，所以时尚中药也包括四个方面：中药的现代化、中药的科普化、中药的大众化和中药的国际化。我觉得在中药的现代化方面，确实我们要与时俱进，我们讲出这些方法，我们的医疗器械、影像这些不是西医的专长，也不是中医的专长，它是共同的、公共的一个手段，中医可以用，西医也可以用，现在我们把它标准化、量化，用一些现代的技术、设备，是不是中药西化呢？不是，我觉得中药可以用，西药也可以用，它是公共的，大家都可以用，不能说我用了这个就是抄袭人家西药的，不是，这是公共资源，中医、西医可以共享一些现代手段。

你看现在很多诺贝尔奖得主也在研究中药、植物药，世界上发现的新药有54%是从植物药里面发现的，已经超过一半了，我觉得很重要，像王老吉，用很多现代的手段，获得国家科技进步二等奖，那也是很正常的，我觉得中药是在现代化当中。

中药国际化也包括几个方面，一个是产品的国际化，像王老吉，现在在六十几个国家销售得很好。还有科研的国际化，我们的板蓝根现在申请很多专利，分析出来很多成分，有些超过达菲，这些都是国际上对我们的认可。大众化和科普化这一块，我们也要借助一些平台。在2006年张德江常委就在广东提出中药强省，上个月省委书记李书记也谈到中药是一个很好的平台，因为要想做到国际化，这个平台要被认可，文化很重要，他说美国有两样东西出口是最厉害的，一个是武器，第二是文化，它的文化出去就什么东西都出去了，好莱坞就是一个传播文化的品牌。文化带动产业，文化输出是产业里面最高级的一个营销方式，我觉得中药文化博大精深，我们要加大力度，我们准备在全球建56个博物馆，现在我们已经建了五六个。中医药科普文化这些东西对产业的带动太大了，我是这么一个看法。

中药的大众化，是指中药应该让男女老少一年四季都可以用，我们知道现在有一个最大的中药就是酒。王老吉有一个例子，中药做成颗粒，到今年做了190周年，才销售了2亿元左右，做成饮料一下就销售200多亿元，我觉得这个是大众化，让老百姓也感受到喝了王老吉很舒服、很爽，酒也是中药的一种。

中药四化，其实也是我们现在说的供给侧改革，同样的东西我们做出来高附加值，企业又好，老百姓又喜欢，所以我觉得中药四化建设很重要，要提倡时尚中药的概念。

第四，我讲讲中药国际化，作为我们行业内的人，确实责无旁贷。因为习总书记曾说，"把中医药这一祖先留给我们的宝贵财富要继承好、发展好、利用好"，我觉得"三好"总结得非常好，现在中药已经立法，并且实施了，所以这是一个历史性的大事件，我觉得我们行业对这一块呼声太小，还应该再继续呼吁，因为从去年7月1日实施到今年6月30日才是第一年，我觉得还应该再努力，大家一起努力，有钱出钱，有力出力，像我去参加达沃斯论坛，我就在那里大声疾呼，建议特朗普应该用中药。现在中医院院长见到我很高兴，他说你说了以后来中医院的人越来越多了，我们是有科研依据的。

屠呦呦教授获得诺贝尔奖，我觉得具有划时代的意义，我去年去德国慕尼黑国家博物馆，里面展示了全世界的科学家，中国只有一个，就是屠呦呦教授，我太骄傲了，中药终于有了一席之地，所以我觉得目前是最好的时代，我们现在是新时代，中药也进入了新时代，所以我们一定会全力以赴，带领广药集团，不断努力，克服困难，所以我觉得今天深圳在这里出钱出力开这个会，应该点赞，我们这么多专家、这么多行家过来，对这一块这么重视，我觉得也应该点赞，如果整个中药界的人都从自我做起，中药国际化指日可待，前途会越来越光明，最后祝在座的各位新年如意，感谢大家多年以来对广药集团的支持。

闫希军　（天士力集团有限公司总裁）

推动中医药形成"顶天立地"之势
着力打造世界大药

以习近平同志为核心的党中央从十八大以来高度重视中医药的地位和作用，十九大又提出来"坚持中西医并重，传承发展中医药事业"，所以我今天给大家提了这样一个题目，像上次张院士说的，应该直起腰杆说，我就直起腰杆说一下，并不是瞎说，我们看看能不能做到。

关于中医药的一系列重要的思想，充分表达了党和国家重视、支持发展中医药事业的态度和决心，给中医药发展奠定了政策基础。

新型医学模式正在探索之中。一个是疾病谱变化引起了现代医疗观念的反思和医学模式的转变，所以对医学发展之路各个国家都在进行调整。中医药在防治常见病、多发病、慢性疾病、重大疾病当中越来越显出它明显的优势。现代生物医学与中医药相互学习、相互借鉴，这样一个大的国际化形势已经悄然出现。我觉得中医药的发展，机遇前所未有，如果中国这一次没有抓住这个机会，可能就会永远失去发展的机遇。在人类历史上，中医药从未像今天这样受到这样的重视和保护，但是也面临着挑战。怎么发展，是我们现在必须面对的。作为企业，必须站在时代的关键节点上，拥有一份担当精神，推动中医药在世界范围内形成人类主流医学。

这也是我多年倡导的，我把它重提出来，现在怎么做中医药，大家每次都提，我觉得中医药发展就必须要分类研究、分类发展、分类指导，分门类进行中医药创新和发展，创造这样一个机遇。

自古以来中医药不分家，而且中医具有浓厚的文化属性、思想属性，使中医和中药保持着不可分离的联动性，但是今天这个时代要对中医药进行多元化的研究，进行探索性的思考，拿出中国的实施方案。我们尝试一个方向，就是要让中药按照中医的思想范畴，要回归到法规药的属性上来。现在是一个法治社会，一个标准化的社会，给你开了一个药方，为什么吃这个药？药还是要回归到药的属性、标准的属性上来。所以要做"顶天"的现代中药——世界大药，达到国际标准，实现疾病症候指导下的精准研究和对疾病网络靶点的精准治疗。

分类研究，多元化探索。基于中药资源库的创新研究，是多元模式分头推动、互相促进的过程。中药行业的管理部门要超前规划，科学指导，使研究单位和企业根据不同的技术基础、资金实力、产品特点、市场需求、应用对象等各方面的因素，作出综合的分析和选择。我们提出了中药五种研究方法，一个是传统中药，第二个是现代中药，第三个是天然药物，第四是化学中药，第五是生物中药。现在国家就有两个，一个是传统中药，第二个是天然药物。所以混淆到一块是没办法研究的。

传统中药，大家都清楚了，国家规定把它放开了，对经典方实行报备制。在传统中药的基础上，怎么能够自动化、现代化，使模糊概念标准化是下一步要研究的。

现代中药，要保持中医的传统理论体系指导，它是来自于临床、长期临床的中药方剂，不改变组方，应用现代先进的种植、提取、分离和制剂技术，去粗存精，以多元活性成分或多元单体组成的有效物质群，改变了中药饮片配方，有效物质组分，形成新制剂、新剂型。

天然植物药，是应用现代医药理论体系指导，开发的天然植物药，这个国家有明文规定。天然植物药研发要达到下面四点：一是产品设计能够及时评价，二是处方合理，三是活性成分过程可以控制，四是明确适应证、安全性、临床价值可评估。

化学中药，这个不用说了，是从中药或植物中分离出有效单体成分，进行深入的化学与生物学活性的研究；或者，作为先导化合物，进行化学结构的修饰和改造；或者，从代谢产物开始进行研发，从而成为结构明确、疗效确切的药物。这个药的代表作品就是青蒿素，还有紫杉醇。

生物中药，利用基因工程技术，来源于基因修饰植物和动物的物质，或者动植物经微生物发酵后的物质，制成中药疫苗或药物制剂。将中药的有效成分融入生物制品中，发挥协同作用，以改善或增强生物制品的功效。

下面讲一下天士力的现代中药，这是从古方来的，它是一个很清楚的配方，明确了它的有效物质，改变传统中药"从药到药""以药研究药"的经验模式，深入到中药的药效成分；还有要回归药品属性，从标准、法规、药效、药理等方面，突出"药"的特性，符合国际药品法规要求的标准。

如果我们研究一个化学药、生物药，万分之一的机会才能做出一个新药。如果我们用现代中药，从临床用的上市中药名方验方，返还到临床二期研究，那我们就省了很多时间，省了很多钱，但是我们国家现在没有。

天士力的现代中药体现了应具备的特点和优势。药效物质明确，作用机理清楚，临床适应证确切。适应现代制造业的工艺技术和质量标准，能够达到现代制剂的安全有效、质量可控、生产规模化、智能连续化的生产新模式。能够实现以专利保护的知识产权，被国际主流医药市场认知、接受并使用，成为与化学药、生物药并立的世界大药，有望实现基因网络创新药物的精准研发，以及针对疾病的基因网络通路的精准治疗。要不了很长的时间，中药是能够实现网络化基因靶点治疗疾病的。

通过这些现代中药的创新，我们就带动了装备的创新，我们现在已经有两个万级无人操作特区，一个是药渣子，一个是提取物，所以完全可以在线控制，完全实现数据及时采集。我们带动了高速微滴丸剂的生产，这是世界唯一一台高速微滴丸机系统。

以复方丹参滴丸探索中药国际化，既然是世界第一个，咱们得把这个事情干到底。到2016年底，全球首例复方中药胜利通过了美国FDA（美国食品和药物管理局）国际多中心、随机双盲、双对照的大样本Ⅲ期临床试验，进入新药申报、补充新试验、材料完善阶段。

试验结果形成了《临床试验顶层分析总结报告》，全球首例试验再次证明复方丹参滴丸组方科学，安全有效，质量稳定可控。复方丹参滴丸在主要临床终点上具有显著的量效关系、增加TED的作用；次要疗效观察终点指标佐证主要临床终点指标，疗效证据成链；整个试验期间没有发生任何与试验方案或复方丹参滴丸相关的严重不良事件（SAE）；按国际通行的平板试验的金指标，抗心绞痛药物的延长运动耐受时间（TED）超过安慰剂20秒以上即可作为临床有效的判断依据，复方丹参滴丸达到了42秒，超过了世界上唯一的治疗心绞痛药物的同类指标。

复方丹参滴丸这个试验完成以后，美国FDA对复方丹参滴丸的三期临床试验结果给出了正面回应，认可其临床价值和6周结果具有统计学显著意义，$p < 0.05$（实际0.02）。需要一个再次验证6周统计显著的临床补充性试验，以达到美国FDA新药申报的2个临床试验同时满足$p < 0.05$的要求。目前，6周验证性试验方案设计已完成，正在与FDA沟通之中。FDA同意将Ⅲ期临床试验的结果在相关的学术大会上交流和发表。

所以我们在这样一个基础上搭建了一个世界联盟平台，现在在国内我们已经有十几家企业在这个平台上，通过我们的服务也在做国际化，所以请大家耐心等待。

借助复方丹参滴丸国际化这个平台和桥梁的作用，拓展了广泛的合作领域，这个对中医和中药都是有很大影响的，慢慢地它的效应就出来了，将显示出它的现实性。

体现国家力量，争夺话语权。要把中国的事变成世界的事，让世界人民接受，有话语权，就必须"顶天"，就是在国际上要站到最高。

经过全球性的推动，按照不同国家研究法规标准，使中药走向世界，追求的目标是成为世界大药，拥有话语权。这项伟大的工程，需要中医药界科研机构和企业的担当精神，不是单枪匹马就能完成的，需要全民的使命意识，联合行动，抱团出海，才能圆中华民族的世界大药之梦。我们说临床再好，是要进历史博物馆还是体现它的价值，这是中国人要回答的问题。中医药走向世界，如同中国的高铁、中国的军工，也是国家力量的体现，国家形象的象征。

第二部分，我们再简单地看一下中医技术和服务模式。

中药的创新和国际化，也需要中医的相应创新和国际化；二者相辅相成，相互促进。对于中医，也要分类研究，分类发展。对传统中医，要继续保持"望闻问切"的诊法以及辨证施治的方法、手段，保持传统文化特色。对现代中医，要在科学论证的基础上，应用现代技术的微观检查、量化检查，实现联合诊断，精准治疗。

我们现在在澳大利亚做了一个模式，就是在海外搭建一个中医与西医互相了解、取长补短、资源整合的技术融合和诊疗服务平台，把西医和中医形成两个网络。因为中医在国外很孤单，我们中间给它提供这个平台，中医就借助现代的终端设备，能够很好地治病。所以我们现在这个模式正在澳大利亚做了一个连锁诊所，在加拿大也正在做，现在也正在向美国延伸。以全科医生为桥梁将中药融入其中，做好中医药康复，现在我们的会员猛增，所以这个市场还是很好的。

现代科技不断为中医药的发展提出问题，指出方向。现代科技不断从物质、能量和信息层面上，揭示生命本质和医药作用机制。现代量子医学与古老的中医药学殊途同归。中药携带的能量与人体生物电同气相求、同频共振，能够调节人体机能，对亚健康和疾病状态有逆转作用。现在我们提出把中医的专属语言变化成现代语言，把中药现代化变成数字化，所以我觉得我们还要探讨中医的系统特色。

第三，是简单提一下"立地"，"立地"是我们的物质保障，就是中药材。

推动中药材产业链重构，打造中药材上游种植、中间市场商贸和终端数字化共享共赢生态系统，将中药材产业带入国际化、智能化变革时代。这是我们现在正在做的，我们现在通过打造两个平台（全国数字农事资源集约平台、全国数字中药都聚商交易平台），通过"五种人"的联动，让种药的人、寻药的人、买药的人、卖药的人、用药的人实现联动，实现数字本草检验检测系统、质量追溯体系和电子商务网络"三网合一"，形成信息服务、仓储物流、金融、标准化和国际化服务五大保障体。我们打造的是行业里面的一个公共服务平台，现在已经使用了，我们正在建二期，给大家提供一个服务平台。

最后提几个建议。

中医药迎来千载难逢的机会，也可能是最后的机会，我们在看这个问题，在研究这个问题，如果我们不抓住这次机会，我们相信全球人类医学飞速的发展的同时我们就永远被其他的医学"边缘化"了。即使在我们中国，咱们毫不客气地说，中医药现在也是"边缘化"。

中医药怎么传承，怎么发展，现在没有好的模式、好的路径、好的办法。现代社会是一个数字化、现实化的时代，人都很现实，人们有不同于过去的需求，中医药不传承不行，没有传承的普及性、广泛性也不行，但是只有传承不创新，就等于不发展，也没法发展。

中医药发展现状与国家的要求、国际化的要求，现在差距还比较大。一个是党和国家对中医药定位很高、政策很明确，但是社会环境不对位，政策落实不对位，与政策要求有差距。国际上寻求具有历史、有系统理论、回归自然的传统医药，认同中医药，全世界保存的最完善的就是中国的中医药，但是中医药与国际标准不接轨，与国际需求差距太大。现在影响中医药发展的，首先不是国际上的问题，而是国内没有真正系统地把它做起来；口号多，实际落实少；概念多，精准方法少；想法多，有效行动少。

中医药的法律地位要在执法中体现，现在体现得太少。中医药在法律上确立了定位，就要求政府执法的理念、信心与定力上要能够相匹配，要求全民参与维护，中医药界能够积极地学法用法。经过几代人的努力，《中华人民共和国中医药法》好不容易颁布了，但目前政策还不配套，没有配套的相应政策，没有落实到地的政策，没有一系列的政策措施构成执法保障环境，没有企业助力赋能，我觉得在这样一个环境下还很难推动中医药发展这么一个伟大的事业。

对中药的市场地位，保护不力。中药在市场上占位不足，给了"出生证"，不给"身份证"，不给"通行证"，更重要的是要市场进入的权力，现在权力还没有，中药在市场通行越来越困难。有的地方，医保药品目录中任意可以删除中药，任意停药，不给合理的保护，也不给合理的解释，那就等于中药没法律地位。既然有中医药法，已经法律保护中药，为什么要剔除？一些地方在招标采购的应用环节，利用医保控费用、控品规，使中药创新药物被"边缘化"。企业不仅需要创新的政策环境，还需要有进入市场的配套机制。

发展政策少，"把门"的关口多，准确的推动少，政策不对位。没有找到改革和发展的通路，没有针对性地分类研究中医药，中医药的研究现在有走低的现象。国家新药审批，这几年中药都在往下走，数量在减。中药注射剂代表着中药技术创新、标准创新，是一个高端的水平，也是中药现代化的方向之一。但现在因为个别产品存在不良反应，以及医保控费，就从大医院到基层医院，限制使用中药注射剂。中药注射剂的不良反应是一个历史问题，有科研能力低下造成的，审批不规范时代批准造成的，也有近几年新批准的产生不良反应，问题交织在一起，但应该是正确疏导研究创新，而不是联合"封杀"。

胡　铭　（四川省浩福集团董事长）

各位领导，各位专家，各位同行，大家好！

从2017年末到2018年初，我两次参加闭门会，为中医药传承与创新发展建言献策，很荣幸。

四川浩福团队，是一支以退役军人为主组成的团队，是一支戍边卫国的团队，是一支从战火中走出来的团队。今天，我们愿意与大家共同肩负起捍卫人民健康的责任和义务。2014年，许嘉璐副委员长为"浩福天府中医药谷"做了顶层设计，项目在成都落地。

我出身中医世家，对中医药的热爱与生俱来，同时也让我更加清醒地认识到中医药人肩负的使命。

据史书记载，从西汉到清末，至少发生过 321 次大型瘟疫，但都因中医药的及时介入得到控制。可以说，中华民族能够生生不息，中医药厥功至伟！

今天，中医中药已经陷入了"能医不自医"的怪圈，它面临的新挑战是：

1. 人才流失、文化散失、传承困难。

2. 难学、难用、难喝没有得到根本解决。

3. 学术价值、经济价值、社会价值还未得到充分体现。

4. 膏、丹、丸、散古法制作几乎失传。

5. 由于生活方式和环境的变化，部分疾病发病率高，疑难杂症越来越多。

与此同时，人们对健康生活提出更高的要求；传统中医药服务方式已经不能满足现代生活的需要。

当前，中医药事业发展，迎来了历史性的机遇。传承、创新、发展已上升到国家战略。我们必须对中医药存在的问题认真把脉，找出症结，开方抓药，提出解决方案。我们认为，中医药的创新发展，以及中医药的现代化和国际化，归根到底，都离不开一个最重要的前提，那就是扎扎实实做好中医药传承。中医药包含的哲理、历史、自然、文化、民俗、道德、知识与技术在中华民族一代代传承，是中医药生存的根本，也是实现中医药创新发展、现代化与国际化的根基。中医药是中华民族献给世界人民的宝贵财富，我国前两批国医大师，去世的已经超过 1/4。无数老中医一辈子的心血和经验，无数中医世家几代人的心血、经验、技术和成果正在不断随着名老中医的去世永远消失，这是整个中华民族的巨大损失。因此，我们深刻地意识到，通过多种方式保障中医药的传承已经刻不容缓！

目前国内的中医药传承，走的是两条道路。一是中医药高校采用西医培养模式，采用"流水线作业"批量生产具备基础知识和技能的中医药毕业生。二是通过硕士、博士以及各级中医药管理局认证的名老中医学术经验传承体系进行高层次中医药人才培养。

但是这两条道路归根到底都是体制内的中医药传承，受自身特点所限，并不能很好地解决以下名老中医经验传承问题：

1. 老专家不具备自主选择传承人的自由。

2. 传承人经过几年短期学习就各奔东西，无法稳定维持老专家学术流派存续和发展。

3. 体制内无法充分实现老专家的经验价值。

可以说，很多名老中医专家培养了大量学生，桃李满天下，但专家们最宝贵的经验却没有传承下来，传播出去。此外，还有更多体制外或民间有一技之长的老中医的文献传承、技术传承、成果转化、商业应用状况更加糟糕，亟待政策扶持。

关于传承教育问题，我们认为中医药文化、理念、品德与技术是几千年传承的根基，中医世家和退休后的名老中医仍是个性化传承教育的载体，需要建立有效的、体制外的、个性化传承教育机制。为此，体制外的传承教育认证亟待解决。

我们呼吁：

第一，充分发挥企业的灵活机制，将中医药文化传承与相关产业深度融合，建立以市场为导向的学术传承与成果转化机制，实现中医药学术价值、经济价值、社会价值，以此推动中医药产业创新发展。

第二，开放优势病种点对面的社会资源配置，重点培育一系列优势病种技术力量的传承，创新中医药商业协作模式，解决中医药人才流失、文化散失、传承困难等问题。

第三，加强现代化、智能化与中医药的有效结合，解决中医药难学、难用、难喝的现状，加快中医药国内外传播。

我认为，中医药产业发展，需要市场整体繁荣，需要实业自强发力。同时，让企业承接或参与由政府主导的产业双创平台建设与运营。在此，我们衷心地希望各位领导在民营企业参与中医药传承事业上给予支持，从政策上给予激励措施。

为了中医药事业发展，我们民营企业将义不容辞地承担起社会责任和事业担当。四川浩福将率先扛起中医药传承的大旗，在浩福天府中医药谷建设国家一流的、面向国际的中医药传承示范基地。以临床疗效为筛选标准，重点推动一批有代表性的名老专家进行临床经验与技能的传承，推动一系列具有国际竞争力的中医特色优势病种的学术经验转化与国际传播。

中医兴亡，人人有责。只要认准目标不放弃，撸起袖子加油干，民营企业必将成为推动中医药创新发展和走向国际化的重要力量。我相信中医药的明天一定会更美好！谢谢大家！

李安平 （山西振东集团董事长）

各位专家、各位老师，大家好。我在 2017 年跑了 19 个县，发现一个问题，中药不做认证，靠农民和农业企业自觉保证质量，我认为这个太可怕了。我们一直在思考中医药如何走向国际，如果这么发展下去，还怎么走向国际呢？我一直认为中国在国际上最有话语权的就是中医药，这是我们的瑰宝，这是我们最最值得骄傲的，所以振东也做了一点尝试，那么我首先讲一讲中医药走向国际的基础象征。

其实中医药传播遍及 183 个国家和地区，现在有 67 个国家的政策正式承认中医药的合法地位，在 193 个世界卫生组织会员国中，有 103 个会员国认可使用针灸疗法。中药呢？那么多的国家和医疗单位认可我们的中药，中成药却只能作为膳食补充进入美国。美国、加拿大、澳大利亚、德国等国，虽然有中医诊所，但主要是以针灸、推拿、按摩、理疗等为主，并且接受者大部分为华裔人群。可以说，中医药国际化进行了很多年，收效甚微，真正意义的中医并没有被认可。

中药至今没有一个以药品的身份被 FDA 认可，欧盟传统药注册（单味药）不能代表中医药，还没有形成规模销售。多年以来，中医药采取产品先"走出去"的战略，走得特别艰难。

中医药起源于中国，国内的西医都不接受中医药，想让国外的西医接受和使用中医药更是难上加难。中医药国际化，根本不是注册了才能"走出去"，中医药要想"走出去"，科研必须先"走出去"，且走得好、走得稳是必须要考虑的关键问题。

科研要想先"走出去"，必须对中医药研发各项流程及环节进行细致评估，尤其是对中西方的擅长领域及研究水平进行评估，在充分发挥双方优势的基础上开展中医药科研合作，同时把西方人最容易理解和最不容易理解的内容也让他们参与或进行研究。总之，让西方科学家在开展研究的过程中真正地了解、理解、认识中医药，进而让西方民众接受使用中医药，这才是打破中医药国际化瓶颈，走向世界的最佳选择。

接下来我介绍一下振东制药在国际化科研合作的成功案例来进一步说明"中医药要想'走出去'，科研必须先'走出去'"这一办法的科学性。

2008 年我们开始尝试"走出去"，我们第一次去美国时，他们非常不认可，根本不相信我们的产品是非常好的。之后，他们的副主任专门来中国看生产工艺，看检测条件，没想到非常标准，回去以后才决定合作。这个例子告诉我们，我们自己一定要认认真真对待自己的原材料，对待自己的工艺，对待自己的质量，这样你才能有资格和他们去商量、去合作，否则的话就没有这个资格。

2012 年 5 月我们和澳大利亚联合建立了振东中澳分子中医学研究中心。振东这两年培养了很多的博士，也联合培养了很多博士，取得了比较好的效果。没想到阿德莱德大学和我们合作以后，他们陆续组织了区域的中医局和中医药大学，为什么呢？一开始合作的时候我就跟他们说，中药有"毒"，你一旦染上它你就会爱上它，就会放不下。

2014 年我们与荷兰 SU 生物医药公司建立传统中药六味地黄片及逍遥丸欧盟注册合作。2015 年和广安门医院成立国际中医药肿瘤联盟，设立美国科研办公室。2016 年启动岩舒复方苦参注射液美国 FDA 注册临床试验。

通过研究，从前年开始不断地有很多论文在国际著名的期刊上发表，特别是 2016 年的这篇文章，得到了美国专家的很好评价，其实有没有用，不要去探讨它，总之这篇文章被欧美专家认可是非常不容易的。

从历史上的根本方法差异、文化的差异、社会方式的差异等方面来看，中医药"走出去"很艰难，经过我们的经验和探讨，科研应该怎么"走出去"呢？应该和国内的科研联合，再和国外的科研机构去做，无论是国内的科研机构还是国外的科研机构，里面一定要有中医和中药两个方面的专家组成，目的是得到他们的理解、认可，我觉得中国的企业和中国的科研机构都要"走出去"。我们如果单纯把在国外注册作为一个"走出去"的途径，我觉得 100 年都走不出去，你想国内的中医都不知道怎么用中药，你怎么能让国外的西医用中药呢？中医是一个非常完整的理论体系，不要一点点拆开去做，那是不太现实的，要拆多少年，根本不知道，所以我觉得振东"走出去"的途径是比较科学、合理的，现在也已经得到了很多专家的认可。

不管怎么说，中医药一定要"走出去"，我觉得作为一个中国人，这是一份责任，作为中医药人，让我们的产品得到国际认可，这个自豪感、成就感是任何事情都无法比拟的，谢谢各位！

张伯礼　（中国工程院院士，中国中医科学院院长，天津中医药大学校长）

首先，中医药国际化要明确是世界需要中医药，不是我们主动地去让别人接受，世界为什么需要中医药？现在看病难、看病贵是全球的难题，现在疾病复杂性的转变，使过去以疾病医学为主的模式遇到了很大的挑战和困境，而中医药这套方法、理念恰恰能应对解决这些问题，不是有钱就能解决健康的问题，很多是理念、方法，中医药这一套更适合自然，更适合整体观念，适合人的自身的需求，所以它能为解决当前全球的健康问题，乃至全球卫生治理的难点问题提供中国经验，解决世界医改问题，所以我想这是一个大的背景。

中医药"走出去"靠的是科技，科技越硬，科技越强，你飞得越高，飞得越远，因为它是一个翅膀。虽然我们强调中医药要国际化，但是它的基点在于国内的工作要好，特别是科技的工作要好。

我想谈三个建议。

第一，应该把中医药的国际化纳入"一带一路"倡议的国家顶层设计之中，不能让它自生自灭，自己发展，不能仅仅鼓励一下就行了，一定要纳入中国大外交的战略之中，把它作为一个国家软实力的杰出代表去做。纳入或不纳入大不一样，特别是在商务部谈判当中，中医药是中国一个有利的工具，我觉得必须要纳入大国外交战略统一的顶层设计之中。

第二，中医药国际化靠什么？应该是靠标准来引领世界，因为我们是中医药原创国，我们应该理直气壮地引领世界，中医药要引领世界的发展，从中医药现代化20年以来，我们基本上做到了这一点。同时中医药的研究方面，在深度、广度上，我们可以和任何一个国家相比，这是国际上公认的。同时我们现在高层次的研究越来越被国际所接受，包括刘教授在去年发的44份针灸治疗老年尿失禁案例，引起了很大反响。现在在标准制定的很多方面国内不接受，我们做了一个中医药传统知识保护目录，现在已经制定出来了，就是我们把自己的土方正式公布，宣示主权，印度、埃及、巴西都在做，而我们在做的时候面临国家的标准化组织方面的问题。我们已经做了两年，但是迟迟解决不了，例如侵权了，谁来告，如果我们宣布了这个是中国人主动发明的，别人再去用它，我们就应该提出诉讼。我们很多的技术诀窍、处方、关键工艺，现在也不能作为专利保护，在专利方面对我们的保护还比较少。

制定国际化标准也面临问题，中医药要引领国际，首先要建立标准，昨天记者问我，为什么在美国做中医药那么难呢？那么长时间不给通过呢？我说不是不给通过，是在路上，因为两种文化、两种技术体系有一个互相沟通、磨合、学习的过程，这是需要时间的，那个路你还没走完，中国也要走这个路，是一样的，专利体现的是国家主权，但是标准是国际的，所以我们说应该要用标准来引领，特别是对传统知识保护目录要给予高度重视，对于符合中医特点的知识产权应该建立特殊的保护制度。

第三，现在国家正提出来要建立以中国为主导的国际大科学计划，我们完全可以主导和引领，这些年世界上有一些知名的院校和研究院所，也在开展这方面的研究，但是应该说水平和我们的差距比较大，所以我们来引领他们一起来做，对扩大中医药的影响、提升中医国际化的水平具有重要意义。但是现在国际大科学计划迟迟没有出台，我们也提了一份报告，但是据说还有很大的难度。像量子通讯这样的科技咱们国家是高度保密的，不可能通过大科学计划把机密都公开，但是中医药可以，因为中医药大科学计划重点是研究，国外对于中医药的接受，往往不是从文化方面，而是要证据。目前复方丹参滴丸三期临床做完了，美国 FDA 说是一个非常好的试验，这个试验不但证明它的疗效，而且证明中医药整体的疗效性是可以被评价的。吃完这个药的效应比西药要好得多，只要是我们有信心，就能够经受得住国际的考验。我们想做的五个药完成了二期临床，都取得了很好的效果，所以希望国家把中医药作为一个重要的项目给予支持，这才能真正地推动中医药的国际化。希望在中医药国际化方面政府能发挥强势作用。

任德权（中华中医药学会临床药理分会名誉会长，国家食品药品监督管理总局原副局长）

从我的角度讲，中医药国际化可概括为三句话，第一句话，过去40年中医药国际化成绩可观。第二句话，现在正处于新的爬坡期，过坎儿，很艰难。第三句话，如果能过这个坎儿，突破现在这样的隔阂、阻拦，那么前景大有可为。

40年的成绩，针灸是最突出的，改革开放大的政策造就了中国针灸大步迈向世界。现已有183个国家正式接受针灸治疗。诸多针灸师在职业针灸的同时，会推荐病人服用中医饮片和中成药，又带动了饮片和中成药的出口。

成绩的第二方面，反映在重要出口市场与身份的变化。出口市场从传统的东亚、东南亚及西方国家唐人街，走向全球各地，走向西方主流社会。出口身份，从一般普通健康用品，开始通过药品注册，上升为"药品"，堂堂正正进入各国包括欧美发达国家主流社会。美欧等国从20世纪90年代中期以来，相继在药品的受理法规上开了口子。对中药制品，只要生产过程可追溯、成品质量一致性符合要求（不必内含成分结构全清楚），就可受理进行临床试验，只要临床试验数据兹证明安全、有效（不必作用机理全明确）就可批准注册作为"药品"上市。欧盟还明确凡有15年以上进口使用历史的品种，作为药品注册可免临床试验。而国内90年代后期以来的重要现代化推进，包括药材生产GAP（《中药生产质量管理规范》）、成药生产GMP（《药品生产质量管理规范》）的实施（体现了现代药品生产可追溯的要求），中成药内含物质指纹图谱相似度质控技术的开拓与普及（体现了成药质量一致性的现代要求），为适应欧美新规，实现突破提供了基础。现在天津天士力"复方丹参滴丸"、上海现代中医药公司"扶正化瘀胶囊"、江苏康缘"桂枝茯苓胶囊"、山西振东"复方苦参注射剂"等相继获得美国FDA受理，进入Ⅱ期临床试验，有的已完成Ⅱ期进入Ⅲ期临床试验。广州香雪制药是国内最早开展口服中成药指纹图谱一致性质控研究的企业，其"板蓝根颗粒剂"以感冒为主要适应证，已于2017年8月正式获得英国药品和健康产品受理的药品注册。

成绩的第三方面，表现在中医药标准国际化的突破。2010年国际标准组织（ISO）成立中医药技术委员会（ISO/TC249），现有中国、日本、加拿大、德国、意大利、韩国、新加坡、南非、澳大利亚、西班牙、瑞士、泰国、越南等 20 个正式成员，奥地利、法国、英国、新西兰、瑞典、津巴布韦等 15 国及香港、澳门地区为观察员，秘书处设在上海。至今已发布了 23 项标准，涉及针灸、脉象、舌象、煎药等中医诊疗设施与装备，尚在进行中的标准还有 50 项。在中药方面，自 20 世纪 90 年代后期起，中方与欧美等国药典机构与专家频繁交流。目前美国药典、欧洲药典都聘请中国专家担任药典专家委员。美、欧药典已相继将人参、丹参、三七等 17 味中成药和 74 味中药材纳入各自药典标准，并还将逐步增添。

虽然 40 年来国际化进展成绩可观，但必须说中医药国际化正处于新的爬坡期，过坎儿阶段。集中表现为：1. 就医而论，国际上广为接受的是针灸，中医尚处于依附于针灸师的尴尬局面；2. 就药而论，目前绝大部分还是以非药品身份进入西方国家，出口额只是内销（200 亿美元左右）的 1% 都不到。即使有的已开始作为药品被受理注册，但其功效必须以西医临床指标来表述并验证。例如在美国已进入 III 期临床试验的两个品种，无论是"复方丹参滴丸胶囊"的心血管改善指标，还是"扶正化瘀胶囊"的肝纤维化的控制与逆转指标，实际上都是按西方植物药对待的。由此可见，这个"坡"与"坎"就是文化的隔阂。历史上鉴真东渡、郑和下西洋为中医药的跨域传播作出了伟大的贡献。那时面临的问题主要是地理的隔阂。今天，地理距离已经不是问题，而文化隔阂的消融要艰难得多。如果哪天"望、闻、问、切"四诊，"阴阳、虚实、表里、寒热"八纲，以及人体"阴虚""气虚""阳亢"等辩证，及相应的"滋阴""补气""潜阳"等功效理念，为世人普遍接受，就是中医药文化真正走向世界之日。这得有个过程，但只要怀有对中医药文化的科学自信，这天终将到来。为了过坎爬坡，从现实出发，我建议从以下几方面努力：

1. 继续努力扩大并巩固针灸在各国大众健康中的服务作用。

20 世纪八九十年代出国创业的针灸从业人员已经开始老化，诊疗所不少存在后继无人状况。应大力培养并选择既有中医针灸功底又有外语基础的新人，组织与各地域前辈对接、承接好。

20 世纪五六十年代增选派优秀中医针灸专家为国际友人，特别是政要服务，取得了较好中医外交作用。现在也可以对各国民众喜欢的公众人物，针对其健康问题，提供合适的中医服务，从而扩大中医针灸的影响。

把来华接受中医或中西结合服务与旅游结合起来，面对中、上层人士开展旅游调养、养生活动。

2. 已有的孔子学院作为中医药文化的重要基地，从中医养生健康管理着手，结合中医体质、中医节气的因人、因时而异的饮食起居养生规则，让当地居民由浅入深地体会中医养生的实用性及其文化内涵。

3. 发挥中医覆盖大健康，从饮料（王老吉、金银花露等）、食品（茯苓饼、芡实糕等）养生品、保健品到药品的多姿多态优点，鼓励企业不拘一格，因地制宜，从易为异国他乡、易为西方大众所喜好的方式，把企业特色好品种做精做好，进入各国地域市场。组织企业与各地使馆结合，了解民俗，有针对性地开发出口品种。

4. 鼓励并支持中药出口企业选择能从西医功效表述的健康产品，大力开展上市后的临床研究。在国内研究取得有效证据的基础上，再与国际或出口国的知名研究机构合作研究，发表结果，开发市场。建议科技、中医药专项把支持证据临床研究，列为重要内容。

在让中医药从西医功效角度为大众、学界接受的基础上，人们自然就会联想为什么这几位药放在一起会有此功效，慢慢就会感觉到中医药的奥妙。让中医药文化润物细无声走向人们的心坎。

5. 进一步"推进中医药现代化，推动中医药走向世界"。文化隔阂的消融离不开中医药现代化。中医四诊采集仪已有突破，有的已列为国家和 ISO 国际标准。建议在四诊仪标准化的基础上，大力推进中医影像学（脉象、舌象等）的研究，进而实现中医药功效指标的量化、可测化。一旦中医药功效可量化，就可运用大数据、云计算、深度学习等新技术实现数字化。那么在数字语言面前，文化隔阂就会自然变小。相信总有一天，像国人测血压、测心电图一样，西方人也想测脉象、舌态。也许那时西方也会受理六味地黄丸作为"补肾阴虚"的药，真正作为中药上市。

王笑频 ［国家中医药管理局国际合作司（港澳台办公室）司长、主任］

我简要向大家报告一下国家在中医药"一带一路"建设方面的工作进展。

关于国家战略和顶层设计，2016 年 9 月 13 日，国家推进"一带一路"建设工作领导小组第四次全会审议通过了《中医药"一带一路"发展规划(2016—2020 年)》（以下简称《规划》），会后由国家中医药管理局会同国家发改委共同颁布实施。《规划》确定了中医药"一带一路"建设的指导思想和工作目标，特别提出配合国家战略在海内外统筹布局：一是在"一带一路"沿线建设 30 所中医药海外中心，由中国政府和沿线政府共同支持，优质医疗资源和产业资源共同参与，打造可持续发展模式。二是在国内建设 50 家中医药交流合作基地，与中医药海外中心形成内外联动效应。三是构建中医药国际标准化平台，开展中医药国际标准制定工作。早在 2009 年行业认识还不完全统一的时候，国家中医药管理局已经开始着手推动中医药国际标准化工作，一方面联合日本、韩国等，将传统医药纳入世界卫生组织疾病分类代码体系，包含传统医学内容的 ICD – 11（国际疾病分类标准第十一版），预计于今年公布，届时传统医药将在国际主流医学体系中占据一席之地，对于奠定国际传统医学临床、科研等信息统计基础，重要意义不言而喻；另一方面，在国际标准化组织里成立中医药技术委员会（ISO – TC249），中国上海承担秘书处工作。目前已发布 20 余个中医药国际标准。四是支持中医药文化海外传播，在双边合作框架下，举办高水平论坛和文化活动，为中医药海外传播营造良好氛围和基础。在国家推动文化"走出去"、建设软力量的文件中，也都纳入了中医药内容。此外，我们还在研究推动在"一带一路"沿线国家以药品、保健品、功能食品等多种方式注册 100 种中药产品。这些都是国家在推动中医药"一带一路"建设方面所做的顶层设计。

在推动中医药"走出去"的同时，我们也积极推动"引进来"。国家中医药管理局会同旅游局签署战略合作协议，共同开展中医药健康旅游。目前海南、新疆、内蒙古都有大量外国消费者入境接受中医药服务，中医药已经成为中国的一张名片，中国的朋友圈越来越大，说明这项工作非常有意义。我局将继续完善配套措施，把这项工作做好。

为推进上述"一带一路"建设工作，国家中医药管理局充分利用中医药部际协调会机制，会同有关部委完善保障措施，建立多部门协调机制，推动将"一带一路"中医药建设纳入国家外交、卫生、科技、文化、贸易等发展战略中，制定扶持政策，实施优惠措施，为中医药与 "一带一路" 沿线国家合作提供强有力的政策保障，同时加大金融财税支持，强化人才队伍建设，并号召地方各级政府加强组织领导，健全统筹协调机制和工作机制，制定具体实施方案，实现各地方分工协作、错位协调发展态势。

在财政支持方面，在财政部的大力支持下，自 2015 年起设立中医药国际专项，连续 3 年每年给予 3000 万经费支持，推动落实《规划》的目标任务。三年来，支持在沿线国家建设了一批中医药海外中心，在国内建设了一批合作基地。中医药国际专项除了服务国家 "一带一路" 大局、产生较好的国际影响、社会效益之外，在建立复合型可持续发展模式方面也取得一定成效。资金带动方面，经过评估，海外中心资金拉动是 1∶21，国内基地资金拉动是 1∶25，即 1 元投入可以带动 21 元和 25 元的社会资本。在王国强副主任的亲自协调下，2018 年国际专项有望继续扩大规模。

关于下一步工作建议，我认为：

一是中央财政继续加大对中医药国际专项的支持规模，并调整支持用途，让专项经费真正能够用在国外。专项设立以来，海外中医药中心服务了包括捷克总统、匈牙利总理等 200 余位国外政要和重要嘉宾，以及数万的海外民众，发挥了巨大作用，但是国际专项经费只能用在国内用于能力提升，不能用于国外，对开展工作形成了一定制约。

二是建议支持成立中医药国际化发展基金。重点对中医药企业 "走出去" 进行支持。中医药国际化的重要标志之一是中国的中医药企业 "走出去"，能够在国际医药保健市场上占有一席之地。鉴于中医药行业的现状以及激烈的国际竞争，像天士力这样有效统筹国际国内资源的企业非常少，而同时中医药企业又在海外面临良好发展机遇，有必要站在更高、更长远的角度从国家层面给予鼓励和支持。

三是支持开展高水平中医药国际科学研究。中医药 "走出去" 有个规律性发展过程，排头兵是中医医疗及其显现出的独特疗效，其次是教育培训，第三个阶段是科学研究基础。三者有个递进的过程，更是相辅相成、相互促进。目前在国家层面应重点对国际间开展中医药科研给予大力支持，针对中医药优势领域和国际医疗保健市场需求，由中国主导，吸引国际一流医学机构的专家，开展国际多中心临床循证研究，让中医药疗效说得清、道得明，使国际社会心服口服，为中医药服务和产品"走出去"打好基础。

四是发挥传统医学大国作用，建立一个机制性的会议交流品牌，每一年或每两年召开一次国际传统医药论坛。

刘保延　（世界针灸学会联合会主席）

对于中医药不只是中国人有需求，外国人也有巨大需求，这也是中医针灸走向国际的基础。我从针灸的角度说说这两年在"走出去"方面的一些体会和遇到的一些问题，并提几条建议。

我主要就世界针灸学会联合会近些年在国家中医药管理局、中国科协支持下，组织开展的"一带一路"中医针灸风采行活动的情况与体会做如下汇报。

针灸已经率先走向国际。中医是我国古代科学的重要组成部分，也是打开中华文化宝库的钥匙，千余年前古丝绸之路传送出中国的瓷器、茶叶的同时也传出了中医药与其承载的中医药健康理念与中华文化。目前国际上已经有 183 个国家在使用中医针灸。最近看到《环球时报》报道"2008 年的一项调查显示，40% 的美国人接受过中医作为补充和替代疗法。对于接受此次调查的美国民众而言，提到中医药大部分人都会想到'针灸'（69.6%）；47.0% 的人想到'中草药'；'拔罐'排名第三，比例为 24.2%"。这项在美国做的调查基本可以代表大多数国家和地区的情况。在国外对针灸的认识程度是很高的。可以说针灸已经率先走向了世界。发源于中国的针灸，现在已经成为世界针灸，针灸的本地化已经普遍展开。据不完全统计，目前在实施针灸与接受针灸的人中华人已经占了绝对少数。世界卫生组织在其报告里说到，尽管针灸源于中国，是中医的特点，但目前已经在世界范围内广泛使用。129 个国家的报告显示，其中有 80% 的国家有针灸使用，针灸是传统医学中使用最广泛的一种。

世界针灸的发展面临诸多挑战。尽管针灸已经在许多国家得到使用，但目前针灸合法化的国家只有 20 多个国家，将针灸纳入医疗保险支付范围的也是寥寥无几；针灸还未被主流医学体系所接纳，学术地位仍然相当低，大多数国家从事针灸者还未进入医师行列；绝大多数针灸有效的治疗并未有高质量的临床证据，在美国 1500 多个临床指南中，只有近 30 种疾病中将针灸作为一种选择；这些都成为当今针灸发挥更大作用的挑战。

建立中医针灸发展命运共同体。中国是针灸的发源地，世界针灸刚刚起步，我们应该成为世界针灸的领跑者，引导整个针灸的发展方向。同时，我们要将国际上的针灸界组织起来，提升当地针灸人员的地位，让他们在当地能够抬得起头，说得上话。能够把针灸堂堂正正地推入主流医学体系中去。通过针灸将中医健康理念、中医药所承载的中华文化带出去，传播到世界各地。我们的具体做法是，以世界针灸联合会作为一个载体、一个纽带，通过"一带一路"针灸风采行活动，充分发挥海外团体会员的作用和积极性，海外活动由他们承办，中国针灸学会以及中国中医科学院发挥专家和学术的优势选派专家参与其中，通过以下五个方面，使此项活动成为引领世界针灸发展的重要抓手。一是高层互动，一般我国驻外使领馆均会积极参与，而当地的医疗主管部门或者当地的西医学会、中医药学会作为东道主，将会作为主体与针灸界互动。二是学术引领，一般都会召开一个高层次的以当地针灸为主体的学术交流会，中国专家的研究成果往往可以体现针灸学术发展前沿技术。三是教育为先，通过举办专题培训班、针灸水平考试等方式，联合成立教育培训基地等提升当地针灸教育的水平。四是民心相通，通过义诊等活动，让老百姓现场体验针灸，接受针灸。五是文化普及，中医针灸作为世界非物质文化遗产，中医的科普宣传、图片展览等也是活动的重要内容。2016 年到 2017 年，我们已经举行了 7 次系列活动，风采行走过了 10 多个国家，大大提升了当地针灸团队的地位和影响力，促进了针灸的国际化发展。

通过"一带一路"针灸风采行的活动以及 30 年来世界针灸学会联合会的发展历程，我深深体会到，中医针灸国际化是我国增强软实力的重要载体，由于中医针灸所蕴含的是一种使人"不得病""少得病""治未病"的健康保障理念，顺应了人类健康需要的发展，体现了中华文化"天人合一""顺应自然"的智慧。"一针二灸三吃药"是呈现给健康世界最现实可行的方案。目前针灸已经率先走向了世界，以针灸为突破口，带动中医、中华文化"走出去"，不但必要而且可行。发挥我国针灸发源地优势、医疗资源丰富、人才济济等优势，领跑世界针灸发展，加强针灸国际化的战略部署，将国内针灸首先做大做强，非常重要。同时，要发挥我国 20 世纪 80—90 年代"走出去"的中医针灸的同仁在国际化过程中的核心作用尤为重要。这部分人在世界各地经过几十年拼搏已经站稳了脚跟，在当地有了相当的地位，帮助他们整合力量，做大做强，是针灸国际化的捷径；针灸作为医学的一个独特的门类，有其系统的理论体系和丰富的诊疗方法，之所以能数千年不衰并走向世界，关键是有疗效，但如今随着循证医学理念被广泛接受，用高质量临床疗效证据体现针灸的作用，成为制约针灸进入主流医学的瓶颈与巨大机遇，如果能够借助循证医学之船，通过大量高质量临床证据，对于针灸立法、进入医保、进入主流医学体系将成为一条捷径。

我就以上体会提以下两个建议：一是创新机制，动员多方力量，将国内针灸做大做强。将"以我为主"的针灸临床评价研究、针灸效应机制研究列入"大科学计划"之中，通过新的组织模式，发挥我国医疗资源丰富、临床研究人才济济等优势，吸纳国际著名团队参与，拿出针灸高质量的疗效证据，揭示针灸效应机制，领跑世界针灸发展。二是启动青年针灸人才国外创业计划。针对率先走出国门的针灸先行者后继乏人的现状，动员和组织我国针灸青年人才（硕士、博士）到国外去创业。借助国外针灸发展潜在的巨大需求和在国外已经站住脚的针灸先行者的帮助，建立系统的设计，鼓励大批青年人"走出去"，传承针灸、发展针灸。以上对于针灸未来的国际发展至关重要。

徐庆锋 （广东省中医药局局长）

广东是改革开放的前沿阵地，是对外开放的窗口，也是海上丝绸之路的桥头堡。现在青蒿素"走出去"是从广东开始的，在总结岭南人民长期与疾病斗争的经验的基础上，广东开始研究青蒿素。青蒿素"走出去"的影响非常大，现在成为我们国家的一个外交名牌，这个成果是非常大的。

广东也是广泛开展科研合作，现在广东的医疗企业与国外30多个国家签订了战略合作协议。广东把中医药"走出去"列入粤港澳大湾区发展规划中，我们希望通过这个窗口再向国家申请优惠政策，现在已经取得了长足进步。我们也重视标准化，深圳是出标准的地方，颗粒剂、中药材等三个标准已经取得了国际认可，所以这些中药材、颗粒剂能够"走出去"，已经取得了"身份证"。

广东是改革开放先行先试区，我们今年就同省发改委联合制定《广东省促进中医药"一带一路"发展行动计划（2017—2020）》，与沿线国家共享中医药服务，准备建2—3个国际化合作平台，4—6个海外中心，2—4个国际交流基地，广东在中医药"走出去"方面应该还是做了一些工作的。

第一，坚持中西并重是"一带一路""走出去"的根本，现在自己都不强，怎么"走出去"？中医药服务站占服务量的17.8%，但是队伍少得可怜。现在中西医资源分配不公，国家这几年，投入严重不足，西医招生和中医招生比例严重失衡，这些培养出来的人很多都没有从事中医服务，培养了85万临床医生，现在真真正正从事中医服务的人数是52万，那三十几万不知道跑哪去了，所以如何坚持中西并重，这是"走出去"的根本。

第二，我觉得文化传承是先导，科技创造未来，没有文化的传承，科技也走不出去，所以要让外国人接受我们的文化，其实中医的健康养生文化是非常容易接受的，所以习总书记讲"努力实现中医药健康养生文化的创造性转化、创新性发展"，理念要创新，模式要创新，服务方法要创新，服务模式要创新，技术要创新与发展，人才培养要创新与发展，文化要创新与发展，科学研究也要创新与发展，让他们接受我们，就是要把文化传承、文化输出作为先导。

第三，标准是核心。我们现在就是没有标准，百家争鸣。中医药品种多，特别像刚才李董事长说的，党参种植、种源、种地，还有采集、加工等，都没有标准，从这个情况来说标准是核心，标准是在一定的范围内就最佳测试、最实际和潜在的问题制定共同的和重复使用的标准，但是我们现在没有这个可以重复使用的标准，标准就是一个工具，西医也可以用，中医也可以用。

第四，理顺中医药的管理体系，这是关键。现在是"九龙治水，各管一段"，中医药是五种资源，这五种资源三层都包含，种在水里的水利部门管，在海洋中的渔业局管，但是发生质量问题是药监局去管，我们整个管理体系需进一步理顺。

第五，知识产权保护是保证，我们必须要绷紧这根弦。

钱忠直（国家药典委员会首席专家）

讲一点体会。一个是问题，我觉得核心瓶颈还是文化，因为中医有文化属性。除了文化这个大的瓶颈之外，我感觉在国际竞争力层面是存在问题的。医药方面的国际竞争力，实际上咱们是弱项，这个行业在国际上就难上加难，所以如何加强国际竞争力，这实际上是一个要正视的问题。

第二个是国家层面，资源没有优势配置，咱们国家现在跟其他国家不一样的就是药品的注册都在药监局，但是中医、中药是专门有中医药局，中医药局是管注册的。中医药国际化目前还没有一个高度的战略布局。当时我是 FHH（西太区草药协调论坛）四个成员之一，当时就是想把它做成中药领域的国际标准，但是到现在一点效益都没有，只有把它定位成国家战略的时候才能有机协调，否则企业得不到支持。

研究层面缺的是什么呢？很赞成刚才李总讲的科技要"走出去"观点，中药在国际上发表的文章还是相对少，虽然这几年数量上去了，但是真正从疗效方面来阐述它的还是少。科技方面要作为重点突破，只有科技突破了，才能够让老百姓认可，在国外去大药店看不到中药，全是在超市、杂货铺，甚至华人的饭店才能看到。大多数人就认可他们习惯的维生素等，所以科研必须要大力发展。

还有就是对政策研究不够，很多是只见树木不见森林，包括中医药局组织的，比如欧盟注册、美国注册。站在世界范围要看见它的脉络，1994 年美国的《美国膳食补充剂健康与教育法》里面已经明确了，1996 年才有了 FDA 的原则，接着有欧洲的植物药和加拿大的天然药物注册反馈，这应该对我们是一个很好的机会，但是我们缺乏从宏观上面来看这个问题，反而是抵触的。从整个国际层面，中药是一个很好的机会，人家是把你当药来看待的，想让中医药堂堂正正走入主流世界，政策研究要从制高点看全世界。

再就是企业，顶着这么多压力，国家对它的支持是有的，但是只限于经济方面。我们过去做的工作实际上就是给企业做基础，我们是把药材饮片做进国外的药店，在欧洲、美国、加拿大你只要进了药店，就给企业减负很多，企业再去注册的时候很多优惠是可以做的，现在走的最前面的就是针对加拿大卫生部的，所以这些核心问题要去解决。

沈远东 （国际标准组织中医药技术委员会副主席）

我有一些在第一线做国际标准化和中医药国际化的切身体会，所以我直接回答这次论坛上的几个问题。

第一，关于中医药国际化面临的挑战，前面有些专家已说到，我把它再罗列一下。挑战大概有这六个方面：一是中西文化的差异对中医药国际化的影响，因为中医药源于中国传统文化。二是中医理论体系与现代医学体系的差异。三是各个国家医疗卫生管理体系与相关法律法规的差异。四是国家与团体经济利益的相关性。我们委员会有三十几个成员国，都要维护自己的利益，成员国里面的各个代表来自不同的商业集团和医药企业集团，他们的利益不同，所以这也成为一种矛盾的焦点。五是中医药本身的质量和安全问题，这个我们不能回避，我们不能一说中医药国际化面临的挑战，都是国际上的问题，其实还有我们自身的问题，比如说中药材的农残量，比如说重金属含量，这些问题也是成为西方建立贸易壁垒的理由，成为阻碍中医药国际化发展一个非常重要的障碍。六是缺乏全球统一的质量和安全标准，刚才各位领导都讲了，我非常同意，而且我有深切的体会。

第二，我觉得做好中医药国际标准是促进中医药国际化和创新发展的一种基础，有一个口号，世界上共同的语言是什么？就是国际标准，不管你的文化不同，还是行业不同，但是有一点是相同的，国际标准就是一种共同的语言，是促进中医药国际化的基础。我们委员会目前有三十几个成员国，大家原来可能想象重视传统医学的都是发展中国家，其实不然，三十几个成员国当中大部分都是发达国家，可以说明中医药在全球的影响力，到目前为止已经发布了23个标准，所以TC249（中医药技术委员会）在整个ISO系统里面是非常有名的，在9年里面是在ISO所有的技术委员会里发展非常快的，目前还有48个标准已经立项，在制定当中，目前发布的这些标准当中，中国完全掌握了标准的主导权、话语权，86%以上的标准都是中国专家提案，这就是中国方案，现在TC249有7个工作组覆盖整个中医药行业，中医药国际标准化现在发展的形势很好，刚才刘院长介绍的世界针灸学会联合会、中国针灸学会、WHO这些国际组织，都是在做国际标准，由于时间关系，我其他不谈，就谈国际化和标准化面临的三个问题和三个对策。

　　我觉得中国是一个中医药大国，但是到目前我们还不是一个做中医药国际标准的强国，这方面我们还没有形成权威性的专家队伍。在国际舞台上，虽然我们在数量上已经占了主导地位，但是我们的权威性还是缺乏的，这个问题分国内和国际两个层面，整个国际化问题主要是有三个方面，两个国内的，一个国际的，一是人才队伍问题；二是机制体制问题，现有的中医药国际化机制与体制跟不上国际发展的需求；三是国际上的问题，中医药国际化发展不仅仅是国内的事情，我这个平台上反映出来的问题是各国发展的情况极不平衡，在中医药国际化方面不平衡。有些国家已经立法，中医药已进入国家医疗服务体系，但大部分国家没有立法，而且从参加到我们这个平台上的成员国的情况来看，有的成员国，比如日韩、德国、美国可以派出20—30个人的专家队伍参加我们的会议，但有的只派出一个人，有的是夫妻店，这种情况反映出中医药国际化要走的路还很长，发展极不平衡，这也是中医药国际化面临的问题。

　　针对这三个问题，我提出三点策略。一是人才队伍的问题。我觉得要坚持文化自信和制度自信，加强中医药国际化人才的培养，这个非常重要。中医药国际化人才的培养，要有中医药的背景，做中医药国际化的专家外语水平不行，到国际舞台上就有难度，还有标准化的知识，这些知识统起来，就需要复合型的人才。另外，怎么吸引优秀的人才到这个平台上工作，为国际化做贡献，为标准化做贡献？需要专业人才的评估考核，晋升体系的标准。做国际标准化不像国家自然科学基金那样吸引人，但做中医药国际标准确实非常重要，像刚才闫总讲的，确实是需要情怀，需要对中华民族科学文化信仰的情怀，需要对制度和政策的自信，这个非常重要。

　　二是机制体制的问题。我觉得创新机制体制十分重要，今天这个论坛也是围绕着创新，所以要创建创新的机制与体制，中医药的国际化平台当中，我们在顶层设计上要把资源优化组合，形成合力，组织形成高效的运行机制和激励机制，这也是一个策略。

　　三是要支持海外的中医药发展。所谓的海外中医药发展是指海外的组织，或者是中医药协会，或者是某些学校和机构的发展，在支持海外发展过程当中，中医药文化的传播对中医传统医学和文化的认同和理解将起到十分重要的作用。这一点我原来没有体会，做了中医药国际标准后我有了体会，认识到中医药文化的传播将会极大地推动中医药国际化发展，就像一个铁轨一样，国际列车要驶向全球，中医药文化传播就像列车的轨道，先行铺设好铁轨，这样国际化的列车就能驶向全球。此外，中医药在国际上的合法地位，也是非常重要的一个方面，一个是文化传播，一个是争取中医药的立法和合法，如果这个不突破，那只能够停留在民间，这也是体现中国方案、中国标准"走出去"，当然可能文化的交流传播是以民间为主，但是立法可能要靠政府来推动。

另外，在上海我们也做了一个探索，如何来支持海外中医药发展，我曾经给中央有些部门领导提过建议，要建立一个基金会，专门支持海外中医药发展的基金，后来王部长来调研的时候我谈了这个设想，现在这个基金会我们已经建立，今年已经开始运作，专门支持那些中医药比较弱小但是对中医药情有独钟的，坚持多年参加国际化工作又对中国十分友好的这些国家和团体。另外，我们希望更多优秀的企业加入中医药国际化、标准化的平台当中来，谢谢。

阎海峰 （华东理工大学商学院院长、教授、博士生导师）

我是做商学方面研究的，跟这个行当接触比较少，是一个外行，今天学到很多东西，我讲一点自己的想法。

第一，我的一个基本看法是，我们一直说中医药，但是实际上从研究企业的角度来讲，中医和中药在国际化过程当中是两个不同的东西，中医属于服务规则，中药属于货物规则，不要混在一起，最好分得比较清楚，西方国家是分得很清楚的，因为他们是那种科学主义的特点，他们那种文化的特点，就要求你什么东西都要分清楚，边界是什么，定义是什么，这个可能就不利于我们"走出去"。

第二，我觉得在中医药行业，问题不在企业，也不是一个商业模式的问题，甚至于现在还不是技术问题，它是整个行业的问题。战略定位应该更清楚，如果一个行业的定位不清楚，通常来说它的发展方向就很模糊。

第三，从这个行业来看，我发现大的企业不太多，一般是中小型的居多，这说明这个行业的成熟度还比较低，它的产业集中度不高，如果产业集中度不够，又要到国际上去竞争，面临的又是西医这样一个对手的话，肯定会遇到诸多困难。

第四，中医药国际化要有强大的资金保证，需要有强大的资金实力，没有一定的行业集中度，没有强大的企业来支持，非常困难，要么就是整个行业联合做才可以，不然的话这个是很烧钱的。医学在全世界都是很烧钱的，它的集中度是很高的，如果集中度不高，可能会有问题。

第五，我想从企业国际化这个基本的路径角度、模式角度谈几点小的建议。一是在进入的过程当中，任何一个企业要进行国际化，主要有三大壁垒：一是市场，要赚钱，要竞争；二是制度壁垒；三是文化壁垒。我暂且不讲从情怀的角度，或从国家这个大的角度，我觉得经济利益很重要，赚不到钱是不可持续的，除非它不是一个行业，所以赚钱是必须的，暂时赚不到钱以后也能赚到钱，不然的话即使出去了也没用。制度约束和文化约束，或者制度壁垒和文化壁垒，对于中医药行业来讲，它受到的约束在制度壁垒方面和文化壁垒方面比一般的产品和服务都要高，因为它太带有不同国家的文化特征了，而且由于它与人命相关，与健康相关，所以各个国家的管制一定是比较严的，跟一般的货品、物品和服务都不一样，所以我认为这两个是我们在国际化进程当中，中医药行业的企业需要慎重考虑的。我把这两个维度分成了四类：

第一类就是跟中国的文化距离近、管制壁垒低的国家，我认为可以优先考虑，假定不谈市场，这个是可以优先考虑的。第二类是管制壁垒低，文化距离比较远的国家，就像非洲的一些国家，也可以考虑，它的难度稍微小一点。第三类是管制壁垒高，但是文化距离近的国家，比如日韩也可以考虑，新加坡的管制壁垒高，因为比较发达，但是它的文化距离近。最后一种最难，管制壁垒高，文化距离又远。尽管它的标志意义很大，但是如果从企业要盈利、要持续发展的角度来讲，我认为它需要面临现实的一些特点，这是第一个建议。从这个角度来看，制度壁垒高进不去，因为不具有足够的正当性或者合法性，如果是文化距离远，接受度低，也很难，没人接受也不行，这个东西和别的还不一样。

第二个是进入模式，以我们这个角度来看，我感觉这个行业的进入模式要分大类的话，除了贸易，就是直接出口药。进入模式基本上就是两类，一类是跟对方合伙干，还有一类就是自己干，独资或直接投资。我感觉这个行业因为需要破解文化壁垒和一些制度壁垒，基本上是以合资合作作为主要进入模式，这可能对企业来说是最重要的。还有就是所谓的点上的突破,刚才针灸其实就是很好的突破,在某一个点上一定要能够形成突破,这样的话它积累到一定程度就会有这种效应,像复方丹参滴丸,它最后会有一个爆发性的效应,我觉得需要做好长期架构的准备,应该是有这样一个点的。

第三是中医药国际化。刚才刘保延会长也讲到了,一个是针灸,针灸可以带医,医可以带药,这个行业就有这样的特点。以医带药,我认为对于中医药行业来说很重要的一点就是本土化,进入任何一个国家都需要本土化,都是为了破解制度和文化这样一个独特的壁垒。

第四是需要人才的培养,现在人才不够,因为我自己也有亲戚学这个,后来也不肯干了,海外的留学生学中医的要很多才行,我们自己的人才要很多才行。

最后一个建议,可以借鉴孔子学院这个渠道的做法,既然要把它上升到一种重要的国家战略,是以一种真正体现中国原创知识产权又有国家特征的这样一个行业进行推动,在"一带一路"倡议下,如果上升到国家战略,可以比照孔子学院那种方式,孔子学院没有专业,中医中药至少是一个专业化的行业,又能够给当地带来福祉,反而更容易被接受,如果这样的话,国际化的速度会更快一些。

熊大经 (成都中医药大学教授、博士生导师)

首先感谢前面六位企业家及各位领导对中医药走向世界所做的努力,对中医药发展的支持。我非常同意天士力裴总的意见,申报一个新中药非常难。

举一例子:我这里拿了一个材料,是国家药监局药物临床试验批件,是2005 年的批件,该文件批复"同意本品进行临床试验","应限定本品临床应用不得超过七天"。申报单位按药监局临床前的要求进行了二期、三期临床试验,当人家把所有工作做完了,再报药监局批准生产时,最后被否决了,为什么否决?有几个理由,很可笑,不知这是否是一个外行所为。他的理由是:"未按常年性和季节性变应原的类型分层分类设计","未充分考虑不同变应原以及接触变应原程度不同,对患者临床症状体征的轻重有明显影响,对照药物的选择欠合理,对照药物辛芩颗粒原标准中规定的疗程为 20 天,而临床试验中仅用了 7 天"。

我们知道近年来过敏性疾病增长迅速，许多疾病都与过敏有关，呼吸道的大部分疾病都跟过敏反应有关，特别是儿童患者，更是与过敏关系密切，加之大气污染的加剧，呼吸道疾病，特别是过敏性鼻炎发病率更是呈上升之势。我从事中医临床工作 48 年，对中医治疗过敏性鼻炎有很深的体会，多年的临床经验告诉我们：中医治疗过敏性鼻炎疗效确切，对改善临床症状有十分明显的疗效，并且有疗程短，费用低，而且没有副作用等特点，是一个非常值得临床推广应用的项目。我们用该中药在临床上治疗过敏性鼻炎 30 多年，并培养了 5 个博士、8 个硕士，发表论文 10 余篇。包括我有一个博士生研究该药，毕业后又到刘保延教授处读博士后。这些说明该品种是一个临床疗效明显的，无毒副作用的中药。而且现在我们临床上还在用这个处方，用得很好，病人反馈也很好。

这样一个临床应用多年，疗效确切的新中药，为什么要让中医做常年性和季节性分层分类的研究？这个给中医出了一个非常大的难题。下面还有一个问题："未按常年性和季节性变应原的类型分层分类设计"，"未充分考虑不同变应原以及接触变应原程度不同，对患者临床症状体征的轻重有明显影响"，我请教了很多西医专家，他们说："目前世界上还没有一个国家能做这方面的研究，而且没有一个临床医院可以做，吸入一个花粉和吸入两个花粉、吸入 10 个花粉、吸入 100 个花粉的差别，这是一个根本无法完成的、无法定量的研究。"这是第一个问题。

第二个问题，我们现在的新中药研究，有一个误区，那就是中医的症一定要与西医的病挂钩，否则不同意申报研究，中医是辨证施治，不是辨病施治，我提一些建议：我们可不可以做中医的症状的研究，比如说讲过敏性鼻炎，我只研究过敏性鼻炎的症状，喷嚏、流清鼻涕、鼻痒，我不做病的研究，我只做症状研究。西药也有只研究症状的药，如西药的麻黄素不治病，它就是通鼻子，缓解症状，西药的止痛片，它也只是止痛而已，也不治病。中药也可以走这条路，将来新药研究，不一定要把中西医挂钩。比如咳嗽，你非要把气管炎、肺炎结合起来，其实可能是其他原因刺激，有一点咳嗽，我非要说你这个是不是支气管炎，是不是哮喘，没有必要，就是一个症状，我吃了这个药不咳嗽了、不打喷嚏了就可以了。新药研究一定要按中医的规律研究新中药。这是第一个建议。

第二个建议，我觉得不能再按照西药的标准对中药来审评了，刚才有一个专家讲，有的老中医的经验是几十年的，是毕生的精力，如果按照西医的标准来要求，很可能将来中医慢慢就失传了。

第三个建议，可以把中医药的名录列为我们的知识产权，列出专科的名录和方剂的名录，比如说日本人把中药学走了很多，其中有一个卖得很好的，改了名就变成日本的，如我们有名的玉屏风颗粒，日本人改为卫益颗粒；我们的通天口服液，日本人改为调顶颗粒等。如果我们有我们的名录，有我们的知识产权，就不会出现这种情况。

亢鲁光　（成都中医药大学教授、博士生导师）

我谈一下我对中医药国际化的理解，第一个是国际吸引力。改革开放以来，我担当了学校的外教带习老师。几十年来我带过世界各地的学生及西医老师。我带学生在病房查房、上门诊，给学生们讲课，中医神奇的疗效，让学生们感受到了中医的博大精深，同时他们也爱上了中医这门医学，回国后从事中医工作。

第二个是国际影响力，近二十年来，我先后到美国哈佛大学、威斯康星大学、英国剑桥大学国王学院等知名大学进行过学术交流，在新加坡南洋理工大学工作过，并受邀多次在德国、泰国进行学术讲座。德国的西医专家多次来成都跟我做临床，最后他们决定让我和德国西医协会副院长、中医学会会长一起编写《糖尿病的中医治疗》，中文全部由我写，德文、英文由他们翻译，《糖尿病的中医治疗》是全球第一本由中外医学专家联合撰写的中医学专著。这本书出版以后，受到了德国、新加坡医学界的热烈欢迎，这本书现在列为德国中医学会官网推荐图书的第一位，目前这本书已经在欧洲、美国、大洋洲18个国家、45个网络平台传播，被13个国外图书馆收录，并被列为德国慕尼黑大学和奥地利两所高校的中医硕士学位课程教学用书，我们在国外用这本书培养了大量的西医。

这本书目前销售量非常好，目前正在出英文版，最后出中文版。在这本书出版的基础上，我们的课题"中国—东盟中医药防治糖尿病的技术交流、示范及推广应用"培训班，得到外交部、教育部、科技部和国家中医药管理局的支持，招收了东盟多国的卫生部领导及学生，我们用讲课、临床结合的方法带教，反映很好，最后促成国家级"中国—东盟教育培训中心"落户成都中医药大学。我们办这个培训班当时是怎么想的呢？当时中国和菲律宾的关系有点紧张，我们说要做一个课题，就做了这个课题，没有想到这个课题一交上去，教育部、外交部、科技部等马上给我们最大的支持，当时我们招收了东盟多国卫生部的领导，还有他们的学生，以及他们认为在当地非常好的西医到我们这里来学习，当时只想是一个小课题，最后这件事情促成了中国—东盟教育培训中心的成立，东盟国家的学生每年源源不断，这些学生跟我们也有很好的关系，所以现在我们学校在领导、师生的共同努力下，留学生是源源不断的，也有很多分校。（2010 年 11 月，由本课题组负责人亓鲁光教授牵头的，国家科技部、外交部合办项目"中国—东盟中医药防治糖尿病的技术交流、示范及推广应用"培训班在成都中医药大学正式开学授课。国家科技部国际合作司亚非处处长徐捷，外交部亚洲司区域合作处处长贺湘琦，四川省科技厅国际合作处副处长胡钢等领导出席开学仪式。来自东盟六国包括印尼、新加坡、越南、泰国、马来西亚和文莱的 27 位中、西医专家参加了培训，由本课题负责人亓鲁光教授等中医药专家悉心教授糖尿病的中医药防治知识和技术，为推动中国—东盟医药技术交流与合作，促进中医药国际推广和增进中国—东盟人民友谊作出了突出贡献。）

中医文化、中医思想已经得到传播，但是我觉得中医文化的传播缺乏载体，美国传播文化是以可口可乐、麦当劳传播到中国，但是我们让世界人民了解中国，除了我们的文化以外，还缺乏载体，我个人觉得中医药走出国门缺少中药这个载体。

因为我是长期从事临床工作的，我们应该把自己的品牌做好，我们学校（成都中医药大学）建院 60 年，获得国家级项目 164 项，部省级项目 348 项，获国家科技进步奖二等奖 2 项，部省级奖 42 项，三等奖 63 项，研究经费 8000多万元，到目前为止院内制剂近十个，包括肾康注射液、鼻窦炎口服液、一清胶囊等。我三十多岁就参加了一清胶囊（卫生部甲级成果奖）的研制，这些产品都是年销售上亿元的好产品。这些产品都是 20 世纪 70 年代转让生产的，我们近几十年来科研能力一天天提高，我们科研经费越来越多，但是没有一个科研成果能转化。原因主要是，周期性太长，不确定性太多，所以现在工厂不愿意再投入新药研究，科研单位成果很多，我这几年出了好多成果，我也有好多获奖证书，就放在那里，没有办法转化成产品，我觉得这是一个极大的浪费。所以今天我发言主要是讲后面这一点，我希望国家能够对工作40年以上的，而且在临床上确实是有疗效的、有科研能力的老中医研究出来的处方开一个绿色通道，我都在临床上40多年了，我治了许多人，我为什么能在哈佛大学讲课？就是因为我当时研究糖尿病，哈佛大学糖尿病研究中心的教授来跟我做临床，我每天上门诊开药。本来他计划待一周，最后他跟了我半年。在此期间，他目睹了很多让他震惊的案例，比如我曾经治好了一个糖尿病引起的坏疽病人，他说他有过类似情况的病人，结果全是截肢，把手切了，左手切了切右手，右手切了切左脚，他说每天给病人换药病人都大叫。

我觉得中医还是很伟大的，它里面还是有很多好东西需要政府给我们扶持，给中医开一点点绿灯。谢谢。

英文版

Opening

January 17 , 2018

Moderator-Xiong Meng: Distinguished Leaders, Dear Guests, Ladies and Gentlemen!

"Even mountains and seas cannot distance people with common aspirations." Today, the International Cooperation Forum for Cities and Industries under the Belt and Road Initiative is jointly held by the China Federation of Industrial Economics and the Development Research Center of the Shenzhen Municipal People's Government. More than 100 government officials, experts, think tanks and entrepreneurs from 23 countries and regions have gathered to discuss the theme of "City Partnership 'Industrial Connection' Think Tank Link". This is of great practical significance for us in achieving closer cooperation among the cities along the Belt and Road, strengthening exchanges and mutual learning among different civilizations, jointly advancing the construction of the Belt and Road and translating the vision of peace, development and cooperation into reality!

Let me begin by extending, on behalf of the organizers of the conference, a sincere welcome and heartfelt thanks to all the distinguished guests and friends attending the Forum!

First of all, welcome:

Mr. Li Yizhong, Member of the Standing Committee and Deputy Director of the Subcommittee of Economy of the Chinese People's Political Consultative Conference, former Minister of Industry and Information Technology of China, President of the China Federation of Industrial Economics;

Mr. Li Zhaoxing, President of the China Public Diplomacy Association, former Foreign Minister of China;

Mr. Yu Hongjun, Vice President of the Chinese People's Association for Peace and Disarmament, former Vice Minister of the International Department of the Central Committee of the CPC;

Mr. Lu Yaohua, Executive Vice President of the China Federation of Industrial Economics;

Mr. Ren Dequan, Honorary Director of the Clinical Pharmacology Branch of the China Association of Chinese Medicine, former Deputy Director of the China Food and Drug Administration;

Ms. Wang Xiaopin, Director of the Department of International Cooperation (Hong Kong, Macao and Taiwan Affairs Office), the National Administration of Traditional Chinese Medicine;

Mr. Liu Qingsheng, Member of the Standing Committee of the Shenzhen Municipal Committee of the CPC, and Executive Vice Mayor of Shenzhen;

Mr. Wu Sikang, Director of the Development Research Center of the Shenzhen Municipal People's Government.

Please come on stage to attend the opening ceremony.

The international guests attending this Forum:

Mr. Stjepan Mesić, General Counsel of the Croatian Chamber of Commerce, Special Representative of Zagreb City;

Mr. Dušan Bella, Ambassador of the Embassy of the Slovak Republic in People's Republic of China;

Mr. Dhia Khaled, Ambassador from the Republic of Tunisia to the People's Republic of China;

Ms. Diana Macarevici, Chargé d'affaires of the Embassy of the Republic of Moldova to the People's Republic of China;

Mr. Cosmin Necula, Mayor of Bacău, Romania;

Mr. Alexandros Modiano, Deputy Mayor of Athens, Greece.

The Chinese guests attending this Forum:

Mr. Li Yizhong, Member of the Standing Committee and Deputy Director of the Subcommittee of Economy of the Chinese People's Political Consultative Conference, former Minister of Industry and Information Technology of China, President of the China Federation of Industrial Economics;

Mr. Li Zhaoxing, President of the China Public Diplomacy Association, former Foreign Minister of China;

Mr. Jin Liqun, President of the Asian Infrastructure Investment Bank, former Vice Minister of Finance of China;

Mr. Yu Hongjun, Vice President of the Chinese People's Association for Peace and Disarmament, former Vice Minister of the International Department of the Central Committee of the CPC;

Mr. Lu Yaohua, Executive Vice President of the China Federation of Industrial Economics;

Mr. Ren Dequan, Honorary Director of the Clinical Pharmacology Branch of the China Association of Chinese Medicine, former Deputy Director of the China Food and Drug Administration;

Mr. Wang Jingsheng, Counsellor of the State Council;

Mr. Sun Weijia, Director of the Second Department of the Counsellors' Office of the State Council of China;

Ms. Wang Xiaopin, Director of the Department of International Cooperation (Hong Kong, Macao and Taiwan Affairs Office), the National Administration of Traditional Chinese Medicine;

Mr. Zhu Huayou, Deputy Secretary-General and Director of the Research Office of the People's Government of Hainan Province;

Mr. Xu Qingfeng, Deputy Director of the Health Commission of Guangdong Province, and Director of the Traditional Chinese Medicine Bureau of Guangdong Province;

Mr. Liu Qingsheng, Member of the Standing Committee of the Shenzhen Municipal Committee of the CPC, and Executive Vice Mayor of Shenzhen;

Mr. Zou Guang, Member of the Standing Committee of the Shanwei Municipal Committee of the CPC, and Executive Vice Mayor of Shanwei.

Experts and think tanks, entrepreneurs and friends of media organizations who have come from countries and regions along the Belt and Road are also attending this Forum.

Let's welcome these leaders and guests with a round of applause!

Now, please welcome Mr. Liu Qingsheng, Member of the Standing Committee of the Shenzhen Municipal Committee of the CPC, and Executive Vice Mayor of Shenzhen, to deliver a speech and announce the opening of this conference.

Liu Qingsheng: Distinguished Mr. Li Yizhong, Mr. Li Zhaoxing, Dear Guests, Ladies and Gentlemen, Dear Friends, Good morning! In this beautiful season, we have gathered in Shenzhen to hold the International Cooperation Forum for Cities and Industries under the Belt and Road Initiative for the purpose of carrying out extensive consultations on innovation and cooperation. Entrusted by Secretary Wang Weizhong of the CPC Shenzhen Municipal Committee and Mayor Chen Rugui, on behalf of the CPC Shenzhen Municipal Committee and the People's Government of Shenzhen, I would like to extend a very warm welcome and heartfelt thanks to our distinguished guests.

In the world today, peace and development are the main themes of the present era, and opening-up and cooperation are the trend of the times. President Xi Jinping proposed the vision of "promoting the building of a community with a shared future for humanity", which points out the direction for creating a bright future for mankind and holds high the banner for China to lead the trend of the times and the progress of civilizations. Against this background, we insist on the close integration of building a community with a shared future for humanity with the construction of the Belt and Road, we insist also on creating a new platform for international cooperation, forming new drivers of common development, upholding the Silk Road spirit of peace and cooperation, openness and inclusiveness, mutual learning and mutual benefit and opening a new window of opportunity for the open cooperation of countries along the Belt and Road.

Shenzhen is the first special economic zone and an important window for China's reform and opening-up. It is the reform and opening-up that has given life, prosperity and strength to Shenzhen. In the past year, in a severe and complicated external environment, Shenzhen worked hard to achieve higher-quality, more effective and more sustainable economic and social development under the guidance of Xi Jinping Thonght on Socialism with Chinese Characteristics for a New Era. According to estimates, in 2017, the city had a GDP of 2.2 trillion yuan and a per capita GDP of 180,000 yuan, which continued to rank among the top cities in the country. The total value of imports and exports was 2.8 trillion yuan and that value has ranked first in China for 25 consecutive years. The city had seven Global 500 companies after two more entered the ranking. It further optimized its industrial structure, continuously strengthened the advantages of innovative development and accelerated its opening-up in an all-round manner.

Shenzhen has historically been one of the important nodes of the Maritime Silk Road. After more than 30 years of reform and development, it has increasingly closer economic and trade relations, scientific and technological cooperation, and cultural exchanges with countries and regions around the world.

In 2017, 41 countries and regions along the Belt and Road invested in Shenzhen and started 302 new enterprises, which had thus increased by 39.8%. The China Railway Express from Shenzhen to Münster and Duisburg opened with 205 container freight liners. Shenzhen also held cultural events such as the Belt and Road Cultural Development Forum and the Belt and Road International Music Festival. Together with countries and regions along the Belt and Road, Shenzhen is willing to adhere to the principles of openness, cooperation and a win-win situation for the future and to jointly construct the Belt and Road to be the road to peace, the road to prosperity, the road to innovation, the road to openness, and the road to civilization.

Outstanding representatives from countries and regions along the Belt and Road have come to attend this Forum for the purposes of benefiting from mutual discussions, enhancing friendship and increasing cooperation. This will blossom and bear fruit in Shenzhen first. Shenzhen will also contribute more wisdom and strength to promoting the construction of the Belt and Road and to building a community with a shared future for mankind. In conclusion, I wish our dear guests and friends good health, happiness in 2018, and I also wish the Forum true success! Thank you!

Moderator-Xiong Meng: Mr. Liu Qingsheng, thank you for your warm speech.

Next, let's welcome Mr. Lu Yaohua, Executive Vice President of the China Federation of Industrial Economics.

Lu Yaohua: Distinguished Mayor Liu Qingsheng, Minister Li Zhaoxing, Ladies and Gentlemen, Dear Guests and Friends, it is such a pleasure to have you with us here in beautiful Shenzhen to discuss cooperation and development under the Belt and Road Initiative. I wish to extend, on behalf of the China Federation of

Industrial Economics and our President Li Yizhong, a very warm welcome and sincere appreciation to all of you, dear guests from home and abroad.

This Forum is being held when the spirit of the 19th CPC National Congress has been implemented throughout the country. It is of important practical significance to focus on international cooperation of cities and industries under the Belt and Road Initiative and have discussions centering on the theme of "City Partnership 'Industrial Connection' Think Tank Link".

Cities and industries are two important carriers to promote the construction of the Belt and Road. For one thing, the Belt and Road Initiative provides golden opportunities for cities along the route to redefine their functions and developmental goals. In the new landscape of opening-up, the system of factors and industrial systems of some node and hub cities will face new changes and restructuring. We should probe into our respective comparative advantages, strengthen cooperation among cities, explore new drivers of economic growth and strive to create new developmental opportunities in the process of globalization.

For another thing, the construction of the Belt and Road also gives renewed vitality to the industrial sector of the countries along the route. The international cooperation of the Belt and Road will break new ground by tapping into comparative advantages of different countries, enhancing technological innovation, achieving the optimal allocation of resources, in particular, strengthening cooperation in emerging industries such as new generation information technology, biology, new energy and new materials, and establishing a mechanism of cooperation for entrepreneurship and investment.

Cities and industries are inseparable from each other. Shenzhen, a city on the frontier of reform and opening-up and a young first-tier city, is actively participating in the construction of the Belt and Road and strives to play the role of demonstration and guidance as a node city. The China Federation of Industrial Economics is committed to facilitating the concerted development of industries along the Belt and Road. This Forum is held by the China Federation of Industrial Economics and the government of Shenzhen for our guests to have discussions, exchange ideas, reach consensus and deepen their cooperation, contribute wisdom and strength for the international cooperation of cities and industries under the Belt and Road Initiative as well as to provide good suggestions for global cooperation, innovation, development and progress, and for building of a community with a shared future for mankind. Thank you!

Moderator-Xiong Meng: Now, please welcome Mr. Sun Weijia, Director of the Second Department of the Counsellors' Office of the State Council of China, to deliver a speech.

Sun Weijia: Distinguished President Li Yizhong, President Li Zhaoxing, Dear Guests, Ladies and Gentlemen, Good Morning! I feel truly honored to attend this forum. First of all, on behalf of the Counsellors' Office of the State Council of China, I wish to extend our warm congratulations to this forum.

In today's world, governments of all countries are faced with unprecedented complex problems and severe challenges in the process of national and global governance. In order to effectively cope with challenges, the government attaches great importance to the wisdom of experts and researchers, listens to the voice of the masses, and constantly improves the scientific and democratic level of decision-making. Thus, think tanks play an increasingly prominent role and have already become an indispensable source of wisdom in global governance.

The Belt and Road Initiative was proposed more than four years ago. From concept to action and from vision to reality, it has become the most popular international public goods to date. It creates a platform for international cooperation with the integration of developmental strategies, mutual complementarity, connectivity, inclusiveness, openness and development, and provides the Chinese approach to cope with the economic problems faced by the contemporary world.

The Belt and Road Initiative belongs to China, and also to the world. The implementation of the Belt and Road Initiative is inseparable from the cooperation of cities and industries along the route. This creates conditions for think tanks to show their wisdom and provides opportunities for exchanges and cooperation among think tanks. In a nutshell, the Belt and Road Initiative will focus on four goals:

First, developmental strategies and policies of the countries should be integrated to achieve mutual complementarity and concerted development and to solve the problems of the unbalanced development of the countries and fragmented international cooperation.

Second, by focusing on infrastructure, the bottleneck of development, we should tap the potential of economic growth from the supply side, promote the radiation effects of cross-border connectivity and achieve the development of all countries in concert.

Third, financial cooperation should be strengthened to build a support system for the sustained economic growth of the world, and to make the regional industrial layout perfect.

Forth, a virtuous cycle of economic cooperation and cultural integration should be formed and a peaceful environment for development should be created by deepening the friendly exchanges of the people in all countries.

In the process of attaining the above goals, exchanges and cooperation among think tanks of different countries can play positive and important constructive roles at least in the following four areas.

First, to interpret the Chinese policies and approach, carry out the scientific research and assessment of the Belt and Road Initiative with professional attitudes and a global perspective, provide solid theoretical support and methodological underpinnings for decision-making consultation on the Belt and Road Initiative, and reach a broad academic consensus, policy consensus, and international consensus to guide the scientific development.

Second, to promote strategic communication, integrate strategies, play the supporting and guiding role of think tanks, deepen the path-opening research of the Belt and Road Initiative, which should be jointly built through consultation to meet the interests of all, clearly understand the developmental conditions, core interests and strategic arrangements of countries along the Belt and Road, and in terms of integrating planning, policies and mechanisms, lay stress on policy suggestions that are conducive to widespread and in-depth cooperation.

Third, to intensify practical cooperation. Not only does the Belt and Road

Initiative require insights, but also project selection and feasibility need profound studies and suggestions from the think tanks. In this regard, think tanks of all countries can reach consensuses on key areas and targets for the implementation of the Belt and Road Initiative, provide intellectual support in further promoting connectivity, capacity cooperation and cultural exchanges, implement more cooperated projects and contribute bits of wisdom to regional economic growth and to the well-being of the people of all countries.

Fourth, to advance cultural exchanges and cooperation. The exchange and mutual learning among civilizations along the ancient Silk Road are regarded as a valuable legacy, and connecting the hearts of the people should be an integral part of the Belt and Road international cooperation. Think tanks in countries along the Belt and Road should jointly promote extensive people-to-people exchanges at all levels covering education, science, technology, culture, health, tourism and sports, and build more platforms for and channels for cooperation. As the bridges of exchanges between people and governments, think tanks should strive to use specialized means of communication, narrow the gap among the peoples of different countries in cognition of the Belt and Road Initiative, create an environment for positive public opinion for the construction of the Belt and Road and enhance the understanding and recognition of the Belt and Road Initiative by people in countries along the route so that they can truly benefit from it.

The Counsellors' Office is a body directly under the State Council of China with the main functions of participating in the administration and discussion of state affairs, making recommendations, consulting on state affairs, and undertaking democratic supervision. Counsellors are directly appointed by the Premier of the State Council, including well-known experts, researchers and officials in the economic and social spheres. The opinions and suggestions of the Counsellors can be directly sent to the desk of the leading comrades of the State Council. This is vividly compared to a "through train". It is an important function of the Counsellors' Office of the State Council to have public diplomacy, broaden international horizons and deepen exchanges and cooperation with domestic and foreign governments, consulting agencies and think tanks. Taking the opportunity of holding this Forum, we hope to deepen cooperation with the think tanks, experts and researchers attending it and to make the international cooperation of cities and industries under the Belt and Road Initiative more fruitful.

To conclude, I wish this forum complete success. Thank you.

Moderator-Xiong Meng：Thank you, Mr. Sun Weijia! Ladies and Gentlemen, the opening speeches have come to an end. Next, our guests will deliver keynote speeches. Please welcome Mr. Zhu Huayou, Deputy Secretary-General and Director of the Research Office of the People's Government of Hainan Province, to preside over the meeting.

Keynote Speech: Create a New Platform for International Cooperation, Promote Economic and Cultural Cooperation, and Form a New Type of City Partnership

Moderator-Zhu Huayou: Mr. Xiong, Thank you! Distinguished Leaders, Dear Guests, I was invited to the meeting as a representative of Hainan, a neighbor of Shenzhen. This year marks the 40th anniversary of Reform and Opening-up, the 38th anniversary of the Shenzhen Special Economic Zone, and the 30th anniversary of the Hainan Special Economic Zone. It is very important to hold this forum at this moment. Peace and development are the themes of the times, and exchanges and cooperation are the foundation of development. Today, the China Federation of Industrial Economics and the Development Research Center of the Shenzhen Municipal People's Government jointly host the International Cooperation Forum for Cities and Industries under the Belt and Road Initiative and welcome over 90 well-known political figures and researchers from more than 20 countries and regions. The theme is "City Partnership 'Industrial Connection' Think Tank Link". Eight speakers have been invited to deliver keynote speeches. They are: Mr. Li Yizhong, Mr. Stjepan Mesić, Mr. Li Zhaoxing, Mr. Jin Liqun, Mr. Yu Hongjun, Mr. Dušan Bella, Mr. Wang Jingsheng, and Mr. Li Huiwu. They will share insights with us on economic and trade cooperation and innovation, and on building of a new type of city partnership.

First of all, let's welcome Mr. Li Yizhong, Deputy Director of the Subcommittee of Economy of the Chinese People's Political Consultative Conference, President of the China Federation of Industrial Economics and former Minister of Industry and Information Technology of China.

Li Yizhong: Distinguished Minister Li Zhaoxing, Dear Leaders, Experts, Entrepreneurs, Friends, to congratulate the successful holding of this Forum in Shenzhen, I was asked to deliver a speech. I have prepared two questions to share with you. First, what is the role of industry and manufacturing in the Belt and Road Initiative? Second, what is the relationship between the Guangdong-Hong Kong-Macao Greater Bay Area and manufacturing in the Pearl River Delta?

First, President Xi Jinping called on us to construct the Belt and Road to be a road of peace, prosperity, openness and civilized conduct. How can industry and manufacturing play a role in this construction? According to our experience over the past few years, we must intensify the practical cooperation in industries driven by projects. I have made a summary in five areas.

1. Transportation, telecommunications and the construction of pipeline infrastructures. Connectivity is the prerequisite for the development of economic and trade relations and cultural exchanges. So far, we have opened hundreds of highway transportation routes with 15 countries along the Belt and Road and 51 freight trains via the China Railway Express to Europe, we have signed shipping agreements with 36 countries, participated in the construction, management and operation of more than 20 ports and we have direct flights of civil aviation aircraft with 43 countries. Then, the sea, land and air jointly constitute a three-dimensional large traffic corridor. In particular, the construction of railways has achieved remarkable results, such as the Jakarta-Bandung High-Speed Railway in Indonesia, and the railway line linking China with Laos already open to traffic. Moreover, the high-speed railway projects in Russia, Thailand, Malaysia, Hungary, Kyrgyzstan, etc. are in their preliminary preparations.

An information network has been jointly built by us and neighboring ASEAN countries. I read a news report a few days ago, which said that Nepal had used the fiber optic cable and communication network constructed by us. China Mobile, Huawei, and ZTE have established more than twenty 4G networks overseas. Oil and gas pipelines linking China with Kazakhstan, Russia and Myanmar have been constructed. In the winter, natural gas has been in short supply, and the project connecting the gas field near the Russian Arctic Ocean to China is under construction. The construction of infrastructure and the efficiency of China's engineering operations, to put it bluntly, are advanced internationally and well acknowledged throughout the world.

2. Investment in industrial projects and the promotion of cooperation in industries. Our third-generation nuclear power technology was applied in the United Kingdom and Argentina. The China National Nuclear Corporation and Argentina cooperated on building two nuclear power plants. CRRC Corporation Limited established locomotive manufacturing bases in Chicago, Boston and Los Angeles in the United States of America instead of exporting locomotives only. In

recent years, our investments overseas have expanded from individual projects to industrial parks. Some of China's rapidly growing enterprises have begun to make mergers and acquisitions. For example, after acquiring shares of Volvo and acquiring shares of Ford in 2010, Geely developed well in these years. Recently, Haier acquired the home appliance business of GE, Hisense acquired Toshiba Visual Solutions Corporation and in particular, the China National Chemical Corporation acquired Swiss Syngenta AG, the world's largest producer of agrochemicals and seeds. By mergers and acquisitions, we have improved industrial development. Investment is a senior form of economic and trade cooperation. Our direct foreign investment should ensure advanced and reliable technology, and we should help the host country with marketing and we should localize our employees. We must be alert to risks, such as social, legal and market risks.

3. Project contracting and labor cooperation. China has obvious advantages with outstanding equipment in projects for the construction of railways, highways and bridges. The China Railway Construction Corporation, the China Communications Construction Company, the China Road and Bridge Corporation and the China State Construction Engineering Corporation have a good reputation. The first phase of Colombo Port in Sri Lanka has been completed. The engineering machinery, represented by Sany Heavy Industry, Xuzhou Construction Machinery Company and Zoomlion, have proved their quality, performance and brand overseas during the construction of the project. Long-lasting quality always comes first in the construction of our projects. But as far as I know, they focus more on the protection of the ecological environment in host countries.

4. Manufacturing provides strong support for foreign trade. China is the largest exporter in the world. Industrial products account for 95% of the exports, and machinery, equipment and electronic products occupy 57%. Two billion mobile phones are produced in China, two-thirds are for exportation and 74% are smartphones. OPPO and Vivo are well-known brands globally. As our traditional export products, infused with advanced technology and modern culture, the textile products are high-end and fashionable. Our food industry and food deep

processing are green and safe. China is the second largest importer in the world. Industrial products account for 72% of the total imports, mostly being parts, components and key raw materials that cannot be made domestically. We also import iron ore and petroleum, which are important raw materials and energy resources for manufacturing. We win the market by exporting high-quality products, but trade protectionism is a big threat. We should safeguard our legitimate rights and interests.

5. Bringing our advantages into full play and promoting cooperation in resources. For example, China Minmetals Corporation ran iron mines in Australia and the China Nonferrous Metal Mining Group developed copper mines in Zambia. Just now, Mr. Yan told me that the Congo had more substantial reserves of copper and nickel mines. China National Offshore Oil Corporation's acquisition of the Canadian Nexen increased its proven crude oil reserves by 30%. China National Petroleum Corporation produced one-third of oil equivalents overseas and helped Saudi Arabia to construct a 20 million-ton oil refinery. The cooperation on resources must be far-sighted and mutual beneficial and it must drive the economic development of the host country forward.

This is a brief summary of mine. By giving these examples, I intend to tell that industry and manufacturing are important for practical industrial cooperation.

Second, the Guangdong-Hong Kong-Macao Greater Bay Area is an important base for the Maritime Silk Road and manufacturing is the economic mainstay of the Pearl River Delta. First of all, let's take a look at the world's famous bay areas, all of which have developed industry at the commanding heights of the world. There are large multinational companies in New York Bay, where the information industry, electronics, biopharmaceutics, high-end equipment manufacturing, nano-materials, and optical manufacturing are greatly developed. The San Francisco Bay area is at the forefront of innovation with high-tech companies, leading aerospace and electronics manufacturing. Japan's Tokyo-Yokohama Industrial Zone in Tokyo Bay, with developed steel, shipbuilding, electronics, and petrochemical industries, is the largest manufacturing center of Japan. For these well-known bay areas, industry and manufacturing lay the economic foundation and create conditions for the development of manufacturing. In turn, developed manufacturing has built the economic pillars of these greater bay areas.

In the Guangdong-Hong Kong-Macao Greater Bay Area ("the Greater Bay Area"), the Pearl River Delta has unique industrial advantages. The Greater Bay Area is an important base for the Maritime Silk Road. Hong Kong is a prestigious financial, shipping and commercial center. Macao is a famous tourist and leisure destination. The manufacturing sector has moved out of Hong Kong. As is known to us, it is less than 1% of Hong Kong's GDP. However, the Pearl River Delta is blessed with powerful manufacturing activities. Guangdong's GDP accounts for one-ninth of the total GDP of China, and its industrial added value is one-eighth of the country's.

Manufacturing activities in the Pearl River Delta are mainly concentrated in the nine cities of the Greater Bay Area. There is a table below. I will analyze it for you.

Data of Shenzhen's Main Manufacturing Indicators from January to October 2017

Projects	GDP Growth (%)	Increase in industrial added value (%)	Share of industry in GDP (%)	High-tech industry accounts for industrial added value (%)	The added value rate of industrial enterprises is regulated (%)	According to regulations, the main profit margin of industrial enterprises is regulated (%)	Increase in total import and export volume (%)	Dependence on foreign trade (%)	Increase in utilization of foreign capital (%)	Number of valid invention patents owned by 10,000 people in 2016 (pieces)
Shenzhen	8.8	9.4	36.3	69.2	27.8	6.4	6.8	143.2	18.4	80.8
The whole country	6.9	6.7	about 33.1	12.5	about 22	6.24	16.6	34.2	-2.7	8

From January to October 2017, the main manufacturing indicators of Shenzhen were clearly ahead of the national average. The data for the whole year have not been released yet. According to the data of these ten months, from left to right, the growth of the GDP and the increase in industrial added value took the lead in the country with obvious advantages. Last year, many provinces and cities reversed the situation of previous years. In Shenzhen, the proportion of industrial output to GDP was higher than that of the whole country, and industrial enterprises above the designated size performed better than those in other parts of China. In particular, the average national industrial added value rate was 21%, 22%, but that of Shenzhen was 27%, 28%, the highest level in the country.

The average national increase in imports and exports was unexpected, but the situation in Shenzhen remained stable. The key lies in the dependence on foreign trade, which is 143.2% in Shenzhen but 34.2% for the national average. What does this mean? These two figures are not comparable. This indicator is often used to demonstrate the export-oriented degree of the country and each region. The figure is 143.2% in Shenzhen, ranking first in China. As of October, 2017, the utilization of foreign capital was 18.4% in Shenzhen but negative for the national average in October, and turning to positive in November. The last figure is the number of invention patents per 10,000 people. The national average is 8, but that in Shenzhen is 80.8, about 10 times the national average. The value added of high-tech industries account for 12.5% of the national industrial added value, but 69.2% in Shenzhen. To achieve the goal of constructing an international manufacturing center, Shenzhen should pay attention to the key role of effective investment.

After boasting the strengths, I will point out some of Shenzhen's shortcomings. Last year I said the same words. Look at the following table.

Main Indicators of Shenzhen's Investment in Recent Two Years

Projects		Ratio of fixed asset investment to GDP (%)	Investment growth (%)	Industrial investment accounts for the total investment (%)	Increase in industrial investment (%)	Real estate investment accounts for the total investment (%)	Real estate investment growth (%)	Bank loan-to-deposit ratio (%)
Shenzhen	2016	20.9	23.6	17	17.1	51.4	26	62.9
	January to October, 2017	23.9	28.4	17.3	40	43.1	25.8	55
The whole country	2016	80.2	7.9	38.2	3.6	22.7	6.8	72.1
	January to October, 2017	about 79	7.2	36.8	3.1	17.5	7.5	73.5

Shenzhen intends to initially shape a world-class industrial system with active innovation, an optimum structure, a leading scale, perfect facilities and developed service sectors in 2025. The vision is very inspiring: to become the domestic pacemaker in smart manufacturing, green manufacturing and high-end manufacturing. Shenzhen drives the economy of the Pearl River Delta forward, and the manufacturing in the Pearl River Delta lays the economic cornerstone for the Guangdong-Hong Kong-Macao Greater Bay Area. Hong Kong and Macao basically have no manufacturing, which is located in the Pearl River Delta. It is unimaginable that a bay area has no manufacturing, so the Pearl River Delta is an important fulcrum of the Belt and Road. Effective investment is a key measure to stimulating economic development and social progress. Investment cannot be excessive, and the economy cannot be over-reliant on investment. Effective investment is very important, as discussed in the Report to the 19th CPC National Congress.

Shenzhen has devoted unremitting efforts in this regard. Our analysis of the situation should also make problems visible, foster strengths and avoid weaknesses. Here, I cite the situations of Shenzhen and the whole country in 2016 and from January to October in 2017. The fixed assets investment had better use the figure for the whole year because often the amount of fixed assets investment in the fourth quarter is relatively large, so I provide two groups of figures. For the ratio of fixed assets investment to the GDP, Shenzhen's investment intensity was much lower than the national average, being 80.2% nationwide and about 20% in Shenzhen. This is too low, the lowest among coastal cities. The total investment in Shenzhen has increased, which is a good sign. The national average investment growth rate was 7.9% in 2016, and 7.2% from January to October in 2017, but that of Shenzhen was 23.6% in 2016, and it was 28.2% from January to October in 2017. There is still a structural problem because adjustment is not easy. Industrial investment accounts for a relatively low proportion of the total investment, only about 17%. What is the reason for this? This is not the case in the whole country. Shenzhen has less industrial investment. This is a structural problem. However, the industrial investment has grown faster, as it was 17.1% in 2016, but 40% from January to October in 2017. Shenzhen has recognized this problem.

Of course, the latter two indicators are not very good. The proportion of real estate to the total investment is about half because the money goes to the real estate industry. The growth rate of real estate investments is not too low, indicating that the structure is adjusting, but the adjustment is still not very effective.

The national average loan-to-deposit ratio is 73.5%, which is reasonable. But this ratio is 55% in Shenzhen, less than the national average. The money sleeps in banks. However, if you have more money, you have greater potential. It is recommended that Shenzhen should estimate the investment demand for future development, moderately increase investments, adjust the structure, and in particular, strengthen the construction of an internationally-renowned manufacturing city.

Shenzhen is expected to make greater contributions to the construction of the Guangdong-Hong Kong-Macao Greater Bay Area, as well as the construction of the Belt and Road. Thank you.

Moderator-Zhu Huayou: Our Minister Li once said that he must tell the truth even after retirement. Thank you, Mr. Li, you told us many truths and gave us detailed data on the role played by industry and manufacturing in the Belt and Road and the Greater Bay Area. You also pointed out problems to be solved in the development of Shenzhen, which was inspirational. Thank you, Minister Li, for your wonderful speech.

Our conference also invites our friend from afar, who is Stjepan Mesić, the General Counsel of the Croatian Chamber of Commerce and the Special Representative of Zagreb City. He attaches great importance to the development of relations and is committed to promoting exchanges and cooperation with China. Welcome Mr. Stjepan Mesić.

Stjepan Mesić: Ladies and Gentlemen, Distinguished Guests! First of all, I wish to express my sincere greetings to you all and my thanks to the organizer's kind invitation. From my point of view, peace is the highest value of international relations. The Belt and Road Initiative put forward by Chinese President Xi Jinping aims to promote the peace and economic development of all countries. Therefore, I couldn't agree with this initiative more after it was proposed. In my opinion, the Belt and Road Initiative is essentially guiding Europe, Asia and Africa to achieve economic coexistence, safeguard peace and develop cooperation.

As China's global initiative for the 21st century, the Belt and Road Initiative itself adheres to the traditional principles of Chinese diplomacy, that is, long-term goals, gradual implementation and use of economic development as a means to build a more stable and multi-polar world. The Belt and Road Initiative connects the three continents with a focus on developing new economic capabilities in countries along the future sea and land economic corridor. Today, for us, the most important task is to implement this initiative. In other words, due to the influx of refugees from the Middle East, North Africa and Ukraine into Europe, the stability of international politics and economy has deteriorated severely. This situation is leading to a destructive trend and will threaten the relationship between states by the power of force, national chauvinism and economic protectionism. Therefore, we must build a new and stable foundation and economic and financial structure in the world to control the situation. I believe that we should always pay attention to and lay stress on the economic and non-economic value of the Belt and Road Initiative. This is both the foothold of the initiative and an important direction for us in maintaining world stability.

In 2011, I was invited to Yangzhou to cut the ribbon on the opening ceremony of the Marco Polo Memorial Hall. In the 13th century, in Venice, Marco Polo published his notes on his travels in Central Asia and China and pointed out that the notes could not even describe half of what he saw and heard.

Marco Polo connected Europe with China. Regardless of China-EU diplomacy or China- Croatia diplomacy, Marco Polo is an indispensable topic. At the mention of Marco Polo, he does not only belong to Croatia, but he is a traveler of the world. Of course, our Chinese friends also know the controversy over whether Marco Polo is Croatian or Italian. What makes me happy is that you are patient enough to hear the arguments of both sides. Referring to Marco Polo, I must underline the fact that the new Silk Road should not simply focus on economy and trade while ignoring exchanges and cooperation in history, culture, science and technology, international students and tourism.

Today's conference aims precisely at enhancing our mutual understanding. Of course, without the mutual understanding of the people, without understanding the current relationship, and without respecting cultural differences, the values of peace, friendship and stability will not be realized, trade cannot be developed, and new roads, ports, railways and logistics centers cannot be built. This is my view on the Belt and Road. Without China's policy of building a community with a shared future for humanity, the Belt and Road Initiative would also be impossible. The initiative is an important part of the strategy of economic development of China, Europe and Asia.

Asia has already become a region that has a decisive influence on the world's economy. Just as what Europe was like in history, from the ancient Silk Road 2,000 years ago to the European Industrial Revolution and colonization, many features can be said to be the precursor of globalization today. Economic globalization has brought many advantages to China. While China is transforming from a country with a large population to a big power with tremendous human resources while achieving balanced economic development and protecting the environment, the world is showing great surprise. China has made great progress through the efforts of all of its people, its reform and its economic opening-up.

Today, the world's economy is interdependent. It does not just rely on the West. The process of economic integration that we are witnessing now is multi-faceted, including intra-Europe, trans-Atlantic, trans-Pacific, Europe and China. This means that Central European countries can participate in the process of economic integration in different directions at the same time. China calls the new policy the "16 + 1" cooperation between China and countries in Central and Eastern Europe. China and these countries are active under the "16 + 1" mechanism because the stability of the European economy can be enhanced by increasing Chinese investment and preferential loans.

The economic crisis of countries in Eastern and Southern Europe can be alleviated with the development of relations with China. When I was in Beijing in 2013, I appealed to Brussels for support in the development of relations with China by 16 Central and Eastern European countries, just as they supported German-Chinese and British-Chinese relations. The reason is that the goal of developing these relationships is the same, that is, economic development. In particular, 16 countries in Central and Eastern Europe have a total population of 123 million. In the field of trade and investment, compared with China's relations with developed EU member states, there is still a big difference in China's relations with Central and Eastern Europe. For my part, the results achieved under the "16 + 1" mechanisms are particularly important because I believe this mechanism is a realistic pillar for achieving the goals of the Belt and Road.

China's leaders have incorporated the relationship between China and Southern and Eastern Europe into the broader foreign policy of the Belt and Road. The ports, railways and highways of the Belt and Road will also cross Central and Eastern European countries and connect with Asia. China's new foreign policy towards Central and Eastern European countries has promoted the development of political relations. More high-level exchanges have led to the growth of investment, trade and new infrastructure projects under the mechanism of cooperation and it has promoted cooperation on education and tourism. China supports financial cooperation and facilitates local cross-border trade, thus making the RMB an alternative for the US dollar.

Finally, I want to emphasize that for the mutual understanding of relations of Central and Eastern European countries, we should jointly maintain and continue to develop this trend, and support and implement all of the facilities from Warsaw to Bucharest, Belgrade to Zagreb. These measures are also important factors for realizing the Belt and Road Initiative. Therefore, the Belt and Road not only has enormous economic benefits, but it also brings non-economic benefits of consolidating peace and cooperation on the three continents. Thank you for your attention.

Moderator-Zhu Huayou：Thank you for the heart-warming speech, Mr. Stjepan Mesić. You are our dear international friend who fully recognized the economic and non-economic value of the Belt and Road. You laid stress on its important role in the prosperity and stability of the world, with particular emphasis on not only economic and trade cooperation, but also cooperation in the fields of culture, science and technology, education, etc. Thank you, Mr. Stjepan Mesić. Special thanks also goes to Marco Polo as a friendly messenger who had been to my hometown, Yangzhou.

Now, please welcome Mr. Li Zhaoxing, President of the China Public Diplomacy Association and former Foreign Minister of China.

Li Zhaoxing：Dear Friends, my colleague and comrade Li Yizhong has indicated exactly what I want to say.

Before retirement, I was invited to Croatia and met with Mr. Stjepan Mesić. I want to thank both of these men and congratulate them on the success of their speeches. I have been lucky recently and feel that I have become younger because I have seen the representatives of the two youngest countries in the world during these months, the leaders of the youngest large company and the youngest modern city. The two countries include the Slovak Republic, newly born after the dramatic changes in the Soviet Union and Eastern Europe. Today, Ambassador Dušan Bella is also attending this meeting. Moreover, Croatia, represented by the former leader Stjepan Mesić, is also a young country. The internationally-renowned young large company I mentioned is the Asian Infrastructure Investment Bank founded not long ago closely connected with the Belt and Road Initiative. Its young president, my old friend Jin Liqun is also here. I feel particularly happy. Two months ago, I met the youngest President of France, only 39 years old. Not long ago, he successfully visited China. Shenzhen, a particularly famous city in our country, is one year younger than the new French President, just 38 years old. I have worked in Guangdong Province for more than three years. I regard Guangdong Province as my second hometown. It is a real blessing that we are attending this forum on the 38th anniversary of Shenzhen.

Now I can only share my personal experience and a story from my diplomatic career of more than half a century.

First, there is only one motherland. Every one of us has a mother; likewise, we only have one motherland. Recently, I find that no matter how far you have gone, for your motherland, you are still a child who has not grown up. Compared with knowledge, you are still a pupil who cannot graduate. I always remember to love my motherland and love my hometown. I was in the United States of America for six years and visited all 50 states. What impressed me most was that I was warmly welcomed in two states, particularly enthusiastic. I was a little bit flattered. I felt like a king, like a hero. Later, I learned that those people did not remember my name. They welcomed me because of my hometown, because of my motherland.

At that time, I was visiting Montana, a state where industry is less developed, but agriculture is very developed. They were lavish with their praises so that I felt very strange. I almost forgot who I was. Later, I learned that the Governor and senators had checked my information and found that I am a Chinese man who grew up in a suburb of Qingdao, Shandong Province, China. They said that they were especially grateful to China, thanked my hometown because if China and the breweries in my hometown had not imported their barley and barley malt, one of the main export products of their state, the common people there could not have lived a well-off life. That's why they welcomed me warmly. It was not because of myself, but because my motherland had contributed to the improvement of people's lives and economic development in that state. On a visit to South Carolina, the Governor sent a plane to pick up my wife and me. Later he told me that he knew I was from Qingdao, Shandong Province, China, and Haier had invested a lot in their state. More than a decade ago, the US immigration policy required a one-time investment of 500,000 US dollars to solve the employment of more than 12 citizens in the United States of America. That company invested more than 500,000 US dollars and employed more than 200 American workers at a time. The Governor felt extremely grateful. We should thank our motherland and rely on our motherland as well.

There is also a little story. I was invited to Liberia for an official visit. After the talks, the female President said that originally it was not convenient for her to walk. After the treatment by the Chinese medical team, especially the traditional Chinese medicine, acupuncture and massage, she could not only walk as fast as the wind, but also play table tennis well. She wanted to thank China and the Chinese people, for both their friendship and the mutual benefit in education as well as for having helped her personally. So, I must thank our motherland. I am ordinary, but my experience has told me that our motherland is our roots. The motherland is the source of our strength. We must participate in the construction of the Belt and Road with the love of our motherland.

Second, always remember that the people are those on whom our livelihood depends. When I think of the people, I will think of three words, four words, five words and six words:

Three words, "people are crucial". My fellow townsman, Mencius, more than two thousand years ago, told us that people are crucial.

Four words, "long live the people".

Five words, "to serve the people wholeheartedly". This will definitely give us confidence and determination to build the Belt and Road.

Six words, "people are the center of work". Xi Jinping has repeatedly emphasized that our work should be centered on the people.

These three, four, five and six words are the mottos and wind vanes of my work and life. Let's study together and work hard with the people at the center, and participate in the construction of the Belt and Road.

Third, always follow the words of the Party. Remember well the words of General Secretary of the Communist Party of China (CPC) Central Committee Xi Jinping. The sentence he always spoke, when receiving foreign and Chinese writers at the 18th CPC National Congress, was that: The people yearn for a better life, and that is the goal we strive for.

I wrote poetry to praise Shenzhen 20 years ago. Shenzhen is a young pioneer of China's reform and opening-up. The fast growth and development of Shenzhen are greatly indebted to the Communist Party of China. We must learn the Xi Jinping Thought on Socialism with Chinese Characteristics for a New Era.

Fourth, unity is power. I studied Chinese history and world history, so we must also remember Lenin's words "Forgetting history means betrayal". The lessons of history must be valued when we are advancing so that we can become forward-looking and we cannot forget history. We must strengthen our unity firmly, we must hold together for warmth, and unity is power. During the construction of the Belt and Road, the people of the countries along the Belt and Road should be closely united. We can learn from each other, strive for cooperation and a win-win situation, and build a community with a shared future for mankind.

I was fortunate to attend the Conference on Interaction and Confidence Building Measures in Asia in 2014. Chinese President Xi Jinping delivered an important speech, he stressed that "China is firmly committed to the path of peaceful development and a win-win strategy of opening up".

Yesterday I visited two big companies. I think they have a lot of things worth learning. I will recommend them to all the entrepreneurs I meet. One is Tencent and the other is Hytera. They have done numerous good deeds. First of all, for targeted poverty alleviation, they have cooperated with some less developed regions in the northwest and the southwest and have provided generous sponsorships, which are really interesting and worth learning from; and their innovation in smart and high-tech products is at the forefront of the country and even of the world. I think other companies and entrepreneurs should learn from them.

It is my pleasure to have had this opportunity of learning. I will take this opportunity to wish everyone happiness and delight. The Chinese New Year is coming soon. I wish you all a happy and successful new year. Thank you.

Moderator-Zhu Huayou: Thanks to Minister Li for his wonderful speech. Minister Li's speech without notes can be summarized in three aspects, two words. The first word is roots. Minister Li told us that our roots are the motherland and the people, serving the people and seeking benefits for the people. The second word is cooperation and win-win. He gave an example of playing table tennis to explain how to achieve exchanges and a win-win situation. We must stick together for warmth and strengthen our unity. We must learn from various civilizations and cultures and achieve cooperation and a win-win situation in this process. Thank you, Minister Li.

The next speaker is Mr. Jin Liqun.

Jin Liqun: Ladies and Gentlemen, I am very happy to attend this forum. Shenzhen is 38 years old this year. It is a year with a clear mind. Today is the first day of the third year of the Asian Infrastructure Investment Bank. Yesterday was our second anniversary. This bank is a new type of international multilateral development institution that reflects China's developmental philosophy and experience and sparkles the spirit of the Chinese era. The bank was initiated by the Chinese President Xi Jinping. He conducted negotiations with 57 countries in just two years and adopted the Charter and other important policy documents. During the preparatory stage, China, in the spirit of democratic consultation, united all countries in Asia and other regions to join the bank. China plays a leading role and receives wide recognition. The Chinese government honors its promises and becomes faithful to its word and firm in its purpose. It operates and guides this institution by international standards. The Chinese government exercises its powers as the largest shareholder through the board of directors. The constructive role played by China has been widely recognized and confirmed by the international community and reflects China's influence.

Asia is a very important region in our world, and the Asian Infrastructure Investment Bank is further committed to advancing sustainable projects and creating a better future for mankind. Today is the first day of our third anniversary. Tomorrow, we will be looking forward to new developments in the coming days.

In these two years, we have launched many projects including the investment of 4.8 billion US dollars and covering the construction of a lot of infrastructures. In 2018 and in the future, we will create more value. We will further cooperate with governments of countries and different organizations. We will invest in different projects to achieve sustainable development. The aim of our bank is to promote such sustainable development. We take this opportunity to provide better infrastructures and create a better life in cities, and we hope to realize a win-win situation around the world.

The Asian Infrastructure Investment Bank and the Belt and Road are two different initiatives. We have different missions, but we are interrelated. On the other hand, we have different missions, so we will further support projects regarding infrastructures in the countries along the Belt and Road. The Belt and Road Initiative and the Asian Infrastructure Investment Bank are two drivers that facilitate each other's tasks. We can also cooperate to further promote the economic development of different countries. We are very proud that such a bank was established and are also grateful to the Chinese government and other shareholders of the bank. I also want to thank our 48 partners. We are looking forward to closer cooperation with Shenzhen.

Moderator-Zhu Huayou: Thank Mr. Jin Liqun for your unique insights, which are refreshing to us. If this meeting discusses the principles, then the Asian Infrastructure Investment Bank promotes the development in practice. Thanks again, Mr. Jin Liqun. Now, please welcome Mr. Yu Hongjun, Vice President of the Chinese People's Association for Peace and Disarmament, former Vice Minister of the International Department of the Central Committee of the CPC.

Yu Hongjun: Your Excellency former President of Croatia, Mr. Stjepan Mesić, Distinguished Minister Li Yizhong and Minister Li Zhaoxing, Dear Leaders, Friends and Experts, Good Morning! I feel grateful for the organizers of this meeting, who invited me to attend the forum in Shenzhen. Nowadays, there is an intensive holding of forums on the Belt and Road, attracting many experts, researchers and very important people.

The Belt and Road Initiative, which reflects the state will, is the joint actions of the 1.3 billion Chinese people. It is of great and far-reaching significance. President Xi Jinping is an advocate of the Belt and Road Initiative and attaches great importance to it. In the report at the 19th CPC National Congress, he mentioned the Belt and Road Initiative. With respect to the major achievements in economic development after the 18th CPC National Congress, the Belt and Road Initiative, the coordinated development of the Beijing-Tianjin-Hebei region, and the development of the Yangtze River Economic Belt have all made notable progress. The Belt and Road is one of the three major developmental strategies. When talking about a new vision of development and a modernized economic system, and explaining the new philosophy of peaceful development and of the building of a community with a shared future for humanity, Xi Jinping said that "China adhered to the fundamental national Policy of Opening-up and pursued development with its doors open wide. China will actively promote international cooperation through the Belt and Road Initiative. In doing so, we hope to achieve policy, infrastructure, trade, financial, and people-to-people connectivity and thus build a new platform for international cooperation to create new drivers of shared development".

In the process of thinking, understanding and promoting, as I see it, we should follow this way of thinking that is easy to understand, grasp and recognize. We must be aware that the Belt and Road Initiative is a solemn commitment made to the world by Xi Jinping on behalf of the Communist Party of China, the Chinese government, and the Chinese people. It is the public goods we provide to the world, and the Chinese wisdom, Chinese approach and Chinese path we contribute against the background of the volatile global situation and anti-globalism. It is a global action led by China for coordinated development, mutually beneficial development, and win-win development.

The key point for advancing the construction of the Belt and Road is the principle of achieving shared growth through discussion and collaboration. We should neither be anxious for quick results and expect results overnight, nor compel other countries, but make progress while maintaining stability. We should not be ignorant of the feelings, interests and needs of our partners with good intentions. Achieving shared growth through discussion and collaboration should be the most basic guarantee for the continuous advancement of the Belt and Road.

The construction of the Belt and Road needs to achieve four breakthroughs, which requires us to break through ideological differences, break through the differences in social systems, break through the gaps in development and break through the new Cold War mentality. After achieving the four breakthroughs, the construction of the Belt and Road can proceed smoothly and overcome interferences. These are not just requirements for us, but also for our partners. The major tasks of the Belt and Road are the five links which we have repeated many times.

At present, the Belt and Road focuses on the six economic corridors, namely the China-Central Asia Economic Corridor, the China-Pakistan Economic Corridor, the China-Indochina Peninsula Economic Corridor, the China-Mongolia-Russia Economic Corridor, the New Eurasian Land Bridge Economic Corridor and the Bangladesh-China-India-Myanmar Economic Corridor. We have done a lot of preparatory work and made investments in the six economic corridors. It build a higher level of regional cooperation platform, create a new regional cooperation model, guide regional cooperation and joint development, achieve global economic cooperation through regional cooperation, start a new trend for economic globalization and lead global economic governance to a new stage.

The Belt and Road Initiative is becoming a global initiative. There are several risks: in case of a change in regime, the change of leaders will impact our construction; in economic, financial and technical fields, whether our technical standards can be interfaced with those of other countries or accepted by them; in social and cultural aspects, in terms of environment, some countries are economically underdeveloped and technologically incomplete and an upgrading is urgently needed, but environmental protection is very important, so we must make adequate preparations; and many companies have suffered from security threats, difficulties and challenges, as well as the threat of terrorism. Finally, due to the new Cold War thinking, the third-party forces have interfered and impacted us.

The last thing I want to say is that yesterday morning, the Central Committee of the Communist Party of China held a work conference on the Belt and Road Initiative, which was a very important meeting this year. The work conference on the Belt and Road Initiative was presided over by Wang Huning, and Zhang Gaoli made an important speech as the leader of the leading group of the Belt and Road work. News media reported his speech, which told us to conscientiously implement the spirit of the 19th CPC National Congress and the spirit of the Central Economic Work Conference, take the Xi Jinping Thought on socialism with Chinese characteristics for a New Era as the guide, adhere to the style of work which calls for steady progress, and promote the construction of the Belt and Road to achieve new and greater development. His speech was informational and could be summarized in the following points. First, it is necessary to reach a broader consensus on cooperation, strengthen strategic docking, planned docking and carry out dialogues on mechanism platforms, as well as enhance the international appeal of the Belt and Road Initiative. Second, we must strengthen connectivity and cooperation, and vigorously promote the hard connectivity of infrastructure and the soft connectivity of standards of planning. Connectivity has two facets: hard connectivity and soft connectivity. Soft connectivity is equally important as hard connectivity. Without soft connectivity, hard connectivity cannot be achieved. We should continue to implement the landmark demonstration projects. Third, we should enhance the level of cooperation in trade and investment, deepen international cooperation on capacity, and add new drivers for the joint development of countries along the route. Fourth, we must innovate financial products and services, bring the role of various financial institutions into full play, and improve the level of financial services for the construction of the Belt and Road. President Jin has shown us many good examples. We have done a lot of work in this area and will continue to increase our efforts. Fifth, we should expand cultural exchanges and cooperation, and consolidate the public opinion base of the Belt and Road construction. Sixth, we should actively fulfill our social responsibilities, strengthen environmental protection, and jointly build a green Silk Road. In the past, some companies have paid insufficient attention to some areas. We again emphasize the importance of environmental protection and the construction of a green silk road in this meeting. Seventh, we must continue to do a good job in risk assessment and emergency response, and strengthen the safety and security of the construction of the Belt and Road. What I have just mentioned is also the seventh challenge. Now the Central Committee of the Communist Party of China attaches great importance to coping with risks and challenges and guaranteeing the smooth progress of the Belt and Road Initiative.

Shenzhen is the pioneer of and the demonstration area for the reform and opening-up. I believe that Shenzhen can give full play to its enormous advantages and potential in the promotion of the Belt and Road, provide first-hand experience in the development of city partnership and our industrial cooperation with relevant countries, including exchanges and cooperation among think tanks, and make greater contributions. Finally, I wish the forum complete success. Thank you.

Moderator-Zhu Huayou: Thank you for your wonderful speech, Minister Yu. Your good insights on how to further promote and how to jointly build the Belt and Road through consultation to meet the interests of all are very inspirational to us. Thank you, Minister Yu. The next speaker is Mr. Dušan Bella, the former Ambassador of the Embassy of the Slovak Republic in China, who has boosted the connectivity of the two countries under the Belt and Road Initiative that benefits the people. Welcome, Mr. Dušan Bella.

Dušan Bella: Honorable guests, dear Mr. Zhu, ladies and gentlemen! First and foremost, I would like to thank organizing committee for holding this event and inviting me to share with you my views on this topic. Today's conference is held under umbrella of Belt and Road Initiative launched by Chinese President Xi Jinping in 2013 , which is embodying the spirit of Silk Road. For thousands of years, the Silk Road spirit has symbolized communication and cooperation between the East and the West, promoted the progress of human civilization and contributed greatly to the prosperity and development of the countries along the Silk Road.

The Belt and Road Initiative aims to promote the connectivity of Asian, European and African continents and strengthen partnership among those countries. And probably there is no better place than Shenzhen with a potential to build a better connected world and make Silk Road spirit happen in the reality of the 21st century.

I think we all know that the city of Shenzhen is home to a great amount of well-known high tech corporations such as Huawei and Tencent. Hi-tech industry has become Shenzhen's pillar industry and Shenzhen indeed lives up to the name "city of innovation". This is resulting from the fact that the level of total R&D investment in Shenzhen is one of the highest in the world (4.1% of GDP). And that international patent applications from Shenzhen has taken up almost half of the national total for 13 consecutive years with a year on year growth of around 50% in 2016.

The issue discussed in this panel is very timely. The innovation has become a driving force of the economic growth of the 21st century, and significant change maker in fierce competition in this world. It does not only deepen our knowledge and satisfy our curiosity, but also spurs progress in our societies and improves people's lives. True innovation can hardly occur in isolation. Only exchanges of ideas and their exposure to the wider picture and different practices can generate new solutions and technology change. I think there is no better way to be intellectually stimulated than "going global".

Having this in mind, I'd like to underline that think tanks have an important role to play in these processes by putting forward ideas and creating a match of platforms for their exchanges. Thousands of years of civilizations prove that there is no better environment for innovation than cities. Especially those with significant volumes of trades and number of visitors which succeed also in attracting talents from everywhere. Think of Athens and Chang'an in more ancient times or the Silicon Valley and Shenzhen in these days.

I would like to take this opportunity to say a few words about my country, the Slovak Republic, its innovation policy and potential for cooperation with Chinese partners. Even though we are a small country, we are the global leader in the number of cars manufactured per capita. We produce 191 cars per 1,000 people. We have an open economy with rich traditions in industry of production and strong results in foreign trade. Being mindful of the major changes currently occurring in the world creation, cooperation in science innovation and technologies have become a clear goal of the Slovak government.

We are currently implementing our national Research and Innovation Strategy for Smart Specialization (RIS3) with specific focus on advanced materials, nano-technology, IT, biomedicine, biotechnology, agriculture, environment and sustainable energy. Equal attention has been given to smart industry and smart cities with individual projects being already implemented.

I would also like to draw your attention to our results. Slovakia is home to a number of startups and innovative companies that have become leaders in their respective fields. Slovak company Spinea is the only European manufacturer of high precision and reduction gearboxes for robots and Slovak AeroMobil, the first flying car aims to revolutionize transportation by the end of this decade. Slovak companies C2i supplies premium carbon fiber composite materials for automotive and aerospace industries. Another Slovak company SYGIG is the global leader in the offline GPS navigation apps and company ESET with its antivirus solution is playing a pivotal role in this cybersecurity.

I would also like to stress the innovation connection with China as we have chosen innovation and technologies as our field of expertise within China, Central and Eastern European countries' format of cooperation. Slovakia hosted the second symposium on innovation between Central European countries and China in Bratislava, which led to the establishment of virtual technology transfer center that encourages further cooperation among China and 16 Central and Eastern European countries. Moreover, the second ministerial conference on innovation between Central and Eastern European countries and China took place in late November 2017 in our capital, Bratislava. The conference specifically focused on biotechnology, green energy and clean technology, and material engineering, offering space for presentations of companies as well as a B2B matchmaking forum.

Speaking about innovation, I should mention also Slovak capital, Bratislava, which scored highl on 2017 EU Regional Innovation Scoreboard as one of two top innovative regions in new member states.

Finally, I'd like to emphasize that 2018 is the year of local cooperation between China and 16 Central and Eastern European countries. In my view, it is a nice opportunity to take advantage of Slovakia's focus on new innovations within this format and establish effective cooperation between Slovakia and its innovation clusters on the one hand, and China's innovational leaders, including our host from Shenzhen on the other hand. I am convinced that both sides would have much to gain and I am ready to offer assistance in building bridges of innovation between our cities and countries. Thank you for your attention!

Moderator-Zhu Huayou：We thank Mr. Dušan Bella for his unique ideas. Now, please welcome Mr. Wang Jingsheng, Counsellor of the State Council.

Wang Jingsheng: Dear Friends, the speeches are really full of insights. I only want to give a brief description of the status and role of the Belt and Road in the

Opening-up of China. The topics are the "The Belt and Road: New stage, new realm and new landscape of China's Opening-up".

Firstly, why is the Belt and Road Initiative regarded as a new stage of China's opening-up? In my opinion, there are three reasons. First, the transition from gradient Opening-up to all-round Opening-up. At the beginning of the opening-up, the coastal regions took the lead before the inland regions, but now they are connected by land, sea, air and the Internet. With the characteristic economic sectors in various regions of China, through developed means of transportation and channels of information, they directly correspond to countries and regions along the Belt and Road, do their best, bring their advantages into play and cooperate to link the global economy.

Second, the transition from shortage economy to spillover economy. The Belt and Road Initiative is not only an intrinsic extension of China's logic of economic development, but it also fits the external needs of China's economic development. Abundant funds and products and a strong capacity for the building of infrastructures provide unique advantages for China's "going global". Equally importantly, the vast population and land and the rapidly increasing middle class demands make China the largest market in the world, and our market will be more active.

Third, the transition from global participants to active promoters.

The second topic is: why is the Belt and Road Initiative a new realm of China's Opening-up?

First, the Belt and Road Initiative is an oath expressed by China's action to take the road to peace. When China declares that it wants to rise peacefully, there are considerable doubts in international politics, diplomacy, and academia; why is that so? Because it seems to be the universal logic of the rise of a big power that a powerful country will surely become hegemonic and make wars. Countries that rose in the past undoubtedly took this road. The reason why we propose the Belt and Road is to let everyone know that China benefits the world through peaceful trade, mutual benefit and shared prosperity. This is true of the Chinese Silk Road and traditional culture, especially true of the Belt and Road in the 21st century.

Second, the Belt and Road Initiative is an oath of China's responsibility to promote globalization and free trade.

Third, the Belt and Road Initiative is an oath of China's commitment to building a community with a shared future for humanity.

The third topic is: why is the Belt and Road the new landscape of China's opening-up?

First, the building of the Belt and Road is rooted in the soil of history, with a focus on the continents of Asia, Europe and Africa and coastal islands, but at the same time it is open to all countries and regions that are willing to join.

Second, it has broad connotations covering not only the economic fields, such as trade, investment and traffic, but also political, social and cultural aspects. This is becoming increasingly prominent, such as politically seeking common ground while holding back differences, social stability and cultural coexistence. The joint construction of the Belt and Road follows the trend of the world's multi-polarization, economic globalization, cultural diversity and social information.

Third, we have broad common interests. Xi Jinping said that "the Belt and Road pursues the great benefit with hundreds of flowers blooming, instead of small gain with only one branch of the tree thriving". As said by Confucius, "treat others as you want to be treated". This is a word that has a great influence on the world. However, another word of his can better represent China's attitude towards the Belt and Road Initiative, that is, "now the man of perfect virtue, wishing himself to be established, seeks also to establish others; wishing himself to be enlarged, he seeks also to enlarge others". This is what we are doing now.

Fourth, the horizons have broadened. With the development of land transportation, the heart of Eurasia becomes the most important strategic area and the renowned theory of the World Island Theory as been proposed. Today, as for how to play the role of the heart region, the Belt and Road gives the answer. For one thing, it is a strategic circle. The Belt and Road reopens the traditional trading channel of Eurasia and avoids possible marine risks, and meanwhile through strengthening investment and trade with developing countries along the route, effectively avoids trade frictions with developed countries and regions. Lao Tzu once said that "the Way of heaven benefits but does not harm, and the Way of man acts but does not contend". In this way, we act on our initiative, ensure security and achieve a win-win situation.

We must maintain a strategic focus, attach importance to economic benefits and follow the laws of the economy, but not be aroused to precipitate action and make decisions intuitively. We should treat investment and benefit as equally important. Since we are doing business, we must not spend money arbitrarily, but make an assessment of scientific efficiency. It is necessary to ensure strategic priorities. The Belt and Road covers vast areas and has a long way to go, thus it's impossible to order at the same time. Sun Tzu always said that "if you know the enemy and know yourself, your victory will not stand in doubt; if you know Heaven and know Earth, you may make your victory complete". Different measures should be taken to ensure the strategic focus for different geographies and the conditions in different countries.

The Belt and Road prospers in trade and matures in culture. To take advantage of this cultural brand, the Silk Road can make a great contribution. Relative to the contribution to the economy, from a historical perspective, its contribution to culture is even greater. It can facilitate cultural exchanges between the East and the West and the world, and thus bringing unique and fruitful achievements through mutual communication and understanding of mankind and in exchange and collision. The unprecedented cultural exchanges can create a great civilization. Cultural self-confidence is inclusive rather than narcissistic. Culture is lovely because of its diversity, and it is not noble because of oneness.

Why did the Silk Road in the history of China attract the world's attention and become popular? It was because our products were great, the quality of our porcelain, silk and other products was good and the Four Great Chinese Inventions were leaders in the world. At that time, the greatness of the Chinese civilization was reflected by our exquisite and advanced products. Therefore, I repeatedly emphasized that the quality of a country's products is the quality of a country's nationals, and the reputation of a country's products is the dignity of a country's products. Quality is the key to the effective implementation of the Belt and Road. Only when the quality of commodities is good, can trade be long-lasting, the Belt and Road can become prosperous, China can gain a reputation and the Chinese people can safeguard dignity. So we must go all out to secure high quality. Thank you.

Moderator-Zhu Huayou：Thank you, Mr. Wang Jingsheng, for giving us a wonderful speech. Now, I'd like to welcome Mr. Li Huiwu, the Deputy Director of Development Research Center of Guangdong.

Li Huiwu: Distinguished Guests, Dear Friends, Ladies and Gentlemen, Nice to see You! First of all, I am very grateful for the organizer's invitation to the forum and for giving me an opportunity to deliver a speech at the meeting.

I will share with you what Guangdong has done for the process of cooperation on the Belt and Road, and my expectations for how the think tank can play its role since I am a member of a local think tank.

When President Xi Jinping visited Central Asia and Southeast Asia in 2013, he proposed cooperation under the Belt and Road Initiative, which is an important platform for jointly creating a partnership of mutual trust and inclusiveness, cooperation and a win-win situation, and for achieving prosperity in the Asia-Pacific region. It is also an important part for building a community with a shared future for humanity. In the past four years, this initiative has become a great cause for active participation and joint advancement of all parties concerned, and it has progressed in an orderly manner towards the goals of openness and prosperity. It provides new opportunities for development of the well-being of people of all countries. The regional GDP of Guangdong reaches 1.3 trillion US dollars, and the total value of imports and exports reaches 1 trillion US dollars. It has been the top economic province in China for 29 consecutive years. Last year, our regional GDP accounted for one-ninth of the national total, and the total imports and exports accounted for one-fourth of the national total. In recent years, Guangdong has responded positively to the country's requirements and has actively participated in cooperation on the Belt and Road. The *Construction Plan*

for Guangdong Province to Participate in the Belt and Road Initiative issued in
June 2015 put forward three goals, namely constructing Guangdong as an
important engine, an economic and trade cooperation center and a logistics hub in
the Belt and Road cooperation. Meanwhile, we also proposed key points for
participating in the cooperation on the Belt and Road, that is to say, promoting the
connectivity of infrastructure, accelerating the pace of industrial investment,
expediting cooperation in the marine sector, propelling energy cooperation and
development, expanding financial business cooperation, improving cooperation
and close cultural exchanges, and advancing the economic and trade cooperation
of countries along the route. At present, the hub ports of Guangzhou Port and
Shenzhen Port in Guangdong have opened more than 300 international container
liner routes, covering major ports on the continents throughout the world. Our
airports are also open onto more than 120 international passengers and cargo
transportation routes. Direct flights cover more than 30 countries and more than 80
cities on five continents.

Guangdong has opened the Guangdong-Xinjiang-Europe international express
trains and the Guangdong-Manzhouli-Russia international multimodal transportation
docking with the Belt and Road cooperation. Both of these activities are running
steadily now. We have also opened the container trains from Shilong in Dongguan
to Yantian in Shenzhen, and the express container trains between China and
South Korea. Our multimodal transportation channel by waterway and railway,
land and railway has also achieved rapid growth. As the Silk Road develops fast
and neighboring provinces are connected by high-speed railways, the international
integrated logistics channel linking ASEAN countries and the southwestern
provinces such as Guangdong, Hong Kong and Macao will be fully connected to
the great corridor of the Silk Road on land. Guangdong makes full use of its
advantage in production capacity to participate in the construction of 16 parks in
countries along the Belt and Road, including six industrial cooperation parks
independently organized and advanced by Guangdong. It has signed a memorandum
of agreements for cooperation on tourism with ASEAN countries. We provide
various forms of aid to them and are actively carrying out cultural exchanges.

Many universities in Guangdong Province have conducted a series of exchanges and cooperation activities with those counterparts in countries along the route.

Because of the nature of my work, I have received more than two delegations of governments, parliaments and political parties from countries along the Belt and Road. In the course of exchanges and cooperation, I feel that the role of think tanks is very important. Here are three suggestions for making full use of their role in the process of cooperation along the Belt and Road:

First, the cooperation and communication of think tanks must be enhanced. Think tanks must concentrate their wisdom, explore new channels and gain new impetus to promote the common prosperity of countries along the Belt and Road. By holding various types of forums, for example, the forum held in Shenzhen today, we can have academic discussions and do collaborative research on policies, forward-looking and pragmatic issues, and we can strive to achieve the sharing of resources, information and achievements.

Second, a platform should be built to allow for practical cooperation, strengthen economic cooperation and exchanges among countries along the Belt and Road and jointly explore ideas for cooperation. It should be constructed as a formal exchange and cooperation platform for governments, think tanks, industry and media to expand the integration of resources in countries along the route.

Third, we should pay attention to the differentiated research and seek points of the convergence of interests. Think tanks must actively understand and study in depth the various information of countries along the Belt and Road, such as economic development, complementary advantages, cultural traditions, habits of consuming and willingness to cooperate, and provide more practical opinions and suggestions for participating enterprises so that they can fully understand and respect the particularities of the society, economy, culture, employment, customs, etc. of the countries along the route, aim at mutual benefit, take account of bilateral and multilateral employment, bilateral and multilateral interests, and find the points of convergence of interests and the greatest common divisor of cooperation.

Distinguished guests and dear representatives, even if the marine navigation technology was not very advanced more than 2,000 years ago, there were not many surplus goods and the exchange was inconvenient due to language barriers, our ancestors overcame numerous difficulties and paved the Silk Road of friendly exchanges and communication between the East and the West. It was a miracle in the history of economy, trade and the exchange of mankind. Today, more than 2,000 years later, we have the technology and equipment to cope with nature, and we have cultural surpluses sufficient for exchanges, so we should strengthen cooperation under the principle of equality, mutual benefit and common development.

Guangdong is an important node of the Silk Road and the province with the highest degree of opening to the outside world. We will share dividends and achieve common development by actively participating in the construction of the Belt and Road.

The Development Research Center of Guangdong is also willing to make our due contributions to the Belt and Road cooperation and give full play to our proper role. Thank you.

Moderator-Zhu Huayou: Mr. Li Huiwu shared some experience and practices of Guangdong in opening to the outside world and explained how we can give full play to our role as a think tank. Thank you, Mr. Li Huiwu. As a moderator, I feel wholeheartedly grateful for the cooperation and wonderful speeches of our guests. If each of you and I have one apple, we will still have one apple each after exchanges; if each of you and I have one idea, we will have two ideas after exchanges. Today, we share the wonderful ideas of our guests and enjoy a feast of great minds. We must thank our guests for their cooperation and wisdom. Thank you all heartily.

Theme Forum: Bringing into Play the Regional and Industrial Advantages, Promoting City Partnerships and Exchanges along the Belt and Road

Moderator-Wu Liang: Welcome to our guests:

Mr. Alexandros Modiano, the Vice Mayor of Athens, Greece;

Mr. Guo Wanda, Standing Vice President of the China Development Institute;

Mr. Axel Goethals, President of the Europe-China Insitiute for Education and Culture (ECEC), CEO of the European Institute for Asian Studies;

Mr. Wang Wen, Executive President and Professor at the Chongyang Institute for Financial Studies, Renmin University of China;

Ms. Jasna Plevnik, Vice President of the Geoeconomic Forum, Zagreb, Croatia;

Mr. Chen Jianke, Vice President of the Chint Group.

Shenzhen is a city of innovation, a city of vitality, and also a model city for the modernization of the country. As for how to practically strengthen cooperation and more effectively promote cooperation under the Belt and Road under the theme of "City Partnerships 'Industrial Connections' Think Tank Links", every one of our guests may share an idea and offer a solution.

Our guests come from think tanks, research institutions, as well as city governments and industries. The first speaker is Mr. Alexandros Modiano, the Vice Mayor of Athens, Greece. Please share with us what is the biggest expectation or point of cooperation of your city for the Belt and Road?

Alexandros Modiano: Thank you for inviting me. Today's forum statement has changed many of my views of cooperation between cities.

A long time ago, we had a lot of city states. They were reshaping the world pattern, in a long history, they experienced a lot of ups and downs. Now we have new internationl relations, uphold a win-win vision, and also get better opportunities to promote urban development.

Athens is an old city and one of the oldest cities in Europe, even the whole world; Shenzhen is a brand new city. We are in the West and East but be it old or new, it makes no difference when it comes to the people. The people in the city have the same aspiration. They want prosperity, health, good environment and good education for their children. And whatever the governing system is, people have the same aspiration. There is a saying that if the goals will benefit you, they will make sure that all your wishes come true. And in Shenzhen, all the wishes of an urbanist are coming true. And we realized that there is no limit on what we can wish, what we can expect. It is a living proof of a laboratory of what can be really possible. And although we cannot just wipe off or erase our history and our cities, we know what is possible and we hope that through the city to city cooperations, we will be able, thanks to the Belt and Road initiative, to focus on specific projects and make them happen.

Moderator-Wu Liang: Which aspects will Athens intend to cooperate on with Shenzhen? Do you have such plans?

Alexandros Modiano: I hope to cooperate more in intelligence, technology and other fields, and expect more investment in innovation. We are looking forward to cooperation in some basic areas.

Moderator-Wu Liang: The topic for today's discussions is city and industry. The next speaker is from industry—Mr. Chen Jianke, Vice President of the Chint Group. What ideas and plans does the Chint Group have for the Belt and Road?

Chen Jianke: My thanks to the moderator. The Chint Group is a company established in Zhejiang Province. We are committed to high-end manufacturing. With the support of Minister Li, we have developed rapidly in the past 30 years. In addition to the innovative development on the domestic market, we have gone global and extended to countries along the Belt and Road. Today's forum involves city partnerships and industrial connections. In my opinion, it is of great significance for industry to go global, integrate with the local development of the city and seek collaborative innovation. Since 2014, the Chint Group has started to cooperate with companies in Frankfurt, Germany. Companies that manufacture solar photovoltaic products in Germany were not well developed. Upon our arrival, we integrated our market, brand, capital and strength with theirs. Now, those companies have become booming, the city council and the state parliament speak highly of us. They renamed a local road, calling it Chint Road and gave a railway station the name of Chint Railway Station. The cultural exchanges have achieved good effects. Now, in the sales revenue of more than 50 billion yuan of the Chint Group, the international revenue accounts for about 25%.

Moderator-Wu Liang: I haven't seen Mr. Chen for 18 years. I still keep the razor you sent as a gift to me when I was a journalist. It is a Japanese brand, but our home-made products are very good now. Our smart appliances, including those made by the Chint Group, are "going global". The Belt and Road brings us more opportunities.

Now we shall discuss some questions. Can our experts from think tanks give an answer to these questions: What are the biggest barriers to the city partnerships, industrial connections and cultural exchanges in the process of the building of the Belt and Road? How can we remove these barriers? How can the Belt and Road Initiative become a broader form of joint actions? The next speaker is Ms. Jasna Plevnik, Vice President of the Geoeconomic Forum, Zagreb, Croatia. Welcome.

Jasna Plevnik: Thank you! It's a great pleasure to be the participant of this forum! And I am glad to be here with all these people who share values and goals to dicuss how to develop free trade, investment, jobs, culture and friendship among nations.

I think that all this value could make economic globalization more fair, balanced and Euro-Asia a stronger integrated continent.

I would also like to stress that two years ago, China's Prime Minister, Li Keqiang, supported and presented one very important initiative and that initiative is also very closely connected with the cities. The development of the cities and this name of this initiative is Cooperation of Three Seas, it is about cooperation between Adriatic, Baltic and Black sea. And the very important part, I will say essential also is industrial cooperation. And through these initiatives and projects, we could see that the Belt and Road is making very good advance in the region.

On the other hand, I would also like to stress that this city cooperation is also very important because I'm seeing it as a great opportunity as an instrument which can be used to deep this coordination between development policies. And that is the best approach to develop cooperation between regions, countries and cities. And that is an approach which is I will say very well accepted at political level in Southeast Europe and Europe. Now city cooperation and regional cooperation and sub-regional cooperation is faced, that all kinds of cooperation are faced with the same opportunities and challenges. And as the biggest challenges for the Europe as a region, I see that an important urge, an important need that all these levels of cooperation, focus themselves on how to comply with European standards and laws. Thank you!

Moderator-Wu Liang：Thank you, Ms. Jasna Plevnik. Croatia is a young but great country. I hope that you may visit China often. Next, Professor Wang Wen from think tank will share his ideas with us.

Wang Wen：Thank you, Mr. Wu. We have some problems to be solved. First, the construction of the Belt and Road is entering a period of hard work. I can't agree with you more. We must be practical, the more, the better. Not just China, but also tens of and even more than one hundred countries along the Belt and Road have signed many agreements. Second, go deep and go into details. Invested projects such as well-developed ports, large infrastructures and hydropower plants must delve deeply and go into details. The situation should not be that a railway or hydropower plant cannot operate further after one or two years. So, this period is very crucial. Third, the comprehensive strength. We should work diligently, pay attention to details and devote comprehensive efforts just like many foreign sectors do. The Belt and Road Initiative is a very complex, integrated and difficult global vision. It is a big program that involves a lot of work in the future. Just like the human body, it involves both the overall health on the surface and the health of every cell in every capillary. This is very difficult, and it requires more comprehensive efforts. Thank you!

Moderator-Wu Liang: Thank you, Professor Wang. Let's welcome Mr. Axel
Goethals, President of the Europe-China Insitute for Education and Culture
(ECEC), CEO of the European Institute for Asian Studies.

Axel Goethals: Thank you very much! It's for me a real pleasure to be back in
Shenzhen again. I had already the honor and the pleasure to be here in 1980s and
to visit the first experimental economic zone in Shenzhen when it started and I've
been many times back to Shenzhen. The only thing I can say is that I'm really
impressed with the achievement of creating a new city of about 20 million people
really from scratch in such a short period. It's really very specific that very few
people are born in Shenzhen, everybody comes from everywhere in China and
even from other places in the world, to move away from your home, to come here
to start a new life, a new career. Shenzhen has attracted a mindset of people really
dynamic people, entrepreneurial people and they really see it in the development
of this Shenzhen city. And I would say there is a parallel with the Belt and Road
Initiative, because also the Belt and Road Initiative, is a new initiative. It's also
very entrepreneurial and it's a visionary platform which at the same time creates
some problems of perception. We hear regularly in Europe comments that yes,
but it's very broad, it's very general sometimes, but it also creates an anxiety, a
suspicion sometimes.

I would say, on the other hand, just because it's such a bold initiative, the Belt
and Road Initiative also gives the opportunity and the potential to develop new
concepts. And it also gives new ideas, new approaches and new strategies. And
that's I would say. It's quite a very open platform still as an initiative, but it
creates the opportunities and the potentials to think further and also for the future.

Now when you look to development of Shenzhen in such a short time, it's not
even 40 years' time yet, where Shenzhen has achieved, the problem is also and it
gives an example of the problem somewhere of the Belt and Road Initiative, for
instance in Europe. There is a problem of perception. The things develop so fast
here in Shenzhen and even in China that people , well, I would say that most of
the people even don't understand it yet in Europe, because the perception is

based on the stereotypes and the stereotypes are mainly on situations of 5 – 10 years ago or more. Now China and Shenzhen 10 years ago or 5 years ago, aren't China of today. So people have a lot of problems to understand what's moving, what's going on in China today.

I think a big part of the Belt and Road Initiative should also be on the connectivity of communication. It means the connectivity of perceptions. In fact what we observe is China and also other speakers have said it already, China is going on the substance and also on improving the quality, and let brands go out, this point is very important.

We should take effective measure to improve the quality of our products. I think the Belt and Road Initiative is not only the hardware, but it's also very important to work on the software. Software is culture, information and education.

And I think it would be very important to give much more emphasis on this, I hope we can pay more attention to the exchange of information in the future, to let Europes know more about China's policies, inculding some new strategies. For instance in Europe, there are a lot of people talking now and initiatives, but it's also part of fake news, In my opinion, problems still exist in this area, and I hope that in the future we can strengthen interactions, including information exchange and cultural communication. Some people in Europe are criticizing the Belt and Road just because they have little knowledge about China, a country that is very distant from Europe. But if the thing is clarified for them, they will have a very direct understanding.

This is the situation regarding Europe, so it is all the more important for us to change it. China must step up its efforts in communication and information updating, and strengthen Europe's understanding of the current situation in China, including some strategies and policies. I believe that Shenzhen has its own problems. Our country has sent numerous delegations to Beijing, Shanghai and Shenzhen, and the Chinese government has also sent delegations to Europe. We have often gone to Beijing and Shanghai, but seldom have we visited Shenzhen. I attended the meetings held in Luxembourg. Last November, I went to Beijing and Shanghai, but it was a pity that I did not pay a visit to Shenzhen. From 2015 to

2016, in order to promote exchanges, Luxembourg also sent some people to learn from Shenzhen and see what was happening there. I think Shenzhen's financial status is no less important than that of other cities, and besides finance, it also plays an important role in the fields of high tech and innovation.

Moderator-Wu Liang: Our experts from European think tanks have given us a wonderful speech. Now, let's welcome President Guo Wanda to make a summary of our discussions.

Guo Wanda: Thank you, Mr. Wu. We have talked about how the Belt and Road can be implemented and how to strengthen city partnerships. There are many barriers to cooperation. According to my observations, think tanks have done a lot of research projects. Let me propose a solution. The most important thing for city partnerships is integrating the developmental strategies of cities, as well as national strategies at the level of countries. The national strategy often ends up with implementation in the nodes of many cities. If the developmental strategies of cities are not integrated, the national strategies will become void. For example, Shenzhen has strategies for connection with some cities regarding several aspects. I think they are very good. When I visited Greece last year, they asked whether Shenzhen was interested in their airport and said that there could be cooperation between us regarding airports. Moreover, they expressed the wish to cooperate with Shenzhen on hot spring tourism. Infrastructure and high-speed railways are not something that a city can do, but airports, ports and subways can be linked to the strategy of a city. Shenzhen's subway company has already gone global, has cooperated with some countries along the Belt and Road and has helped them to operate. This is the first of this kind of cooperation, which is very great.

Mr. Axel Goethals from the European Union also mentioned that many cities along the Belt and Road lay stress on the smart city and the Internet. Shenzhen is no exception. I have a project in progress that helps Indian cities connect with the smart city. Shenzhen has many good companies. They are leaders in payment and do well in B2B and B2C platforms. I think that Shenzhen can provide a package of solutions regarding the smart city, including Huawei's basic channel construction.

Another plan for integration focuses on parks. Shenzhen has a variety of parks, such as industrial manufacturing parks, logistics parks, and free trade parks. In general, there are many parks called special economic zones by us. I haven't been to Croatia, but I have visited Montenegro. Montenegro is a relatively small country. They asked us to construct a port park as we did in Shenzhen. They said that their park was small, but they wanted to know if it was possible for them to develop like Shekou in Shenzhen within ten or twenty years? I told them that it would be very good. In order to construct a park, legislation must come first. Shenzhen was originally granted the legislative power by the National People's Congress. It would be difficult to do it well without laws. After legislation, we could have plans to attract investors from Shenzhen.

In a word, the city partnership is the integration of national strategies to some extent, but must be finalized on the strategic integration of cities. A city must have its own strategy. How can they connect with Chinese cities? The infrastructure, smart city and parks mentioned just now are only what we should do from the perspective of the think tank. I think there are still many other aspects that can be linked. Thank you.

Moderator-Wu Liang: Thank you, Mr. Guo. What we just talked about was concentrated on one point. Exchanges and cooperation necessitate specific carriers for city partnerships and cooperation of industrial chains. We can enhance communication, exchanges, mutual benefits, cultural integration and emotional links based on specific carriers. Just now, everyone has talked about what we want to discuss and what we want to do. I hope that everything can become better and better in the future. Today's discussions have come to an end. Thank you.

Sub Forum 1: Think Tank Link

Subject: Strengthening Communication about Policies,
Building a Think Tank Partnership Network among Cities

Session 1

Moderator-Wang Yiwei: The first speaker is Kim Seok-Hwan, President of Korea Institute for Eurasian Studies, welcome.

Kim Seok-Hwan: Thank you, moderator. First of all, I have a wealth of first-hand experience of exchange and cooperation among think tanks. Recently, I have been serving as the chief editor of a policy-oriented journal published jointly by Hankuk University of Foreign Studies and a Russian institution, for the purpose of expressing ideas. I think that the cooperation between the two think tanks is very meaningful. In my own institute, the Korean Eurasian Institute, we have also initiated a forum as a very important exchange platform between Korea and Russia. Well-known experts from the Eurasian continent have been invited to speak on the forum, which was held two years ago in Moscow for the first time, and then in South Korea. This year the forum will probably be held in Kazakhstan. This platform for Eurasian scholars was proposed by myself and my colleagues. It is a very good model of cooperation among think tanks which can be used for reference.

Of course, as far as the experience of think tank cooperation was concerned, we cooperated with a Russian think tank — Valdai Discussion Club. Against this background, we carried out a three-year research program with a number of think tanks from Norway, Singapore, Japan, China and Russia. This program was mainly funded by the Norwegian side, but they were not directly responsible for the management. The program was under the management of the Singaporean think tank, so we had an equal partnership with the sponsor. The win-win cooperation of our think tanks continued, and we made good progress on how to enhance the understanding of all sides and how to achieve common goals, and so on. The final results were published by the Russian think tank. In the past three years, this program has been very successful. Although it had come to an end, from this year on, the Korean side, the Russian side and the Japanese side have decided to expand their cooperation to include more European think tanks and private think tanks, and we are currently negotiating.

The second topic of the discussions involves the difficulties and problems in cooperation. In the morning, we discussed the role and difficulties of think tanks. From my point of view, think tanks need some new standards, new forms. Their traditional role is disappearing, so we need some innovations in this area. The role of think tank was defined many years ago when traditionally, a think tank was writing memos, doing research and sharing ideas to the government or the parliament, and simultaneously tracking how those ideas were implemented in the real world. However, such a model now lags behind or is becoming outdated. For example, it is a consensus of Brookings Institution, other leading Western think tanks, and our Korean counterparts that think tanks need a new model of development. Why? First of all, the policy focus has begun to shift from the central government to the urban and metropolitan, transcontinental and intercontinental levels, so beyond the traditional seats of the central governments in Washington, Beijing, Tokyo and Seoul, we have more say and voices, and the distribution of resources has changed dramatically. For example, some private investors are now playing a more important role than public investment in some small countries. Second, the policy has shifted from the national level to the local level, and our public institutions are also playing more roles. Accordingly, the role of think tanks also needs to be adjusted. In the past, think tanks were able to share their experience and ideas through the Internet after writing research reports. With innovations to and advancement in technology, our audience has also undergone changes. We find that there are more and more "individual think tanks" and even just one person can be a think tank. This phenomenon is very common in many countries, so the traditional think tank model of the 20th century has become outdated. I believe that a new model of think tanks is urgently needed, and our new model can respond to the transfer of new resources.

In my opinion, the Belt and Road is a very successful and meaningful initiative. China has never before gained such great influence in the world, and the Belt and

Road Initiative allows this to come true. From such a perspective, it is successful, but of course it also faces some big problems. For example, how will China implement the Belt and Road Initiative in reality and how will it put these concepts and plans into practice? Of course, there is now some propaganda in China that aims at the world. Integration and connectivity are very important, and only mutual integration and connectivity can bring prosperity and peace to the world. This rule, which is based on mutual understanding, is logical in itself. But at the same time, we must be clearly aware that the lack of communication or lack of consensus poses some barriers among us. Of course, the disregard for new technologies and new advances is also a big problem. Currently, science and technology have changed dramatically and have had a significant impact on our workforce in all aspects. Therefore, in the process of developing mutual connectivity and achieving integration, there is an even greater need for a deep and broad ideological understanding of the present problems.

Connectivity and integration not only create an opportunity for development, but they also bring big risks, including social risks. For example, Vietnam now lacks such connectivity and experience in communication, automation and digital management. The difficulty faced by Vietnam are actually more serious than those of China and South Korea, because 75% of the workers are under pressure. If we can promote connectivity with each other and carry out some projects regarding infrastructure and transportation facilities, then that won't be an issue for our future workforce, so more attention must be paid to some issues of principle and where those strategies ultimately work. Thank you.

Moderator-Wang Yiwei : Thank you. You may further share your ideas in the discussions. As you just talked about, the Institute for Eurasian Studies also analyzed the risks and crises we faced. I think we really need to pay attention to them. I also like the new type of think tank you mentioned. China proposes a new pattern of international relations, and I think that think tanks also need to have a new pattern. I think this is not just about Asia and the Belt and Road. The next speaker is Yi Peng, President of the Pangoal Think Tank.

Yi Peng: We belong to a private think tank, and I will simplify my ideas into three points. First, we have attended more than 150 exchanges of think tanks. We must have exchanges. More exchanges allow us to avoid misunderstandings and to reach consensus. Being candid is the basis of exchanges. Without candor, sincerity and honesty, we cannot go directly to the point.

According to my experience, think tanks from different countries and in different forms have differences in culture, values and national interests. We often think along the lines of our own perspective. This may not be conducive to solving the problem. A consensus is that putting yourself in another's shoes may be good for the exchanges of think tanks. There may be persistence or stubbornness, but I think it is necessary to improve the quality of exchanges of think tanks by putting yourself in other people's shoes.

Second, because the city partnership network of think tanks is to be constructed under the Belt and Road Initiative, we are also willing to participate in this network.

Third, the core of think tanks lies in the implementation of the project. Currently, most think tanks talk about macroscopic aspects and directions, but we should focus more on problem-solving. For example, the cultural and people-to-people bonds in the Belt and Road, but in my opinion, the projects must also be connected. Currently, countries along the Belt and Road aim to achieve cooperation on the project by integrating industries and cities, with cities as the theme. For example, Shenzhen is the epitome of the Reform and Opening-up. It sets a good example for the integration of industries and cities in China. Moreover, can India and Indonesia or other countries along the Belt and Road implement more successful projects like the city-industry integration of Shenzhen, through a series of cooperation projects under the Belt and Road Initiative and by the design, planning and schemes of think tanks? The implementation of these projects is not only conducive to the integration of industries and cities along the Belt and Road, but it is also beneficial to the economic development of this country and can produce an increase in the employment and income of its people. This model for the bilateral and multilateral benefit can be implemented.

The first suggestion is that, like our face-to-face exchange, we advocate the Internet-based think tank connection by applying the video technology. During the course of the year before last, we established a Pangoal Think Tank Link in Beijing. We adhere to new technologies. For example, the remote video technology of Huawei is well developed. Such technological progress enables us to communicate and exchange 24 hours through the Internet. There may be extensive and broad discussions in the communication and exchanges among cities.

The second suggestion is that currently the participation of think tanks is divided by countries. Another dimension is multinational companies. Their influence might be even greater than that of a country. On the whole, the power of international organizations is changing. We should focus not just on the exchanges of countries, but also on those between multinational companies and cities, multinational companies and countries, and multinational companies and think tanks. The reason is that the Belt and Road construction is not only a concept, but also the implementation by different organizations.

Finally, on behalf of Pangoal Think Tank, I invite you to communicate and exchange in Xiangshan, Beijing. I also wish this conference a great success. Thank you.

Moderator-Wang Yiwei : Thank you, Yi Peng. You mentioned we can have communications from different dimensions to solve our problems and strengthen cooperation. Probably in the future, we may achieve a very idealized state, which allows every one of us to become an intelligent person. The next speaker is Ms. Jasna Plevnik, the Vice President of the Geo-economic Forum, Zagreb, Croatia.

Jasna Plevnik: As the moderator has just introduced, I am the Vice President of the Croatian Geo-Economic Forum. We have had efficient cooperation with the Chinese Government throughout many areas, and we have also had high-level economic dialogues with the relevant institutions from Beijing over the past two months. These activities effectively promote high-level dialogues and economic connections among us. We are pleased to reach the consensus that we urgently need further development of international cooperation of cities under the Belt and Road Initiative, and more transparent and interactive communication and cooperation among every countries under the Belt and Road.

I want to point out that today, under the Belt and Road Initiative, we have a very good structure and network and we need to understand the many facets of think tanks before we get acquainted with new think tanks. From my own experience, the Belt and Road think tanks have multifaceted meanings. In the past, we often focused too much on introducing projects and situations, so that we could constantly extend our influence, continuously promote more transparent exchanges among small and medium-sized enterprises and at various levels, and effectively enhance the influence of the Belt and Road, all of which I believe are quite crucial.

On the other hand, I would like to say that each think tank has its own area of expertise, and we also need each think tank to have the programs that it specializes in, and realize that not everything is doable. China's think tanks are arguably in a highly leading position, and we would like to see more open and transparent cooperation, which would require us to work together, share and bear the pressure on each other, so that we can progress together.

Another goal is to extend our influence and localize the work of think tanks for the benefit of local businesses. In the building of the Belt and Road, I have a new idea, that is, think tanks should also pay more attention to the financial and commercial areas, and connect countries, regions and cities so that they can be better integrated. Hopefully in the future there will be a little more transparency in this regard and we will be able to see how it works.

Meanwhile, it is crucial for us to promote and publicize the projects under the Belt and Road Initiative. For example, some self-sufficient projects can bring substantial benefits to various countries along the route, rather than to just one country. We must have such regional cooperation. Of course, when talking about high-level cooperation, we also need some high-level development strategies; more often than not, we need to further transform them into more realistic and concrete strategies. Cooperation is very important, especially for the Belt and Road Initiative to be implemented under our system in a practical way.

From the perspective of our institution, we hope that the Belt and Road Initiative can become a very good leadership program that enables us to cooperate better with China, and through this program, we hope to have better interaction not only with China but also with all Asian countries. We need to develop new forms and explore more new things under the Belt and Road Initiative so that we can benefit from it. Of course, we also have to be aware of the downside. The European Union and other countries seem to have bias or an assertion that is not based on data and facts, and if there is such a bias or assertion, personally I would not like to comment on it. But I think this situation is very common in Southeastern Europe, where many countries are members of the European Union and three countries are already candidates for the European Union, and there is an atmosphere in these countries that the regulations of the Belt and Road Initiative and the rules of the European Union are opposed to each other. Personally speaking, I don't think that is the case, but we need to do something to solve the existing problem. In this regard, I believe that there is a lot of potential for think tanks, and we can influence the prevalent thoughts.

We must point out that the Belt and Road Initiative is a great promotion for and support to the European Union, and it is not just because China wants to make more friends in Europe through the Belt and Road Initiative. For example, on the Belt and Road forum last year, the European Union sent observers. Many documents and policies can demonstrate that the Belt and Road Initiative is extremely valuable. I think this is related to our mutual blending and integration, so we need to seek common ground while holding back differences, find more commonalities under the Belt and Road Initiative, and further achieve cooperation.

Finally, all countries participating in the Belt and Road should be supported by relevant think tank studies to some extent, so as to understand the strengths, weaknesses and risks at the regional, sub-regional, urban and other levels of the Belt and Road Initiative. In the first place, we have to have local insights on the Belt and Road, so that local communities can really benefit from it. This is a starting point. Thank you for your attention, thank you.

Moderator-Wang Yiwei: Thank you, Jasna. Croatia is the youngest member country of the European Union and also an active participant of the "16 + 1" cooperation program, so you have set a good example for other countries in the European Union, which may follow suit. I cannot agree more with you on the synergy of "16 + 1" cooperation and the Belt and Road Initiative so that the initiative can be better accepted by the European Union. I also hope that Southeastern Europe can join the European Union as soon as possible. We need cooperation either at the national level, the city level or even the continental level. We need such interaction and links. European think tanks often see the Belt and Road as an emerging Silk Road project of China because Japan, South Korea, Turkey and Russia had initiated many Silk Road projects. However, this is not the case for China. The Silk Road is about culture. However, the Belt and Road goes beyond culture and focuses more on policy collaboration and finance. The name of the New Silk Road cannot fully embody the essence of the Belt and Road. It is a brand-new project with the connotation of the Silk Road, but it is not all. The next speaker is the dean of the School of Innovation and Entrepreneurship, Peking University, Mr. Chen Dongmin.

Chen Dongmin: Good afternoon, ladies and gentlemen. I'm Professor Dongmin Chen, I'm from Peking University. Our School of Innovation and Entrepreneurship is focused on understanding national innovation systems and equal development. In terms of how we are developing an innovation and technology capacity to support a national strategy on innovation or global strategy. So I'm learning a lot today from this morning's sessions and I also have some opinions. I believe the previous speakers all made very good points: the Belt and Road is a new pattern.

I think to begin a think tank must have an objective and the Belt and Road as a prime vision that we all now continue to embrace it and now we think the think tank model is to really understand the issues and address differences to how to facilitate in communication of this primary vision. As the moderator just mentioned actually, given the Belt and Road has quite complex dimensions, some are just trade, culture but also ecological cooperation, industrial cooperation and innovation and technology. Actually, in every aspect of today's modern economy and therefore probably there's no single think tank that can really lead in all these issues. And I think it is important seeing as, I'm an engineer, we like to have a road map to define a goal of different stages and identify critical issues. The think tank actually makes a difference. I think it's difficult to put a model without understanding what problem you are trying to address. In innovation technology, we try to understand the problem first and based on the real problem, then we create a model to attack the problem. I think by this new model, it will not be resolved purely by creating a model to say but to identify a road map, different regions probably have different road map, and identify key issues where think tank can truly makes a critical difference. And I do believe think tank could do a lot in terms of addressing differences in new areas, facilitating communications and help to deliver the benefits of multilateral cooperations.

So perhaps, I would give a more concrete example. So, this is about this model, I think the model shall not be dual-carriage based on what problems we find. I'll give a concrete example, I know more about innovation and entrepreneurship. But the more recent innovation, one of the key issues is intellectual property (IP). Intellectual property is the most single universal role in intellectual property, is every time there's some intellectual property, and one of the impediments of encouraging the deepening of cooperation among countries in the industry is the patent, the IP protection. So I believe a think tank probably could help address differences among different parts of the world if we rely on patent system, that will not be very helpful. Actually no one wants to go through litigation and we create a difficult litigation actually. To try to follow the patent litigation system as much as possible so that we can quickly enable a multi-national and multilateral cooperation. And this is true by building technologies with China and other countries. China has made great progress in protecting intellectual property rights, and now our reputation in this area is getting better and better. Everyone is also realizing that China's legal system is protecting businesses. Recently, there was a domestic lawsuit in which a foreign company won and a Chinese company lost. This could demonstrate that our legislative system is becoming increasingly robust in protecting intellectual property rights.

In terms of cooperation in innovation among countries, I would like to focus on networks. There are different areas for think tank networks or think tank partner networks. Technology, intellectual property and talents are important. The public talent think tank network is what we need to take further advantage of. Currently we have established more cooperation with universities in countries along the Belt and Road. We want to further promote partnerships through education. Nowadays, it is an age of the Internet and technology when more and more young entrepreneurs are emerging, so we are interested in encouraging new entrepreneurs and university students who have the spirit of entrepreneurship. We also hope to build such a network in countries along the Belt and Road to help everyone. Thank you.

Moderator-Wang Yiwei: Thank you, Professor Chen. Innovation is a keyword. President Xi Jinping had an innovative idea at the Belt and Road International Forum for International Cooperation held in May. He mentioned, " First, we should build the Belt and Road into a road for peace." "Second, we should build the Belt and Road into a road of prosperity." "Third, we should build the Belt and Road into a road of opening-up." "Fourth, we should build the Belt and Road into a road of opening-up." "Fifth, we should build the Belt and Road into a road connecting different civilizations." In fact, they are also the problems of all mankind is facing at the moment. That is to say, there are shortcomings in our development. Of course, President Xi Jinping also mentioned that innovation was based on our entrepreneurship and entrepreneurial spirit, not just on technological innovation, so at the institutional level, we need more innovations. At this point, our think tanks are also very promising. We must come up with some new models and shape think tanks adapting to the new situation. In the morning, our speakers also mentioned that the Belt and Road is a new type of industrialization.

Industrialization actually originated in the United Kingdom. Both Europe and America experienced a wave of industrialization. But there are billions of people in China and India. We cannot simply replicate their model of industrialization but we have to rely on more technologies. Now our world is facing an unprecedented emergence of new ideas. Our experience and ideas are different from those in the past.

The fifth speaker is my former colleague from Fudan University. Lin Minwang is the Deputy Director of the Center for South Asian Studies, Institute of International Studies at Fudan University, and he will talk about the international cooperation project of the think tank network.

Lin Minwang: I come from a university. I will focus on three points. The first point is the necessity of a link to think tanks and the role of universities in the building of the Belt and Road. I think that all of us have a clear idea of this point because after the Belt and Road Initiative was proposed by President Xi Jinping at the end of 2013, he called for the construction of think tanks in China at the beginning of 2014. So, the construction of the Belt and Road and that of the think tanks are closely linked. Why? My understanding is that both of them are the inevitable result of China's expansion of its global horizons. Because of the Belt and Road Initiative, China needs the think tank to broaden its understanding of the whole world. As is known to us, many European researchers come here today. In my opinion, the European's understanding of the world was also mostly because of the broadened horizons and expanded interests. Several years have passed since the Belt and Road Initiative was first proposed. We have found many problems. In this process, think tanks and universities can play a very important role. I am interested in the studies of Southern Asia and India. For example, India's GDP ranks seventh in the world and will surpass Britain and France soon to rank fifth. I think that few people in China really understand India.

I think it needs to do a lot of field survey to study a region or a country. If not, how could there be high-quality results? So, this is a big problem. After the construction of the Belt and Road began, we have even little understanding of

India, let alone other countries. China not only lack understanding of the countries along the Belt and Road, but also other countries. I mean, it is necessary for think tanks and universities to provide effective and reliable knowledge about different regions and countries.

The second point is that we need to integrate the knowledge of think tanks and universities regarding different regions and countries through cooperation. Each researcher has his or her own limitations, and each institute has its own limitations. I have the advantage that I know a lot about international relations. I think it is also because I was a diplomat in India, and I keep in contact with some official institutions in India and China. President Yi Peng and Pangoal Think Tank are interested in economic studies. He keeps frequent contact with many Chinese enterprises. After we met, he decided to set up an Indian Research Center to effectively integrate our knowledge. I think this is a very good idea and practice. Both domestic and international think tanks should cooperate to achieve more effective results and promote the sharing of benefits.

The third point is that since the Belt and Road attracts a lot of foreign researchers, many researchers, including those from India and Pakistan, have often quoted words of Chinese researchers. But some researchers have often told me that they made sacrifices for China because they joined the construction of the Belt and Road so that China could realize its strategic needs. I said that this idea was wrong. China has so many neighboring countries. There are so many places China can invest in. Countries along the Belt and Road have relatively poor market conditions. China does not have so many geopolitics, and the Belt and Road Initiative is mainly an economic consideration, so it is still based on the logic of the market. These are my personal points of view.

Moderator-Wang Yiwei: Thank you, Professor Lin. You mentioned the campaigns and publicity of China regarding the Belt and Road. In fact, we need to make a lot of ideological changes. We need to look at other countries from more objective perspectives. We may not know much about some countries, such as India. We need to strengthen our learning from each other. Similar examples also include the United Kingdom and Germany. In fact, we have learned a lot from India and other neighboring countries, such as regarding Buddhism. On the new continent, we need to understand the Old Continent and the situation of different continents. The next speaker is Gunter Siegfried Heiduk, Professor of the East Asian Research Unit at the Warsaw School of Economics, Poland, who is studying relevant economic policies in Poland.

Gunter Siegfried Heiduk：Good afternoon, everyone! I would like to talk about something different from what the other speakers have spoken about. I want to show you more of our research, show you our data, and show you what the Belt and Road Initiative and the Brexit look like. As we all know, there were many changes before and after Britain's leaving the European Union, and we hope to analyze it all by considering the actual situation and making adjustments according to China's Belt and Road policy and the situation in Britain.

First of all, I would like to talk about the Belt and Road. I am mainly concerned about some key points on how to achieve mutual benefits and maintain the balanced cooperation in development. When we look at the relationship between China and Britain, we first look at some of our political rhetoric from the high levels, and cooperation on the political side. More often than not, we can find the cooperation between China and Britain on news frontpages. On the other hand, besides the agreements signed by the former Prime Minister David Cameron with China, there are many other agreements. We need to check whether these government initiatives are good for cooperation and development. Moreover, there are a number of specific projects under those initiatives. When we talk about the relationship between China and Britain, particularly in the near term, both sides are committed to building a global comprehensive strategic partnership faceing the 21st century, not only between China and Britain, but also between China and other EU countries.

Now, let's focus on some areas of the economy. When we look at the Sino-British trade data, it can be found that the trend in trading has been declining since 2014. China is now Britain's seventh largest trading partner with a contribution rate of only 4.4%, which is very low. Then, when it comes to investments, we can find that Britain is the largest destination for China's foreign investment in the whole of Europe, but such an investment is insignificant compared with that in the United States of America. China is increasing its investments in Germany, and its investments in Britain are decreasing, with the largest part of its investments in the real estate industry. It is known to us all that China has introduced new regulations since August last year, which restrict three types of investment, including foreign real estate, entertainment, sports and clubs. Looking at the investment of China in Europe in 2015 and 2016, the top three European countries are Britain, France and Germany, followed by countries along the Belt and Road, and then the whole European Union.

Let's look at the comparison of the Belt and Road before and after Brexit. I would like to compare four projects: first of all, the Yiwu-London railway project, second, the nuclear power plant project I mentioned earlier, third, an investment plan of China's in the City of London, which is actually a port project, and fourth, the City of London. I would like to see what role the City of London plays in promoting China in the Belt and Road. This morning the president of the Asian Infrastructure Investment Bank said that the bank has never ruled out the possibility of building a local office in London, and this is possible, and it is also one of the bank's related projects.

My point is, what is the influence of Brexit on the projects that have been decided before? First of all, the Yiwu-London railway does not mean a direct train from Yiwu to London, but stops in Germany, where the containers are unloaded onto smaller trains, and then the trains enter Britain through the Channel Tunnel. That is to say, the train unloads containers in German cities, from where they are transported to London, vice versa on the return trip. Will there be more barriers after Brexit as Britain is no longer a part of the European Union? We find that this railway is not the same as before, and that German cities are not as attractive as they used to be. And if Britain is reluctant to make adjustments, the barriers will exist after Brexit. So, is it possible to have a project straight from China to Britain without passing through continental Europe? Here is a proposal for a railway line that we call the North Sea or Arctic Route. It can depart from Shanghai, Hong Kong or Shenzhen and would take 22 days to reach London directly, without having to pass through any city on continental Europe. Such a route takes less time than the previous route through continental Europe because the former takes 22 days, while the latter requires 37 days. "But the problem is that a project like this that goes to the Arctic Ocean needs a lot of preliminary investment", here I also quote comments from COSCO executives, because it is after all a sea transportation project.

Next, the nuclear power plant project. A thorny problem is that the project was initiated through cooperation with Electricite De France, and later China General Nuclear Power Group joined. According to the current EU laws, it is based on the EU standards for nuclear power plants, which we all know are very high. These are conventions on safety standards established in 1952. Since Britain left the European Union, it has also withdrawn from the Euratom conventions. Things will become complicated after Brexit, especially with regard to safety standards. The European nuclear reactor project will be delayed because Britain will also withdraw from Euratom and the nuclear supply chain after Brexit, including equipment and staff training. There are many other similar projects that will be delayed, and China is negotiating because China is also negotiating nuclear power projects in Britain, one in Somerset and the other in another place. China has built the nuclear power plants in three locations in Britain.

The third affected project is a partnership project in London, which is co-financed by China's ADP and China CITIC Bank and is expected to be completed by 2026. Before the project actually starts, there will be a very complicated process of consultation and negotiation. The British government would like to start such a project before Brexit because that would be much easier. Starting these projects now requires compliance with EU-based rules, but Britain will definitely need to make changes to these rules and regulations after Brexit. This is also one reason why Britain wants to leave the European Union.

Another project is the City of London, which is very important from China's perspective, because an increasingly greater number of Belt and Road projects will involve more and more capital. How can these projects be financed? London is still the largest financial center in the world. Of course, some banks now intend to withdraw from Britain, but London is still the largest global financial center. From an economic point of view, this is a "lock-in effect". The key is how to keep it active, and currently I have come to some conclusions that I'd like to briefly discuss with you.

First, the view from the British side. Britain after Brexit needs to support China's Belt and Road projects, as pointed out by the Chancellor of the Exchequer. Despite Brexit, Britain remains an important country and will continue to play a very vital role under the Belt and Road Initiative. It is very important to note that China will still feel interested in Britain after Brexit, because London is still the largest financial center in the world and extremely crucial for the internationalization of the RMB, or it can serve as an offshore trading center. More than half of RMB, including loans, are realized not in Asia or the USA, but in London. Of course, I have some policy suggestions regarding the fact that China should pay more attention to London's role as the global economic center, and if necessary, China should make some assumptions about worst-case and best-case scenarios. For example, how should China respond if London loses its advantage as a financial center? What should China do if its position as a financial center is further consolidated after Brexit? My point is that China should envision different scenarios, and what should China do if any changes occur to London as a financial center?

The second point still involves the nuclear power plant project. I believe it is necessary for China to build an entirely new business model for operating nuclear power plants. There are two partners, the European Union and Britain. How can China's industrial standards and technologies be integrated with British standards after Brexit? This problem needs to be solved by a new business model.

The third point is about the idea of the Yiwu-London railway. As we know, there is a land and sea express route that goes through cities like Belgrade and Budapest. I think that will involve the EU budget for 2021–2027. My suggestion is that the Chinese government should get involved in this cooperation framework and have some of the budget. If the Chinese government has the opportunity to get involved in relevant projects, by new framework functions, combining the ideas of Britain and China, different sectors of each country, such as agriculture, can accelerate a coordinated type of regional development. This can create a better future for us and integrate the advantages of Chinese cities and industries.

As a think tank, we analyze data and build different models for economic development, mainly from an economic perspective. Hopefully, we can all benefit from building good network connections with China, sharing some information, and integrating resources with the Chinese government and relevant think tanks. Because a lot of think tanks are based on data or models, sometimes research is more than just an idea and needs to be based on many statistics. These are my points, thank you.

Moderator-Wang Yiwei: Thank you, Heiduk. It can be said that you have shared a lot of relevant specific content. Of course, you have also analyzed some uncertainties. We need to understand that we will not both be losers, but we will achieve win-win results. You mentioned the need to further share data and strengthen mutual cooperation under the framework of the Belt and Road. In fact, many think tanks in China also hope to continuously share our knowledge and data. Next, Professor Tao Yitao from Shenzhen University, welcome.

Tao Yitao: Ladies and Gentlemen, Good Afternoon! The topic of my speech is "The institutional and cultural constraints on the implementation of the Belt and Road Initiative." I would like to talk briefly about two issues. The first one is the institutional constraints on the implementation of the Belt and Road Initiative, and the second one is the significance and value of inclusive development.

Fundamentally speaking, the implementation of the Belt and Road Initiative is not a simple economic issue for China or countries along the route, but a non-economic issue in which culture is greater than capital, and technology is more important than institutions. The technological and cultural constraints are both the softest and the most fundamental constraints, which are actually behaviors of the social community and individuals defined by common values and laws. Informal institutions, such as habits and values, developed and shaped by the social community, not only constitute an integral part of the institutional system, but also an integral part of the system of culture. So, I think that across institutional and cultural constraints, a cognitive community of inclusive and operable institutional culture may be useful for the implementation of the Belt and Road Initiative. It should be a strategy of priority or consideration of wisdom, both logically and realistically.

The most important issues in the promotion of the Belt and Road Initiative are our own mindset, way of thinking and behaviors. The experience of China's Reform and Opening-up for nearly 40 years proves that the state-sponsored system is effective. It has the efficiency and advantage that are unmatched by other systems in terms of concentrating resources, rapidly mobilizing the people to participate in big projects and efficiently solve mass incidents. However, we cannot simply use such a way of thinking and customary Chinese style to cope with projects of the Belt and Road, especially big projects directly involving the interests of local residents and even cultural beliefs. We must act according to law and international practices, abandon the mentality of quick success, spend time reaching consensus, achieve win-win results through understanding and protect our interests with laws. These are issues we must take into careful consideration.

This is the first facet of the topic. The second issue is the significance and value of inclusive development. The concept of the Belt and Road means the information and value orientation that China conveys to the international community. It is also a new change in the way China cooperates with the world. In the past 40 years, China has changed from a planned economy to a market economy and has explored the path from universal poverty to common prosperity. China has been successful in taking this road. It is a difficult and tortuous process in which a country adheres to independence and self-reliance and combats poverty and backwardness, and also a beautiful story that a country is committed to the reform and opening-up, opens up to the outside world and seeks peace and development. The value identity is the potential institutional cost of China's cooperation with neighboring countries and with the world. Building a value-based community with a consistent understanding can be helpful for the evolution of the internal system of the community and make it more predictable. For the evolving internal system of the community, the common values play the role of a filter. The inclusive development is not the values among countries or regional communities, but the real cooperation, and the ideological foundation for effectively seeking common prosperity and development and entering into agreements.

In this sense, concept, values and consensus themselves are resources, the wealth that creates wealth, and intangible capital and guarantees that can bring prosperity. Inclusive development aims at common development and prosperity; however, this process is by no means a process of defeating ideas with ideas, but an acceptance of simple values and ideas of mankind. Ideas can change people, and people can change society. Meanwhile, inclusive development also aims to confirm and support the development of member countries. It is the acceptance and respect of country differences, rather than an attack on each other. The realization of economic globalization provides not only room for the growth, development and prosperity of the community in the economic system, but it also means unlimited possibilities for the common prosperity and development of the community. A more important premise of inclusive development is the protection and respect of each other's core interests. The market is based on fair exchanges. The market is not a battlefield. The market must foster rivals and business partners, and a healthy business partnership is conducive to a healthy and orderly market.

The inclusive development must, of course, be confronted with contradictions, differences and even conflicts, because they are inevitable in regional cooperation. Each country has its own national interests, values, value judgment and even political inclination. However, the key lies in how to resolve, reduce, weaken and solve the above issues. In this regard, the ideas of Lao Tzu and Chuang Tzu are worthy of our compliance.

Finally, I will share several points. The first point is that the Belt and Road Initiative is by no means a short-term program, but a great move to change the world's political landscape. Second, the most important task for implementing the Belt and Road Initiative is establishing mutual trust. Mutual trust among countries can be achieved through cultural and value identity. It does not mean simple recognition of one culture by another culture, but achieving a win-win situation in mutual respect. I believe that the most important issue for common prosperity and development is that all people and all countries can benefit from the Belt and Road Initiative. This is very important. This is the end of my speech, thank you.

Moderator-Wang Yiwei: Thank you, Professor Tao. The Belt and Road is not just a process of learning from the West, but also from developing countries and the entire external world. In many countries, the economy and infrastructure are not well developed and the political system is influenced by the West, so it is impossible for those countries to directly replicate the successful model of China. The inclusive development you mentioned is very important. I also had the concept of the inclusive globalization in my book. This concept is identical to what you have talked about. The next speaker is Professor Shahab Enam Khan, the Director of Bangladesh Enterprise Institute.

Shahab Enam Khan: Thank you, everyone. Good afternoon! First of all, I would like to thank the moderator for his introduction. I think the discussions are truly significant. You talked about all kinds of issues, our uncertainties, our new models and other aspects, and of course we find that we are entering a new dimension of development. So we must be certain about our ideas, and what differences there are between ours and those of others. Asia is a significant region of the Belt and Road, and of course there are other significant regions. In our opinion, the economy is very important for development. Previous speakers talked about the role of think tanks, relevant experience and the manner of our interaction. Professor Tao also mentioned the relevant framework model. I would like to talk about what contributions think tanks can make under the Belt and Road Initiative from a technology perspective. Professor Kim pointed out that the traditional think tank model is outdated and we need to have a new model. I completely agree with this idea. In the past, think tanks gave advice to the government, but now think tanks need to interact more with the public. We need to take into account new technologies and social media because people have more tools for acquiring information. That is to say, the traditional model is outdated, we need to reach a greater number of audiences. Think tanks need not only to do research, but also to disseminate our findings and our ideas. We need to establish very good connections between the rulers and the public. In my opinion, we need to use social media and other new technologies.

It is interesting to find that the development of think tanks in China is very different and there are a lot of new types of think tanks, previously concerning trade, economics, international relations, foreign policy and so on. As a matter of fact, I personally focus on the field of foreign affairs as well. I find there is a problem in Asia, and more specifically, in Southeast Asia. Generally, connectivity is believed to be a problem, but I think the problem is more one of financing and the very slight interest shown by the government. Some projects give more consideration to the interests of the donors before investment or financing, and this problem is quite obvious in Southeast Asia. These projects are subject to market restrictions and ideological issues on financing that think tanks should pay attention to.

It is also important for think tanks to carry out capacity building. I come from the Bangladesh Enterprise Institute that has a lot of partner institutions in cities. How can we expand the dissemination of information? We have an official website for publishing information. President Xi Jinping's visit to Bangladesh in 2016 facilitated relations between our two countries, and we are now strategic partners. We want to make sure that Bangladesh is one of the partners of the Belt and Road Initiative. I hope that South Asia and South-east Asia can play a greater role in that initiative. Of course, we have some extremely fundamental problems, that is to say, many countries may not be fully strategically connected. A country, especially a small country like Bangladesh, must achieve balance in this process.

We hope that these projects are not only what Bangladesh needs, but also what China and other interested parties (such as South Korea) need, and that they represent our common interests. We also hope for a pool of resources that can be shared, in order to make the Belt and Road better connected. We need more ways and models of cooperation. We are not in the 19th or 20th century, but in a new era, so we need new interpretations and new partners.

The moderator also mentioned that we need to achieve economic integration and strengthen cooperation, not only at the monetary level, but also at the financial level. Our cooperation must be supported by very good research results. As pointed out by the moderator, there are numerous projects regarding infrastructure and energy that can benefit both sides. If such projects can be boosted by our research, the Belt and Road construction will become better. We now have a very fashionable term called "interactive research" or "interpretable research". Once research results can be interpreted, relevant policies may be formulated to carry out reforms in the country, which will be a good impetus for changes at the national and regional levels.

As far as South Asia is concerned, it is a very large market. However, the integration of South Asia as a whole is relatively worse as compared with East Asia and Southeast Asia. In my view, the reason is that we have not achieved good connectivity among various regions and groups, and our system is a very big problem that we think tanks need to think over. Under such circumstances, think tanks can intervene and play a very positive role in promoting countries along the Belt and Road that are mutually integrated and connected. Faced with crises, this mechanism can be used to solve problems and provide some support in funding. We can play the role of our institute well in this way.

In the meantime, think tanks can also be a good link between authorities and the public, building bridges between them, and become fully aware of differences, common interests and commitments. I suggest cooperation in the areas of understanding, such as production and supply networks; on the other hand, cooperation among small and medium-sized enterprises; third, the issue of income inequality, as well as technology and social media issues. Promoting such cooperation and market collaboration can lead to greater integration, while meeting political and social needs, maintaining security and strategic coordination, as well as coordinated cooperation on changes in food, energy, environment and water resources. The mutual trust of countries is essential for economic integration and cooperation. Think tanks should promote dialogues to help resolve disputes and differences so that the Belt and Road can understand the concerns of all stakeholders on this issue, while at the same time we need to take account of decision-making processes and reforms in a comprehensive manner. Perhaps think tanks can help coordinate regional and national goals, because the regional interests are mutually complementary and reinforcing.

Think tanks should look for solutions to geopolitical problems and ways to connect countries, and offer them with mutual benefits, for example, one benefit is that the infrastructures are used to strengthen ties among Asian neighbors. Of course, when we think from an economic perspective, we need to continually strengthen ties between Asia and one another via infrastructure. This is also a common concern in the region from which I come. In my opinion, not only governments, but also institutions like the Asian Infrastructure Investment Bank, can lay a basis for the further cooperation of think tanks between Asia and other regions. It is not just cooperation within Asia and with other countries. Asian countries will be different. For example, my country, Bangladesh, is already the 32nd largest economy in the world. According to projections, our GDP will grow to $1.32 trillion by 2030, the economy will become bigger and the growth will be more diversified. We must be well prepared for the changes. There are many factors behind these changes, such as the development of artificial intelligence, which we all know better, and the changing demographics of the youth. Therefore, we must build new systems and new forms of information technology and media, all of which are crucial for us.

Finally, the Belt and Road Initiative is also very good for innovations, because it allows us to continue our reform. Sometimes, something may be overlooked in some developing countries. We suggest that there should be more cooperation among think tanks so that we can continuously integrate and become an equal and mutually beneficial community. These efforts can eventually lift us out of poverty and help us become prosperous. Thank you.

Moderator-Wang Yiwei: Some comments to Mr. Khan. First of all, Bangladesh is not a small country. You have a population of more than 100 million people. We need to rediscover the importance of some countries. For example, your neighbor Myanmar is a very important country, as well as Pakistan. East and Southeast Asian countries are very important participants in the Belt and Road Initiative, which has a very good impetus to our continuous promotion of each other's civilization.

Second, you mentioned two kinds of artificial intelligence. Professor Chen Dongmin also discussed two innovations, one is to save energy and resources and another is to save labor. The saving of energy and resources can be helpful for our developing countries, it can maximize our use of resources and achieve the best results. This is also the new development of industrialization.

Finally, I want to briefly summarize the problems discussed by our speakers. There are many important tasks for think tanks because they are located in big cities. We encourage them to learn from each other. This is our top priority.

The second job is that think tanks must solve practical problems. We have some tactical collaboration. We are able to solve problems of different facets, either by applying Chinese technologies or adopting the laws and regulations of the United Kingdom. You did not discuss one problem. There is an important think tank in Brussels called CEPS, where participants from many countries do a lot of work. This is a new direction that can help many people. For example, it can be helpful for solving the problems of refugees and environmental improvement. This think tank aims to not only find solutions to contemporary problems, but also discover potential problems and solve them promptly. This is a long-term comprehensive solution that we need to further understand.

Session 2

Moderator-Kim Seok-Hwan: Welcome to the second session. As we agreed, we have discussed many interesting issues, which have been very effective and have enhanced our mutual understanding. In particular, we have paid attention to the Belt and Road Initiative and now we know where the problems are. The second session will be simpler than the first one because we are now familiar with each other. Next, I would like to hand over the stage to professor Mao Yanhua, from Institute of Guangdong, Hong Kong and Macao Development Studies, Sun Yat-sen University.

Mao Yanhua: Thank you for the invitation. I come from Sun Yat-sen University, which has an Institute of Guangdong, Hong Kong and Macao Development Studies. It is a high-level think tank specializing in the studies of regional development. The topic of my speech is building a first-rate think tank to serve the construction of the Belt and Road.

The first point is that the Belt and Road Initiative accords with the construction of the first-rate think tank. I think there is a demand for first-rate think tanks. Since the global financial crisis in 2008, the process of globalization has reached an inflection point. According to economic data, for example, we mentioned that the growth rate of global trade was lower than the global economic growth in the past five years after the outbreak of the financial crisis. This is rare in the globalization of the past 20 years. Global investments have also seen a sharp decline. In addition, the rapid globalization in the past two or three decades has led to great changes in the global network of production. Europe, the United States of America and especially East Asia with the revival of China, have become a trio on the global landscape. Similarly, in the global value chain, many developing countries are still in a very low-end position, so this is a new problem and an imbalance in globalization.

I think economically developed regions of China are participating profoundly in globalization. For example, Guangdong has experienced 40 years of the reform and opening-up. It is a region open to the outside world. In Shenzhen, its foreign direct investment reached 85.2 billion US dollars in 2016. From the perspective of Guangdong as a whole, the foreign direct investment is concentrated in the Pearl River Delta, which reached 125 billion US dollars and accounted for 23.9% of China's total foreign direct investment. Hong Kong, adjacent to the Pearl River Delta, is a channel for linking the global market to the market of mainland China, and also the channel for capital, logistics and trade. About 29% of the foreign direct investment in China comes in through Hong Kong. Similarly, 60% of China's foreign direct investment goes out via Hong Kong. Therefore, Hong Kong, Macao and the Pearl River Delta are involved in the global economic division of labor to a very great degree.

In the new stage of globalization, including the new developmental stage of China's Belt and Road Initiative, local think tanks of cities should be able to participate in international exchanges and in consultations on policies. This is the first point. Shenzhen needs to build a center of think tanks, communication, and allocation of resource factors.

The second point is, as mentioned by the leaders of think tanks attending this conference, that the think tank plays some very important roles in the new development of globalization. First, it conducts theoretical research. What are the differences between the Belt and Road Initiative as a global solution and globalization in the past? What are the fundamental differences between the initiative and the globalization led by the multinational companies in the past? On the construction of global value chain, how can the Belt and Road Initiative drive the economic development of participating countries? These are all new theories that need to be explored.

Second, consultation and advice. After the Belt and Road Initiative has been proposed, many countries benefit from it. The construction of industrial parks, cooperation on production capacity and infrastructure has more or less influenced these countries. However, in the process, there are also many problems, such as inconsistency of standards, difference of investment management systems, fluctuation of exchange rates and conflicts of laws. There are some cultural and religious factors, all of which need to be solved by us together. Think tanks can play a very important role in consultation and advice.

Third, theoretical research and guidance. When visiting Dubai in July 2017, we found that in an international city like Dubai, the publicity of the Belt and Road is not enough. Our think tanks must be guides to publicize the concepts about the Belt and Road.

Another role is the professional evaluation. For example, international organizations need to carry out evaluations. Our think tanks may also participate in the evaluation of cooperation projects under the Belt and Road. For example, we are evaluating the construction of the pilot zone. Our think tanks can play their roles in evaluating the effectiveness of the pilot zone's institutional innovation, investment environment and business environment.

The Belt and Road Initiative lays stress on the joint building to meet the interests of all. Which areas should our think tanks focus on? I think we must pay attention to the following aspects.

First of all, think tanks should pay attention to the construction of New System of Open Econnomy. On many occasions, President Xi Jinping proposed to build a New System of Open Econnomy. How to integrate the open system is still a problem of many developing countries which desire to participate in economic development, such as facilitation cooperation, investment cooperation and so on.

The second aspect is to focus on cooperation regarding industry and innovation in the process of the construction of the Belt and Road, such as the issue of Industry 4.0, the emergence of the Internet, artificial intelligence, etc. The development of these areas provides new opportunities and presents new challenges for our cooperation on the global value chain, including how to apply new technologies, certain rules of the digital economy, better integration of small and medium-sized enterprises into the global market to take advantage of the new economy, as well as cooperation in the field of property rights. We should also pay attention to the youth. In fact, this is a global issue. The younger generation is faced with a developmental environment different from our rapid development in the past. The youth issue more or less exists in each country or region. Think tanks should have exchanges and discussions on the youth issue. Of course, we may also show concern for the issue of sustainable development and green development.

Finally, I'd like to talk about the key to the role of the think tank. First, we must bring about some innovations to the operating mechanism of think tanks. For example, China proposed building new high-level think tanks, which should have a good operating model to give play to the role of third parties, closely linked to the government and connected with the society. Second, the link with the government should be enhanced. This is conducive to solving some problems in economic development and regional cooperation, better reflecting the requests and making suggestions to the government. Third, the network of city think tanks should be expanded. Through "going global" and conducting research, today we talk about the building of a network of city think tanks. This is very important. Think tanks of countries and cities should strengthen cooperation, interact with each other, carry out research and solve problems together in the process of economic development. Fourth, an analysis must be made with the big data technology. As we have just now discussed, our think tanks are different from traditional ones. We should have new tools and applications. We should apply big data to strengthen the analysis. Last but not least, we should enhance links with enterprises and society and solve the problems faced by enterprises in the process of "going global". Thank you for listening to my speech.

Moderator-Kim Seok-Hwan：Thank you, Mao Yanhua, for your wonderful speech and insights. The next speaker is Axel Goethals, President of the Europe-China Insitute for Education and Culture (ECEC) and CEO of the European Institute for Asian Studies.

Axel Goethals: I have a "problem". It is not really a problem, but something that many speakers have mentioned. It can be said that we share the same idea on the same line. We attach importance to the potential cooperation and future opportunities among think tanks, and we want to continuously promote the cooperation of think tanks. At first, think tanks prevailed in European countries, such as the United Kingdom, and later in the United States of America. China, with the introduction of the Belt and Road, has also taken the initiative in this regard. It is positive and brings us a lot of new energy. This is a very good phenomenon and provides us with different perspectives.

In fact, we have considerable experience at this point. We established the first inter-Eurasian think tank in Brussels, covering a lot of research institutes and full-time researchers. In the early days, we focused only on simple issues without in-depth discussions. We had discussions in general terms, which cannot be comparable to the situation today. At present, we are cooperating with over 2,000 think tank members from all over the world.

The second problem is that we sometimes need to consider the limitations of financial support, such as projects involving the EU, which require financial support. When we complete a project, we need to get additional funding support. Sometimes the funding is so limited that it is very difficult for us to launch other projects after we complete one.

The problems I have just mentioned are faced not only by us, but also by other think tanks. After many years of efforts, our think tank in Brussels have done a lot of work and have built some networks. More often than not, we focus on the dialogues regarding various projects. We have relevant senior think tank members to lead the implementation of the whole guideline. Of course, we also have some ongoing projects that are very flexible and dynamic. Personnel with the ability to work flexibly are essential for such projects. No matter what views these think tank members have, they need to be ahead of the times in various fields, and constantly unlock new potential. For us, these think tanks not only pay attention to the relationship between Europe and Asia, but also to the situation in China and the potential for future development. In the meantime, these think tanks should be able to predict what the next 5 – 10 years will look like in the current 5 – 10 years, and find out viable solutions in the context of potential analysis. There are people in our organization who are older, for example, some people are well into their 50s and 60s. They have a clear understanding of what has happened in the past fifty or sixty years and can come up with specific solutions. We are now witnessing a very rapid development of China, but new problems may emerge in the next 5 – 10 years, so a better analysis must be made on what will happen in the future. This is the direction for our work. It is the guideline of our institute in studying how to solve problems that will arise in the next 5 – 10 years. This guideline can continually urge our think tanks and members to always be ahead of the times, and analyze and integrate the problems.

As think tanks, we pay attention to three areas. We focus on academic institutions, big companies, the short-term situation at the company level as well as the government side. Think tanks not only analyze problems from an academic perspective, but they also focus their attention on practical problems. We need to understand the operation of various institutions at the government level, and integrate the different aspects. At the leading position, you may have some ideas and directions which are different from the mainstream media. A think tank must keep moving forward to be a leader and stay ahead of the times. Sometimes, our new ideas are not accepted, or even considered as incorrect, but that should not be a problem.

We should not position ourselves as a NGO promoter or a campaign promoter, but we need to have clear concepts and theories that can find solutions to problems. Sometimes problems can be discussed further, but not truly solved. As think tanks, we have the desire to improve our ability to influence governance in a constructive and positive way for the benefit of our society. Nothing is perfect. The EU is not perfect; on the contrary, there is still much room for improvements. I think Europe has developed a lot in the past 100 years. I remembered my life in Belgium when I was young. I drove 2 hours from Belgium and needed to pass through two countries. Different passports were required to complete the 2-hour drive. Now, it is unnecessary to show different passports in EU countries, and there is traffic integration within the EU. This is the concept of EU unification.

Of course, we should also see that as think tanks, we need to strike some balance, and we need to find balance between being politically correct and being politically incorrect. Sometimes, we must accept some restrictions to make ourselves politically correct. But if it is too politically correct, there is no way to provide good advice to those who govern. In the long run, there will be slow changes and shifts in the mainstream views, which will slowly merge with our personal views. The views that we originally found very strange will gradually become the mainstream views, so trade-off is something that think tanks need to make.

In the process of trade-offs, we have to consider the interests of the region, the society and the people. In fact, some think tanks are official think tanks established by the government, some are privately funded, some are established by political groups, some are academic think tanks, such as educational institutions, and there are also independent think tanks. A diversity of think tanks exist. That's why we must consider the issue of funding. We must observe which sponsors are behind an institution, a think tank. Although the think tanks can be counted as a social group, there are a variety of think tanks, so different approaches are proposed. We can seek common ground while holding back differences, and learn from each other, in order to achieve further development.

Today's think tanks have very close ties. We have very meaningful cooperation in China too, because now we share the same direction, that is, to build a new network of think tank partners. In this way, China, Europe and the rest of the world can be connected. In this way, we can realize a new type of think tank partner network, but in my opinion, one network of think tank partners is not enough. We need more networks, because think tanks involve many aspects. Think tanks can better play their role through the establishment of the networks of think tank partners, so as to create greater value for the society. Thank you.

Moderator-Kim Seok-Hwan: Thank you. The speaker has shared his ideas with us. He talked of the history and possible future direction of think tanks. Thank you very much. Next, I will hand over the stage to Deputy Director of Development Research Center of Shenzhen Municipal People's Government

Deng Shenghua.

Deng Shenghua: Thank you, our dear guests for coming. I am the leader of the Development Research Center of the Shenzhen Municipal People's Government, one of the organizers of this forum.

Today, I will share information regarding three aspects: first, an introduction to Shenzhen, the basic economic situations of Shenzhen; second, specific actions or areas of cooperation of Shenzhen in the construction of the Belt and Road Initiative; third, some ideas and suggestions.

In our mind, Shenzhen was a small place 30 or 40 years ago. After 40 years of development, it has changed a lot. Some experts and researchers may not understand this. So I can report some basic information to you. This year is particularly important in the history of Shenzhen's development. This year, the economic aggregate of Shenzhen has exceeded that of Hong Kong for the first time. It exceeded Guangzhou last year, and its regional GDP reached 350 billion US dollars, which is equal to 2.24 trillion yuan. According to the speed of development, the ranking of Shenzhen in the Chinese city landscape will further change. For example, compared with Shanghai, China's largest city, our economic aggregate is 55% that of Shanghai ten years ago, 64% five years ago and currently 74%. That is to say, we have increased by 20 percentage points in ten years. We might even grow to be the largest city in China.

Shenzhen has a land area of about 1,950 square kilometers, where 21 million people reside. It is one of the most densely populated cities in the world. Judging from the relationship between local finance and central finance, the central government can get the financial revenue of more than 530 billion yuan from such a small piece of land. Our local financial revenue is 332.2 billion yuan. This year, we are closer to Hong Kong. In other words, our economic aggregate will further increase, the quality of economic development is very good and we are also one of the cities achieving the most remarkable economic results in China. From the perspective of industry, our information industry, biotechnology and six emerging industries are leading in China. From the perspective of urban construction, we are now the city with the largest number of buildings over 150 meters in height in the world. Last year, four of the world's 20 tallest buildings were located in Shenzhen, including those under construction. Three years later, the number of tall buildings over 120 meters will exceed that of Hong Kong because there are a lot of buildings over 100 meters in Hong Kong. Since our city is small and there are many mountains but few plains, we can only develop up. The new information technology and new planning methods have been applied in our urban development. For example, the double-layer urban expressway will be constructed on a large scale. The upper layer is the road linked to urban communities, and the lower layer is the direct long-distance expressway. This construction model is an advanced one in the world. There are currently 40 international airlines in Shenzhen, and we will plan for 200 lines in the future. Shenzhen now has a tanker port. It also has the largest number of ocean-going shipping lines in the world. Its ocean freight capacity ranks third among the world's top ten seaports. If Hong Kong is counted, the two cities rank number one in many fields in the world. This small piece of land in the southern part of China is becoming the global hub and hotspot of information, capital and goods.

As an emerging city, we hope to develop towards several distinctive directions in the future. This is also the second aspect I mentioned, that is in which areas can Shenzhen cooperate better with you.

In terms of technological innovation, the total investment in R&D accounts for 4.13% of the GDP, which reaches the level of Israel. We are aiming at the Silicon Valley. We hope to create in Silicon Valley and develop in Shenzhen because the manufacturing chain in Shenzhen is absolutely perfect and the cost is relatively low. We have a lot of opportunities to cooperate with the world at this point. In the past few years, Shenzhen has attracted many students returning from Europe and the United States of America. It is one of the cities that attracts the greatest number of scientific and technological talents, about 80,000 people a year.

The construction of infrastructure is another area of cooperation. Large companies in Shenzhen have a lot of experience in overseas projects such as in Sri Lanka. Shenzhen also has many opportunities for cooperation in the field of innovation and finance. The RPU of the Shenzhen Stock Exchange has ranked among top ones globally recently. We hope to build a global cluster of innovative companies in the future. If there are good companies, the information may be linked with us.

The third area of cooperation is tourism. The new cruises of Shenzhen also exert certain influence. We have our own advantages in ocean shipping, especially in terms of trade. We used to go towards developed countries in Europe and America, but now we are turning to new markets. There is a great deal of room for our development under the Belt and Road Initiative.

Finally, I would like to share two ideas on cooperation. The first idea is that we hope to work hard with all of you for this forum. This is the second time we have held this forum, which needs support from you. We also hope to strengthen the role of think tanks in the process of cooperation. I hope that everyone can communicate with Shenzhen more, and introduce projects to Shenzhen. We will provide support as always. Thank you very much.

Moderator-Kim Seok-Hwan: Thank you for the wonderful introduction. Mr. Deng Shenghua has shared many practical content and some new information with us. Shenzhen's environment is very special. It is a leader compared with China's inland cities. It can be said that Shenzhen has played a leading role as a window to help China change some of its past conditions. Just now you mentioned that China's future depends on the development of Shenzhen. This is indeed a very ambitious commitment and also a very ambitious concept. The next speaker is Vasyl Yurchyshyn, the Director of Economic Programs, Razumkov Centre, Ukraine.

Vasyl Yurchyshyn: I would like to talk about how we understand and communicate with each other because mutual understanding and communication can help us to establish good cooperation mechanisms, which are crucial for all countries. Our country is a little bit different. I know the situation in many other countries, and Ukraine is also very keen on participating in the Belt and Road

Initiative.

However, we are facing some problems. We must not only facilitate the development of the initiative in other countries, but also respond to some specific challenges, especially in my country, Ukraine. As a think tank, we are working side by side with the government. In the modern world, we are confronted with many problems, we can accumulate more experience from different countries and different situations, and we hope to pay more attention to the analysis of some successful cases, especially the cases of China, which can provide very efficient guidance for our future actions. I have read some books and the documents published by our government. Our country is becoming increasingly interested in this area, so we need to focus more on the successful projects and learn from their experience. We need to understand their potential for development. Most of the projects we are talking about here are related to the Belt and Road. It can be said that the Belt and Road projects may have different repercussions. We must take actions to enable different countries to cooperate with each other and use others' strengths to make up for our weak points. I have to emphasize that Ukraine's agreement with the EU is still in force, and of course there are other agreements that can help us cooperate with China. Surely, we have also entered into agreements with Canada. The cooperation projects and agreements are all areas of interest to us. Many people do not believe that the Belt and Road Initiative is good for Ukraine. Our suggestion is that the projects can reflect more of the interests of the people, and promptly give return to the public, because this can strengthen coordination and communication between the government and the public, promote cooperation between think tanks and the government and businesses, and enhance understanding and communication within the government.

With regard to the financial support, as a matter of fact, I don't know much about finance. For example, for some projects proposed by China, I don't understand the financial content, but I have some knowledge about projects in Southeastern Europe. Of course, some projects are carried out in Ukraine by countries in Southeastern Europe. These projects are very practical and helpful for the locals; and there are also good think-tank projects that are beneficial for development. For us, for the purpose of project development, we must focus on the relevant financial mechanisms, such as the Silk Road Fund and the Asian Infrastructure Investment Bank. This financial support is undoubtedly very helpful. We hope that there may be long-term joint activities and projects by investment institutions, including opinion polls, which are particularly beneficial. Thank you.

Moderator-Kim Seok-Hwan：Thank you for some very real insights. Thank you for sharing your ideas. Next, I will invite Wang Yiwei, Professor of the Renmin University of China. Welcome.

Wang Yiwei：I think that connectivity determines the competitive strength of cities, instead of labor and technology. It was not the peace of some countries, but the peace of cities. A new type of human civilization is emerging. Therefore, the Belt and Road is a new type of industrialization and urbanization of mankind. If the urbanized infrastructure cannot keep up with the times, there will be problems in cities. Last year, President Xi Jinping emphasized during the Belt and Road Forum for International Cooperation that "concentrate on efforts on key passageway, cities and projects". Although a city may have a small GDP, it is a key node and a smart city. We must explore its importance in global interconnection. This is the topic of my speech.

Historically, cities could connect different regions of a country. Since the Europeans went to sea, many cities have mainly been concentrated in coastal areas, and 90% of the trade is carried out via the sea. Today's Belt and Road intends to change the backwardness of inland areas. The ocean-type globalization should be changed to a great extent. The night lights of the United States of America are concentrated in coastal areas, and the vast inland areas are dark. The Belt and Road will turn on the lights and leave nowhere invisible during globalization. The division and fragmentation of the world should be changed. In ancient times, our tools were horses and camels, but today we use the Internet and high-speed railways. China is leading the world in both fields. In particular,

Shenzhen can link the world in the field of the Internet, and it can change the situation in which some cities and countries are marginalized because of the lack of connectivity.

China has built high-speed railways overseas, which have connected a number of ports and have linked the world. There is also inclusive development. Inclusive globalization on a global scale largely overcomes the unsustainability of globalization. China's rate of urbanization is now 60%, still falling behind the 70% and 80% in Europe. The GDP of Guangdong and Jiangsu has exceeded that of Russia. These urban agglomerations have become China's main sources of population, GDP and information. Inland cities in Yunnan and Sichuan Provinces are connected by high-speed railways because they can make up for the disadvantages of inland areas. For information connectivity, Alibaba and cloud computing enables Guizhou to change from a backward province to a province at the frontier of reform and opening-up.

This is a map of city development. Most of the fifteen fastest growing metropolises in the world are concentrated in developing countries. There is a common urban problem of overcrowding in developing countries. Now we should consider whether the countries along the Belt and Road can avoid this urban problem. I think to introduce a new type of urbanization can rely only on new technologies. China is cooperating with Europe. ZTE, Huawei and Nokia are studying 5G to help the construction of smart cities and smart medical care. This is the Belt and Road in industrial and information development.

We are cooperating with Southeast Asia and have a port alliance with 17 cities in Southeast Asia. For the construction of information-based ports, ports should not only be the centers of trade, but also the centers of finance, information and education. The interconnected development is an essence. To apply for the world heritage site, the maritime trade network, maritime cultural exchange, maritime medical care, tourism, training and education are not just friendship cities in the original sense. The Belt and Road transforms the original cooperation of cities from political friendship cities to interconnected nodes. The concept of the network can be said to take central cities as the fulcrums, invigorate cities through the network of the inland areas and key ports, keep the culture and spirits of cities alive, interconnect more cities and allow for the connectivity of countries and regions. Based on the construction of urban agglomerations, the interconnection of trade, facilities and finances can improve the level of connectivity of the Belt and Road.

Finally, international cooperation. Shenzhen is the epitome of China's Reform and Opening-up. Shenzhen has become a global Shenzhen. A large number of countries come to and learn from Shenzhen. The Belt and Road should run a college in Shenzhen. Many political parties are studying the reform and opening-up of China, including city governance. Shenzhen is the global Shenzhen model. The understanding of our reform and opening-up by many regions begins in Shenzhen. It is very interesting. In the future, Shenzhen will become one node and center for city diplomacy or interconnection along the Belt and Road. The urban population of China is on the increase. Many initiatives and spirits of China's Belt and Road are reflected more in cities at the frontier of reform and opening-up. The concept of city diplomacy should not just focus on foreign affairs, but the role of interconnection and pacesetter. It is not only the interconnection of countries, but also of cities. Cities can demonstrate the achievements of China's reform and opening-up. City governance and urbanization are important contents of city diplomacy. It enriches the original form of diplomacy and makes Chinese cities internationalized in terms of entities and missions. For instance, Shenzhen will become a diplomatic special zone in the future, so there should be new functions for them.

Shenzhen has new innovations, new pilots, new special zones and new work in the background of the Belt and Road, so the city makes life better and the Belt and Road makes life better. Connectivity lights up the Belt and Road and surpasses the old civilization. Today, the Belt and Road has already been printed on currencies of some countries. There are also many related books. All of them are in local languages, not just official languages. I have written four books. The fourth book is about to be published. Some content of my books have even become the topic of questions in middle school classes.

This is my report. I will share more with you later. Thank you.

Moderator-Kim Seok-Hwan: Thank you, Professor Wang, for your wonderful sharing and introduction to some details of the Belt and Road. After your speech, I have a clear idea of the specific connotations of the concept of the Belt and Road. The last speaker is Anastasia Likhacheva, the Deputy Director of the Center for Comprehensive European and International Studies (CCEIS), Higher School of Economics in Moscow, Russia.

Anastasia Likhacheva: I'll give a brief speech. It's my pleasure to be invited here. We do have a lot of similar projects, and many of them are related to the Belt and Road. Now I will give some details.

We are divided into three main sectors, official content, academic affairs and the release of some relevant publications. We have established a committee and published the publications, which will also be integrated. These materials give us a direction for specific work. Our goal is to enhance mutual understanding through these projects. Some projects are not very easy, and despite difficulties in the process, they all end up with very good results. Our goal and results, which are clearly planned, can be elevated to a very high level. We are also working on two books that cover not only the research of related projects, but also international cooperation, the regional situation, etc.

We need to know exactly what we are facing and how to improve. They are track records for us to become aware of what we are doing now and what we will be doing in the future. We have also had a lot of academic discussions. We make the specific research projects public with the hope to promote our future work and build a very good open platform. We have a specific action guide that explains how we can seek cooperation. For cooperation and development in the Far East, we focus on the global economic corridor and our specific situation, and this surely covers many countries, such as China and Japan. In the past three years, we have organized many international cooperation projects and held forums in Moscow, Tokyo and Singapore, so as to strengthen continuous connection and communication among different countries, enhance bilateral and multilateral links and promote the implementation and development of specific projects.

Next, I would like to talk about the future. As mentioned by Professor Kim, when looking to the future, we not only anticipate the present situation, but also understand each other's needs. We need to further strengthen cooperation with China, Japan and European countries, and focus on the economic area and other areas of cooperation. If China feels interested in these areas, we can integrate with each other on similar projects.

Russia also desires to be connected to one another and work together on this mechanism. The Belt and Road Initiative is very good because it can connect with our country and other countries in Europe. In May 2016, President Xi Jinping mentioned a lot of relevant content. In fact, we have recently spoken of a lot of ongoing projects. Russia hopes to strengthen cooperation with Europe and other countries. This is an important mechanism for us. We are now working on some research projects regarding stocks, and have made good progress. They play a very positive role in furthering cooperation with Europe. Moreover, we hope to develop in a healthy way through continuous cooperation and competition. Chinese investors are welcome in Russia. If there are any projects you feel interested in, we can have further discussions in details.

Moderator-Kim Seok-Hwan: Thank you. All attendees have had the opportunity to share their ideas. Unfortunately, Mr. Stavros from Greece was not present, and Mr. Axel Goethals who is the CEO of European Institute for Asian Studies did not have enough time to explain all of his content.

Axel Goethals: I had sometimes visited Shenzhen in the 1980s, and it can be said that I have first-hand experience. Changes in Shenzhen are so radical that if I had invested in a piece of land then, I could have become a billionaire by today. Shenzhen's miraculous changes are known far and wide around the globe. Its industrial structure is very good, and the innovative spirit of entrepreneurs in Shenzhen is amazing. It brings a new perspective to the world.

Further, the Belt and Road Initiative is a very good platform for us to focus on different needs and to achieve a balance. It is very good, opens up more possibilities and enables us to join new initiatives. All of us hope to build a good friendly network with Asia and carry out relevant work. This is something that we must focus on. I believe that through the initiative it is possible to build an Asian network, and that we can look at the initiative from a new and interesting perspective. I am very happy and honored to be here in Shenzhen. I can feel the spirit of Shenzhen. It is a nice choice to host this meeting in Shenzhen because it is a gorgeous city.

Moderator-Kim Seok Hwan: Thank you. Marvelous words. I sincerely thank all the speakers for their participation and wonderful speeches. I sincerely thank you for your great ideas and understanding of the initiative. Thank you very much for coming. I am grateful for the wonderful arrangement and considerate service of the organizing committee. I also want to thank Shenzhen and the Chinese people. Thank you.

Sub Forum 2: City Partnerships

Subject: Strengthening Cultural, Economic and
Trade Relations and Building a Network of
Think Tanks and City Partners

Stjepan Mesić (General consultant of Croatian National Chamber of Commerce, special representative of Zagreb City)

For many years, I have always advocated and adhered to multilateralism policies and economic cooperation to strengthen Croatia's ties with Europe and the world. Today, if the European Union and China continue to promote free trade and globalization, these views remain practical. I believe that the Belt and Road Initiative proposed by Chinese President Xi Jinping is a very important economic initiative and a civilized initiative because it has the ability to deepen China-European relations and enhance global economic ties.

I hope that the presidents of all European countries can understand the Belt and Road Initiative, because it will have an important influence on the world's development and stability, and will also advance the growth of international trade and investment. Under the framework of the Belt and Road, industry in Europe and Asia will further develop through various centers of innovation. Just as the Belt and Road Initiative advocated by Chinese President Xi Jinping should follow the principles of "Consulation, Contribution and Shared Benefits", I believe that China and Europe are natural partners in achieving the goals for the Belt and Road.

The building of the Belt and Road connects the three continents. It is currently progressing smoothly, and the economic and cultural interdependence between Europe and Asia is also enhanced. The Belt and Road provides a new mechanism for various countries and global governance. I would like to emphasize the fact that we should work together under the framework of the Belt and Road to consolidate and develop multilateral cooperation, so that the Belt and Road can increase the openness of the global economy, improve global governance and cope with global challenges together, just like the European Union and other models of integration. The world needs such a power that can guide the development of multi-polarization and establish a new type of international relations of mutual benefit and win-win results. Under the premise of respecting the standards and transparency of the WTO international trading system, we should seize the new opportunities brought by the Belt and Road Initiative in

Central Europe, and extend them to regional and local cooperation levels.

Today's world is more closely connected than ever before. Ma Yun, a Chinese entrepreneur who supports the Belt and Road Initiative and Chairman of the Alibaba Group, is building an electronic platform around the world, allowing entrepreneurs to buy and sell on mobile phones anytime and anywhere in the world. Here, I want to point out that the Belt and Road will also promote the digital connection between Asia and Europe.

The Belt and Road is not only an important initiative, but also the best opportunity to mobilize all resources in private and public sectors to accelerate global economic development. Looking to the future, we must strengthen cooperation and connectivity in various fields between China and Europe, thus not just providing good opportunities for the economic development of Eastern Europe and Asia, but also providing ample room for the world's peace. Peace is not everything, but without peace, you can do nothing. Thank you.

Zhu Huayou (Deputy Secretary and Director of Research Office of The People's Government of Hainan Province)

Let me give a brief introduction to the business environment. Creating a good business environment is the focal point of international cooperation and trade of cities. The business environment is productivity. It means foreign investment and development. Hainan is the largest special zone of China established by proposal of Deng Xiaoping in 1988. Shenzhen is the earliest special economic zone. Three months from now is the 30th anniversary of the Hainan Special Economic Zone. Hainan is an island in the South China Sea, with a land area of about 35,000 square kilometers. When I had supper last night, several foreign guests said that Hainan Island is very beautiful. You are welcome to go on holiday there.

We have five large ports and only a high-speed railway of more than 700 kilometers that goes around the island. It takes one hour to travel throughout the island without stopping, and one and half hours if you stop at all the stations. There are 475 domestic and international airlines, including 100 international lines. Why do we talk about this? Because the airlines are very important for the investment environment. We have always negotiated an investment with Hawaii. They were willing to invest in Hainan Island for planting flowers, a relatively high-efficiency industry. We also felt interested. Unfortunately, it came to no avail. An important reason was that we had very few international airlines then, so the flowers could not be picked today and sold on the markets of London, Paris and New York tomorrow. For this reason, the flower industry could not develop on a large scale. International airlines could improve our tourism environment while developing the economy. At the end of 2009, Hainan was officially classified by the central government as an international tourist island that mainly develops the service sector. At present, the service sector is growing at around 70% . By the end of 2017, we had received 70 million domestic and foreign tourists.

Further, an open environment. For example, we currently have 26 countries exempt from visas, and soon they will increase to 59 countries. In other words, foreign friends present here can pay a visit to Hainan only by holding a passport. There is also duty-free shopping. The central government allows Hainan to have duty-free shopping. That is to say, all mainland guests can travel to Hainan for purchasing goods valued at 16,000 yuan without tax. This is also attractive to mainland tourists.

Third, we have a Hainan Boao Lecheng International Medical Tourism Pilot Zone. The Boao Forum for Asia is an important international forum for us. Many foreign guests present here should have been there. In April this year, the Boao Forum for Asia will be held with very high standards. On a land of more than 20 square kilometers, the central government approved the development of Boao Lecheng International Tourism Medical Pilot Zone. Many Chinese and foreign medical institutions are investing there. For example, foreign doctors can practice there for three years and foreign medical institutions can invest solely in Boao. No other places enjoy this policy. Foreign drugs, including those sold in Europe, the Americas and the United States can be used simultaneously here. Foreign medical equipment can enter the zone duty-free. This policy is unique in the country. Now many Chinese and foreign medical companies are settling in Boao. In the future, we can provide a good platform for medical cooperation between China and Asia-Pacific and attract tourists from Southeast Asia and other countries to Lecheng for medical examinations, cures, health care and cosmetology.

In addition to the particular focus on the opening of infrastructure, we also pay special attention to the security of basic power, mainly nuclear power and clean energy. A few days ago, President Emmanuel Macron and President Xi Jinping signed contracts in Beijing, and Hainan attended the signing ceremony. We have a cooperation project with Électricité de France on the Hainan Clean Energy Demonstration Zone. We are willing to participate in the construction of the Belt and Road actively by taking advantage of the characteristics of Hainan. We are part of the Maritime Silk Road because our island is situated in the South China Sea. We should make full use of this advantage and strengthen our cooperation with cities along the Belt and Road, of course, including cooperation with the Guangdong-Hong Kong-Macao Greater Bay Area. We have tens of cruise routes directly arriving in Southeast Asia. We hope to bring into play our unique advantages and participate in the industrial cooperation of the Belt and Road. Thank you.

Wu Sikang (Director of Development Research Center of Shenzhen Municipal People's Government)

I will talk about the focus on industries and think tanks of cities. The first point is that city cooperation can provide important support for the construction of the Belt and Road. Why? Because I have collected some data, that is, cities are the hubs of global economic cooperation. At present, more than half of the world's population lives in cities, and 70% of the economic activities take place in cities, or from cities. According to the data of a US research institute: the world's 300 largest cities have a population that is 20% of the world's population and an economic aggregate that accounts for 50% of that of the world. Also, there are cities even wealthier than countries. If a city is seen as an economy, some cities are already very large. For example, the GDP of Shanghai in 2016 was about 400 billion US dollars and equivalent to that of Thailand, which ranked 26th in the world. The GDP of Shenzhen in 2016 was more than 290 billion US dollars and equivalent to that of Ireland, which ranked 40th in the world. In 2017, Shenzhen's GDP was more than 340 billion US dollars and ranked further ahead. This also proves my point that some cities are a large economy. The conclusion is that in the construction of the Belt and Road, the country sets up the framework for cooperation, and cities should play an important role as pivots and carriers.

Second, industrial cooperation is the most important point we need to pay attention to. I have also collected some data here. Countries along the Belt and Road are mostly developing countries. The important problem they face is still development. Here are also the data of 2016. In more than 60 countries along the Belt and Road, there were approximately 40 countries with a GDP of more than 100 billion US dollars, that is to say, one-third of them had a GDP of less than 100 billion US dollars. This figure was only one-third of that in Shenzhen. From per capita GDP, we found that 32 countries had a per capita income of less than 5,000 US dollars. That is to say, half of these countries are still underdeveloped. This means that industrial cooperation is the most important thing we should pay attention to.

China also attaches great importance to cooperation on capacity. By March 2017, we had established 56 industrial parks in the countries along the Belt and Road, with an investment of more than 18 billion US dollars. Only the data from 2016 can be obtained by us. In 2016, we paid taxes of more than 1 billion US dollars and created 160,000 jobs for the host countries.

Third, think tank cooperation can be an important support for the Belt and Road Initiative. Why? Because the religions, cultures, languages, laws, and customs of the countries along the route vary greatly, and so we need the research of think tanks to deepen mutual understanding and reach consensuses. Religions include Buddhism, Christianity, Islam, etc. Actually, there are many other religions. Big cultural differences also exist. In the East, the Confucian culture is the mainstream, and our cultures are quite different from Western culture and Arab culture. The differences in customs are even greater. The simplest difference is the way we eat. We use chopsticks, but they use knives and forks or they eat directly with their hands. This indicates that there are very large regional differences that need to be studied.

Think tanks not only play a role in institutional planning, program design, policy consultation, etc., but also play a unique role in removing doubts, reaching consensuses, and policy communication. The think tank cooperation is conducive to sharing developmental experiences, reaching consensuses, enhancing policy communication, promoting the integration of strategies and proposing solutions.

Then, let me talk about Shenzhen's practice and some of our ideas about the future. Shenzhen has unique advantages. First of all, we are adjacent to Hong Kong, an international center, and located in the hub of international trade. Look at this route from the Pacific Ocean to the Indian Ocean, Shenzhen is situated on the left, close to the main route. It is also the developed city of China closest to countries along the Maritime Silk Road. We have well-developed ports. Last year, the container throughput reached 25.2 million TEUs, ranking third in the world.

The advantages of economy and trade. In 2017, the GDP of Shenzhen was estimated to be 2.2 trillion yuan (about 340 billion US dollars), ranking among the top 25 cities in the world. The total value of imports and exports was 2.8 trillion yuan (about 430 billion US dollars), including the exportation of the value of 1.67 trillion yuan (about 260 billion US dollars), ranking first in China (excluding Hong Kong, Macao and Taiwan) for 25 consecutive years.

Also, industrial and financial advantages. The city is an important world base for the electronic information industry. The output value of this big industry last year reached 1.6 trillion yuan, about 250 billion US dollars. Emerging industries accounted for about 41%. Shenzhen is also one of the three major financial centers in China. As a financial center, it ranks around 20th in the world.

The advantage of companies. There are many companies in Shenzhen. Yesterday, a mayor told us that the city had 3 million commercial units and 1.8 million registered companies, including seven Fortune 500 companies. Two hundred and eighty Fortune 500 companies invest in Shenzhen. A total of 382 companies are listed at home and abroad. There are 11,200 national high-tech companies.

We have an innovative advantage. Shenzhen is a national innovative city and a national independent innovation demonstration zone and was called "Silicon Delta and Innovation Greenroom" by the *Economist* magazine. In 2017, the total amount of research and development investments accounted for 4.13% of its GDP, comparable to that of Israel and South Korea. Metamaterials, gene sequencing, new energy vehicles, drones and terahertz technology are at the frontiers of the world, and the communication technology is also advanced globally.

Shenzhen's future developmental goal is to build an innovation-driven global city. To achieve this goal, we need to further take advantage of the platform of the Belt and Road Initiative and strengthen economic and cultural cooperation with countries, cities and regions along the route. Shenzhen is always an open and inclusive city. We have partnerships with 83 cities around the world. The circle of friends of Shenzhen includes Busan, Kathmandu, Almere, Athens and so on. In the future, we will strengthen cooperation with cities along the Belt and Road, improve multi-layer communication and exchange mechanisms, take think tanks as a link, build a network of city partnerships, and carry out closer exchanges and cooperation.

Fourth, we will vigorously promote industrial cooperation with countries and regions along the Belt and Road. Companies from Shenzhen have invested in or set up 5,689 branches around the world, and 137 projects are located along the Belt and Road.

As is known to us, Huawei has implemented 26 industrial projects in countries along the Belt and Road with a total investment of 12.5 billion US dollars. We still have more companies like this. In the future, we must make full use of our industrial and financial advantages. Shenzhen is a city with abundant funds and also a financial center. We should continue to give full play to our advantages of industries and finance, encourage our companies to invest in and set up factories, build bonded warehouses and construct industrial parks in countries along the Belt and Road, and export our products, technology, capital and management expertise. Companies from countries and regions along the route are also welcome to settle in Shenzhen and expand in the Chinese market. Our country's policy is also encouraging consumption. China recently launched a particularly favorable policy, that is, reducing the tariffs on imported products. Therefore, we are also very happy and encourage companies from Shenzhen to cooperate with foreign companies and establish joint market organizations to develop in the Chinese market.

Fifth, we will strengthen cooperation with think tanks along the Belt and Road. In February 2016, we held a Belt and Road International Think Tank Conference, which was attended by seven former political figures and more than 120 think tank experts from 50 countries along the route, and the Belt and Road Think Tank Alliance was established.

As a policy advisory body of the local government, we hope to increase the intensity of personnel exchanges, carry out research projects together with other cities, find solutions in special research on some issues in our cooperation and put forward some plans and suggestions.

Dušan Bella (Ambassador Extraordinary and Plenipotentiary of the Embassy of the Slovak Republic in China)

Thank you for allowing me to share my point here. I think that this is very good. This initiative is also very good. Especially in terms of economic cooperation with China, Slovakia is a close partner of China. Under the Belt and Road Initiative, our exchanges and cooperation are constantly expanding. The goal of the Belt and Road Initiative is to cooperate regarding transportation, infrastructure and personnel. Here, I would like to talk about how we promote our business projects under the Belt and Road Initiative, those in Slovakia. First of all, the route connecting Slovakia with the northern part of China has been open to traffic since November 2017. I must point out that with this project, it takes us only a short time to achieve train transportation between the two countries. We also intend to connect five cities in China to promote our exchanges and cooperation.

Moreover, in the field of digital cooperation, how can our cities cooperate under the Belt and Road Initiative?

Before we learned about ICTs, and we cooperated on the corresponding technology and technological innovations under the cooperation mechanism of

Slovakia and Eastern Europe, we studied how to apply this technology to improve our health, hygiene and public safety. Our citizens are also very grateful for our achievements in technology, business development and public health. All of these technologies can help us solve many problems and realize the management in all aspects of a smart city and intelligent management. We need to understand the smart city, which can help us manage cities and urban hygiene. For the concept of the smart city, Huawei can provide more than enough solutions for cities that can be promoted to 111 countries. Now Huawei is still working hard to frame the concept of more convenient urban facilities. "Smart" enables us to promote information, link us together and allows us to share the convenience of life. Smart applications and smart test devices can make great contributions and lead to the development of health undertakings. This kind of solution can help us solve all the problems. The digital system can drive us to better manage the city so that our city government can play a better role in finance and national governance.

After building smart cities, we can construct smart countries and provide benefits to mankind. The existing urban cooperation projects use the concept of innovative smart devices to cope with climate changes and solve water pollution and various other problems.

My point is to build up this kind of urban partnership under the Belt and Road Initiative, carry out multilateral cooperation and apply the smart city solution to all aspects of cities. Thank you.

Zou Guang (Member of the Standing Committee of Shanwei Municipal Committee, Executive Vice Mayor of Shanwei)

Thank you, Mr. Wu Sikang, for your invitation. I come from Shanwei, Guangdong Province. Chinese friends ask me where you are in Guangdong, what is your relationship with another special economic zone called Shantou? Foreign friends ask me whether there is any delicious food or anything interesting in my area. Now I will answer these two questions.

Our city is located 150 kilometers to the east of Shenzhen. We are brother cities with Shantou, another special economic zone; our transportation is very convenient. If you travel from Shenzhen to Shantou, you must pass through Shanwei. If you are interested, it would take you an hour in the afternoon to get from Shenzhen to Shanwei. I will invite you to have afternoon tea at Shanwei.

The second question was asked by Dušan Bella. In Shanwei, we have the mountains like those situated in South California. Once, a friend of mine visited the mountains, the coastal areas and the sea in Shanwei. Then, he showed me the photos and said that Shanwei closely resembled his hometown. If Mr. Clayton Dube could be here, he would tell us whether the cities are similar. Here, I invite all our audience to pay a visit to Shanwei and enjoy a scenery that resembles Mr. Clayton Dube's hometown.

We are neighbors to Shenzhen, Guangdong, Hong Kong and Macao. The Guangdong-Hong Kong-Macao Greater Bay Area is a world-class Greater Bay Area with a population of 60 million. It has the most complete industrial chain, the most abundant funds, the most developed market mechanism, and the most active talents. The global talents, including everyone present here.

The nine cities in the Pearl River Delta, such as Guangzhou, Foshan, Zhaoqing, Shenzhen, Dongguan, Huizhou and Zhuhai, etc., are also accelerating their integration. We have seen the Hong Kong-Zhuhai-Macao Bridge, Guangzhou-Shenzhen Cooperation, and the Guangzhou-Shenzhen-Hong Kong High-Speed Railway, as well as a lot of close cooperation regarding traffic, talents and industries.

In Guangdong Province, the remaining twelve cities, except for the nine cities in the Pearl River Delta, are located in the east, west and north of Guangdong, so they are normally called Yue East-West-North, with a land area covering 69.5% of the entire land area, a population accounting for 49.5% of the whole population and the GDP accounting only for 20% of the whole GDP, and the fixed assets investment and fiscal revenue account for about 12% of that of Guangdong Province. This means that the developmental stage and situations are very imbalanced. Last year, the 19th CPC National Congress was held, which proposed to solve the problem of imbalance in the development of our country. Our twelve cities have an important mission, that is, how to link with city partners of

Guangdong, Hong Kong, Macao and the Pearl River Delta. We now advocate the word "cohesion", but before we only got "radiation".

In the past, we talked about radiation and spillover, but now it is cohesion. The two words reflect a change from passive to active. From the perspective of city development, we have taken a few actions recently.

We are very happy to join the round table, a meeting for the club of the rich. It was originally the Shenzhen-Dongguan-Huizhou Economic Circle, but now it becomes "3 + 2", plus Shanwei and Heyuan, two cities located in the Yue East-West-North. Just like today's exchanges at the conference, we can get more information about Shenzhen, Dongguan and Huizhou. A lot of our demands can have a resonance and wishes can be realized together.

In 2013, Shanwei began the construction of railway lines connected with Guangzhou and Shenzhen. There are three railway lines under construction. On December 28, 2013, the Xiamen-Shanwei Railway opened to traffic, and last year the railway line from Guangzhou to Shanwei opened. Just in one hour, you can travel from Guangzhou to Shenzhen and bask in the sunshine of "Southern California".

In order to enhance the functions of these railway lines, the rapid transit line from Shenzhen to Shanwei opened to traffic on January 5 last year, and the trains from Shenzhen North to Shanwei were opened point-to-point, amounting to 10 trains of 5 pairs per day. They achieved good benefits after operating for one year. Before, the railway company was worried about the number of passengers, but last year they added carriages from 5 to 8. I asked the boss of the Guangzhou Railway whether this line would be terminated. He answered absolutely no because the benefits were very good. There are intercity links between us now.

A total of 468 square kilometers of land in Shanwei was handed over to Shenzhen for management, operations, development and integration of resources. That is to say, by this round of changes, as mentioned just now, we are 150 kilometers away from Shanwei City where we are right now. In the future, we will be zero kilometer away from Shenzhen, that is to say, some of the land in Shenzhen will be turned over to Shanwei. Due to these three roles, the city partnership is getting closer and closer, and we cannot waste that kind of management. From October 2016 until now, every day we select 100 passengers at the high-speed railway station for a questionnaire survey. Volunteers will ask those passengers three questions. If you pay a visit to Shanwei, please cooperate with our volunteers. They will ask where you are from, how long you are going to stay here and what you are going to do there. Every month, we will analyze the questionnaires. We are very happy to see more and more guests coming from the Pearl River Delta willing to stay more than one month or one year in Shanwei, and more guests are doing business in Shanwei. We hope that the questionnaire survey will continue so that we can observe changes in 10 or 20 years, and we hope that everyone can participate in this survey.

Today, the theme of this forum is city partnerships under the Belt and Road Initiative. Through our cooperation with Shenzhen and the Guangdong-Hong Kong-Macao Greater Bay Area, we grasp these points. First, the cities have the strength to get along with each other. Second, collision causes sparks, in other words, we get more opportunities and new ideas after exchanges. Third, uniqueness is charm. Every city, as we cannot step into the same river twice, is a different city with a different charm even on the same land. I hope that our friends from all cities, regions and countries along the Belt and Road get along with each other and have exchanges with us. Each of us has unique charm and can bring better glory. Thank you.

Alexandros Modiano (Deputy Mayor of Athens, Greece)

Dear leaders, you are very welcome to come here.

First of all, I want to ask you a question. Why are you here? Like me, there are some other guests here. They come here from far away. Why do we come here for this meeting by plane for more than ten hours? Do we just want to enjoy the journey or just come here to take photos and make friends? What is our purpose?

Because China has achieved more and more success, we will learn from it. We are all a community. Many of our friends come from Europe. Greece is also the only place for Europe to go to China, so Greece's position is very unique. China is also more and more open. We see that China is now our friend. China can do anything to make Europe stronger. China can do anything to unite Europe, cooperate with 16 European countries, and constitute a very powerful force.

I think the only way out is to cooperate with China. We can help each other and connect with each other very well. We can see that many cities are totally different, "several ups and downs". The state and the country are also different. The formation system of each country is different. Some central governments can manage the government very well, such as Singapore is a centralized urban country, which has decision-making power in many cases, so it's unfair to simply compare what a country or city can do. They have many differences.

On the other hand, China can express ambition and vision. After a long period of time, China can keep an open system and trade. The Belt and Road Initiative is very conducive to the development of the country, enabling us to exchange information and support each other with our respective resources. China can make many countries achieve a win-win situation with such initiatives.

Let's first understand that if we want to focus on the government's advantages to make our regions accessible and promote economic integration, from the perspective of the city, the first issue to be considered is to make people to people relations more convenient, so that both sides can enjoy mutual benefit. A new model of multilateral or bilateral development must be adopted, and I also mentioned green cooperation this morning as well as multilateral cooperation, I hope that many countries can tolerate, embrace and cooperate with each other. Do not be afraid to embrace the whole world and the diversity of the whole world. I hope that all of us will not pursue isolationism.

The compass has eight angles, every angle should be embraced. The Belt and Road Initiative can guide us and let us lose our way in the trend of globalization, just like Marco Polo. To find their own direction, first of all, we should join the corresponding organizations and share the mutually beneficial and win-win methods.

First, there should be a top-down approach. For example, what projects is Sri Lanka going to carry out? To carry out these projects, two or more countries should be considered from a multilateral perspective. With a multilateral perspective, it can solve many problems and build very well.

Second, we must stick to our plan, study strategies, focus on innovation and support all services.

The third is to continuously promote the cooperation and development of synergism. In fact, many times, we see that some regions are in unbalanced development. We need policy support. First of all, we need to understand where the imbalance is. Countries are all unbalanced and development is different. We can understand the problems and demands of many countries. We need to take corresponding programs to make our country better than before.

Fourth, investment. China has made a lot of investment, which is not easy. Many countries avoid investment. In fact, there are many risks that need to be considered when it comes to capital investment. Many countries want to do PPP (government and social capital cooperation). Now I want to tell them that infrastructure construction needs to be built according to local conditions. For example, infrastructure investment in our region needs the ministry of public, private, and third sectors participate in the process of infrastructure construction. Therefore, in order to better understand the needs and maintain social security, we must maintain a balance among the three parties so as to ensure the smooth investment in infrastructure construction. In addition, we need to implement some key projects. First of all, we need to keep pilot projects and use very easy strategies to carry out investment projects.

Fifth, we must make innovations in finance, such as Alipay or WeChat in China, rebuilding the financial system and conducting multilateral financial cooperation.

Sixth, the role of the city is to establish ties between people, which is very important. On the one hand, the ties between people should be conducive to culture and the country, which is also related to the corresponding soft power. We need to understand how the city can expand its soft power and see how the culture of a powerful country has penetrated and expanded in history. In particular, these powerful countries can integrate culture and values into the spirit of young people, such as China, which can influence generations of young people. Let's take a small example. There are 6 to 7 communities in Athens, most of which are Chinese residential areas. Their facilities are also well built. They have a good spirit. Chinese children come to our public schools to study, but they understand Chinese language and culture, learn Chinese dishes, and keep Chinese culture well. At home, they need to learn from their parents Chinese culture, in Athens, they can also contact with local historical sites, learn local culture, these children learn both Chinese culture and Athenian culture at the same time. What I want to say is that this model is very applicable to these realities, and China has done a very good job in this regard. Athens will become an important city along the Belt and Road in 2018.

Seventh, we must give full play to the role of the "compass", and we must have a sense of direction to carry out global cooperation. Just like the compass, we need to build urban partnership. In addition, we need to build think tanks. Think tanks need to spread suggestions to many people in various languages and answer many questions. They need to put their views and their advanced concepts into well spread. In cooperation, we should also guarantee sovereignty.

Eighth, I would like to say that we need to strengthen security. We need to enhance the construction of business monitoring and supervision mechanisms while investing. Many countries attach great importance to national security when they cooperate. China also attaches great importance to national security when it cooperates with other countries. Therefore, we need to ensure bilateral security, a security system that can guarantee security and eliminate all risks. Thank you.

Chen Youwen (President of CCCC-Institute of Urban & Regional Development Planning)

First of all, an introduction to my employer. CCCC is a Fortune 500 company and ranks 110th. CCCC has 110 overseas offices in more than 100 countries throughout the world. Next year, a business turnover of 300 billion yuan will be realized overseas. This year, with the implementation of the Belt and Road Initiative, CCCC has a lot of project investments in Asia, Africa, Latin America and Eastern Europe, and a great number of cooperation projects with new urban areas and new industrial cities in countries along the Belt and Road. It also undertakes the cooperation of large channels and large hubs within the country, helps companies to go global and assists the domestic and foreign governments in doing a lot of work.

We are a think tank within CCCC. In the past few years, we have participated in many international investment projects that everyone is familiar with. Today, my speech mainly focuses on two points: First, how can our domestic companies find the entry point in cooperation with countries along the Belt and Road? Second, what is the role of Shenzhen in the Belt and Road international cooperation?

First, the entry point. According to our profound cooperation projects in dozens of countries abroad over these years, there are different opportunities, areas of cooperation and directions in cooperation with countries at different stages of development. To put it simply, it is divided into three scenarios: developed or post-industrialized countries; emerging countries in the middle and late stages of industrialization; and countries in the early and middle stages of industrialization.

Let's take a look at countries in Africa, represented by South Africa and North Africa. The level of industrialization is very low, but the illiteracy rate is as high as over 80%. In this region, we have to distinguish between several situations. Some areas have abundant labor resources. There is a lot of agricultural land and a large population. For example, Victoria in East Africa has 60 million people. In our proposal, we proposed to promote the modernization of agriculture, extend the industrial chain of agriculture, and develop the agricultural processing and trade. This, for one thing, can unleash the population, and for another, increase people's income. As for countries with abundant mineral resources but without other pillars, the general idea is to assist them in direct trade, further develop them into a processing industry chain, and facilitate the industrialization of resource-based countries.

Important nodes of the Belt and Road can function as trade hubs that provide good support for inland countries. This is also the enhancement of the hub function and an important future direction of cooperation, so China has cooperated to construct many nodes like this, such as Sabah.

Many regions lack infrastructure but have a good amount of demand. In the initial stage of cooperation, trade is relatively easy. If a country is very backward in infrastructure, urbanization must solve the problem of urban infrastructure. We invested heavily in Africa in the past to improve the conditions of local infrastructure through the government's framework of cooperation.

The second scenario is that China is basically a coastal country in the late stage of industrialization, which achieves its economic growth by exporting products to external markets. Similarly, cities in countries along the Belt and Road are confronted with the same problems as we are in China, such as the upgrading of the industrial structure and the transformation of the model of economic growth. These cities are unwilling to establish partnerships with respect to the labor-intensive industries, but long for only high-tech industries. Our cooperation with them must take account of these factors. At this point, Eastern Europe also has great advantages because the people there are well educated. We have established corresponding research centers in Eastern Europe. The conditions are good. In countries in the stage of post-industrialization, the infrastructure is still lagging behind for various reasons, including land and continuous improvement. Therefore, opportunities exist, including the railway line in which CCCC invested 70 billion yuan in Malaysia.

There is also a third scenario, that is how to cooperate with developed countries. Northern and Western Europe have good technological advantages, but China has a good foundation of manufacturing capacity and a strong market promoting ability. There are opportunities for cooperation with developed regions and Eastern Europe in advanced technology and advanced capacity. After these three types of countries are included, the future-driven and market-driven factors of China will become increasingly greater in the future. As China's urbanization makes progress, it will become the world's largest market. In the past 30 years, the global market has been driven by Europe and the United States, and even China was initially driven by external demand of the European and American markets. In the future, China's internal demand will gradually become an important driving force of the global market. Technological service is the future direction for the market driver of China.

Now let's talk about the role of Shenzhen in the Belt and Road international cooperation.

The municipal party committee and the municipal government has made it very clear that from our perspective, according to the status of gateway and hub with countries along the Belt and Road, in this framework, what role can Shenzhen play? We believe that the role of Shenzhen is unique. Shenzhen can't do everything in the Belt and Road Initiative, but it can do many things that other regions cannot do, that is, Shenzhen is a global model. We have met many presidents and leaders from developing countries who asked for a visit to Shenzhen. Why? Because Shenzhen is the dream of their countries, a city growing fast from zero to one. There are various ways of bringing about innovation in the long-term development of Shenzhen, all of which are valuable for developing countries, so Shenzhen provides the invaluable experience of city development to developing countries.

The second role is because Shenzhen is ahead of many cities in China, and the Pearl River Delta was dependent on Hong Kong-driven development in the first 30 or 20 years since the reform and opening-up, now Shenzhen can become a new engine driving that development. Such a transformation is unique among all cities of China. Such technological innovation-driven capabilities can not only drive the transformation of Shenzhen but also drive the transformation of other cities. For example, Shenzhen's manufacturing and R&D move to Dongguan and provide very good opportunities for the future transformation of Dongguan. Similarly, some regions or cities in developing countries would like to create such a situation. The spillover effect of Shenzhen's technological innovation can bring opportunities to other cities.

Another point is that the whole system centered on Shenzhen is quite complete, including financial centers, international shipping centers, and a capacity for world-class production, so these capabilities enable Shenzhen to provide a fast channel for the transformation of Western high-tech achievements. This point can be a very promising direction for future development.

Therefore, according to this understanding, our recent suggestions include:

1. For countries in the early and middle stages of industrialization, Shenzhen has no advantage in labor-intensive production capacity cooperation, and the focus should be on the export trade of technological products.

2. For emerging countries entering the middle and late stages of industrialization, Shenzhen has a great advantage of high-tech capacity cooperation.

3. For developed or post-industrialized countries and regions, Shenzhen has the advantage of absorbing Western high-tech achievements and carry out rapid industrialized transformation through advanced manufacturing in the Pearl River Delta.

Finally, I want to talk about the Shenzhen model and the sharing of Shenzhen's experience. Firstly, Shenzhen is a unique city name card of the Belt and Road, so it can promote the brand of the Belt and Road and share the Shenzhen model and Shenzhen's experience. Secondly, based on universities and scientific research institutions in Shenzhen, it is possible to provide consulting support for the construction of a framework for a model system of city governance for cities in countries along the Belt and Road. Thirdly, it can participate in overseas special economic zones through government cooperation.

Philip McConnaughay (Dean of School of Transnational Law, Peking University)

I am the dean of the School of Transnational Law of Peking University. This law school is quite unique because it can integrate and study laws of all regions, such as laws of the European Union, and also the legal systems of many countries. Our school is known for such a creative process. We believe that what we do can participate in the process of the world, and China's global influence is increasing rapidly. The legal system in the Pearl River Delta is different from that in other regions. We have cooperation and exchanges with many countries and regions. Many of our students are also studying the legal systems of countries along the Belt and Road. We also have exchanges with the University of Athens. In our opinion, to realize the Belt and Road, we must understand the local legal systems.

On the other hand, to promote the Belt and Road Initiative, we must do a good job in education and the rule of law. We are also concerned about some investments, the investment in and construction of infrastructures. Two issues are very important. First of all, we must apply this principle of investment. These cities are unique, and the Pearl River Delta is also the most densely populated region. The second issue is that the economy transforms from specialization to technology. We need to transfer the center of manufacturing to other regions, such as biological systems and pharmaceutical systems. So, what we can do and what we are concerned about is how to promote the process of industrial upgrading by our understanding of the legal systems or our study of laws. For example, when the industry is being upgraded, it will inevitably involve the issue of government regulations, as well as the issue of laws. These are our concerns. Thank you.

Clayton Dube (Dean of of US-China Institute of USC)

I am very grateful to be here at this meeting. I admire Shenzhen very much. When I first came to Shenzhen, there was basically nothing. That was in 1982. From 1982 until now, the city has changed in all aspects and has influenced the world. So, I am very grateful to the organizer and their cadres. I must express my gratitude.

What is my mission today? For foreigners here, we attended the meeting held in Wuzhou Hotel, which means five continents. I come from Southern California in America. We have come to the Belt and Road conference, so we know a lot about the Belt and Road. My question is, in your home countries, have the people heard of this, and has it made some sort of impact? And in my country, almost none at all. In my country, the United States, most Americans have never heard of the Belt and Road, but they have all heard of China, they have all heard of China's remarkable economic progress, but they don't generally know about this gorgeous initiative. And they have some awareness of China's going out, and everyone in America knows that because there are many Chinese in America. The exchange of talents is increasing at the university level and at other levels.

Averagely every day, about 6,000 Americans come to China and 8,000 Chinese come to America. So, here is a question, at what point will Americans know everything about the Belt and Road Initiative? Or when will they know about it?

Is it impossible for the Belt and Road Initiative to become something that people in the United States and people in Europe will all know about? This is the first question I would like to ask you. There is a song on the video you watched just now, and this song was composed by some Chinese in the United States, singing a song about the Belt and Road Initiative. They know that the Belt and Road crosses many countries, including different cities in America, even Texas. Therefore, the Belt and Road involves various languages, for example Spanish and English. Many people are doing business in China. After knowing more about China, everyone may have met this word, "guanxi", which means connections. Chinese people often tell foreigners that "guanxi" is very important in China. If you don't have good "guanxi", you cannot succeed in business. Therefore, many people have said that if a foreigner could speak Chinese and when he/she communicates with foreigners, they would say that if you have good "guanxi" with somebody, this would be really helpful.

However, "guanxi", as I mentioned just now, is originally a Chinese term, and now many Westerners have begun to consider the importance of guanxi because its meaning is extended. And for many years I have talked about this as a joke. It's not a joke anymore. As you can see on the screen, guanxi became part of our English dictionary. Guanxi is different from other translated words because it is spelled in Pinyin. Everyone knows that it is important. Many people will think of the Belt and Road Initiative and will pay attention to it. So, when President Xi Jinping announced the Belt and Road Initiative, a lot of people paid attention. I am from North America, but I am here to talk a little bit about South America. Actually, the South Americans are quite eager for the Belt and Road to reach South America. So, here we can see that President Xi Jinping has visited these various countries. This desire will also probably gradually spread to other countries. On the screen, you can see the Chinese investment in countries along the Belt and Road. If the plan on our screen is successful, these investors will have made a very big and very successful investment.

Therefore, the countries shown in the picture are quite eager to establish diplomatic relations with China and then be impacted by the Belt and Road; Panama is one of these countries. In fact, we can see that many investors are curious about this idea, and come to learn it.

California is the number one exporter to China. Americans are aware that the Chinese market is generating economic opportunities in America, Tencent purchased a gaming company in Los Angeles; other companies purchased AVP or supermarket and retail companies. A total of 1,800 Californians work in Chinese funded companies. I think this is pushing back against negativism towards China, it's very important and we see more of this. We heard more and more examples of China investing in the United States to make acquisitions of American companies. Huawei employs a lot of people in America. Now China's reasons for doing it are because we all will benefit as a result. In California, two governors from the Democratic Party and from the Libertarian Party both want to work with China. They discuss with China about building high-speed railways and have signed agreements with China. We can see opportunities on the Belt and Road. This company is promoting cooperation between China and the United States.

Two of our Los Angeles companies want to participate in the Belt and Road Initiative. One of them built the tallest building in Shanghai, and they want to create better lives in other cities. Shenzhen is one of these kinds of cities.

Since the 1990s, some countries have adopted what they called the "East-Asian Development" model, but it was very difficult. So, the Belt and Road is very important for them and also an important part of China's strategic cooperation. China will become a very promising and influential country among them.

So, I'd like to conclude that I am impressed with this bold initiative that will be important not just for the population of China, but the people of the world. The United States is not directly connected, but I hope that America can also participate in China's Belt and Road Initiative. Thank you.

Dhia Khaled (Tunisan Ambassador to China)

Today, I feel honored to come to Shenzhen, a beautiful city. I have just heard the wonderful speech of the last speaker. I am very honored to be able to speak after him.

First of all, I would like to thank the government leaders here for their support, because they provide us with the opportunity to attend the forum. Another point I want to emphasize is, congratulations to the successful holding of the 19th CPC National Congress. It will surely lay a good foundation for better development of China in the future.

Sitting here today, we are discussing cooperation in the future, especially economic cooperation among various countries. We know that cooperation among cities is very important. Also congratulations to city partners for great success in their partnerships. I also hope that China will have a better future.

The theme of this speech today is, of course, related to the Belt and Road. Everyone knows that cities play an increasingly important role and involve various industries, so the successful developmental experience of various cities can be a lesson for other cities. Of course, we also know that we are facing other challenges. Also, I am very happy that the Tunisian government is cooperating with China, especially with Shenzhen. Although I haven't been here in Shenzhen for very long, my experience is very positive, and I know that Tunisia and Shenzhen cooperate very closely.

In particular, the policy dividend between the two countries, that is, our connections, are getting closer. Therefore, our two countries have very great potential for cooperation. I hope that you can invest in our country. Today, I have a proposal, that is, we can cooperate to establish an entrepreneurship park based on the Belt and Road Initiative. I think this can greatly unlock the potential of cooperation between our two countries. We can increase cooperation in areas of manufacturing, new energy, IT and the Internet of Things. As you know, our country is located in the middle of the Mediterranean region. We know that China is working hard to promote a partnership between Africa and China, and we are also planning to organize the second forum of China and Africa. So, I hope to emphasize that Tunisia is very important for the Belt and Road. Tunisia will become a very large market for Chinese investments, and we signed a free trade agreement with China in 1995. This is also our policy dividend and is also the promotion of our network of cooperation. We have a lot of achievements that can be displayed in figures. And you know that the Tunisian economy is relatively fragile, and cooperation with China can enable us to greatly enhance our resilience to various challenges. I must underline the fact that we established an economic cooperation center in 2000 to study economic cooperation. There are two Chinese companies, ZTE and Huawei, operating in Tunisia, and I hope that more companies will come to Tunisia.

In 2000, I came to Shenzhen for the first time. Eighteen years later, I have found that great changes have occurred in Shenzhen and it is very beautiful. I am very happy to witness this. We must look to the future. I have to take this opportunity to congratulate Shenzhen and even Guangdong for their great success in urban planning and construction and thank the organizer for giving us this opportunity to look into the future, discuss global issues of different themes and to achieve a win-win situation. In this way, we can greatly improve the connectivity of cities, countries and inland regions. Tunisia is one of the fastest-developing economies in the world. We are seeking cooperation with China and want to become an active participant in the Belt and Road Initiative. We hope that the Belt and Road Initiative can continue for a long time. Thank you.

Feng Jian (The Xinhua News Agency)

On the waves of modernization and globalization, in such an era, it is beyond doubt that the media image of a company, a city and a country is very important. But the necessity of the image is usually not in our own hands. With social development and progress, people become increasingly aware of their images and pay unprecedented attention to image building. Now we take the initiative to build up our image for strengthening soft power and enhancing our attraction, appeal and leadership. Under the big framework of the Belt and Road, how to build up an image is a topic faced by many companies.

In my opinion, the media, especially important media, play a very important role in image building. The emergence of media or the development of science and technology provide a big platform for information sharing and increase the speed for the gathering and dissemination of information. The media has three roles: information collection, bridge of friendship, builder or shaper.

Needless to say, media can play a role of information collection. Everyone knows this very well. For example, big media, either mainstream media such as Reuters, AFP and Associated Press in the West, or CCTV in China, are very important for the collection of information. For example, the Xinhua News Agency has more than 50,000 information users and 6 million periodicals. It is also the largest news group in China. Also, there are very influential websites in the world. The media can play a unique role and the Internet will connect more and more people and equipment. With the development of information technology, it will become faster and more convenient for us to connect, and the cost will also decrease.

The media is a link of communication and a bridge of friendship. It not only disseminates information, but also communicates culture and enhances understanding. In the Belt and Road Initiative, we talk about the people-to-people bonds, for which the media can play an irreplaceable role.

President Xi often tells us to "tell China's stories, spread China's voice". The first half-sentence means we should report the news of people-to-people bonds in the Belt and Road for developed countries. As we all know, people-to-people bonds are the premise for international exchanges, and enhancing mutual understanding is the basis for cooperation and the glue and booster for sustainable development and cooperation. After the Belt and Road Initiative was put forward, big media began to report the news of society, culture and people's livelihood and to promote a culture of harmony.

The media is the shaper of influence. It has the functions of collection and dissemination of information and builds up an image by deciding what kind of information is collected, how to disseminate that information, and how to disseminate useful information. From a country to a group or a company, all of us are disseminating information to the outside world, and the media can build up an image. A positive image may be built if positive news is disseminated more and on a broader scale, but if negative news is disseminated more and on a broader scale, there will be a negative image.

It is the necessary value judgments of media to decide on what information to select, what kind of information is collected, and what kind of news is reported. Another point depends on the field of information dissemination and also the influence of the dissemination of information. The third point is the ability to set the topics based on the information regarding those topics. The setting and the expression of the topic are very important. Where there are no refreshing and fascinating topics, the audience will not be interested, the influence will not be produced and the image-building will not be good.

The next step for a company or a city should be strengthening its image-building. A good image is inseparable from media support. To build a good image, we must actively cooperate with the media, dream up good ideas, and enhance our product image on media communication platforms, thereby improving appeal of our products.

We should take the initiative in building up our image. As a saying goes, you will win with a plan. The plan means the setting of the image and the planning, which is also a function. We should know how to prepare plans and what to publish. Nowadays, many countries are also aware of the importance of topics and they promote their bright points. There are many events, such as cultural weeks, corporate exhibitions, etc. I think they are topic-setting activities.

Powerful communication determines influence. It is very important to have an influence on the topic. It is necessary to set different topics by considering factors such as country, region, audience and local culture. For example, in the Arab world, the setting of the topic must consider the features of Arabic culture.

Both the government and companies should enhance image awareness with synergy. Now everyone in the world is a disseminator of information. Everyone is a kind of media. Everyone is a planter. Everyone has a microphone. It is one facet of image-building by strengthening the training of every person, every group and every company and further enhancing the awareness of image-building. The government may increase training in this regard, organize various projects to enhance the awareness, raise awareness of citizens and heighten their senses of belonging, honor and pride. The achievement of a city is that of every person and every organization. Showing off our achievements can enhance the senses of belonging, honor and pride. Learning and training are required.

It is also necessary to sharpen the sense of social responsibility of our companies. Companies investing in developed countries should not only pursue profits, but also shoulder the responsibility for the image-building of the country, and exhibit the image of the city and the country locally.

Diana Macarevici (Temporay Agent of Moldova Embassy in China)

The people of the Republic of Moldova express their strong support for the Chinese people and their deep admiration for the achievements made by the Chinese people unswervingly following the past and heralding the future with the wisdom from the history of thousands of years. Today, China is a modern country that has achieved historic and great success in economic construction, science and technology and culture. This success sets a shining example with the ancient civilizations of China. China is not only the world's second-largest economic power, but also an important partner of all countries in the world, including the Republic of Moldova. The Republic of Moldova is willing to make every effort to continuously strengthen bilateral relations with the People's Republic of China.

Last year, China and the Republic of Moldova celebrated the 25th anniversary of their diplomatic relations. Although 25 years is a short period of time, our two countries have always maintained friendly and mutually beneficial cooperative relations, and continued to diversify and develop such relations in various fields. The Belt and Road Initiative proposed by Chinese President Xi Jinping in 2013 brought great opportunities to the Republic of Moldova and China and created new areas of cooperation. The Moldovan government strongly supports the Belt and Road Initiative. We believe that this will greatly strengthen the friendship between the governments and people of our two countries and push the economic and trade cooperation between us into a new stage.

Therefore, the establishment of a sustainable city partnership will play an important role in promoting regional economic integration, exploring new areas of cooperation and making new room for development. I would like to thank the Shenzhen Municipal Government and the Development Research Center for giving me the opportunity to become well acquainted with Shenzhen's business environment and economic advantages. Shenzhen has left me with a strong impression that the city itself is a legend. In less than 40 years, Shenzhen has developed like a bolt of lightning. In just a few decades, its economy has undergone radical changes, thus attracting the attention of the international community. Shenzhen has significant advantages in the fields of distribution, logistics and manufacturing, and these can offer numerous possibilities for strengthening economic and commercial cooperation between Shenzhen and Moldovan companies.

In May 2017, Mr. Octavian Kalmyk, the Vice Premier and Minister of Economy of Moldova, attended the Belt and Road Forum for International Cooperation and signed *Initiative on Promoting Unimpeded Trade Cooperation along the Belt and Road.* We hope that this document of global importance will not only facilitate bilateral cooperation between the Republic of Moldova and China, but that it will also bring opportunities for cooperation among major cities in Moldova and Shenzhen. The economic and trade cooperation between Moldova and Shenzhen will be open. With the support of the governments of both sides, the cooperation of cities will also be enhanced.

The Republic of Moldova also hopes to take this opportunity to develop its economy and attract more Chinese investors and tourists to Moldova. For Moldova, China is a very trustworthy and reliable partner. For the benefit of Moldova and the Chinese people, we hope to continue to develop excellent bilateral cooperation between the two countries.

The Republic of Moldova, situated between the European Union and the Commonwealth of Independent States, has the geographical advantages of close proximity to the western and oriental markets, thus ensuring communication and ties between the East and the West. We can take full advantage of our geographical advantages to become a bridge linking Europe and Asia. This will open a window for Chinese investors to a market with 800 million consumers. The Moldovan government advocates economic openness and has signed several bilateral and multilateral trade agreements. The Republic of Moldova continues to explore new sustainable developmental strategies to create a good business environment for Chinese investors and improve the country's overall competitiveness.

The industrial projects to which priority is given for attracting investment and promoting exports are listed below: information technology and telecommunications; machinery and equipment manufacturing (vehicles); activities of management and support services; machine and spare parts manufacturing; textiles; electrical equipment; food industry and agriculture, including the wine industry.

In order to facilitate trade exchanges and allow citizens of both countries to understand each other and enter each other's markets, the governments of both countries began discussions on the signing of a free trade agreement. Over the years, we have had many preparatory discussions on this issue, and successfully signed a memorandum of understanding to officially launch free trade negotiations. We hope to complete the negotiations and sign the agreement by the end of this year. The signing of a free trade agreement will be a milestone in strengthening economic relations between the two countries and increasing the volume of trade.

Wine is the most important Moldovan product exported to the Chinese market. We hope that the free trade agreement can also promote the exports of Moldovan wine. The wine industry is an important pillar of the Republic of Moldova's economy. The country has a history of wine making for more than 3,000 years. It has the world's largest underground wineries: Cricova and Milesti Mitz, each of which has the wine cellars with a length of more than 120 kilometers. Also, we have the largest stock of wine, more than 1.5 million bottles, recorded by the Guinness World Records.

The Chinese market is one of our target markets, and we have made a plan for the development of the market for it, including a series of promotional activities such as participation in China's largest wine exhibition, wine tasting events and wine culture training for Chinese consumers.

Shenzhen is one of the largest cities in China and a very important market. Companies and friends from Shenzhen are welcome to visit the world's largest underground wine cellars in Moldova, taste the mellow wine culture lasting for thousands of years and see the possibilities of cooperation in the exportation of and investment in wine.

Here, I would like to point out that in order to enhance direct exchanges between our two countries and their peoples, the Government of the Republic of Moldova has adopted a decision on simplifying visa formalities for Chinese citizens. From August 1, 2017, any Chinese citizen who holds a valid visa issued by any member state of the European Union or Schengen countries may enter Moldova during the period of the validity of the visa. We hope that this decision can increase the number of visitors and the interaction of business people, with a view to encouraging both sides to facilitate new cooperation projects.

I would like to reiterate the fact that the Moldovan government attaches great importance to developing relations with China and agrees to work with China to implement the consensus on cooperation reached by officials of the two countries during mutual visits, advance the relations and cooperation within the framework of the Belt and Road Initiative, enhance the well-being of the people of the two countries and achieve more fruitful results. Meanwhile, the Embassy of the Republic of Moldova will do its best to further develop the relations mentioned above and strongly support and deepen cooperation at the local level and among the companies of the two countries.

Finally, I would like to thank the organizers of this forum again for their sincere invitation and warm welcome. Here, I sincerely hope the discussions we have today can yield fruitful results, flexibly interpret the theme of the forum and achieve mutual benefits in a real sense. Thank you.

Marie Chan (Executive Chairman of Hong Kong East Timor General Chamber of Commerce)

I am a third-generation overseas Chinese born in Timor-Leste. My grandfather moved to Timor-Leste 100 years ago. Our family is in the business of plastics, sandalwood and coffee. We have our own business there. In the 1970s, there was a coup in Timor-Leste and a big conflict with Indonesia. Only 30 years later, in 2000, we separated from Indonesia. I happened to meet our new president, who asked me to return to Timor-Leste and rebuild our country. When I went back, he first wanted me to set up a Chamber of Commerce in Hong Kong because I am an overseas Chinese in Hong Kong, I know the language of the motherland and understand the language of Timor-Leste. So, in 2013, we established the Timor-Leste General Chamber of Commerce with an aim to facilitate economic trade cooperation with Hong Kong, the ASEAN community and other regions and help China to go global and bring in. Our Timor-Leste General Chamber of Commerce will bring more entrepreneurs, businessmen and citizens from mainland China and the ASEAN countries to visit, invest in and sightsee in Timor-Leste. Especially in Shenzhen, we have met more than 50 of them. When talking with them, we hoped that they could bring high-tech industries from Shenzhen to Timor-Leste, invest in and cooperate with Timor-Leste, and set up training classes and centers in Timor-Leste. Timor-Leste has good geographical advantages. Today, Minister Li Zhaoxing told me that Timor-Leste had a very good advantage of being a natural tourist attraction. He had been to Timor-Leste. At the sight of the beach every day, you can't help but go swimming in the sea there. Timor-Leste is a tourist attraction. There are also a lot of natural resources, oil, solar energy reserves, natural lake reserves, collective agriculture and construction industry. Now we are constructing airports and roads. Timor-Leste is a very young country with unlimited business opportunities. In recent years, Timor-Leste has introduced companies, and Chinese entrepreneurs may find business opportunities there. Timor-Leste is a developing country. It will certainly strengthen its cooperation with neighboring countries, make greater contributions to the development across the straits, to the prosperity and stability of China and to the development of ASEAN, and it will provide a platform for more exchanges in culture, sports, high tech and talents.

The Timor-Leste General Chamber of Commerce in Hong Kong has been following up the Belt and Road promoted by our motherland. Timor-Leste borders on and is a neighbor of Indonesia. On Zheng He's Voyages to the Western Seas, he had been to Timor-Leste to pick sandalwood. Many people in Southeast Asia don't know what the Belt and Road is. Last year and the year before last, I went to Malaysia and they asked me what the Belt and Road was. When I came to Shenzhen, Hong Kong, Macao and mainland China, everyone knew what the Belt and Road is, so I answered that the Belt and Road was the road to the alleviation of poverty, because President Xi Jinping encourages connectirity and adjacent road towards the alleviation of poverty.

Timor-Leste is a country which is blessed with favorable weather, natural conditions, harmonious people and abundant resources. There are unlimited business opportunities. We attract investment from China and benefit from each other. Especially under the leadership of Shenzhen, we will focus on the economic development of companies, actively implement the Belt and Road Initiative advocated by President Xi Jinping.

Cosmin Necula: (Mayor of Bacǎu, Romania)

First of all, I would like to thank the Forum for International Cooperation and thank you for your invitation. I would also like to thank the Shenzhen Government for its kind invitation. Romania regards China as a brother country. We did not hesitate to establish diplomatic relations with China in 1949. Although we did not know much about each other then, Premier Zhou Enlai visited our country in 1961. The Belt and Road Initiative proposed by President Xi Jinping aims to bring about peace, rise peacefully and develop peacefully. We are brother countries that share economic similarities and implement economic development plans. It is important to create opportunities for dialogues and to share experience, because this allows more people to learn how to develop and spread the experience of success. Ideological differences will not hinder our cultural and economic exchanges. In Romania, we have good measures and mechanisms for promoting economic growth, which coincide with the Belt and Road Initiative. The cooperation mechanisms are necessary for cities to find ways to facilitate business cooperation. We must treat each other like brothers, expand our initiatives and implement policies and measures to countries along the route of the Belt and Road. Economic development is important, but we should have a good understanding of cultural education as well. We must understand the differences and cultural commonalities of our two countries. We should achieve economic and cultural exchanges, so that our cooperation can rise to a higher level. In my view, the Belt and Road Initiative can serve as a driving force for our economy, boost all aspects of smart development and benefit the people's lives.

This is the first time I have come to China, and to Shenzhen. Shenzhen is a city of miracles. For me, Shenzhen is a model city. As the mayor of Bacau, Romania, I take the development of Shenzhen from scratch over these thirty years as an example. In fact, I want to learn from the model of Shenzhen, and apply it to our city. In Europe, we are passionate about smart cities, intelligent cities, and everything needs to be intelligent and smart. I feel that we can find the answer to the creation of a smart city in Shenzhen. For example, Huawei and ZTE are all from Shenzhen. Shenzhen is a smart city whose relevant experience we can learn from.

In terms of cooperation, there are many issues that need to be considered, such as economic and cultural issues, as we mentioned just now. It is also necessary to link up with Shenzhen. In my opinion, our next step, an important step under the Belt and Road Initiative, is to make full use of this platform, to cooperate through this very good system. We can have systematical cooperation in this way, and through this platform. I believe that it is the platform developed by you that can lead our development in the general direction. Thank you again for your invitation. I hope to invite you to our city, Bacau, to share your experience at the right time. Thank you.

Qian Xiaoqin (The representative of Xuzhou Handler Special Vehicle Co., Ltd.)

Dear Leaders, Ladies and Gentlemen, Good Afternoon! It is an honor to make this speech on behalf of Ms. Yang Ya, the Vice Chairman of Xuzhou Handler Special Vehicle Co., Ltd., and the Chairman of the Board of the Shenzhen Lianshuo Educational Investment Management Co., Ltd.

Our company manufactures hardware for new energy and new materials, especially motherboards. My department is communication and positioning. I am very happy to meet with you here. I wish to give my special thanks for the organizer's invitation for me to give a speech here. We often keep in contact with each other. I want to ask a question: What is the relationship between your country and the Belt and Road Initiative?

Here, I would like to report what we have done under the Belt and Road Initiative. Our parent company has a long history of cooperation with countries along the Belt and Road and supplies a lot of equipment. Lianshuo Education Investment Management Co., Ltd. has some international cooperation with ZTE and other high-tech companies in Shenzhen, that is, cooperation under the Belt and Road Initiative. We are a pilot or experimental unit that received strong support from the Ministry of Education at the end of last year as well as the support from the city government of Shenzhen. We are running a school, which is developing very well and is training many talents. One of the missions of our organization is to make a contribution to the Belt and Road Initiative. We also devote great efforts to industrial integration.

I have just now introduced what we have done. Probably some people may ask why we have done this as a private company? Is this not something the Chinese government should do? Despite being a private company, we have a department called the social responsibility department, so we also provide them with information services and systems, such as ZTE. We also cooperate with many countries along the Belt and Road.

Some countries along the Belt and Road are short of comprehensive talents, and our company can solve this problem. Skilled talents are very scarce. If economically underdeveloped countries can have more talents to help them, I believe that they will develop better.

Finally, one of the topics of the forum today is the "think tank". Ms. Yang Ya also mentioned that I could share her idea here. In her opinion, the cooperation of think tanks is a trend. Our company temporarily can't provide such services because we are incapable of providing training to policy-makers. I think this topic needs the participation of companies. With their participation, we will be able to do better, and we would be passionate and enthusiastic about doing better. Our company actually has experience in marketing and other aspects as well.

Roi Feder (Managing Director of APCO Worldwide's Tel Aviv Office)

I would like to thank the Shenzhen Municipal Government for inviting me and the organizers for their hard work in organizing the conference.

I am very happy to attend such a conference because I can get more information and make observations as well. As the executive president of a public relations company, what I need to do is address the issue of international communications. We have 36 offices in the world, and 3 in China. In the past, we provided the consultant services to the Israeli government and supported the trade links between China and Israel. I still remember when I first came to China in 2010, I paid a visit to some technology companies. Several companies get together, Huawei, ZTE and others. I was fortunate enough to see the advanced technology in China, to see that China had done very well, to see the pace of the globalization of China, and to see its great development. I felt that many companies have encountered problems in the last few years, and I am able to help them solve those problems.

It's my honor to share my points with everyone. For me, Shenzhen is the best place for sharing my ideas. SIGNAL (Sino-Israel Global Network of Leadership) is the only Israeli think-tank platform that has access to the Belt and Road, and it can promote academic cooperation and network cooperation among countries. Israel is also a relatively large country in terms of GDP. Israel also has a nickname — the global technological and industrial innovation center, and Shenzhen is the "Silicon Valley" of China. The two regions represent the transit stations of innovation.

China is taking off due to many technological factors, Chinese enterprises will become more and more powerful, and Chinese enterprises will invest hundreds of billions of dollars in the next few years. Therefore, we will have great cooperation in artificial intelligence or healthcare and education.

Israel, despite being a small country, can be supplementary to China. I would like to talk about how to achieve better cooperation under the Belt and Road Initiative. Cooperation between our two countries is not limited to technical aspects, but also involves economic aspects. Here, I will give details about the drivers of the Israeli economy and look at how Israel and China are mutually beneficial.

Natural gas is an important promoter. In the past, everyone said that Israel did not have any energy, but in fact we had a lot of energy. In 2010, we found 1,000 BCM (billion cubic meters) of natural gas (but the total consumption of Israel is is 7 BCM per year), which can better promote human development. Such large natural gas reserves can promote economic development, earn revenue and provide the fund of $1.1 billion to our country. It can boost the cooperation between China and Israel and reduce manufacturing costs. For China, the cost of importing natural gas from Israel is lower than the cost of China's producing its own natural gas. It is a favorable industry for China. Our location is very close to the European market. More importantly, China can move the production center to Israel, closer to our market.

Speaking of ports, the northern Israeli seaport becomes a trade route to Jordan and other Arab regions. After a bridge was built over the Jordan River to connect Israel and Jordan's Free Trade Zone, Israel has achieved a favorable position.

What is also happening is the network connection from the Israeli border to Beit She'an. We share common economic interests, so we have closer relations with Greece and Cyprus. We have built natural gas pipelines linking up with Southern Europe for energy sharing and mutual connection. We have agreed to build 1,000 miles of cable so that we can share electricity with Europe.

Most workers in Israel deposit money into pension plans. Last year, the national pension plan was established. This means that Israeli financial institutions now manage more than $400 billion of functional savings, and financial institutions can have opportunities and advantages. In fact, many financial institutions in our country have the desire to seek investment opportunities because they are relatively cash-rich. I think this is very good for the Belt and Road Initiative. In my view, we are facing great opportunities, and we can develop ourselves through opportunities no matter what happens.

Some very interesting research was a project regarding risk assessment of the Israeli Belt and Road Initiative market by the EIU (Economist Intelligence Unit), which found that the risk was lower than that for Singapore. This is very important because it is beyond technology with unstable factors. Our investment environment is very stable, and we are a very safe investment system. Thank you.

Sub Forum 3: Industrial Connection

Subject: Innovating the Cooperation Model and
Constructing a Network of City Think Tanks
and Industrial Partners

Session 1: Sharing Experience and Building the New Model of Cooperation for Enterprises under the Belt and Road Initiative

Zhu Guangchao (Deputy Chief Engineer of the State Grid Corporation of China)

Ladies and Gentlemen, Dear Guests:

I am very pleased to attend this forum on behalf of the State Grid Corporation of China. I will report our achievements, experience and understanding on how to serve and promote the construction of the Belt and Road.

1. Cognition and understanding of the Belt and Road Initiative

The Belt and Road Initiative proposed by Xi Jinping is an important measure for China to actively participate in global governance, promote in-depth development of economic globalization, and build a new pattern of opening-up to the outside world. The Belt and Road has already become the most popular international cooperation initiative in the world. It is an important cooperation platform for relevant countries to achieve common development. With the active support and participation of more than 100 countries and international organizations, the initiative, coming from China, will turn into a reality that will benefit the world.

Most countries along the Belt and Road are developing countries with enormous market potential. According to the predictions of many authoritative organizations, in the next five years, the demand for power investment in countries along the Belt and Road will reach 1.5 trillion US dollars, and the consumption of electricity will grow at an average annual rate of more than 4%, higher than that of developed countries and other developing countries. This provides a rare market opportunity for China's power companies. The State Grid Corporation of China, the largest public company in the world, is the second-largest energy and power company in the Fortune 500 list. It has the responsibility, obligation and ability to effectively play its role as a backbone and leader in the construction of the Belt and Road, share our technology and experience with countries along the route and support local economic and social development.

2. Serving and promoting the Belt and Road by the State Grid Corporation of China

In recent years, the State Grid Corporation of China has implemented the Belt and Road Initiative, adhered to the principle of extensive consultation, joint contribution and shared benefits, and regarded the service and promotion of the construction of the Belt and Road as the core of international development. It has formulated the *Plans for the Construction of the Belt and Road* and the *Action Plan for the Cooperation on International Capacity*, it gives full play to its comprehensive advantages, facilitates the coordination of policies by planning integration and standards, it promotes the connectivity of facilities by investment and the construction of infrastructure, it achieves unimpeded trade by cooperation on international capacity, boosts financial integration by international capital operations, and realizes people-to-people bonds by "localized operations" and international exchanges and cooperation. Therefore, it plays a role as a backbone of and leader in the construction of the Belt and Road.

First, to steadily invest in energy and power infrastructure. Our company has successfully invested in the backbone energy network of the Philippines, Brazil, Portugal, Australia, Italy, Greece and other countries with the scale of overseas assets up to 60 billion US dollars. All projects are running stably and profitably. These projects are important infrastructure for economic and social development and the focus of the Belt and Road Initiative. Our operational efficiency and the safety of our projects have been steadily improved and have won recognition by local social and regulatory authorities. Our good reputation can effectively promote facilities' connectivity and people-to-people bonds.

Second, to actively promote the connectivity of power infrastructure. A total of 10 transnational transmission lines, including China-Russia, China-Mongolia and China-Kyrgyz, have been built, with a trading volume of more than 24 billion kWh, which facilitate the optimal allocation of energy in neighboring countries. By means of investment and project general contracting, we promote and participate in the network projects of countries along the Belt and Road, we are building the network projects of Ethiopia-Kenya and Turkey-Iran, we actively advance the connectivity project on the islands of the Philippines and Greece, and we follow up potential cross-border and intercontinental power grid connectivity projects.

Third, to facilitate cooperation on international capacity with high quality and great efficiency. According to our comprehensive advantages, we establish the model for cooperation on capacity for the entire industry chain "going global", from investment and operations, planning and design, project construction, equipment manufacturing to technology and standards, so as to serve the construction of infrastructure of countries along the Belt and Road. We participate in the construction of backbone power grid projects in Pakistan, Ethiopia, Egypt, Poland, Myanmar, Laos and Brazil, share our technology and experience, improve the level of local power grid infrastructure, and make positive contributions to the local power supply and to the better use of clean energy.

Fourth, to vigorously promote the Chinese standards to go global. We adhere to independent innovation, comprehensively master a number of core technologies such as UHV transmission and smart grids, and take the lead in establishing a complete set of technical standard systems for UHV AC/DC and smart grids. The State Grid Corporation of China is responsible for the formulation of China's standard system of electric vehicle charging and battery swapping, which is one of the world's four major standard systems in parallel with that of the United States, Germany and Japan. We have led the formulation of 47 international standards. Some countries along the route have further improved their systems of national technical standards by adopting Chinese standards. Our company standards are widely used in power grid construction and operation in countries such as the Philippines, Brazil, Pakistan, and Egypt.

Fifth, to actively enhance the people-to-people bonds. In the process of serving and promoting the construction of the Belt and Road, the State Grid Corporation of China, which is a long-term strategic investor, insists on the concept of sustainable development, adheres to market-oriented operations, professional management and localized operations, continuously improves asset operation indicators, provides safe and good quality services, fulfills the corporate social responsibility, focuses on publicizing the developmental achievements of the State Grid Corporation of China, exhibits our philosophy of development, and tells the story of China. Therefore, we have been spoken highly of and enhanced the people-to-people bonds. For example, the 500 kV power transmission project of the Grand Ethiopian Renaissance Dam was identified by the local government as an educational base for the patriotism of youths. The World Bank and African countries praised the quality and technical level of our project.

3. Experience in the construction of the Belt and Road

First, to continuously exert our comprehensive advantages and build up our core competitive power. The State Grid Corporation of China has leading technologies in the fields of UHV, smart grids and new energy access, and considerable experience in the construction, operation and management of large power grids, which provide a solid foundation for and guarantee of service and the promotion of the construction of the Belt and Road. In recent years, an important reason for us to make breakthroughs in "going global" has been to give full play to the advantages of technology, capital, operations, management and brand, and to shape our core competitive power for service and promotion of the construction of the Belt and Road.

Second, to adhere to standardized operations and achieve long-term stability. In the process of advancing international projects, we abide by international rules and laws and regulations of the countries where we operate. On the one hand, we standardize examination and approval. We have a concession bill after winning the bid in a Philippine project so that the project can maintain relatively stable operations. During the acquisition of Redes Energéticas Nacionais, SGPS, S. A., CDP Reti and the IPTO, our company applied for anti-monopoly approval according to the rules of European Union. On the other hand, the structure of governance is scientifically set. In all overseas investment projects, we won the board seats corresponding to our shareholding proportions, and assigned our senior managers to participate in the company management, thus ensuring our management and control rights corresponding to the equity.

Third, to adhere to long-term strategic investment and to maintain steady and sustainable development. The State Grid Corporation of China insists on the concept of sustainable development, it sticks to long-term strategic investment and cultivates intensively. In Brazil, our company achieves the continuous enlargement of stock asset acquisitions, greenfield project development and cooperation on international capacity, and our business covers power transmission and distribution, new energy and equipment manufacturing. In Pakistan, we have not only built the country's first HVDC transmission project, but we will also be training a large number of technicians in Pakistan during the 25-year period of operations. In Ethiopia, on the basis of constructing the 500 kV power transmission project of the Grand Ethiopian Renaissance Dam to become the most advanced power transmission and distribution project in Africa, we won the contracts for the light rail power supply project in the capital city, the medium and low voltage distribution network upgrading project and the Ethiopia-Kenya grid connection ±500 kV DC power transmission project.

Fourth, to adhere to the principle of extensive consultation, joint contribution and shared benefits and achieving win-win cooperation. In the Philippines, after entering the National Grid Corporation of the Philippines, we helped them to establish a grid accident repair command center and system. The grid accident repair time and fault recovery power transmission time were greatly reduced, and we also received regulatory rewards. In Brazil, after entry into the Brazilian market, we actively shared our technology and experience on the basis of actively operating the stock assets. After several rounds of communication with the Brazilian power authorities and power counterparts, we introduced UHV transmission technology to Brazil, invested in the construction of the first and second phase of licensed beautiful mountain and water UHV projects, and transmitted abundant hydropower in the Amazon basin in northern Brazil by long-distance and in a large capacity to the southeastern load center, which became a "clean energy highway" running through Brazil from north to south. President Xi Jinping witnessed the signing ceremony of the first phase of the project and Premier Li Keqiang laid the cornerstone. In December 2017, the project was completed and put into operation two months ahead of schedule; it set a historical record of electric power construction in Brazil, realized the goal of promoting the technology and standards of the State Grid Corporation of China to go global, reflected China's quality and speed, allowed the Chinese equipment to go global, creating more than 10, 000 jobs for Brazil and promoting the development and utilization of clean energy in Brazil.

Xia Zhong (Deputy General Manager of the State Power Investment Corporation Limited)

State Power Investment Corporation Limited is mainly doing business in industries of nuclear power, thermal power, hydropower, new energy, railways, ports, coal mines, electrolytic aluminum as well as sectors of environmental protection, capital and finance. The proportion of clean energy is relatively high, about 26.7% when it was first established, and increased to 45% after 15 years of our hard work. In several big groups, the proportion of clean energy is the highest, and our goal is that the installed capacity will reach 50% by 2020.

After more than five years of Belt and Road practice and learning the spirit of the 19th CPC National Congress, central owned enterprises have a deeper understanding and cognition of the importance, urgency and arduousness of the Belt and Road Initiative. In the past five years, our corporation actively promoted economic development and international development. The 19th CPC National Congress of the Communist Party of China proposed to "remain true to our original aspiration and keep our mission firmly in mind", "work tirelessly to realize the Chinese Dream of national rejuvenation", "not only must we finish building a moderately prosperous society in all respects and achieve the first centenary goal; we must also build on this achievement to embark on a new journey toward the second centenary goal of fully building a modern socialist country". We can become a great power in science and technology, national defense and diplomacy only after growing to become an economic great power. An important signal that we have become an economic great power is that there should be world-class enterprises here. In the report at the 19th CPC National

Congress, President Xi Jinping clearly proposed the goal that "central enterprises should be built to be internationally competitive world-class enterprises". Compared with world-class enterprises, there is still a long way to go for our Chinese enterprises. There are no specific quantitative indicators for world-class enterprises. Currently, the overall situation is positive. China has more than 120 enterprises ranking among the Fortune 500. However, exactly they are the 500 largest ones. Many enterprises are large but not strong. In particular, in comparison with global prestigious enterprises, there are still considerable gaps in our abilities of scientific and technological innovation, sustainable profitability, modern corporate governance structure and international business performance and scale. Now, I will give a brief introduction to the developmental concepts and experience of our Group:

1. To adhere to the concept of green economic development.

From the *Kyoto Protocol* to the *Paris Agreement*, the green development and low carbon emissions have become an irresistible global trend. For example, in Africa, although being underdeveloped, their awareness of environmental protection is stronger than ours, so we must adhere to the concept of green and clean development in the Belt and Road and our international development. Especially through the efforts in recent years, the grid parity of wind and photovoltaic power is very close to reality. The National Energy Administration required grid parity of solar power by 2020. In provinces with good resources, like those in northwestern and northern China, such a goal can be basically achieved. With technological advancement, clean development has very obvious long-term resource advantages in terms of cost and electricity price.

2. To adhere to the innovation-driven developmental philosophy.

The idea of "bringing in" and "going global". Our corporation has undertaken key special scientific research tasks for the country. First, nuclear power, just like the introduction of technology by the United States to construct a high-speed railway, through introduction, absorption and then "going global", the nuclear power project in Shandong Province is preparing for charging and will soon be put into operation and will generate power. To go global, the preliminary work of nuclear power in South Africa, Turkey and other countries is advancing. Second, heavy-duty gas turbine technology. On the one hand, we achieve the integration of industry, university and research with Dongfang Electric, Harbin Electric, Shanghai Electric, Tsinghua University and the Chinese Academy of Sciences, as well as foreign companies such as Japan's Mitsubishi, GE and so on. Third, solar power generation. A national-level demonstration base was built in Qinghai, and the largest hydropower and photovoltaic complementary project was completed. Domestic enterprises must strengthen this point for "going global" under the Belt and Road Initiative.

3. To adhere to the concept of cooperation and win-win development.

We must work closely with local governments and enterprises in foreign projects, either investing in EPC projects or power plant service projects. Our projects already put into production and under construction and some reserve projects under negotiations have adopted the model of shareholding by local enterprises and being controlled by us. This model can achieve good and steady benefits and be effective in risk control, so those projects generally achieve good results.

I have several points on the mechanism of synergy for Chinese enterprises to go global and actively participate in the construction of the Belt and Road.

First, it is very important to realize win-win cooperation and share benefits. From preliminary planning to the entire implementation process, we must consider the interests of local governments and local enterprises, as well as the interests and demands of local people. Cooperation can notch up the success of projects.

Second, we must actively localize talents for the Belt and Road projects on the basis of internationalization, employ as many local talents as possible, and allocate talents internationally. Currently, in Australia, Brazil and Japan, most of our employees are locals, some are Japanese and Japanese Chinese and some are European professional project managers employed to do this work, but the biggest difficult is still lack of talents. How to fill the gap of talents is a common problem that we face.

Third, especially central enterprises must cooperate with world-class enterprises, and compete with them on the same stage. From domestic competitions to international competitions, through such cooperation and competitions, we can practice and improve the competitive power of central enterprises. Now, many enterprises are big but not strong. We must cooperate and compete with the best enterprises to become truly strong and outstanding.

Qin Gang [Assistant President of the China International Marine Containers (Group) Ltd.]

Although the name China International Marine Containers (Group) Ltd. contains the word "containers", the container business only accounts for about 30% of the Group's total revenue. Currently, it mainly supplies equipment, projects and services to the logistics and energy industries. The Group, with a history of 35 years, owns more than a dozen of the world's leading products. Last year, the semi-submersible drilling platform for mining flammable ice in the South China Sea was manufactured by our Group. The base is located in Yantai and the trial mining was operated by us. Our Group originated from Shekou on the frontiers of reform and opening-up, so it has market-oriented genes. Originally, we manufactured containers and focused on the so-called import and export business. The starting points of our international business were imported raw materials, overseas orders and equipment and China's labor resources. Since the early period, the Group established eight sectors and developed the logistics and energy industries in accordance with strategic global planning. At present, there are more than 60 overseas companies, including operating entities and production bases. Overseas revenues, including the export business and overseas sales, account for 60% of the total revenues of the Group. Our total number of employees is about 50,000, including 7,000 overseas employees. These are the main businesses of the Group.

Next, I would like to report our strategy of globalization and implementation of the Belt and Road. In the process of our strategy of globalization, our development underwent such a process. From the market point of view, first, we entered the

European and American markets, exported many products to them, and gradually developed into emerging markets and the third world. In terms of investment, it began with the acquisition of manufacturing companies in Europe and America, and then to alternative investments, new projects and new investments. The scope of business started from equipment manufacturing, including energy equipment and semi-trailers, extended downstream to marketing and product design, and provided funding for projects, including contracting overseas EPC projects.

From investment and operations to international industrial cooperation, against the background of the Belt and Road, the Group created new business opportunities with new values and acquired companies in Southeast Asian countries. How to achieve a good performance of these companies is an important issue for us. We did the following work:

1. Training

The adjustment of management. We seldom dispatched cadres, but basically selected and trained them locally and allowed them to establish growth targets. The companies we acquired were profitable by ordinary performance but without growth. By our efforts, basically, all of their performance grew.

2. Upgrading and transformation of production lines.

Even in European and American companies, the production methods, capacity and facilities are relatively old without any investment for many years; the interactions between China and Europe or the United States can create synergy so that the production capacity can be raised.

3. Increasing in the sales revenue of acquired companies.

The market networks including the network of the Chinese market and overseas markets are used, the financial knowledge for financing and guarantee are applied in case of business needs, financial means and incentives are employed and the well-performed incentive policies are applied to overseas companies. Therefore, they are stimulated and guided to expand on the international market, including the Chinese market and the Southeast Asian market. For example, we have a natural gas company in Bonn, Germany, whose business is LNG receiving stations. In the past ten years, China's LNG imports increased sharply and new receiving stations are needed. We helped Chinese companies win orders and provided financing support for them, basically covering major orders of Chinese LNG receiving stations. At the end of 2013, we acquired a fire engine company. From 2012 to 2017, the Group helped that company in marketing. Last year, it became the top brand of Chinese imported overseas fire engines.

Our Group invests, does business and makes acquisitions overseas. It is important to pay taxes and create employment in the localities. Regardless whether it involves European or American companies or those in Southeast Asia and Africa, through investment, market expansion and improvement of management, the business performance is improved, the sales revenue rises, the tax payment grows and the number of people hired also increases. After several years of development, the Group's concept of globalization can be summarized as: global operations and local wisdom. Overseas companies are supported by a structure of governance, management systems, sharing, funding, technology, talents, raw materials and sharing platforms. Local wisdom means fully respect the local management team that is familiar with the market, give them more authority, manage the team through the board of directors, and play their role.

The theme of today's conference is the Belt and Road. According to the implementation of the strategy of globalization during these years and our efforts in countries along the Belt and Road, I would like to talk about a few points:

First, for a company, it is necessary to find the intersection of the Belt and Road policy and market opportunities. We must sufficiently survey the market demand of countries along the Belt and Road according to our business abilities and the direction of development, and find a convergence point of business abilities and market demand. There are many oil and gas-producing areas in countries along the route. Our energy, ocean and natural gas business abilities can be connected with these countries. For example, the Caspian Sea is an inland sea, so the semi-submersible drilling platforms could not be transported there to drill for oil. We cooperated with a Russian shipyard on the Volga River, transported the main components made in Yantai, and supervised and cooperated with them for installation in Turkmenistan.

Second, in addition to simple product sales and project deliveries, for the implementation of the Belt and Road Initiative, Chinese companies and industries should strive to build up industrial chains overseas. Companies should go global and cooperate to extend towards operations and services. China International Marine Containers (Group) Ltd. and Shenzhen Gas cooperated in a Southeast Asian country to invest in LNG receiving stations. Through investment and operations, it will extend downstream in the future, thus prolonging the industry chain of natural gas to Southeast Asian countries and gain mature experience and competence.

Third, we should give play to the role of integration of core cities. Shenzhen has a lot of resources. For projects involving energy or tourism in countries along the Belt and Road, if the government plays a role in matching, coordination and organization, and holds relevant companies together, the results will be better than they achieve alone.

In the process of Belt and Road practice, we improved our strategy of globalization and the cognitive level of market development and seeking business opportunities and enriched our practical strategy. In particular, business promotion and investments in countries along the Belt and Road raised our actual performance. For example, Southeast Asia was short of electricity infrastructures. We created designs and made products using natural gas facilities and power generation technology to help them. With the implementation of the Belt and Road Initiative, we increased our investments in developing countries and achieved remarkable results. For example, at the end of 2013, we acquired a German fire engine company whose subsidiary is located in Indonesia. Thanks to the guidance of the Belt and Road, the business performance of its Indonesian subsidiary improved and the number of orders increased.

Under the Belt and Road Initiative, we actively took actions, invested in the Djibouti Free Trade Zone and constructed modularized buildings, which could be completed within one year after the signing of orders, while traditional local concrete buildings took several years to complete. It is our further direction to enhance cooperation with other central owned enterprises and strengthen integration with the government.

Zhang Jianwei (Deputy Chairman of the Board of the Sinotrans & CSC Group)

The Sinotrans & CSC Group is a subsidiary of the China Merchants Group. As early as the beginning of 21st century, it had already started to build up an overseas logistics network, which also fits well with the Belt and Road Initiative. In the early 1980s, the Chinese economy was still in the process of transition from the traditional planned economy to the market economy. Sinotrans was among the earliest companies to go global. The adjustment of the domestic economic structure prompted us to seriously review our gains and losses in the development of overseas business, so we began to build a comprehensive overseas logistics service network oriented to customers. The Belt and Road Initiative is essentially an important structural adjustment of economic globalization. Reconstruction is both an important opportunity and a severe challenge. Some countries along the Belt and Road are economically underdeveloped, and their political and cultural environments sometimes lead to unexpected problems in normal development and construction, which cannot be avoid.

We have both successful experience and lessons of failure in the process of development. Even when we had equity cooperation with our long-term partners, after we really went deep into the country, there were still many problems requiring us to deepen our understanding. The implementation of the national strategy of the Belt and Road Initiative is also the responsibility of our central enterprises. We must accelerate development pursuant to the strategic requirements of the central government, but we should not ignore the existing problems and new problems arising from our contacts with the locals in the future process of development. This is true for ocean shipping and railway transportation. For the simplest example, as the operator of the Eurasian trains, we found no matter how smoothly we operated domestically, the port entry took considerable time. For train operations, how to shorten the port entry time is a very important topic.

I have two points of view on the construction of the prevention and control system for various risks in overseas investments and operations.

First, the cultural environment, ideology, religious beliefs and infrastructure in countries along the Belt and Road are different. Without clear cognition and an in-depth understanding of these countries, we will inevitably encounter problems that are difficult to overcome. In the past few years, there were many successful companies going global, which summarized a lot of successful experience, but a few lessons of failures. These lessons are our precious wealth. Is it true that all companies can meet the conditions for development along the Belt and Road? Our strategic choices are very important. We must figure out what our companies are going to do overseas. Of course, without good teams of talents, even a great strategy cannot be implemented. The internal mechanisms of our companies should also be flexible, including employment and incentive mechanisms.

Enterprises, especially central enterprises and local state-owned enterprises, have long adapted to the government-led economic developmental environment during the transition from the planned economy to the market economy. Once we leave the government and enter other markets, our market adaptability is not enough, so the government should provide guidance in the process of our enterprises going overseas and developing under the Belt and Road Initiative.

Second, when our enterprises are going global, even the national strategy of the Belt and Road is painstaking, and there will inevitably be problems. We cannot be victorious every time, so it is very important to establish a fault-tolerance mechanism and a mechanism for the management of risks.

Yan Diyong [Deputy General Manager of China Nonferrous Metal Mining (Group) Co., Ltd.]

Today, my speech mainly focuses on three points: first, the basic situation of the international operations of the China Nonferrous Metal Mining Group; second, the basic experience of our group in the capacity of international cooperation; and third, the choice of a path.

First, the main business of the China Nonferrous Metal Mining Group is the development of mineral resources and project construction, including related trade and services. It is also a company in the non-ferrous metal industry that began international operations early. Ten years ago, Minister Li Yizhong gave instructions that the China Nonferrous Metal Mining Group should start early and go far and steadily. Meanwhile, we are one of the companies with many overseas investments and a great deal of cooperation. We have overseas heavy metal resources, mainly 20 million tons of non-ferrous metals, as well as seven mines, seven smelters and one economic and trade cooperation zone in the world. Now our businesses cover more than 80 countries and regions, including more than 30 ones along the Belt and Road. Our products are mainly non-ferrous metals and we have over 40 types of those metals.

Second, our new experience in cooperation on international capacities under the Belt and Road Initiative. In recent years, the Group has been developing and growing together with countries where our projects are located. We have gone global in practice and have fulfilled the economic potential of countries where our projects are located. The Group acquired a copper mine in Zambia in 1998 and invested in and constructed the Chinese economic and trade cooperation zone of Zambia in 2007. It was also the first cooperation zone established by China in Africa, with a total area of nearly 18 square kilometers, and created a new model of China-Africa cooperation. Based on the advantages of our Group, the cooperation zone is positioned as mainly dealing non-ferrous metals, extending to the non-ferrous metal processing industrial chain, appropriately developing supporting industries and service sectors, and constructing a comprehensive park of non-ferrous metals with radiation and demonstration effects. China's engineering technology and mining process were introduced to Mongolia and have achieved good economic benefits. It was praised by former President Hu Jintao as a model for China-Mongolia cooperation.

Third, to promote the process of industrialization of countries where our projects are located and achieve the sharing of cooperation on international capacities. The China Nonferrous Metal Mining Group has already reached the advanced level in the world in copper, lead and zinc of the non-ferrous metal industry. Mining is a pillar industry for many countries along the Belt and Road, which have an urgent need for the development of resources. This need is the direction for our cooperation. We have independent Chinese intellectual property rights and have successfully gone global in Iranian aluminum oxide in the Middle East, copper mines in Southeast Asia, electrolytic aluminum in Kazakhstan in Central Asia, and in the Indian lead and zinc project in South Asia. So far, our Group has completed contracts for overseas construction projects valuing a total of more than 100 billion yuan. We constitute an inseparable community of common interests and development with our host countries. We seek the support of countries where our projects are located. The China Nonferrous Metal Mining Group always adheres to the principle of integration and synergy and we try our best to fulfill our corporate social responsibility, make our tax payments according to law, maximize the localization of employment and enthusiasm for public welfare, especially in the non-ferrous metal industry. Our Group takes the lead in releasing social responsibility reports in Zambia, Mongolia, Myanmar and other countries, and has trained a large number of local industrial workers who are familiar with Chinese traditional culture and mining culture through the pilot work of actively promoting vocational education. We construct environment-friendly companies. Moreover, we have built the China-Zambia Hospital and hospitals solely owned by China.

Enterprises that go global must still bear in mind their mission and responsibilities. In particular, for international enterprises, it is also our core competitiveness to establish social responsibilities. In order to go global, enterprises need to constantly adjust and meet staffing needs. Enterprises that go global must make friends and build mutual trust, not only Chinese friends, but also foreign friends and local friends. We should insist on cooperation, a win-win situation and joint development.

Zhang Peng [Deputy Chief Economist of Anhui Jianghuai Automobile Group Corp., Ltd. (JAC)]

Recently, China's auto exports to Belt and Road countries have grown substantially and have accounted for more than half of China's total exports. JAC exported 65,000 vehicles in 2017, ranking fifth in the industry. The export of mid- to high-end light trucks and SUVs ranked first in China and JAC exported 40,000 vehicles to 30 countries along the Belt and Road, accounting for more than 60% of the total exports of the Group. We constructed a total of 19 overseas factories, 11 of which were situated in countries along the Belt and Road.

First, to adhere to collaboration and inclusiveness, and add new impetus to development. The economic development of countries along the Belt and Road is very uneven, particularly the unbalanced and inadequate auto development. Ever since the reform and opening-up, China has accumulated considerable successful experiences in promoting economic development and industrial transformation and upgrading. Meanwhile, to respect differences among the countries along the Belt and Road, we should jointly explore the developmental path suitable for the national conditions of each country, combine deeply with regional developmental strategies of the countries concerned, recognize the industrial developmental needs of countries along the route, consider the advantages of both sides in the cooperation, integrate resources by the concept and mechanism of synergy and win-win results, create advantages, gradually realize the coordination of industrial planning and system compatibility and seek long-term common development. Through the achievements of demonstration projects, we should continuously enhance the participants' sense of gain and sufficiently arouse their enthusiasm and creativity in all aspects. Our light trucks exported to Algeria ranked first because we were the first Chinese automaker that met local standards after their technical standards were upgraded higher than those in China. Our construction of an assembly factory locally is close to completion now. Local industrial policies and foreign investment policies are constantly changing. Therefore, we are very grateful to the Ministry of Commerce and the Ministry of Foreign Affairs for their coordinated support. The activity of integration is progressing smoothly. At the country level, how to cooperate with developing countries is very important. Their industrial planning and developmental path must enhance communication and synergy based on inclusiveness.

Second, to seize the opportunity of the "five-pronged approach" and create a new platform for industrial cooperation. From the perspective of the automobile industry, the construction of a large number of infrastructures and the formation of logistics and transportation networks in countries along the Belt and Road will promote the growth of the consumer demand for commercial vehicles. The economic development, improvement of infrastructure and amelioration of people's lives also provide an opportunity for the entry of passenger vehicles. The auto industry has a strong driving effect for economic development. Automobile development has a strong driving effect for auto equipment manufacturing, and will also lead to the development of wholesales, retails, finance, insurance, advertising, logistics and other service sectors. For example, JAC's project in Kazakhstan is a model of strategic cooperation between China and Kazakhstan and also the only auto project among 32 industrial revitalization projects of Kazakhstan. It has attracted the attention of the leaders of the two countries. Auto assembly utilizes the idle production capacity of the local partner, JAC provides technology, products and management, and another central enterprise provides funds for local partner. Products are not only assembled and consumed in Kazakhstan, but also exported to Russia and other countries in Central Asia. It not only produces fuel vehicles, but also electric vehicles. This project contributes greatly to the growth of the big logistics channel of the Belt and Road and is also supported and welcomed by the Ministry of Railways of Kazakhstan.

In terms of industry, China has a unique advantage in that it has a complete set of industrial categories subject to balanced development. Such an advantage exists in both manufacturing and service sectors, both traditional and emerging industries. Cross-border cooperation and integration are the potential for our development in the countries along the route, and also the most indispensable momentum for our medium and long-term development.

Third, to adhere to the innovation-driven development and cultivation, and accelerate the formation of new competitive advantages. At the enterprise level, product competitiveness is very important in developing countries. Our products have made a lot of adaptive improvements and incremental innovations based on the needs of our target countries, including adaptation to emissions standards, O1 to O6. A great number of adaptive improvements have been made to the environmental conditions of plateaus, mountains, of alpine environments, high temperatures and high humidity content. First of all, our products are very reliable and mature, not just relying on the cost-effective advantage, but finally, from product to technical management and capital, we have a full range of commercial and passenger vehicles in 19 overseas factories.

If the development of an enterprise lies only in manufacturing, there is no way to achieve medium and long-term development. In foreign countries, we should pay attention not only to manufacturing, but also to marketing and services, including some considerations for adaptive research and development, as well as the provision of auto financial services and promotion of the full auto value chain "going global". At the enterprise level, we provide solutions to the entire product lifecycle and full value chain system through innovation-driven, transformation and upgrading to enhance our core competencies.

There is much to be done for today's innovative cooperation model in countries along the route at the national, industrial and enterprise levels. Here are some of our suggestions for building an international brand and improving the quality image.

The competitiveness of enterprises can be divided into product competitiveness, marketing competitiveness and brand competitiveness. The product has three characteristics: reliability, which means that the product should have higher reliability on the international market than on the domestic market because developing countries and the spare parts process lag far behind China's existing systems, and for developed countries, due to high labor costs, the high reliability of products is the first priority to avoid problems in foreign countries; adaptability, which means that we need many improvements because the local environment and working conditions are very different from those in China, including fuel standards, road conditions, air temperature and terrain; and complexity, which means that we must conform to industry standards, technical standards and to consumer culture.

Tong Laiming (Vice President of China Chengtong Holdings Group Ltd.)

The Chengtong Holdings Group is one of the two companies operated by state-owned capital as determined by the State-owned Assets Supervision and Administration Commission of the State Council. In the construction of the Belt and Road, we are always thinking about how to participate in cooperation and give better play to our unique role as a company operated by state-owned capital.

In recent years, we have made some explorations with Chinese enterprises "going global" and countries and regions along the Belt and Road. The general idea is to persist in serving the global deployment of state-owned capital and the overseas development of state-owned enterprises. In summary, there are mainly three forms, which will be shared with you by combining some specific practices:

First, empowerment cooperation. We should rely on the capital of the China Structural Reform Fund Corporation Limited (hereinafter called the "China Reform Fund"), take advantage of our professional investment capabilities, give play to the empowerment roles of capital in guiding and supporting investment and promoting operations, and serve state-owned enterprises' participation in the Belt and Road construction and the "going global" strategy. In 2017, the China Reform Fund participated in the non-public offering of Power China (SH601669) and the funds raised were invested in important projects of infrastructure construction of the Belt and Road, such as the Phase-II hydropower plant project of the Nam Ou River in Laos. Moreover, we also invested in China Molybdenum (SH603993) to support their overseas project development. Companies operated by state-owned capital also assisted other central enterprises and local state-owned enterprises to go global and explore new models of overseas mergers and acquisitions and attracted the attention of international capital markets.

Second, platform-based cooperation. We mainly invested in the construction of overseas economic and trade exchange platforms, went deep into local markets, promoted the cooperated development of economic and trade relations of China with the host country, and provided public services for Chinese enterprises to go global. The Chengtong Group invested in Russia to construct the Moscow Greenwood World Trade Center (the "Greenwood Center"), which is China's largest overseas commercial and trade investment project. The Greenwood Center provides comprehensive services such as business offices, commodity display transactions, conferences and exhibitions, hotel and catering, legal and financial services, customs clearance and logistics. It is an overseas display marketing center for Chinese brand enterprises and a public service platform for Chinese enterprises "going global", as well as a practical platform integrated with the Belt and Road Initiative and the Eurasian Economic Union. At present, more than 300 enterprises from 14 countries and regions are operating there. Chinese-funded enterprises such as the Industrial and Commercial Bank of China, Huawei, Haier, Liugong, Brilliance Auto, China National Heavy Duty Truck and BOE account for one third, create 12,000 jobs to local people and increase the trade volume by 2 billion US dollars. It has become a cornerstone for Sino-Russian trade and investment and an important node project of the Belt and Road. In the future, this model is expected to be replicated and promoted along the Belt and Road.

Third, service-oriented cooperation. This model mainly focuses on the traditional advantages of the Chengtong Group in the fields of warehousing and logistics, bulk commodity trade and so on, with stress on the Belt and Road, extending the global deployment, opening up international and domestic business channels through business model innovation and providing professional supply chain services for Chinese enterprises "going global". In 2015, CMST Development (SH600787), a listed company affiliated to the Chengtong Group, acquired 51% of the controlling shareholdings of Henry Bath & Son Limited (the "HB Group"), an internationally renowned commodity delivery warehouse operator, and became the only multinational logistics operator in the world with the qualifications for delivery warehouse operations on domestic and international major futures exchanges. After becoming the shareholder of HB, CMST Development practiced the Belt and Road Initiative, executed the intention of cooperation between the two countries during the visit of President Xi Jinping to Britain, and signed a *Memorandum of Understanding on Strategic Cooperation* with the London Metal Exchange (LME). The LME Shield new inventory system was introduced along the Belt and Road to promote investment and trade activities along the coast of Central Asia, Russia and inland Europe, as well as in Southeast Asia and the Indian Ocean, activate the trading of bulk commodities and boost the construction of infrastructures and industries. Meanwhile, CMST Development cooperates with the HB Group and the Shanghai Futures Exchange to design and explore the two-way business linkage model between international and domestic markets, which has already successfully realized the whole process of services for the import business of international customers, as well as the integrated services of the domestic logistics supply chain for domestic customers + exportation and international market delivery. This innovation to the business model has attracted the widespread attention of international business partners.

Further, we are working on cooperation on international capacities, such as some explorations in the Far East of Russia, in order to enhance corporate cooperation under the Belt and Road Initiative and strive to play our unique roles.

Li Xiaoqiang [Financial and Senior Executive Director of CLP Holdings Limited (Hong Kong)]

CLP Holdings Limited, established in 1901, currently has a market value of approximately 200 billion HK dollars. Here, I will give a brief introduction to our company's practice in the construction of the Belt and Road and some thoughts. We contribute electricity to 80% of the population in Hong Kong. In China's reform and opening-up, we also play the role of pioneer and bridgehead for "bringing in". In 1979, we supplied electricity to Guangdong. In 1980s, we invested in Daya Bay nuclear power. With the deepening of China's reform and opening-up and the reform of the power system, we invested in thermal power, hydropower, wind power and solar energy. In 2002, we invested in India and are still one of the largest foreign power investors in India. Moreover, under the Belt and Road Initiative, for example, although we are 100% shareholders in the power plant we invest in India, the engineering design, equipment manufacturing and construction contracting of the two units of 600, 000W in India were undertaken by domestic state-owned enterprises. This is also a successful model of the Belt and Road. Now our investment in Vietnam also invites domestic power companies and banks, which expressed their willingness to provide support, to participate. Our thoughts about future cooperation on the Belt and Road are still deepening.

Hong Kong-funded enterprises, especially those who have been deeply plunged for many years in some countries along the Belt and Road, basically achieve localization of employees. Like us in India, we are 100% shareholders, but the presidents and employees at the grassroots level are all Indians. If we cannot fully match the investment in the future, we can at least provide some services to domestic enterprises "going global", such as business negotiations, due diligence and human resources. In the past, Hong Kong played a good role of pioneer and bridgehead for "bringing in" during the period of domestic reform and opening-up. In the future, under the Belt and Road Initiative, Hong Kong enterprises should be able to play a better role as a bridgehead.

Now I will share the unique advantages and suggestions of Hong Kong enterprises in the construction of the Guangdong-Hong Kong-Macao Greater Bay Area and the Belt and Road. Investments and trading already existed among the three regions before the concept of the Greater Bay Area was proposed, thus laying a good foundation during these years. Beyond doubt, it will have good effects on the further synergy among Guangdong, Hong Kong and Macao. Hong Kong has very good advantages compared with Macao and Guangdong, especially in terms of the soft environment such as talents and systems, which are more unique than those of the other partners. In particular, over the years, we held the Guangdong, Hong Kong and Macao Power Summit Forum to regularly exchange with leaders of the China Southern Power Grid, the Guangdong Power Grid, Macao Power and China Guangdong Nuclear Power. To further advance the cooperation of the Greater Bay Area, in addition to investments and trading, communication cannot be ignored, the more exchanges, the better. This should be emphasized at this stage.

Dmitry Chukhlantsev [Chief Executive Officer of the TONAP Group (Russia)]

The TONAP Group is a company producing laser heat treating and surface hardening equipment. The group has six subsidiaries, all of which are leaders in their respective industrial sectors. The products of our group have some unique characteristics in the industry because we have technologies that other companies do not have. In addition to the equipment for laser heat treating, our group also produces raw materials and powders for laser printing. Only five companies in the world have this technology. Therefore, we hope to find investment partners in China. We can provide the patented technologies and related documents in the process of cooperation. China will have great potential in future industrial development and I am willing to bring our technology to China for production.

Our group also plans to build a joint venture of laser heat treating. After preliminary research, the current plan is to cooperate in four cities in China, including Shanghai, Taizhou, Shenzhen and Dongguan. Through research, we have found that many industrial enterprises in China have a large demand for our technologies and products. Taking advantage of the Belt and Road Initiative, we hope that this project can be incorporated into this policy. The first step for cooperation is that we provide technology-related documents, including patented technologies, as well as staff training. The next step is the batch production phase. To build a joint venture, we provide technology and the Chinese side provides infrastructures, including aid regarding local laws, company registration and management.

Tan Sri Dato' Sri Lim Sing [President of the Associated Chinese Chambers of Commerce and Industry of Malaysia (Malaysia)]

The Associated Chinese Chambers of Commerce and Industry of Malaysia, founded on July 2, 1921, is the largest and most representative Chinese chamber of commerce in Malaysia. It has 17 branches and offices, and its network of contacts spreads all over the country, directly and indirectly including more than 100,000 Chinese companies and firms. Its membership firms cover many domestic business and trade areas. Besides active participation in China-Malaysia commerce and trade, it assists the development of construction in other neighboring countries. After the Belt and Road Initiative was proposed, we found the great mission of the times, continuously increase the intensity and depth and participate in this trend towards globalization. The Belt and Road Initiative is an upgraded version of the trend towards globalization. Although the Belt and Road Initiative was proposed by China, the specific actions and voices benefit all the countries along the route and also coincide with the willingness of every countries to develop.

In fact, movements towards globalization in the past had loud voices and took many actions. However, we are far from enough in terms of how to eliminate the gap between the rich and the poor and narrow the developmental imbalance, and how to set the rules of the game in other fields and achieve mutually-beneficial cooperation. The actions and voices of the Belt and Road are full of the genes of innovation and sharing. After further optimization and refinement in the future, we can truly make breakthroughs from one point and then comprehensively, and assist countries along the route in realizing the happiness and dreams in the new century.

The Belt and Road Initiative aims to help countries along the route achieve the great undertakings of country construction, combine the resources and strength of the entire large region, complement and benefit each other and promote large-scale development and construction. The Belt and Road indeed achieves a two-pronged approach, proposes an individualized guideline to construction for accurate requirements of countries along the route, converges resources and strengths of countries and regions, and facilitates specific transformation and change. This is already a remarkable innovation and reform. Countries along the route participating in the construction and development of the Belt and Road can feel the true win-win situation and sharing. Through this meeting, we will work harder for the happiness and dreams of people with greater confidence and perseverance.

Since the start of the Belt and Road economic cooperation framework, we have set new targets for work, deepened bilateral exchanges, extended interaction and integration and guided our merchant members to walk through the days of learning and promotion. At the Associated Chinese Chambers of Commerce and Industry of Malaysia, I am responsible for receiving the Chinese delegation all year round. After the Belt and Road Initiative was launched, we adhered to the policy of "going global". Before the Belt and Road, our trade delegations often attended and participated in the Xiamen Investment Fair, the Spring and Autumn Canton Fairs, Nanning China-ASEAN Expo, the Kunming China-ASEAN Chinese Business Forum, and so on. After the Belt and Road was proposed, we decided to attend the Dongguan Maritime Silk Road International Expo. In June and November 2017, we further expanded our scope to attend the Asia (Shanghai) International Food & Beverage Expo, and also the Harbin International Economic and Trade Fair and the China, Mongolia, Russia and Malaysia Economic Cooperation Forum.

After the launch of the Belt and Road, the actions for and voices in favor of the integration and exchanges of Malaysia and China last for a longer time. In this process, together with other new selling points, we will strive for innovation and improvement. The future will become more exciting and gorgeous. It is an inevitable evolution. In the past two years, our trade delegation has visited local departments of commerce, industry and commerce federations, overseas Chinese affairs offices, it has returned to overseas Chinese federations and overseas exchange associations in the three provinces of Northeast China, Jiangsu, Anhui, Zhejiang, Shanghai and Yunnan. Under the arrangement of relevant units, our delegation has also visited local emerging development zones and explored the commercial arteries of Chinese mainland within a short radius. During our surveys and visits, we signed bilateral friendship agreements, and since then, we have been able to integrate bilateral trade in a more systematic, institutionalized and efficient manner, and enhance our corporate exchanges and information swappings. Over the past two years, organizations and units that signed enterprise friendship agreements with us included Industry and Commerce Federations of Zhejiang, the Returned Overseas Chinese Federation of Yunnan Province, the Overseas Chinese Businessmen Federation of Fujian Province, the Kunming Municipal People's Government, the Jilin Provincial Department of Commerce and so on.

Looking into the future, we will continue to promote institutionalized bilateral integration. Our goal of 2018 will be Shaanxi, Ningxia and Sichuan. We firmly believe that China is a vast territory with abundant resources. The economic production and structure, commodity features, market characteristics and cultural coefficients are different for provinces in the east, south, west and north of China. Therefore, we will lead our merchant members to do more research and make more visits, establish institutionalized bilateral relations, and continue to optimize and refine, with the hope of instant online access. Chinese enterprises are developing very fast and the economic ecology is prosperous, so they are worthy of continuous investigation and study by global enterprises and market players. Of course, with the rise of China's national strength and prosperity, the business ecology of Chinese mainland will become sustainable. Soon, every economic hotspot can become a place of legend and create and realize dreams pursued by overseas business circles.

Session 2: Pioneering Innovation and Constructing a New Pattern for Industrial Cooperation under the Belt and Road Initiative

Yu Zenggang (Deputy General Manager of China COSCO Shipping Corporation Limited)

China COSCO Shipping Corporation is a shipping logistics company that went global as of the 1960s. At present, it has branches in more than 100 countries around the world, with over 10,000 overseas employees and more than 600 Chinese employees in various countries. Its ships spread all over the world. Now,

I will share the experience and thinking of our company in implementing the strategy of "going global" and in promoting the construction of the Belt and Road in the past five years:

1. To adhere to the cluster development and achieve mutual benefit and win-win results.

Our investment in countries along the Belt and Road involves some relatively large-scale infrastructure projects. The construction period is relatively long and the demand for funds is relatively large. Therefore, a cluster of enterprises can reduce the financial pressure and the financial leverage ratio of a single enterprise. For example, in the past two years, our company has invested heavily in foreign ports, especially in Abu Dhabi, the Middle East, and European countries. We are actively cooperating with some large Chinese financial institutions for fundraising. We cooperate with central enterprises on construction. This can be very helpful for preventing risks in all aspects of politics, law, credit and exchange rates, and in improving our comprehensive influence and ability to respond to emergencies.

2. To adhere to the innovation of the business model, and strive to enhance the international competitiveness of shipping companies.

The Belt and Road Initiative has brought new opportunities for China, especially state-owned shipping companies, to expand international markets and improve international management capabilities. Meanwhile, there are new challenges coexisting with new opportunities. First of all, the relatively weak recovery of the global economy and trade continues to fluctuate at a low level. Second, cross-border competitions break the original competitive landscape of industries, weaken the overall profitability of traditional industries and present enormous challenges to the continued profitability of the traditional businesses of our shipping companies. If we want to take a favorable position in the competition, we must adhere to the innovation of the business model.

3. Organic integration with the supply-side structural reform.

The Belt and Road program is undergoing transformation and upgrading. For state-owned shipping companies, it is necessary to recognize that the fleet restructuring can play an important role in enhancing our competitiveness on the Maritime Silk Road, and organically integrate the removal of the excess capacity of old ships with the development of the Belt and Road construction projects. We should pay more attention to shipbuilding while eliminating excess capacity by dismantling old ships. Over 1,100 ships of our company have an average tonnage of about 100,000 tons and the age of 8 years. Our ships and technologies are new, so we have certain advantages in competition with other international shipping companies. This is helpful for enhancing our competitiveness on the Maritime Silk Road.

4. To strengthen cultural integration and realize the localization of overseas investment projects.

To become international, our company must adhere to peaceful cooperation, openness and inclusiveness, mutual learning and construction, mutual benefit and win-win results. How to integrate our senior management talents with local employees in culture, way of thinking and operations is a question we are constantly thinking about. We encountered a labor issue while acquiring the Port of Piraeus. The first reaction of 1,200 Greek workers was unemployment after our acquisition of the port. At this point, our company communicated with them effectively, guaranteed their jobs and told them that after the Chinese company acquired the terminal, the local business would flourish. Our barriers were eliminated through a series of cultural integration activities, which achieved good results.

Qin Weizhong (Deputy General Manager of the China National Petroleum Corporation)

Here, I will talk about a few points:

1. Energy cooperation and development with countries and regions along the Belt and Road will become an important choice for international energy companies.

Countries along the route are rich in energy and resources. Their proven reserves of petroleum account for 55% of the world's total and their remaining proven reserves of natural gas account for three-fourths of the world's total. Since the 20st century, countries and regions along the Belt and Road have been the focus of global oil and gas cooperation. In 1997, we signed a large-scale oil and gas cooperation project in Kazakhstan and took the first step towards the Belt and Road oil and gas cooperation. By now, we have cooperated in more than 50 projects with 19 countries along the Belt and Road. Our equity oil and gas production accounts for 60% of China's total oil and gas production. We have a natural gas pipeline transportation capacity of 67 billion cubic meters per year, which plays an important role in guaranteeing the natural gas supply for China during the winter periods.

2. We are committed to the transformation and upgrading in the Belt and Road oil and gas cooperation.

As an early pioneer of the "going global" strategy of central enterprises, looking back on our practice in the past 20 years, we have promoted our own transformation and upgrading during international oil and gas cooperation. First, we became more international. We planned for development with a global vision, cooperated under international standards, and competed with large international companies. Our internationalization index increased from 2% twenty years ago to over 30% today. Second, our market competitiveness was enhanced significantly. Our upstream and downstream, domestic and overseas business chain of production, refining, marketing and trading gradually improved and perfected. Investment and services promoted each other and enhanced our competitiveness. We built up the good image of a responsible large company on a global scale. We adopted the upstream and downstream integrated cooperation model in Central Asia, built a long-distance oil and gas pipeline across the three countries of Central Asia, and started a new model of cooperation between governments and enterprise. Our exploration and development of overseas oil and gas fields won the first prize in the National Award for Science and Technology Progress of China. Through Belt and Road cooperation, a high-quality overseas team of talents was built up, which has played a very important role in promoting the transformation and upgrading of our corporation.

3. Several suggestions.

First of all, we should continue to regard energy, the development of resources and the construction of infrastructures as the key areas of Belt and Road industrial cooperation. Adhering to the ideas on the "sharing of resources and market, joint construction of channels and industry", we should strengthen our investments and cooperation in regional energy, resource development and oil and gas channel infrastructure, advance policy coordination by energy cooperation, facilitate the connectivity of facilities by channel construction, realize unimpeded trade by energy investment, achieve financial integration based on large projects and establish people-to-people bonds by fulfillment of corporate social responsibility. Second, we should attach importance to promoting complementary cooperation with high starting points, high standards and high-quality projects. The laws, taxation systems, markets, technologies and standards along the Belt and Road have long been under the influence of Western countries, and international companies have taken root in these regions for many years. Chinese companies should uphold high starting points, standards and quality when advancing project cooperation, and boost complementary and mutually beneficial cooperation by industrial development and technological innovation. Third, we should establish a corporate-led, government-driven collaborative mechanism of development. The industrial cooperation of the Belt and Road cannot be separated from government support, especially energy cooperation projects, but our enterprises should take the initiative. Central enterprises can play a leading role, drive domestic social investments, build a union of the entire industrial chain, and create competitive advantages of Chinese enterprises. Fourth, we should strengthen security prevention and control along the Belt and Road. It is recommended that the government establish a Belt and Road risk assessment and early warning mechanism to help enterprises to prepare and take security measures, thus enabling the Belt and Road international energy cooperation to become a safe, reliable, prosperous, stable, beautiful and harmonious large corridor.

Yang Guangyao (Chief Operations Officer of the BROAD Group)

The BROAD Group is a private enterprise founded in 1988. At present, we have two parks, four core business sectors, ten branches and subsidiaries and 4,000 employees. Our products are sold to more than 80 countries and regions, including 30 countries along the Belt and Road. Here are our three points of experience:

First, BROAD's disruptive technology and strict safety, technology and quality standards have achieved a higher degree of product quality than global industrial standards and have taken the lead in the progress on global technology. By the refrigeration technology with waste gases of power generation, we have created the world's most efficient cooling-heat cogeneration system and continue to be a global leader in the field of non-electric air conditioning. Our energy efficiency has increased from the traditional range within 35% to 40% to over 85%. We maintain the largest market share in this industry. These projects are widely applied in Europe, Pakistan, India, Turkey, Southeast Asia, Russia and countries in the America. Istanbul Airport in Turkey and the Hilton Hotel are very typical representatives of our cooling-heat cogeneration projects and they have achieved good social and economic values in terms of energy conservation and emission reduction. Moreover, we further enhance innovation in the comprehensive utilization of energy technology and apply low-temperature technology to developing the low-temperature flue gas recovery for large thermal power plants in South Korea, Denmark, Russia and other countries. Taking the project in South Korea as an example, the waste heat of flue gases recovered from the Seoul Thermal Power Plant reached 200 MW, supplied heating to more than 40,000 households, and created values in waste gases. In our projects in cities such as Copenhagen, we advocated green heating projects, which also have very significant social and economic benefits. In the field of construction, we innovated steel-framed prefabricated buildings in 2009 and achieved a speed of construction that led the world. In the 1990s, Shenzhen set a world record of constructing one floor in three days. In 2015, BROAD established a record of constructing three floors in one day. The result and embodiment might be fast, but we laid more stress on energy saving and environmental protection. All buildings adopted thick thermal insulation, three or four-layer windows and external window systems and a system of fresh air and heat recovery. Our sustainable buildings could save 80% of the energy consumption compared to traditional buildings. The combined energy consumption of newly-fabricated buildings is only 20% of the energy consumption of traditional buildings.

Second, for innovations to businesses and business models, we have shifted from a traditional manufacturing enterprise to that of manufacturing plus services, provided customers and society with total solutions, and exceeded the actual expectations of the government, society, and owners. In terms of products and supply and demand, we export design and manufacturing engineering technology and provide a complete package of solutions to our customers and local projects. For example, we contributed a great deal to the energy and carbon saving for IKPP in Indonesia. Manufacturing plus extension to services, through our exportation of equipment and technology as well as energy-saving services, can provide customers with a higher quality experience. With the increase in project operations, we continuously expand technology and engineering, broaden our horizons in product design, engineering construction, investment and financing risk control, improve our risk control ability, further enhance product performance and smoothly advance orientations towards intelligent systems and the Internet.

Third, we promote the progress of localization of overseas companies. Under the Belt and Road Initiative, we set up our branches in many countries, such as Indonesia, Denmark and Turkey. Our headquaters appoint core executive teams, recruit local employees, achieve a good cultural identity, and promote the brand perception of BROAD within the locality. By building platforms with the local community, we can truly achieve cooperation and win-win results, take root on local markets and cooperate with local capital and consortiums. When we provide good services, this can further extend and consolidate our value chain, and capital return.

As a promoter of ecological advancement, we have several ideas:

First, in the process of infrastructure development, especially in the development of energy infrastructure, energy development and energy resource conservation should be combined and China's experience should be summarized. Our construction of cities along the Belt and Road should not replicate China's old path in the 1990s and the early period of 21st century. We are unwilling to see smog in cities along the Belt and Road, just as that in London, Los Angeles.

Second, we should further increase cooperation and enhance platforms. Chinese enterprises in the industry should actually compete and cooperate instead of competing only. Both regarding state-owned enterprises and private enterprises, we have many profound lessons in the process of "going global". The government's guidance is very important.

Third, in terms of platform construction, the combination of our enterprises and capital must be rapidly upgraded, and the influence and creativity of capital and the "created in China" must be enlarged. Thank you for your attention.

Yan Yunfu (Chief Engineer of Shanghai Zhenhua Heavy Industries Co., Ltd.)

Zhenhua has long been committed to being the pioneer of independent innovation. In the global port equipment industry, it has ranked first in the world since 1998. In those 19 years, it has maintained the global market-leading position in the port equipment industry. The reason is technology. We invest around 800 million yuan for R&D every year. We undertake 5 to 10 national R&D projects and our company's independent R&D projects, and also the construction of four national engineering centers.

The economic affordability of countries and regions along the Belt and Road is quite different. We must, through technological innovation, develop technologies, products and projects that are suitable for local conditions so that these infrastructures can be built quickly, be affordable, and benefit local people as soon as possible. Zhenhua and its controlling shareholder, China Communications Construction, are good at the Beidou satellite navigation and communication technology, replacement of concrete structures with steel structures, prefabricated buildings, the overall transportation and installation technology of wind power, ship unloading equipment with high-energy consumption at ports and terminals, and production bridges with high-energy batteries and LNG as the power. Our technology and equipment are close to zero emissions, green and low consumption. There is a very good demand for them in countries along the Belt and Road.

The Zhenhua Group has always focused on technological innovation in the field of logistics automation to promote intelligent development. At present, although there is so much e-commerce in China, most of the cargo identification, sorting, dispatching, handling and delivery in the logistics field is manually carried out. Zhenhua constructed automated terminals. We are grateful to China COSCO Shipping Corporation because they decided to take the lead in building an automated terminal offshore and handed over this important task to Zhenhua. Last year, we built an automated terminal for Qingdao Port, and the Yangshan Phase IV Terminal officially opened for navigation. They were developed by us together with port users. Our continuous efforts were praised by the leaders of our country. There were two Zhenhua's projects that were mentioned by President Xi Jinping in the New Year Speech of 2017. One is the Hong Kong-Zhuhai-Macao Bridge and the other is the Yangshan Phase IV automated terminal project.

The automated terminal equipment developed by Zhenhua can realize the automation of planning, dispatching, handling operations and power of handling equipment, and the information connectivity of terminals and people, vehicles, ships, containers, cargoes and handling equipment, and provide equipment support for the terminal industry. We are expanding our research on this set of intelligent equipment systems and we are ready to use it for intelligent logistics for general cargoes. There is also have a very large demand for intelligent equipment in the countries along the Belt and Road.

With the focus on digital, intelligent and networked manufacturing innovations and the promotion of the transformation and upgrading of traditional manufacturing, our technology can be widely applied. We still cannot create the technology for discrete industrial intelligent manufacturing. If the complete intelligent manufacturing or industry 4.0 is achieved, the first problem is the technology barriers and the other problem is affordability, so it is unnecessary for us to achieve intelligent manufacturing or industry 4.0. We should do research on robots that are suitable for some selected links and certain types of work, such as work that is dangerous, tiring, heavy, full of suffering, terrible and mechanically repetitive, replace labor with robots, establish an information logistics system, achieve the vertical, horizontal and end-to-end information interconnection of people with equipment, materials, process and environment, improve production efficiency and ensure the level of quality and management. The levels of development of manufacturing are very different in different processes and links, some are industry 1.0, 2.0, and 3.0, but finally, they should develop to industry 4.0. There is a great potential for the upgrading of traditional manufacturing and a lot of space for cooperation. This is another important aspect of technological innovation and industrial cooperation.

Liu Hui (Deputy General Manager of China National Agricultural Development Group Co., Ltd.)

1. Agricultural Cooperation Practice under the Belt and Road Initiative

The China National Agricultural Development Group, the only comprehensive central agricultural enterprise under the administration of the State-owned Assets Supervision and Administration Commission of the State Council, is a pioneer of China's agricultural "going global" that has the experience of overseas cooperation of more than 30 years. At present, our overseas business in the fields of fishery, animal husbandry and planting has spread across dozens of countries and regions in Asia, Africa, the South Pacific and Latin America along the Belt and Road. Our operational areas have spread throughout the four oceans, and the overseas business has become a beautiful business card of our group. In the new stage of development, based on our strategic plans during the period of the 13th Five-Year Plan, surrounding the construction of the Belt and Road, the Group will continue to actively promote the "going global" of agricultural products, technology and capital on the basis of continuously summing up overseas developmental experience.

The animal husbandry of the China National Agricultural Development Group is the national team and main force for prevention and control of critical animal diseases in China, with a leading comprehensive market share and a focus on the business of veterinary drugs and vaccines. In order to optimize the industrial structure and achieve transformation and upgrading, we chose to enter the dairy industry and lay stress on dairy investment projects in New Zealand. By investing and control of two raw material and processing plants in New Zealand, we increased our capital to acquire controlling shares of Shanghai Nouriz Sales Co., Ltd., built a whole industrial chain of infant formula milk powder, and created our dairy brand from source to terminal. The innovation of this project is reflected in three aspects.

First, in terms of cooperation model, we built a whole industrial chain of the dairy industry. The project realized the control of high-quality dairy resources from the source, integrated world-class technology into production, leveraged the mature terminal network in sales, achieved the upstream and downstream linkage of the industrial chain, and completed the deployment of the whole industrial chain of the dairy industry.

Second, in terms of brand building, we made full use of both domestic and foreign resources and the two markets. The project combined the brand influence of the central enterprise, New Zealand's high-quality dairy resources and the domestic market demand for high-end dairy products, thus constituting a far-reaching significance for establishing an image of safe Chinese food.

Third, in terms of strategic advancement, we changed from pure resource development to building a comprehensive product service system. Through deployments in key and weak links of China's dairy development, the project enhanced the core competitiveness and boosted the transformation and upgrading of China's dairy industry.

As known to all, on January 1, 2018, a new policy was implemented for domestic infant formula milk powders, and we will advance this project in accordance with the requirements of the new policy. At present, we are the only central enterprise that enters the dairy and milk powder industry except for Mengniu, a subsidiary of COFCO.

We were committed to becoming a high-quality offshore fishery product supplier that is the best in China and a leader in the world. In 1985, the China National Agricultural Development Group set the first offshore fishing fleet sailing from Mawei in Fujian, which marked the beginning of China's offshore fishing activities. From the cooperation area at the beginning of the sailing route to the current business deployment, there was a high degree of coincidence with key countries along the Belt and Road. The whole route from Mawei to Singapore's Strait of Malacca, the Gulf of Aden, the Suez Canal and then to Spain, Africa was the route of the Maritime Silk Road. Under the leadership of our group, more than 3,000 vessels went global and expanded China's rights and interests under the conditions of the management of the world's fishery resource quota. Today, our ocean fishing is still at the forefront of the industrial chain, but insufficient on the terminal market. We should continuously give play to the leading role of our offshore fishing sector, further improve regional deployment and boost the construction of comprehensive service bases for offshore fishing, such as fishing for tuna in Vanuatu. We also invest in the construction of wharves, cold storage warehouses, we innovate and develop comprehensive service capabilities of fishery and strive to become an internationally competitive and influential fishery enterprise.

In the field of planting, we will continue to enhance foreign cooperation. Focusing on the promotion of the Belt and Road, our Group has established more than a dozen overseas farms in Africa, Southeast Asia, Eastern Europe and Australia, and undertaken cooperation projects of the Chinese government on foreign agricultural technology. In recent years, we have continuously expanded the scale of cultivation of featured agriculture, increased our support for the base for the planting and processing of sisal in Tanzania, the base for the planting of wheat in Ukraine, the base for the planting and processing of rice in Cambodia and the base for the breeding of livestock in Australia, and we have played an important role as a central enterprise in promoting the structural reform of the agricultural supply side and realizing the transfer of agricultural technology.

2. Opportunities and Challenges for Agricultural Cooperation under the Belt and Road Initiative

Today's speakers have mentioned a lot of cooperation in industry, manufacturing, resources, etc., and they have focused on the long-term mutual benefit and win-win results. "Food is the first necessity of the people", but agriculture needs large investments in the long term, and with a long term of return. Connectivity on the Belt and Road lays a solid foundation for and provides a good opportunity for us to carry out agricultural cooperation. Most of the countries along the Belt and Road are developing countries. For example, countries and regions where our projects are located, such as Kazakhstan and Cambodia, have good agricultural endowments with flat land, good agricultural species and resources and pleasant climatic conditions, but there are also problems of weakly developed infrastructures, backward agricultural production technology, an imperfect industrial system, insufficient developmental funds and no exploration of domestic and international markets. Therefore, they are strongly complementary with Chinese enterprises in terms of capital, technology, talents and markets. Countries in today's world pay more and more attention to the fundamental role of agriculture, focus more on the integration and utilization of global agricultural resources and the deep development of agricultural products, and have a stronger demand for international cooperation in agriculture, thus providing rare historical opportunities for China's agricultural cooperation.

Meanwhile, we should also notice that China's investments in countries and regions along the Belt and Road are mainly concentrated on leasing and commercial services, manufacturing, energy, wholesale and retail, mining, finance, construction and so on. Agricultural cooperation still has great potential to be tapped. The challenges faced by agricultural cooperation along the Belt and Road include frequent extreme weather incidents, a monopoly of international grain traders, and the competitive power of Chinese agricultural enterprises yet to be upgraded. The lack of sustained growth of agriculture and the significant changes in the structure of supply and demand of agricultural products have become new problems and challenges that all countries in the world need to face together. It is necessary for countries to strengthen their agricultural cooperation and jointly promote the sustainable development of agriculture.

Under the new situations, it is necessary to uphold three concepts in international agricultural cooperation. The first concept is shared development. International agricultural cooperation is not simply the possession and control of agricultural resources in the host country. Instead, it should realize the discovery and utilization of bilateral resources, the demonstration and promotion of advanced technologies, and the cultivation and allocation of technical and management talents in the process of cooperation. The second concept is innovative development. Agricultural development is important for the national economy and people's livelihood, and hence a pillar industry of many underdeveloped countries, but it is confronted with the problems of large investments, long cycles and high risks. We should get rid of the practice of single-handed efforts for many years, and combine with energy, infrastructure, manufacturing and other industries to achieve cross-industry cooperation and the development of innovative models. The third concept is green development. Agricultural resources should not be developed at the expense of destroying the natural environment and the cultural environment, but harmoniously to produce safe and environmentally-friendly green agricultural products.

The Belt and Road Initiative means the innovation and exploration of the mechanism of the development of regional cooperation, which is actually win-win cooperation. It can be expected that China and countries along the Belt and Road will continue to deepen their cooperation in all aspects, the scale of investment will continue to expand, and the investment fields will continue to diversify. As a central agricultural enterprise, we are also willing to cooperate with domestic and foreign partners to further explore the path for agricultural cooperation and innovation under the framework of the Belt and Road and contribute to the building of a community with a shared future for humanity!

Li Xinhua (Vice Chairman of the Board of the China National Building Material Group Co., Ltd.)

Dear President Lu, Entrepreneurs present here, it is my honor to attend this forum. I am Li Xinhua, the Vice Chairman of the Board of the China National Building Material Group. Just now, General Secretary Yansheng introduced the building materials of China. We have three main business sectors, including traditional production and sale of cement, glass and other basic building materials, international engineering services, and new materials business.

At the beginning of 21st century, our Group began to go global to engage in cooperation of international capacities. We began with the EPC business of dry process cement and float glass and constructed turnkey projects around the world with technology driving equipment and services. In more than a decade, we have built 312 cement lines and 60 glass lines in 75 countries and regions (in North America, South America, Europe, Africa, the Middle East, Southeast Asia, etc.), with a global market share of 65%, which ranked first for ten consecutive years.

Our country has put forward the Belt and Road Initiative. We are also constantly thinking about and summing up our experience in turnkey projects. There are several principles for "going global" and participating in cooperation on international capacities: First, to build a good image of our Chinese enterprises. "Going global" means that we represent not only the China National Building Material Group but also China. When Premier Li Keqiang visited our carbon fiber factory in Lianyungang, he said that besides economic, political and social responsibilities, central enterprises must also assume state responsibilities; second, to promote local economic and social development; third, to work with our partners, local people and even competitors to achieve win-win cooperation.

We propose the "six-one" strategy of "going global". First of all, to build 10 mini industrial parks with an average construction fund of 500 – 1,000 million US dollars, instead of large ones, and 2 of them have already started; second, to construct 10 overseas warehouses distributed along the Belt and Road as overseas warehousing and transit hubs; third, to have 10 overseas regional testing and certification centers, because we have an affiliate, the China Building Material Test

& Certification Group, which is responsible for certifications of all domestic building materials, including those used for buildings holding G20 and other summits; fourth, to own 100 distribution centers and supermarkets for building material chains , and we have already built about 40 to 50 of them in the past several decades; and further, 100 smart factory management projects and 100 EPC turnkey projects.

In the past, we took the path of technology driven equipment and services. Now we will invest money. In this respect, we have just starated. Our total overseas investment is around 26 billion yuan so far. Take Zambia as an example for explaining how we are deeply involved in local development. In a small town 20 kilometers away from the capital city of Zambia, we built a mini industrial park. The town mayor claimed it as a magnificent blueprint painted after the independence of Zambia, but no changes occurred to the town. It was our presence that changed their lives. Our work there was to paint on a piece of white paper. The town was very underdeveloped, so we did everything for them, including the construction of roads, a mosque, schools and hospitals. It was expensive for the local people to dig wells, so they used to drink the bitter and unsanitary water on the shallow land surface. We spent tens of thousands of dollars digging a few deep wells, which they called sweet water wells. All the people in the town were very grateful for us. We also invited Chinese art troupes to put on performances for them. Once, some drunken people made trouble, and local villagers came before the arrival of the police to solve this problem for us. Our relationship with the villagers was very harmonious. In this way, we spent very little money to get along very well with local residents. The President of Zambia also said: "I will cut the ribbon for you personally when you finish the work!"

There are also many other good points for building up a good image of our central enterprises. For example, we invested 520 million US dollars in Egypt to build a 200, 000-ton fiberglass project, which had three highly intelligent production lines. We recruited 2, 000 local employees, about 98% of the total number of employees, and more than 200 employees were sent to China for training. The fiberglass products, with Egypt as the core, could be sold to Africa, Europe and the Middle East, thus achieving very good results. For another example, we acquired a research institute for thin-film solar cells in Germany. This research institute originally belonged to Siemens, and we invested heavily after our acquisition. At the end of 2017, we built a 300 MW production line in China. The efficiency of the conversion of thin-film solar power generation was over 16%. They could be hung on the exterior wall of buildings without occupying the floor space. Their efficiency was much greater than the traditional polysilicon. We are not only going out and building research and production institutions abroad, but also bringing back some technologies and products that can be industrialized according to the characteristics of China.

Doruk Keser (Chief Representative of Isbank Shanghai Representative Office)

First of all, I would like to express my gratitude to the speakers and the organizers. It's a great pleasure and honor to be here today. Guangdong has a GDP of more than $1 billion, which account for 1/9 of China's GDP. It's a major economic zone in China. And Shenzhen shows us a very important fact, that the business models are keeping changing. Yesterday we had a visit to Tencent and another company. We witnessed that China adapted to the new technologies. So Shenzhen is now a base for Internet of things and smart manufacture. And we witnessed that the industry restructuring is changing the way we do our businesses and there is no competitive edge in cheap labor anymore.

We talked about Shenzhen and Guangdong just now. Let's take a look at Turkey. Now China often mentions the vision of reaching industry 4.0 by 2025, which coincides with our national strategy. It will take some time to industry restructuring and industrial restructuring. I want to share our experience with you here. In our country, the Belt and Road can bring more opportunities. So the Belt and Road enhanced connectivity but in order to be value added, it shows certain and important things, which are connected with the intellectual capital which means human resource, connectivity of financial capital like the launch of capital market and connectivity of technology which means transfer of technology. So these points are in my opinion will make a lot more sense between those countries which already put their will to be a part of this.

And in my field, since I come from the financial side, I will briefly try to put forward how can we cooperate on financial innovation, especially, particularly in the Belt and Road framework. In my opinion, We have a way for inclusive finance, which means that finances shall be eligible and connected to every feasible project, not just a government project, but also private sector projects. Private capital which will help us to finance and innovate the projects which we see China is now being very well on it, especially Shanghai to be the leading financial connected centers in Asia, our suggestion is that in the Belt and Road projects we can not only use loans with banks, but we can also use capital markets, because the capital markets are right in order to attract inefficient savings of individuals to the market. In the morning, a guest said that 55% of Shenzhen's money is in banks, so there is a great potential in investment.

So the suggestion is to stopping banks and capital market product to put forward and to pull back some individual savings and trying to fund more loans or capitals for these projects. Our bank has branches in Shanghai, and we have invested in many projects. Both the government and the enterprises can make loans in our bank. RMB can be used as the main currency of investment, because China has made great contribution to the world now, but compared with the US dollar, the international influence of RMB is not big enough.

As for the risk management of the project I think we can have a letter of guarantee. The interest rate is relatively low and the loan time is relatively long. Chinese can also make loans here and invest in other countries. We are a relatively large bank in Turkey, and more tourists from Turkey will come to China. I also hope that more Chinese tourists will come to Turkey for tourism. Now there are mobile payments. WeChat payment and Alipay are developing very fast and hope to have some cooperation in mobile payment.

Andreas Hube (Vice President and general manager of China Affairs Department)
Distinguished speakers and guests, it's an honor for me to speak here on behalf

of SAP. SAP is a German company and is the world's largest supplier of enterprise management and collaborative solutions. We provide solutions for different industries, with many consumers and many customers in China. Some of our customers want to enter the Chinese market and understand the situation in China. They will corn to our company for consultation when we entered the Chinese market in 1998, we cooperated with local companies in China, such as Huawei. Alibaba and other famous companies in China and achieved good results.

Speaking of cooperation, under the framework of the Belt and Road Initiative, we are very much looking forward to implement the good initiatives proposed by President Xi Jinping, for example. "Internet +" and other good ideas. As a German company, we are very willing to provide assistance in these areas.

We saw it already there, the China 2025 is actually much broader and much more affected to the manufacturing field and we want to make sure that we are able to offer solutions in China which are relevant to project China 2025. For example we recently created an innovation center in Ningbo and Ningbo is a center for Made in China 2025, we are very much looking at how can we cooperate. And this is a key aspect, when we're looking into cooperation and innovation process, when we look into what are the challenges of the companies or the challenges of the government and how can we find the solution and then apply the right methodology. So we are less looking to technology but we are looking to the solution and by this applying technology, so fields like AI, machine learning, big data, all those aspects will be considered and will be included when we talk about the solution.

We take it as a very good opportunity. Many companies will come to China. and many Chinese companies will go out. How to solve some of the challenges in China needs to listen to more international experiences and introduce them to Chinese enterprises. There are some problems we will encounter overseas, but may won't be such problems in China. Maybe there are some things that are easy to do in China but not easy to do in Germany. In view of the mutual advantages, we can introduce the mutual advantages into China or lead them out from China to solve our potential problems. We are willing to discuss the challenges we face with you further.

Sub Forum 4: The Internationalization of Traditional Chinese Medicine (TCM)

Subject: The Road to Innovation and Development of
TCM Internationalization

Li Chuyuan (Chairman of Guangzhou Pharmaceuticals Co., Ltd.)

Today, our theme is "The Road to Innovation and Development of TCM Internationalization". In the past few decades, Director Ren Dequan, Academician Zhang Boli and Director Wang Xiaopin led our industry to continuously explore and bring about innovations to the internationalization of Chinese medicine and made a lot of achievements. All of us present here are experts in the industry. I would like to share a point on the internationalization of Chinese medicine.

First, we must have confidence in Chinese medicine. There are different voices on traditional Chinese medicine in these years, but our voices on Chinese medicine must be heard internationally because we probably have a feeling that the Chinese medicine in Japan and South Korea seems to have surpassed that in China. I don't think so. They feel that many things seem to be very similar. So, when attending the Davos Forum and the Fortune 500 Sub Forum last month, I spoke with a loud voice saying that Chinese medicine is the best in the world. Every one of us must have confidence in Chinese medicine.

In fact, we now have expectations for a long life and a high quality of life. Chinese medicine is very important to these two aspects. Chinese medicine has made great contributions to our longevity. As early as 2,000 years ago, a person named Xu Fu told the First Emperor of Qin that he could find him an elixir of life. Later he went to Japan. No matter what the result was, Japan now has the longest life expectancy in the world. Japan also likes Chinese medicine, maybe they were taught by Chinese, so Chinese medicine is really good for prolonging life. Chinese cultural symbols are composed of Chinese food, Chinese medicine and Chinese Kungfu. To internationalize Chinese medicine, first we must have confidence in Chinese medicine. We must be self-confident and then the world can be confident in us.

Therefore, from the perspective of the philosophy of human health, we really need to promote China's healthy ideas and solutions to the world. In fact, our Chinese people are very great. At the time of Three Emperors and Five Emperors 8,000 years ago, the *Book of Changes* written by Emperor Fuxi said that "Taiji generates two complementary forces, two complementary forces generate four aggregates, and four aggregates generate eight trigrams". This is the earliest binary system. Even though science is well developed today, the computer is still binary, without ternary or quintuple systems. China has this invention in the world, which is not outdated even after thousands of years, so we should contribute to world health and promote our concepts and solutions to health. This is the second point I would like to talk about.

Third, we must advocate traditional Chinese medicine. Our aim is to become a millennium enterprise. We have always attached great importance to traditional Chinese medicine, and we also have an accumulation of experiences and many ideas. Chinese medicine should give people a real sense of gain so that they can feel its helpfulness and value for internationalization. It is necessary for us to advocate fashionable Chinese medicine. What is fashionable Chinese medicine? This concept means using modern technology and an easy-to-accept market model to manufacture healthy products that everyone likes. Therefore, fashionable Chinese medicine also includes four aspects, modernization, science, popularization and internationalization of traditional Chinese medicine. It is true that we have to keep up with the times about the modernization of traditional Chinese medicine. The methods, medical devices and images are not specific to Western medicine or to Chinese medicine, but they are common and public so that both Chinese and Western medicine can use them. Now how can we standardize and quantify it? If some modern technology and equipment is used, does that mean that Chinese medicine has been westernized? No, both Chinese medicine and Western medicine can use them. It cannot be said to have copied from Western medicine, but they are public resources. Traditional Chinese and Western medicine can share some modern means.

Nobel Prize winners are also studying Chinese medicines and herbal medicines. A total of 54% of the new drugs in the world were discovered from herbs, already more than half. I think this is very important. For example, it is appropriate for Wanglaoji to have won the Second Prize of the National Award for Progress in Science and Technology because it uses many modern methods and it is being modernized.

The internationalization of Chinese medicine also includes several aspects: First, the internationalization of products, like Wanglaoji, which now sells well in more than 60 countries, and also the internationalization of scientific research. Our Banlangen (Indigowoad Root) has applied for a lot of patents and analyzed many substances, some of which have better effects on Tamiflu. It is international recognition for us. Moreover, in terms of internationalization of research, popularization and popular science, we also need some platforms. In 2006, Zhang Dejiang proposed building a strong province of traditional Chinese medicine in Guangdong. Last month, Secretary Li of the Provincial CPC Committee felt that Chinese medicine was a good platform because we have always talked about internationalization, this platform must be recognized and culture was very important to it. He pointed out that the United States had two very important exports, weapons and culture. Their products were sold out with cultural promotion. Hollywood is a brand that spreads culture. Culture drives this industry. Culture is the most advanced marketing in the industry. In my opinion, Chinese medical culture is profound, so we must increase our efforts. We are preparing to establish 56 museums of Wanglaoji in the world, and now five or six have already been completed. The popular culture of Chinese medicine can be an important promoter for this industry.

The popularization of Chinese medicine means that Chinese medicine should be available to men, women and children all year round. We know that there is one of the biggest Chinese medicines, that is wine. Take Wanglaoji as an example, when it is made into pills, although this year marks the 190th anniversary, the sales revenue is only 200 million yuan. When we make it as a drink, the revenue is 20 billion yuan. I think this is popularization. Every person feels good after drinking Wanglaoji. Wine is also a kind of traditional Chinese medicine.

The four requirements of Chinese medicine are actually the supply-side structural reform we are talking about now. Our products must have high added value, that is favored by our people, so the four requirements are very important. This is the meaning of the concept of fashionable Chinese medicine.

Fourth, the internationalization of Chinese medicine. It is our responsibility in this industry. Xi Jinping said that "we should inherit well develop well and make good use of the Chinese medicine which is the precious wealth left by the ancestors". The summary is very good. Now there is a law on Chinese medicine, so it is a historic event. The voices of our industry are too weak, and we should continue to speak loudly. This law was promulgated on July 1st last year, and June 1st of this year marked the end of the first year of this law. I think we should work hard. Everyone should work hard by spending money and contributing efforts. Just like what I did on the Davos forum, I was there to speak loudly that Donald Trump should use Chinese medicine. Now the president of the Chinese Medicine Hospital is very happy to meet me. He said that more and more people go to Chinese medicine hospitals after my speech. We have a basis of scientific research.

Professor Tu Youyou won the Nobel Prize. I think it is also of an epoch-making international significance. I went to the National Museum in Munich, Germany last year, which showed scientists from all over the world. There was only one Chinese, Professor Tu Youyou. I said that I was so very proud. Our Chinese medicine can be accepted by the world, so I feel that we are in the best era. We are now in a new era, and Chinese medicine has also entered a new era. I will definitely do my best to lead the Group to constantly work hard and overcome difficulties. I am grateful to Shenzhen for holding this conference today, and also for so many experts who are attending it. If the whole Chinese medicine industry starts from ourselves, the internationalization of Chinese medicine is just around the corner, and our future will become brighter and brighter. Finally, I wish all of you here a happy New Year. Thank you for your support to our Group for many years.

Yan Xijun (CEO of Tianjin Tasly Pharmaceutical Co., Ltd.)

A "Dominant" Trend in Chinese Medicine
An Important Part of the World

The Central Committee of the Communist Party of China with General Secretary Xi Jinping as the core has attached great importance to the status and role of Chinese medicine since the 18th CPC National Congress. The 19th CPC National Congress also proposes to "support both traditional Chinese medicine and Western medicine, and ensure the preservation and development of traditional Chinese medicine". Therefore, I have this topic for my speech today. As the Academician Zhang said last time, I should air my views out loud, but not blindly, because we can do it.

A series of important ideas on Chinese medicine fully expressed the attitude and determination of the CPC and the State to attach importance to and support the development of Chinese medicine, and laid a policy foundation for that development.

New medical models are being explored. First of all, the changes in the spectrum of disease cause a reflection on modern medical concepts and the transformation of medical models, so all the countries are making adjustments to their roads of medical development. Chinese medicine has increasingly shown its obvious advantages in the prevention and treatment of common diseases, frequently-occurring diseases, chronic diseases and severe diseases. Modern biomedicine and traditional Chinese medicine learn from each other. Such a big international trend has quietly emerged. The development of Chinese medicine offers an unprecedented opportunity. If China does not seize this opportunity, it may lose the opportunity for development forever. In the history of mankind, Chinese medicine has never been so valued and protected as it is today, but it also faces challenges. How to develop is what we must consider now. As a company, we must stand at the key node of the times and keep a sense of responsibility to make it possible for Chinese medicine to become part of the mainstream medicines of mankind.

This is what I have been advocating for many years, but now I highlight it again. Every time we discuss how to make Chinese medicine. In my opinion, Chinese medicine must be developed by classified research, classified development, a guidance in its classification for innovation and development of traditional Chinese medicine, thus creating an opportunity for us.

Since ancient times, it has not been possible to separate doctors from medicine. Traditional Chinese medicine is characterized by profound cultural and philosophical attributes so that the Chinese doctors are closely linked to traditional Chinese medicine. However, today diversified research and exploratory thoughts are required for Chinese medicine to come up with their own solutions. We try one direction, that is, according to the philosophical domain of traditional Chinese doctors, Chinese medicine should return to the attributes of prescription drugs. Now our country is ruled by law and has standards. You write a prescription, but why should I follow it? So, its attribute as drugs and the attribute of standardization are very important. To become "dominant", an important medicine in the world, we must meet international standards, achieve accurate research under the guidance of disease symptoms, and provide accurate treatment of the targets of the network of diseases.

Classification research, diversified exploration. Innovative research on the resource pool of the traditional Chinese medicine is a process of promotion by different directions and mutually in a diversified model. Competent authorities of the Chinese medicine industry must have advanced planning and scientific guidance so that research institutes and enterprises can make comprehensive analysis and selection according to various factors such as a different technological basis, financial strength, product characteristics, market demand and application objects. We have proposed five research methods of traditional Chinese medicine. The first method is traditional Chinese medicine, the second method is modern Chinese medicine, the third method is natural medicine, the fourth method is chemical Chinese medicine, and the fifth method is biological Chinese medicine. At present, China only has two methods, traditional Chinese medicine and natural Chinese medicine, so there is no way to study it because we are confused.

Everyone has a clear idea of what traditional Chinese medicine is. Our country opens this area and records classical prescriptions. But based on traditional Chinese medicine, how can we achieve automation, modernization and standardization of fuzzy concepts? This is the next step.

Modern Chinese medicine should follow the guidance of the traditional theoretical system of Chinese medicine. It means prescriptions of Chinese medicine generated from long-term clinical practice. We may not change the prescriptions, but modern advanced planting, extraction, separation and preparation techniques should be utilized to refine and preserve. The groups of effective substances made up of multiple active substances or multi-monomers change the formula of Chinese medicine decoctions, and the effective substances can constitute new preparations and new forms of dosage.

Natural herbal medicine should be developed by applying the guidance of the modern system of medical theory. Our country has stipulated clear policies. The following four requirements must be satisfied. First, the product design can be evaluated promptly; second, the prescription is reasonable; third, the process of active ingredients can be controlled; and fourth, the indications, safety and clinical value can be evaluated.

Chemical Chinese medicine, needless to say, separates effective monomers from traditional Chinese medicine or herbs for in-depth studies on the chemical and biological activity; or, as lead compounds, for the modification and alteration of the chemical structure; or, starting from the research and development of metabolites, to become well-defined and effective drugs. The representative drugs are artemisinin and paclitaxel.

Biological Chinese medicine, based on genetic engineering technology, uses substances sourced from genetically modified plants and animals, or substances of plants and animals after fermentation by microorganisms, to make vaccines or pharmaceutical preparations. Active ingredients of traditional Chinese medicine are integrated into biological products and play a synergistic role in improving or enhancing the efficacy of biological products.

I would like to talk about Tasly's modern Chinese medicine which derives from an ancient prescription. It is a very clear formula. We make clear its effective substances, change the empirical model of traditional Chinese medicine "from medicine to medicine" or "studying medicine by medicine", and go deep into medical ingredients of Chinese medicine; and we also return to the properties of drugs, highlight the characteristics of the "medicine" from standards, regulations, efficacy and pharmacology, and meet the requirements of international drug regulations.

If we study a chemical or a biological drug, a new drug can be made only one in ten thousand. If we use modern Chinese medicine and resort to the Phase II clinical study according to clinically listed Chinese medicinal prescriptions, then we will save a lot of time and money, but our country fails to do this.

Tasly's modern Chinese medicine reflects its due characteristics and advantages in that the pharmacodynamic substances are clear, the mechanism of action is clear, and the clinical indications are exact. It adapts to the technological standards and those of quality of modern manufacturing and can build a new production model of modern preparations that is safe and effective, quality controllable, able to be produced on a large scale of production, and intelligently continuous. The intellectual property rights that are protected by patents are recognized, accepted and used by international mainstream pharmaceutical markets, and become one of the three world's major medicines together with chemical drugs and biological drugs. We are expected to achieve the precise development of innovative drugs for genetic networks and precise treatment of genetic network pathways for diseases. In the future, it will not take a long time for Chinese medicine to realize the networked gene targets for treating diseases.

Through the innovation of modern Chinese medicine, we bring about innovations to the equipment as well. Currently, we have two 10,000-level unmanned operation areas, one is the medicine slag and the other is the extracts, so we can achieve online control and prompt data collection. We realize the production of high-speed micro-dripping pills, the world's only system of a high-speed micro-dripping pill machine.

The Compound Danshen Dripping Pill explores the internationalization of

Chinese medicine. Since it is the first in the world, we have to notch up success. By the end of 2016, the world's first compound Chinese medicine successfully completed the Phase III clinical trial with a big sample size in multiple international centers, by randomized double-blind and a double control by the FDA. Now it has entered the phase of the declaration of a new drug, supplementing new tests and material improvement.

The test results generate the *Top-Line Analysis and Summary Report of a Clinical Trial.* The first trial in the world once again has proved that the prescription of the Compound Danshen Dripping Pill is scientific, safe and effective, with a stable and controllable quality. It has a significant dose-effect relationship and increases the effect of TED at the main clinical endpoints; the endpoints of the observation of secondary efficacy corroborate the main clinical endpoints, and the evidence of efficacy is chained; no severe adverse effects (SAE) related to the trial plan or dripping pills occurred during the whole trial period; according to the international gold standard for plate test, if the total exercise duration (TED) of antianginal drugs exceeds placebo for more than 20 seconds, it can be used as a clinically valid piece of evidence. The Compound Danshen Dripping Pill reached 42 seconds and surpassed similar indicators for the only anginal drug in the world.

Upon completion of this trial, the FDA gave a positive response to the results of the Phase III clinical trial of Compound Danshen Dripping Pills and recognized its clinical value and the statistical significance of 6-week results, $p < 0.05$ (actual 0.02). A clinically complementary trial is still required to revalidate the statistical significance of 6-week results so that it can meet the requirement for two clinical trials meeting the requirements of $P < 0.05$ in the declaration of a new drug. Currently, the 6-week validation trial design is complete and being communicated to the FDA. The FDA agrees to exchange and publish the results of the Phase III clinical trial in academic conferences.

Therefore, we have built a platform like that of the World Alliance on this basis. Now we have more than a dozen companies on this platform in China, and we are also internationalizing our services, so please wait patiently.

With the support of the platform and bridge of Compound Danshen Dripping Pills, we are expanding to a wide range of cooperation areas. This will have an infinite effect on Chinese medicine, which will slowly emerge and be turned into reality.

We must reflect on the power of the State and compete for the right to speak. We are discussing about Chinese medicine here. We should allow it to go from China to the world and be accepted by people around the world. To make our voices heard, we must be "dominant" and stand at the top in the international arena.

Through global promotion, according to the research standards of different countries, Chinese medicine can go global. Our goal is to become a world medicine and have the right to speak. This great project requires the sense of responsibility of scientific research institutes and enterprises in the Chinese medicine industry. It cannot be accomplished single-handedly, but it requires the consciousness of a mission on the part of all people, joint action and going global together. Only in this way can our dream of becoming a world medicine become reality. In clinics, a history museum or a reflection of its value, this is a question to be answered by our Chinese people. Chinese medicine goes to the world, like China's high-speed railway and military industry, it is also the embodiment of the country's power and the symbol of the country's image.

Second, let's take a look at the technology and service model for Chinese medicine.

The innovation and internationalization of Chinese drugs require the corresponding innovation and internationalization of Chinese medicine; the two complement each other and promote each other. Chinese medicine needs research and development by classification. For traditional Chinese medicine, we will continue to maintain the four diagnostic methods of "observing, listening, asking and feeling" and the methods and means of dialectical treatment and preserve the traditional cultural characteristics. For modern Chinese medicine, on the basis of scientific validation, microscopic examination and quantitative examination of modern technology are applied to achieve joint diagnosis and precise treatment.

We have now developed a model in Australia to build a service platform for the integration of technology and for diagnosis and treatment for Chinese medicine and Western medicine to understand each other, learn from each other and integrate their resources. Western medicine and Chinese medicine are designed as two networks because Chinese medicine is very lonely abroad. We provide this platform for it. Chinese medicine can cure diseases with modern terminal equipment. So, we are now working on chain clinics in Australia and Canada, and then extending them to the United States. Chinese medicine is integrated into the bridge with general practitioners at the center and focuses on rehabilitation. The number of our members is soaring, so this market is very good.

Modern science and technology constantly raise questions for Chinese medicine and points out the direction, and they also constantly reveal the essence of life and the mechanism of action of drugs from the levels of substance, energy and information. Modern quantum healing has the same goal as ancient Chinese medicine. The energy carried by traditional Chinese medicine and body bioelectricity are in the same gas phase and resonant at the same frequency so that it can regulate the function of the human body and have a reversal effect on the state of sub-health and disease. Now we are exploring how to change the proprietary language of Chinese medicine into a modern language and how to modernize Chinese medicine into a digital one. Therefore, I think we should also explore the characteristics of the system of Chinese medicine.

Third, our material guarantee, in other words, Chinese herbal medicine.

We should promote the restructuring of the industry chain of Chinese herbal medicines, create a sharing and co-win ecosystem of upstream planting of Chinese herbal medicine, intermediate market trade and terminal digitalization, and bring the Chinese herbal medicine industry into an era of internationalization and intelligent transformation. This is what we are doing now. We are building two platforms (National Intensive Platform of Digital Farming Resources and Anguo Digital Chinese Medicine Conglomeration Trading Platform), linking "five kinds of people", namely those who plant, look for, buy, sell and use drugs, realize the "integration of three networks into one", that is, the digital herbal inspection and testing system, the quality traceability system and the e-commerce network, and shape the five guarantees of information service, warehousing logistics, finance, standardization and international services. We are constructing a public service platform for the industry. We have done that and we have used it. Now the second phase is under construction to provide us with a service platform.

Last but not least, several suggestions.

Chinese medicine ushers in a golden opportunity, which may also be the last chance. We are looking at this issue and studying this issue. If we cannot seize this opportunity, with the rapid development of global medicine, we will always be "marginalized". Even in China, to put it bluntly, Chinese medicine is now "marginalized".

How to inherit and develop Chinese medicine? There is currently no good model, good path or good way. Modern society is in a digital and realistic era. People are very realistic. People have needs that are different from those of the past. Traditional Chinese medicine must pass on with universality and extensiveness of inheritance. However, if the inheritance is not innovative, it means no development.

The current development of traditional Chinese medicine lags far behind the requirements of the country and the requirements for internationalization. Although the CPC and the State put Chinese medicine at a high position with clear policies, the social environment is inadequate, the policy implementation is not proper and the policy requirements still cannot be met. The world pursues traditional medicine with a history, a systematic theory, and return to nature. They recognize Chinese medicine. Traditional Chinese medicine is the most perfect inheritance of mankind, but our Chinese medicine is not in line with international standards and lags behind international demand. Nowadays, the development of Chinese medicine is not affected by the world, but we cannot develop it well domestically. There are too many slogans, but few practical implementations; too many concepts, but few accurate methods; too many ideas, but few effective actions.

Traditional Chinese medicine does not have a legal status, which should be reflected in law enforcement and governance, but there is too little of this. There is a law regarding traditional Chinese medicine, but the government should have the corresponding concept, confidence and determination to enforce the law and all the people must participate in its maintenance. Practitioners in the traditional Chinese medicine industry must actively learn and use the law. After so many years of hard work, after several generations of efforts, the *Law of the People's Republic of China on Traditional Chinese Medicine* was promulgated, but the policies lag behind. The law has been promulgated for almost a year now, there is no supporting policy, no policy for implementation, and no series of policy measures that constitute a law enforcement environment. Without the empowerment of enterprises, it is very difficult to have such a great cause in the development of traditional Chinese medicine remain in such an environment.

The market position of Chinese medicine is subject to inadequate protection. Chinese medicine does not have a sufficient share of the market because we issued the "birth certificate" without an "identity card" and "passport". More importantly, we do not have the power to enter the market. It becomes increasingly difficult for traditional Chinese medicine to enter the market. In some regions, traditional Chinese medicine can be deleted from the list of drugs with medical insurance, without reasonable protection or reasonable explanation. Traditional Chinese medicine has no legal status. Since we have the *Law on Traditional Chinese Medicine*, how can it be possible to delete them from the drug list? In the application process of bidding and procurement, the regulations on the control of medical insurance expenses and quality "marginalize" innovative drugs of traditional Chinese medicine. Enterprises not only need a policy environment for innovation, but also a supporting mechanism to enter the market.

There are few developmental policies, but many barriers "at the door"; there is little targeted driving, but a lot improper policies. Without the correct path of reform and development and without the targeted classification of traditional Chinese medicine, our study is declining. In the country's new drug approval, the number of traditional Chinese medicines has been decreasing in recent years. Traditional Chinese medicine injections represent technological and standard innovations of traditional Chinese medicine. It marks a high-end level and also one of the directions of the modernization of traditional Chinese medicine. However, due to adverse reactions in individual products and control of medical insurance expenses, the use of traditional Chinese medicine injections has been restricted from large hospitals to primary hospitals. The adverse reaction of traditional Chinese medicine injections is a historical problem that is caused by the low competence of scientific research, irregular approval in the era of non-standardization, and also new recent approval medicine which produce bad reaction. We should guide research and innovation, rather than jointly put up a "blockade".

Hu Ming (Chairman of Sichuan Haofu Group)

Distinguished Leaders, Dear Experts and Colleagues, Good Morning!

Between late 2017 and early 2018, it was my honor to attend two closed-door meetings and make suggestions for the inheritance and innovation of Chinese medicine.

Sichuan Haofu has a team made up of veterans, which is a team defending the country and a team that has the experience of fighting in war. Today, we are willing to work together with you to shoulder the responsibility and obligation to defend the health of the people. In 2014, Vice Chairman Xu Jialu made a top-level design for the "Haofu Tianfu Chinese Medicine Valley" project launched in Chengdu.

I was born in a family of Chinese medicine practitioners, and the love for Chinese medicine was born with me. I am also well aware of the mission of Chinese medicine practitioners.

According to historical records, from the Western Han Dynasty to the late Qing Dynasty, at least 321 large-scale plagues occurred, but they were all controlled by the prompt intervention of Chinese medicine. It can be said that the Chinese people can grow and multiply primarily indebted to traditional Chinese medicine!

Today, traditional Chinese medicine has fallen into a trap of "good doctors do not treat themselves", and faces new challenges:

1. Brain drain, loss of culture, and difficulties in inheritance;

2. Difficulties to learn, to use and to drink without fundamental solutions;

3. Academic value, economic value and social value being not fully reflected;

4. No inheritance of the ancient manner of production of pastes, recipes, pills and powders;

5. Changing lifestyle and environment, high incidence of diseases and increasing hard-to-cure diseases.

Meanwhile, people have higher requirements for a healthy life; and methods of traditional Chinese medicine can no longer meet the needs of modern life.

At present, development of Chinese medicine ushers in a historic opportunity. Inheritance, innovation and development have risen to a national strategy. We must take the pulse of the problems existing in traditional Chinese medicine, find out the crux of those problems, prescribe drugs, and propose solutions. We think for the innovative development of Chinese medicine, as well as the modernization and internationalization of Chinese medicine, that is, the good inheritance of Chinese medicine. The philosophies, history, nature, culture, folklore, morality, knowledge and technology contained in traditional Chinese medicine, which are passed on from generation to generation among the Chinese people, are the foundations of Chinese medicine and the basis for the new development, modernization and internationalization of Chinese medicine. Traditional Chinese medicine is a precious treasure that our Chinese people contribute to the world. More than a quarter of the first two batches of Chinese medicine masters in China have already passed away. The efforts and experience of countless old Chinese medicine practitioners for life and the efforts, experience, technology and achievements of countless generations of Chinese medicine practitioners are permanently disappearing after the death of prestigious old Chinese medicine practitioners. This is a huge loss for the entire Chinese nation. Therefore, we are deeply aware that it is imperative to guarantee the inheritance of Chinese medicine through various means!

Currently, the inheritance of Chinese medicine in China is going in two directions. First, universities and colleges with specializations in Chinese medicine adopt the Western model of training in medicine and use the "streamline technique" to mass-produce graduates with the basic knowledge and skills in Chinese medicine. Second, high-level Chinese medicine talents are trained by the master and doctor degree programs and the experiential inheritance system of prestigious old Chinese doctors certified by the National Administration of Traditional Chinese Medicine.

However, these two directions are ultimately the inheritance of Chinese medicine in the system. Due to their own characteristics, they cannot solve the problem of the inheritance of prestigious Chinese medicine practitioners.

1. Old experts do not have the freedom to choose their own inheritors;

2. After several years of short-term study, the inheritors follow their own directions and cannot maintain the continuity and development of the academic affiliation of old experts.

3. The experience and value of old experts cannot be fully realized within the system.

It can be said that many old Chinese medicine experts have trained a large number of students all over the world, but their true and most valuable experience fails to be passed on. Moreover, the situations are even worse for documentary inheritance, technical inheritance, transformation of achievements and commercial application of old Chinese medicine practitioners not within the system, so policy support is urgently needed.

Regarding the issue of inheritance education, in our opinion, the culture, concept, morality and technique of traditional Chinese medicine are the foundation of thousands of years of inheritance. Families of traditional Chinese medicine and old Chinese medicine practitioners after retirement are still the carriers of individualized inheritance education, and it is necessary to establish an effective individualized mechanism for inheritance education outside of the system. To this end, the educational certification of inheritance outside the system needs to be resolved.

We call for:

First, giving full play to the flexible mechanism of enterprises, deeply integrating the cultural inheritance of Chinese medicine with relevant industries, establishing a market-oriented mechanism for academic inheritance and transformation of achievements, and realizing the academic value, economic value and social value of Chinese medicine, so as to promote the industrial innovation and development of the Chinese medicine industry.

Second, opening the allocation of social resources for points of dominant diseases, focusing on the inheritance of a series of dominant disease technologies, innovating the business cooperation model of Chinese medicine, and solving problems of talent drain, cultural loss and difficulties in inheritance.

Third, enhancing the effective combination of modernization, intelligence and traditional Chinese medicine, solving the current difficulties in learning, use and taste of Chinese medicine and accelerating the spread of Chinese medicine at home and abroad.

I believe that the development of the Chinese medicine industry requires the overall prosperity of the market and self-improvement. Meanwhile, enterprises should undertake or participate in the construction and operation of industrial innovation and entrepreneurship platforms guided by the government. Here, we sincerely hope that all leaders can support the participation of private enterprises in the inheritance of Chinese medicine and initiate policy incentives.

For the development of Chinese medicine, our private enterprises will be duty-bound to assume social responsibility and career responsibility. Sichuan Haofu will take the lead in flying the banner of Chinese medicine inheritance and will build a leading national and internationally-oriented Chinese medicine inheritance demonstration base in the Haofu Tianfu Traditional Chinese Medicine Valley. Taking clinical efficacy as the screening criterion, we will focus on the inheritance of clinical experience and skills from a group of prestigious old experts and on the transformation and international communication of the academic experience of a series of internationally competitive specific diseases to be cured by Chinese medicine.

The rise and fall of Chinese medicine is everyone's responsibility. As long as we never give up the goal and work diligently, private enterprises will become an important force in promoting the development and internationalization of Chinese medicine. I believe that traditional Chinese medicine will have a brilliant future! Thank you!

Li Anping (Chairman of Shanxi ZhenDong Group)

Dear experts and teachers, good morning! I visited 19 counties in 2017 and identified a problem that Chinese medicine is not certified but requires the spontaneity of farmers and agribusinesses. This is incredibly horrible. We are always thinking about Chinese medicine going international. If this situation continues, how can we go international? I always think that Chinese medicine should speak out loud internationally. It is our treasure that we should be proud of, so Zhendong also makes some attempts. First of all, I would like to talk about the symbol of Chinese medicine going international.

In fact, Chinese medicine is prevalent throughout 183 countries and regions. Now 67 countries officially recognize the legal status of Chinese medicine. Among 193 WHO members, 103 member countries have approved the use of acupuncture. What about Chinese medicine? So many countries and medical units recognize our Chinese medicine, but Chinese medicine can only enter the United States as a dietary supplement. In the United States, Canada, Australia, Germany and other countries, although there are Chinese medicine clinics, they are mainly acupuncture, massage, physical therapy, and so on, and most of the patients are Chinese. Chinese medicine has been internationalized for many years, but the effects are minimal. True Chinese medicine is not recognized.

No Chinese medicines are approved by FDA as drugs. The registration of traditional medicines in the EU (single herbs) cannot represent Chinese medicine, and they have not yet been sold on a large scale. For many years, it is particularly difficult for Chinese medicine to adopt the strategy of products "going global" first.

Traditional Chinese medicine originated from China, but Western medicine in

China does not accept Chinese medicine. It is even more difficult for Western medicine in foreign countries to accept and use Chinese medicine. The internationalization of Chinese medicine is not "going global" after registration, but scientific research should take the lead and doing well and steadily is the key issue that we must consider.

In order to take the lead in "going global", scientific research must conduct a careful evaluation of various processes and links in the research and development of Chinese medicine, especially the areas of excellence and research proficiency of both China and the West, and cooperate on the scientific research of Chinese medicine while giving full play to the advantages of both sides. Meanwhile, Westerners should participate in or conduct research on the content that can be understood most or least easily. Anyhow, Western scientists can truly understand and recognize Chinese medicine in the process of conducting research, and then the common people will accept the use of Chinese medicine. This is the best choice to break the bottleneck of the internationalization of Chinese medicine and of its going global.

Next, a successful example of Zhendong Pharmaceutical in international scientific research cooperation is used to further explain the scientific nature of the method that "scientific research should take the lead in 'going global' before Chinese medicine".

In 2008, we started to go global. When we first went to the United States, they did not recognize us very much. They did not even believe that our products were very good. Later, their deputy director came to China to observe our production process and testing conditions, which were unexpectedly standardized. Then they decided to cooperate. This example told us that we must take our raw materials, process and quality seriously, and then we can qualify for cooperation with them. Otherwise, we would be disqualified.

In May 2012, we, together with the Australian side, established the Zhendong China-Australia Molecular Chinese Medicine Research Center. Zhendong has trained a lot of doctors independently or jointly in recent years and has achieved good results. Unexpectedly, after cooperation with us, the University of Adelaide successively organized the regional Chinese Medicine bureau and the university of Chinese medicine. Why? Because I told them upon our initial cooperation that Chinese medicine was "poisonous", and once you had contact with it, you would die for it.

In 2014, we cooperated with SU BioMedicine in the Netherlands for the registration of our traditional Chinese medicines Six Ingredient Rehmannia Pills and Xiaoyao Pills in the EU. In 2015, we cooperated with Guang'anmen Hospital to establish the International Consortium for Chinese Medicine and Cancer, and set up the American Research Office. In 2016, we initiated the clinical trials for the FDA registration of the Yanshu Compound Kushen Injection.

Through research, many articles are reported in famous international journals since the year before last. In particular, an article in 2016 was spoken highly of by American experts. In fact, regardless of its usefulness, it is very difficult for this article to be recognized by European and American experts.

Due to the fundamental differences in history, culture and society, it is very difficult for Chinese medicine to go global. According to our experience and discussion, how can scientific research go global? We should work together with the domestic scientific research circle and hand it over to foreign research institutes. Either in domestic or foreign scientific research institutes, there must be experts in the fields of traditional Chinese medicine and Chinese drugs. The purpose is to earn their understanding and recognition. Both Chinese enterprises and research institutes must go global. If international registration is simply regarded as an approach to going global, we cannot achieve our goal, even after 100 years. If Chinese medicine practitioners do not use our Chinese drugs, then how can you expect foreign doctors to use our Chinese drugs? Chinese medicine has a very complete theoretical system that should not be split up. That is not realistic. It is impossible for us to know how many years are needed for such splitting. So, in Zhendong, the approach of going global is scientific and reasonable. Now it is also recognized by many experts.

Eventually, our traditional Chinese medicine must go global. As a Chinese person, I regard it as a responsibility. The international recognition of our products can give us an unprecedented sense of pride and accomplishment. Thank you for your attention!

Zhang Boli (Member of the Chinese Academy of Engineering, President of the China Academy of Chinese Medical Sciences, President of Tianjin University of Traditional Chinese Medicine)

First of all, the internationalization of Chinese medicine should make it clear that the world needs Chinese medicine. It is not that we take the initiative to let others accept it. Why does the world need Chinese medicine? The difficulty and high cost of seeing doctors is a global problem. Due to complex changes in diseases today, the model of disease treatment in the past is faced with big challenges and difficulties. The methods and concepts of Chinese medicine can solve these problems. It is not a matter of money to solve health problems, but one of concepts and methods. Chinese medicine is more suitable to nature, more suitable to the overall concept and suitable to people's own needs, so it can solve the current global health problems, and even provide China's experience for resolving difficult issues in the global health governance, and solve the world's problem of medical reform, which I think is the background.

Chinese medicine "going global" relies on technology. The better the technology, the stronger the technology, the higher you fly, the farther you fly, because technology is our wings. Although laying stress on the internationalization of traditional Chinese medicine, we must take root and do a good job domestically, especially in science and technology.

Here, I would like to make three suggestions.

First, the internationalization of Chinese medicine should be included in the national top-level design of the Belt and Road Initiative. We must not allow it to fend for itself and develop itself. It must be included in the big diplomatic strategy of China as an outstanding representative of our soft power. It will make a difference after such inclusion. Especially in the negotiations of the Ministry of Commerce, it is a good tool of China's. It must be included in the organic top-level design as an inseparable part of the overall diplomatic strategy of our country.

Second, what should the internationalization of Chinese medicine rely on? It should rely on standards to guide the world. Because we are the country where Chinese medicine originated, we should lead the world with confidence. Twenty years after the modernization of traditional Chinese medicine, we have basically achieved this. Moreover, we can be comparable with any other country in the depth and breadth of the research on Chinese medicine, which is internationally recognized. Our high-level research is now increasingly accepted by the international community, including 44 cases of acupuncture treatment of senile urinary incontinence by Professor Liu last year, which caused a sensation. At present, many standards are not accepted at home. We have prepared a catalogue of the protection of knowledge for traditional Chinese medicine. This means that China has officially announced our prescriptions and ownership. India, Egypt and Brazil are doing this work. We are faced with the organization of standardization when we are doing this work. No one has been able to solve this issue for two years. In case of infringement, who will file a lawsuit? If we announce that this is a Chinese invention, we can file a lawsuit against anyone who uses it. Much of our technical know-how, some prescriptions and some key processes cannot be protected as patents. We are less protected by patent rights.

There are also problems in formulating international standards. Chinese medicine must lead the international market. First, we must set standards. Yesterday, a journalist asked me, why is it difficult for Chinese medicine to enter the United States? Why hasn't it been approved after such a long period of time? I answered that we were still on the road because two cultures and two technical systems must have a process of mutual communication, understanding and learning. It takes time. There's a long way to go. China should also take this road. This is sovereignty, but the standard is international, so we must be guided by standards. In particular, the catalogue of the protection of traditional knowledge should be given a high priority. The intellectual property rights that coincide with the characteristics of Chinese medicine should have a special protection system.

Third, China is currently proposing the International Big Science Program. We are competent in guiding and leading such a program because some well-known universities and research institutes in the world are also carrying out research in this area, but they lag behind us. We can lead them and work together. This may be of great significance to extending the influence of Chinese medicine and improving the level of internationalization of Chinese medicine. The program has not been promulgated. We also submitted a report, but it is said that there are still a lot of difficulties. Quantum communication can be a big science program, but it is strictly confidential and cannot be disclosed by such a program. However, Chinese medicine can establish the program because we focus on research, and foreigners accept Chinese medicine not because of culture but because of evidence. The third phase of clinical trials of the Compound Danshen Dripping Pills has been completed, and the FDA said that it is very good, since it can not only prove the efficacy, but also evaluate the overall effectiveness of Chinese medicine. The efficacy of taking this medicine is much better than taking Western medicine. As long as we have confidence, Chinese medicine can withstand international tests. We have completed the second phase of clinical trials for five kinds of drugs, all of which have achieved good results. Therefore, we hope that the goverment can support Chinese medicine as one of the earliest scientific programs. This is the true support for the internationalization of Chinese medicine. We hope our government can play a strong role in our internationalization.

Ren Dequan (Honorary President of the Clinical Pharmacology Branch of the China Association of Chinese Medicine, Former Deputy Director of the China Food and Drug Administration)

From my point of view, the internationalization of Chinese medicine can be summarized into three sentences. The first sentence is that the internationalization of Chinese medicine in the past 40 years has made considerable achievements. The second sentence is that Chinese medicine is now in a difficult period of climbing up. The third sentence is that Chinese medicine will have a promising future if the difficulties and barriers can be overcome.

Acupuncture has had the best performance in the past 40 years. The policy of

Reform and Opening-up allows China's acupuncture and moxibustion to become familiar to the world. Acupuncture treatment has been officially accepted in 183 countries. Many acupuncturists recommend drug pills of traditional Chinese medicine to their patients, which in turn drives the exportation of drug pills and proprietary Chinese medicines.

The second aspect of our achievements is the changes in important export markets and our identity. The export market spreads from traditional East Asia, Southeast Asia and Chinatowns in Western countries to all over the world and the mainstream communities in the West. The export identity is elevated from general health products to "drugs" through the drug registration and then officially enters the mainstream community of developed countries including Europe and the United States. Since the mid-1990s, countries, such as the USA, and regions, such as Europe, have successively opened the acceptance of drugs. Clinical trials can be accepted as long as the process of the production of drugs can be traced and the quality of the finished product meets the requirements (not necessarily having a clear idea of ingredients and structure), and they can be approved and registered as "drugs" if the clinical trial data proves their safety and effectiveness (not necessarily having a clear idea of the mechanism of action). The European Union also makes it clear that clinical trials may be exempted from drug registration if a drug has a history of importation and use of more than 15 years. The important advancements in modernization since the late 1990s in China include the implementation of the GAP for the production of medicinal materials and GMP for the production of finished medicines (reflecting the requirements of traceability by modern pharmaceutical production); the exploration and popularization of quality control technology for the similarity of the fingerprint spectrum of substances contained in proprietary Chinese medicines (reflecting the modern requirements for the consistent quality of finished medicines) provide a basis for adapting to new European and American regulations and making breakthroughs.The Compound Danshen Drilling Pills of Tasly in Tianjin, the Fuzheng Huayu Capsule of Shanghai Sundise Traditional Chinese Medicine Co., Ltd., the Guizhi Fuling Capsule of Jiangsu Kanion

Pharmaceutical and the Compound Kushen Injection of Shanxi Zhendong were accepted by the FDA and entered Phase II clinical trials, and some of them even proceeded to Phase III clinical trials. Guangzhou Xiangxue Pharmaceutical Company Ltd. is the earliest enterprise in China to carry out the research on the consistent quality control of the fingerprint spectrum of oral proprietary Chinese medicines. Its "Banlangen Granules", with the cold as its main indication, officially obtained the drug registration accepted by the Medicines and Healthcare Products Regulatory Agency in August 2017.

The third aspect of our achievements is reflected in the breakthroughs in the internationalization of Chinese medical standards. In 2010, the International Organization for Standardization (ISO) established the Technical Committee on Traditional Chinese Medicine (ISO/TC249), currently with 20 official members including China, Japan, Canada, Germany, Italy, South Korea, Singapore, South Africa, Australia, Spain, Switzerland, Thailand, Vietnam, and 15 countries or regions including Austria, France, Britain, New Zealand, Sweden, Zimbabwe, as well as Hong Kong China and Macao China as observers. The secretariat is located in Shanghai. 23 standards have been issued so far, involving acupuncture, pulse, tongue, decocting and other Chinese medicinal clinics and equipment, and there are still 50 standards in progress. In terms of traditional Chinese medicine, since the late 1990s, the Chinese side has frequently exchanged with pharmacopeia institutions and experts in Europe and the United States. At present, the United States Pharmacopeia and the European Pharmacopoeia employed Chinese to serve as pharmacopeia experts. They have successively included 17 Chinese herbal medicines such as ginseng, salvia miltiorrhiza and panax notoginseng, and 74 Chinese medical materials into their respective pharmacopeia standards. The number is still increasing.

Although we have made impressive progress in the past 40 years, the internationalization of Chinese medicine is still in a new period of ascent that has met with many difficulties, which are reflected as follows: 1. In terms of medical treatment, acupuncture is widely accepted throughout the world, and it is embarrassing that traditional Chinese medicine is still attached to acupuncturists;

2. As far as drugs are concerned, most of them are still exported to Western countries as non-drugs, and our export value is less than 1% of domestic sales (about 20 billion US dollars). Even if some drugs are beginning to be registered as drugs, their efficacy must be expressed and validated by clinical indicators of Western medicine. For example, for the two drugs that have entered Phase III clinical trials in the United States, either the cardiovascular improvement indicators of "Compound Danshen Dripping Pills" or the control and reversal indicators of liver fibrosis of the "Fuzheng Huayu Capsule" are treated as Western herbal drugs. Thus, these difficulties are actually cultural barriers. In history, the Voyage to the East of Jian Zhen and the Maritime Expeditions of Zheng He made great contributions to the cross-border spread of Chinese medicine. The problem then was the geographical barrier. Today, geographical distance is no longer a problem, but it is much more difficult to break cultural barriers. The culture of Chinese medicine can be truly recognized by the world only when the four diagnostic methods of "observing, listening, asking and feeling", the syndrome differentiation with eight principles of "Yin and Yang, Excess and Deficiency, Exterior and Interior, Cold and Heat", syndromes of "yin deficiency", "qi deficiency" and "hyperactivity of yang" as well as the efficacy of "nourishing yin", "tonifying qi" and "repressing yang" are widely accepted by all of the people. There is a long way to go, but as long as we have the scientific confidence in the culture of Chinese medicine, this day will come. In order to overcome these difficulties, from a realistic point of view, it is recommended to work hard on the following aspects.

1. To continue to work hard to expand and consolidate the role of acupuncture in the public health of all countries.

Acupuncture practitioners who started their business abroad in the 1980s and 1990s have become elderly and are without inheritors. We will vigorously train and screen newcomers who are good at both acupuncture of the traditional Chinese medicine and foreign language and organize them to link with their predecessors in various localities.

In the 1950s and 1960s, excellent acupuncture experts were selected to serve as friendship ambassadors, especially politicians, and Chinese medicine played a good diplomatic role. Today, we may provide proper Chinese medicine services to public figures that are popular among people of all countries and thus expand the influence of Chinese medicine and acupuncture.

The medical services by Chinese medicine or the combination of Chinese-Western medicine are integrated with tourism, and the rehabilitation and healthcare activities of tourism are provided for middle or upper classes.

2. The existing Confucius Institute is an important base for Chinese medicine culture. Starting from the health management of traditional Chinese medicine, they can experience the practicality and cultural connotation of traditional Chinese medicine from the surface to deep down, and consider the dietary, living and healthcare rules of traditional Chinese medicine that vary according to physical quality and different times.

3.We should give full play to the advantages of diversified coverage of good health from beverages (Wanglaoji, distilled liquid of the honeysuckle flower, etc.), food (Tuckahoe Pie and Semen Euryales Cake, etc.), health products and drugs. Enterprises are encouraged to be eclectic and adapt to local conditions, do well in characteristic varieties favored by people in foreign countries and enter the local markets of all countries. Enterprises should coordinate with local embassies, understand folk customs and develop varieties of export products in a targeted manner.

4. Enterprises exporting Chinese medicines are encouraged and supported to select health products that can be expressed from the efficacy of Western medicine, and vigorously carry out clinical research. After obtaining valid evidence from domestic research, they should cooperate with famous research institutes abroad to publish research results and expand markets. It is suggested that importance should be given to the clinical research of supporting evidence.

After the efficiency of Chinese drugs is accepted by the public and academic circle, it is natural to ask oneself why these drugs are effective. Gradually, they will feel the advantages of Chinese medicine and Chinese medicine will become deeply rooted in our mind.

5. To further "promote the modernization of Chinese medicine and the internationalization of Chinese medicine". Breaking cultural barriers is inseparable from the modernization of Chinese medicine. There have been breakthroughs in the four instruments of the diagnostic techniques of Chinese medicine, and some have been prepared as national and ISO international standards. On the basis of the standardization of the four instruments of diagnostic techniques, it is recommended to vigorously advance the research on the imaging of Chinese medicine (pulse, tongue, etc.), and then to quantify and measure the indicators of the efficacy of Chinese drugs. Once the efficacy of traditional Chinese medicine can be quantified, it can be digitalized using new technologies such as big data, cloud computing and deep learning. Then with the digital language, cultural barriers are naturally reduced. I believe that one day, like the measurement of one's blood pressure and the electrocardiogram, the Westerners also want to measure their pulse and tongue images. Perhaps then, the West will also accept Six Ingredient Rehmannia Pills as medicine for "reinforcing kidney yin deficiency" and our Chinese medicines can be truly marketable.

Wang Xiaopin [Director of the Department of International Cooperation (Hong Kong, Macao and Taiwan Affairs Office), the National Administration of Traditional Chinese Medicine]

Here, I would like to report the progress of our work on Chinese medicine in the development of the Belt and Road.

With respect to the national strategy and top-level design, on September 13, 2016, the Fourth Plenary Session of the Leading Group for Promoting the Belt and Road Initiative reviewed and approved the *Belt and Road Development Plan for Chinese Medicine (2016 - 2020)*. After the meeting, the National Administration of Traditional Chinese Medicine, together with the National Development and Reform Commission, jointly promulgated and implemented the plan. It determined the guiding ideology and work objectives of the construction of the Belt and Road regarding traditional Chinese medicine. In particular, it proposed to coordinate with the national strategy at home and abroad. First, 30 overseas centers of Chinese medicine are to be constructed along the Belt and Road with joint support from the governments of China and other countries, common participation of high-quality medical and industrial resources, so as to build a sustainable model of development. Second, 50 Chinese medicine exchange and cooperation bases are to be constructed at home and linked with overseas centers of Chinese medicine. Third, an international standardization platform for Chinese medicine is to be constructed to formulate international standards. As early as 2009, when the industry's understanding was not completely unified, the National Administration of Traditional Chinese Medicine had already begun to promote the international standardization of Chinese medicine. On the one hand, it united Japan and South Korea and integrated traditional Chinese medicine into the WHO's classification code system of diseases. ICD-11 (11th Revision of International Classification of Diseases) is expected to be announced this year. Then, traditional Chinese medicine will have a place in the international mainstream medical systems and will lay the foundation for the statistics of clinical and scientific research on international traditional medicine, thus being of great significance. On the other hand, the Technical Committee on Traditional Chinese Medicine (ISO-TC249) was established under the International Organization for Standardization, with the Secretariat in Shanghai, China. Currently, more than 20 international standards for Chinese medicine have been released. Fourth, we should support the overseas spread of Chinese medicine culture and organize high-level forums and cultural activities under the framework of bilateral cooperation to create a good atmosphere and foundation for the spread of Chinese medicine overseas. Chinese medicine is also included in the government files on promoting culture "going global" and the building of soft power. Moreover, we are also researching and promoting the registration of 100 kinds of traditional Chinese medicine products in the forms of drugs, health products and functional foods in countries along the Belt and Road. These belong to the top-level design made by the State in promoting the development of the Belt and Road for Chinese medicine.

While boosting Chinese medicine's "going global", we also actively focus on "bringing in". The National Administration of Traditional Chinese Medicine signed a strategic cooperation agreement with the China National Tourism Administration to jointly carry out health tourism for Chinese medical. At present, there are a large number of foreign consumers entering China from Hainan, Xinjiang and Inner Mongolia to get Chinese medical services. Traditional Chinese medicine has become a business card for China, and China's circle of friends is expanding. It indicates that this work is very meaningful. Our administration will continue to improve the supporting measures and do a good job in this regard.

In order to promote the aforesaid development of the Belt and Road, the National Administration of Traditional Chinese Medicine will make full use of the ministerial mechanism of coordination and render the guarantee measures perfect together with relevant ministries and commissions. A multiparty mechanism of coordination will be built to include the development of the Belt and Road of Chinese medicine into the national developmental strategies of diplomacy, health, science and technology, culture and trade, formulate supporting policies, take preferential measures, provide strong policy support for the cooperation with countries along the Belt and Road in the area of Chinese medicine, increase the financial and taxation support, enhance the building of talent teams, call on local governments at all levels to strengthen organization and leadership, improve the overall coordination and working mechanisms, make specific plans of execution and achieve a local division of labor and developmental trend of misaligned coordination.

With respect to financial support, under the vigorous support from Ministry of Finance, the special international program of Chinese medicine was established as of 2015, and a financial subsidy of 30 million RMB was allocated for three consecutive years to promote the implementation of the objectives and tasks of the Plan. Over three years, a number of overseas centers for Chinese medicine have been constructed in countries along the route and a series of cooperation bases were built in China. The special international program of Chinese medicine, in addition to serving the overall arrangement of the Belt and Road and having a good international influence and social benefits, also made certain achievements in building the comprehensive model of sustainable development. In terms of capital, through evaluation, the driving effect of overseas funds is 1:21 and that of domestic bases is 1:25, that is to say, an investment of 1 yuan can drive the social capital of 21 yuan and 25 yuan, respectively. With the coordination of Deputy Director Wang Guoqiang, the special international program is expected to continue to expand in 2018.

Regarding suggestions for further work:

First, the central government should continue to increase its support for the special international program of Chinese medicine and adjust supported goals so that special funds can be truly used abroad. Since the establishment of the special program, overseas centers for Chinese medicine have served more than 200 foreign political figures and important guests including the Czech President and the Hungarian Prime Minister, as well as tens of thousands of overseas people. The program plays an important role, but special international funds can only be used for domestic capacity-building instead of that of abroad, thus restricting international development.

Second, it is recommended to set up an International Development Fund for Chinese Medicine. We should focus on the support of Chinese medicine enterprises in "going global". One of the important signs of the internationalization of Chinese medicine is that Chinese medicine enterprises in China can go global and have a place on the international medical and health care market. In view of the current situation of the Chinese medicine industry and fierce international competition, there are very few companies like Tasly that can effectively coordinate international and domestic resources. Meanwhile, Chinese medicine enterprises meet with good developmental opportunities overseas and it is necessary to provide encouragement and support at the national level from a higher and longer-lasting perspective.

Third, we should support high-level international scientific research on Chinese medicine. It is a regular process for Chinese medicine "going global". The forerunner should be the traditional Chinese medicine and its unique efficacy, followed by education and training, and the third phase is scientific research. This is a gradual process the phases of which complement and promote each other. At the national level, it is important to provide strong support to international research on Chinese medicine. Based on the advantages of Chinese medicine and the demand of the international health care market, guided by China, experts from world-class medical institutions should be attracted for conducting international multi-center clinical evidence-based research so that Chinese medicine can be made clear, convince the international community and lay a good foundation for Chinese medicinal services and products "going global".

Fourth, we should give play to the role of a big country of traditional Chinese medicine, build a brand for meeting exchange mechanisms and hold the international traditional medicine forum once every year or every two years.

Liu Baoyan (Chairman of World Federation of Acupuncture-Moxibustion Societies)

Chinese medicine can not only meet the needs of Chinese people, but also the huge demand of foreigners. This is also the basis for acupuncture going global. From the perspective of acupuncture, I would like to talk about some experience and problems encountered in "going global" in the past two years and make several suggestions.

I will focus on the acupuncture and moxibustion activity organized by the World Federation of Acupuncture-Moxibustion Societies in recent years with the support of the National Administration of Traditional Chinese Medicine and the China Association for Science and Technology.

Acupuncture takes the lead in going international. Traditional Chinese medicine is an important part of ancient Chinese science and the key to opening the treasure house of Chinese culture. More than a thousand years ago, the ancient Silk Road not only transferred Chinese porcelain and tea, but also spread Chinese medicine and its traditional concept of health and the Chinese culture. At present, Chinese medicine and acupuncture are prevalent in 183 countries across the world. According to a report of the *Global Times*, "A survey in 2008 showed that 40% of Americans had taken Chinese medicine as supplements and replacement therapy. For those covered in this survey, the mentioning of Chinese medicine, brought 'acupuncture' (69.6%) to mind; 'Chinese herbal medicine' (47.0%) and 'cupping' (24.2%)". This survey in the United States basically represents the situation in most other countries and regions. Acupuncture is well recognized abroad, and it can be said that acupuncture takes the lead in going global. Acupuncture, which originated in China, has now become acupuncture for the world. The localization of acupuncture has been widely carried out. According to incomplete statistics, there is only a minority of Chinese who practice and get acupuncture. The World Health Organization reported that although acupuncture originated in China and represents Chinese medicine, it was widely used worldwide. According to the reports of 129 countries, 80% of them use acupuncture, which is the most popular among traditional Chinese medicinal treatments.

The development of acupuncture in the world faces many challenges. Although acupuncture has been adopted in many countries, it is legalized in only more than 20 countries and few countries cover it in their medical insurance payments. Acupuncture has not been accepted by the mainstream medical system and its academic status is still quite low. Acupuncturists in most countries have not yet been regarded as physicians. There is no high-quality clinical evidence for most acupuncture treatments. Of the more than 1,500 clinical guidelines in the United States, acupuncture is an option for only 30 diseases. These factors become the challenges that acupuncture faces today.

We should build a community of acupuncture with a shared future. China is the birthplace of acupuncture, but it has just started to appear throughout the world. We should become the world leader and guide the development of acupuncture. Also, we should organize an international acupuncture community and raise the status of local acupuncturists so that they can be respected. Acupuncture must be officially incorporated into the mainstream medical system. Through acupuncture, the health concept of and the Chinese culture carried by Chinese medicine can go global and become popular around the world. Our specific approach is to take the World Federation of Acupuncture-Moxibustion Societies as a carrier and a bridge, and by virtue of the Belt and Road acupuncture and moxibustion activity, play the role and arouse the enthusiasm of overseas members, who will hold overseas activities with the participation of experts from the China Association for Acupuncture and Moxibustion and the China Academy of Chinese Medical Sciences. This activity can be important for leading the development of acupuncture in the world in five aspects. First, high-level interactions, generally with the active participation of Chinese embassies and consulates abroad, and local medical authorities or associations of Western medicine or Chinese medicine as the host for interaction with the acupuncture community. Second, academic guidance, generally holding a high-level academic exchange meeting on local acupuncture, and the research of Chinese experts can often reflect the frontiers of academic development. Third, to improve the level of local acupuncture education by organizing special training classes and acupuncture examinations and building education bases. Fourth, people-to-people bonds, allowing the masses to experience acupuncture in volunteer services. Fifth, cultural popularization. The scientific popularization and photo exhibitions are also important because acupuncture is one of the world's intangible cultural heritages. From 2016 to 2017, we held seven series of activities and traversed more than 10 countries, thereby greatly enhancing the status and influence of the local acupuncture community and promoting the international development of acupuncture.

Through the acupuncture and moxibustion activity of the Belt and Road and the development of the World Federation of Acupuncture-Moxibustion Societies over the past 30 years, I deeply understand that the internationalization of Chinese medicine and acupuncture is an important carrier for enhancing the soft power of China, because Chinese medicine and acupuncture convey the concepts of health protection consisting of "no disease" "little suffering" and "early treatment". It coincides with the health needs of mankind and reflects the wisdom of the "unity of man and nature" and "accommodating nature". "Acupuncture-moxibustion-drugs" is the most realistic and feasible solution for human health problems. Currently, acupuncture takes the lead in "going global". It can be taken as a breakthrough point to drive Chinese medicine and Chinese culture to go global, which is necessary and feasible. It is very important to give full play to the advantages of China as the place of origin of acupuncture and moxibustion with abundant medical resources and talents, lead the development of acupuncture in the world, strengthen the strategic deployment of acupuncture and moxibustion and help it grow to be big and strong domestically. Besides, it is particularly important to allow the pioneers of acupuncture and moxibustion who went global in the 1980s and 1990s to play a central role. They have gained a firm foothold in the world after several decades of diligent efforts. A shortcut to the internationalization of acupuncture is to integrate their strength. Acupuncture is a unique category of medicine with its systematic theoretical system and a wealth of methods of diagnosis and treatment. The key to its success in thousands of years and in the world is efficacy, and today it is widely accepted with the concept of evidence-based medicine. It is a bottleneck and a good opportunity to restrict the entry of acupuncture into mainstream medicine that the efficacy of acupuncture can be reflected by high-quality clinical evidence. If the evidence-based medicine is applied to provide a large number of high-quality clinical evidence, it will be a shortcut to the legalization of acupuncture and its coverage by medical insurance payments and of its becoming a part of the mainstream medical system.

I have two suggestions based on the above experience. First, the mechanism should be innovated and multiple sides should be mobilized to make domestic acupuncture stronger. Our research on clinical evaluation and the effects of acupuncture should be included in the "big science program". Through the new organizational model, we should give full play to the advantages of abundant medical resources and talents in clinical research in China, attract the participation of famous international teams, obtain the evidence for high-quality efficacy of acupuncture, reveal the effects of acupuncture and lead the worldwide development of acupuncture. Second, we should launch a foreign entrepreneurship program for young acupuncture talents. According to the current situation of no inheritors of acupuncture pioneers who went global early, young acupuncture talents (masters and doctors) should be mobilized and organized to start businesses in foreign countries. Given the potentially huge demand for acupuncture development in foreign countries, with the help of acupuncture pioneers who have already taken root, we should establish a systematic design, encourage a large number of young people to go global and pass on and develop their acupuncture ability. It is crucial for the future international development of acupuncture.

Xu Qingfeng (Director of Traditional Chinese Medicine Bureau of Guangdong Province)

Guangdong is the frontier of reform and opening-up, a window for opening up to the outside world, and a bridgehead for the Maritime Silk Road. "Artemisinin" goes global from Guangdong. By summary of the experience of the people in South China struggling with diseases, Guangdong began to study "Artemisinin". "Artemisinin" is very influential and has become a diplomatic brand of our country. This is a really great achievement.

Guangdong is also cooperating extensively in the field of scientific research. Now Guangdong's medical enterprises have signed strategic cooperation agreements with more than 30 countries. Guangdong has included the going global of Chinese medicine into the construction of the Guangdong-Hong Kong-Macao Greater Bay Area. We hope to apply for preferential policies from the State through this window. Now we have made great progress. We also pay attention to standardization. Shenzhen is a place of standardization. Three standardization methods of granules and Chinese herbal medicines have been internationally recognized. Therefore, Chinese herbal medicines and granules have the "passport" for "going global".

Guangdong is the first pilot zone for reform and opening-up. We jointly formulated the *Action Plan on the Belt and Road of Developing Traditional Chinese Medicine in Guangdong Province (2017—2020)* with the Guangdong Provincial Development and Reform Commission this year, we have shared Chinese medicine services with countries along the route, and we are preparing to build two or three international cooperation platforms, four to six overseas centers and two to four international exchange bases. Guangdong has made a number of contribution to Chinese medicine's "going global".

First, attaching equal importance to Chinese medicine and Western medicine is the foundation of "going global" under the Belt and Road Initiative. If we are not good enough, how can we compete in the world? Chinese medicine service stations provide only 17.8% of the services with a small number of doctors. At present, medical resources are not fairly distributed between Chinese medicine and Western medicine. In the past few years, the investment is seriously inadequate. The proportions of student enrollment in Chinese medicine and Western medicine are seriously unbalanced. Many students are not working on Chinese medicine services. A total of 850,000 clinical students have been trained, but only 520,000 of them provide Chinese medicine services. I don't know where the remaining 300,000 students are. Therefore, attaching equal importance to Chinese medicine and Western medicine is the foundation of "going global".

Second, cultural inheritance is the forerunner, and technology creates the future. If there is no cultural inheritance, technology cannot go global. It is necessary to make our culture accepted by foreigners. In fact, the health culture of Chinese medicine is very easy to accept, so Xi Jinping emphasized "strive to achieve the creative transformation and innovative development of Chinese medicine health culture". We must innovate our concept, model, service methods and service style, and innovate and develop our technology, talent education, cultural innovation and scientific research. Let them accept us, that is, cultural inheritance and cultural output should be the forerunner.

Third, standardization is the core. Now we have no standards but hundreds of schools. There are many varieties of traditional Chinese medicine. In particular, as President Li mentioned just now, we have no standards for planting, seeding, land, collecting and processing of codonopsis pilosula. In such a case, standardization is the core. Standardization means the common standards that can be repeatedly used within a certain scope or formulated according to the optimum tests and the most practical and potential problems. But now we do not have reusable standards. Standardization can be counted as a tool that can be used both by Western medicine and Chinese medicine.

Fourth, we should rationalize the system of management of Chinese medicine, which is the key. It is now in a chaotic state in that there are many administration authorities. Chinese medicine has five resources, which grow in three types of places. Those growing in water are administrated by water conservation authorities, those growing in the sea are administrated by the fishery bureau, but the issue of quality is administrated by the food and drug administration. Our entire management needs to be further improved.

Fifth, the protection of intellectual property is a guarantee and we must tighten control over it.

Qian Zhongzhi (Cheif Expert of Chinese Pharmacopoeia Commission)

I would like to share some of my experience. The first point is the problem. The core bottleneck is culture because Chinese medicine has cultural attributes. In addition to the big bottleneck of culture, there are also problems at the national level. International competitiveness of Chinese medicine is actually our weakness. It is difficult to develop this industry around the world. So, how to strengthen national competitiveness is actually a problem to be addressed.

Second, at the national level, resources are not optimally allocated. China is different from other countries because drugs are registered at the Food and Drug Administration, but Chinese medicines are registered at the Administration of Traditional Chinese Medicine. The internationalization of Chinese medicine has not yet a high strategic layout. I was one of the four members of the FHH. We wanted to make it an international standard in the field of Chinese medicine. But now we have no benefit at all. Only when it is included in the national strategy can it be organically coordinated, otherwise, the current status of enterprises cannot be supported.

What is missing at the research level? I cannot agree more with Mr. Li's idea, that is, that technology must go global. There are relatively few articles published internationally regarding Chinese medicine. Although the number of articles has increased in the past few years, only a few of them explain the efficacy. We should make key breakthroughs in science and technology. Only when science and technology achieve breakthroughs, can Chinese medicine be accepted by common people. We rarely see Chinese medicines in big pharmacies, but they are sold only in supermarkets, grocery stores and even Chinese restaurants. Everyone recognizes only vitamins they are used to taking, so research must take the lead.

In addition, there is not enough research in terms of the policy. We can see trees only, but not the forest, including those organized by the Administration of Traditional Chinese Medicine, such as registration in the EU and the USA. In the world, we must see the "veins". It has already been clarified in the *Dietary Supplement Health and Education Act* which was promulgated in 1994, and then there are the principles of the FDA in 1996, followed by the registration feedback of herbal medicines in Europe and natural medicines in Canada. This should be a good opportunity for us, but we lack a macroscopic view of this issue and even raise an objection. At the international level, there is a good opportunity for Chinese medicine because ours are treated as drugs by them. Chinese medicine needs to be recognized, and our research on policies should view the world at a high level.

Also, enterprises are faced with so much pressure, but support by our State is limited to only the economic field. The work we have done in the past is actually to lay the foundation for enterprises. Our drug pills are sold in foreign pharmacies. In Europe, the USA and Canada, particularly Health Canada, if drugs are sold in pharmacies, this can reduce the burden on our companies. When they go to register, there are many preferences, now we have done a lot of work aim at the Ministry of Health of Canada. So these core issues should be solved.

Shen Yuandong (Vice Chairman of the Technical Committee on Traditional Chinese Medicine of the International Organization for Standardization)

I would like to directly answer the questions raised in this forum because I have had some personal experience on the front line of formulating international standards, international standardization and the internationalization of Chinese medicine.

First of all, regarding the challenges faced by the internationalization of Chinese medicine, some experts have already talked about this topic. The challenges can probably be divided into six aspects. First, differences between Chinese and Western cultures affect the internationalization of Chinese medicine because Chinese medicine originates from Chinese traditional culture. Second, there are differences between the theoretical system of Chinese medicine and the modern medical system. Third, differences exist in the national health management systems and relevant laws and regulations of different countries. Fourth, the economic interests of countries and groups. Our committee has more than 30 member countries, each of which needs to safeguard their own interests. Different business groups and pharmaceutical enterprises in member countries have different interests. As a result, this becomes a focal point of contradiction. Fifth, the quality and safety of Chinese medicine itself, which is a problem we cannot shy away from. Challenges to the internationalization of Chinese medicine are not totally international issues. In fact, we have our own problems, such as pesticide residues and the heavy metal content of Chinese herbal medicines, which are the reasons for trade barriers in the West and a very important obstacle to the internationalization of Chinese medicine. Sixth, we lack globally uniform quality and safety standards. As mentioned by leaders just now, I can't agree with you more because I have a deep understanding of the issue.

Second, formulating international standards for Chinese medicine is the basis for promoting the internationalization and innovation of Chinese medicine. There is a slogan. What is the common language in the world? It is international standards. Regardless of your culture or industry, one thing is the same all over the world. International standards are regarded as a common language and the basis for promoting the internationalization of Chinese medicine. Our committee currently has more than 30 member states. You may imagine that our developing countries attach importance to traditional medicine. In fact, most of them are developed countries. This can prove the global influence of Chinese medicine. Twenty-three standards have been published so far. TC29 is very famous in the entire ISO system because the technical committee has developed the fastest among all of the ISO technical committees. At present, 48 standards are being prepared. Among standards currently released, China is totally dominant and has the final say. More than 86% of the standards were proposed by Chinese experts. This is the Chinese program. Now TC249 has seven working groups covering the entire Chinese medicine industry. The current situation of the international standardization of Chinese medicine is very good. The international organizations, such as the World Federation of Acupuncture-Moxibustion Societies, the China Association of Acupuncture-Moxibustion and the WHO, introduced by President Liu just now, are formulating international standards. Due to the time limit, I will focus only on the three problems and three countermeasures that internationalization and standardization face.

China is a big country of Chinese medicine, but until now we are not a strong country in terms of international standards of Chinese medicine. In this regard, we have not formed an authoritative team of experts. In the international arena, although we have a dominant quantity, we lack authority. This should be viewed both domestically and internationally. The issue of internationalization mainly has three aspects, two domestic ones and one international one: first, talent teams; second, system and mechanism because the existing international system and mechanism for the internationalization of Chinese medicine cannot keep up with the needs of international development; third, international and overseas. The internationalization of Chinese medicine is not only a matter for China. The problem reflected on this platform is that countries have extremely imbalanced developments in the internationalization of Chinese medicine. Some countries have already enacted laws and Chinese medicine has entered the national medical service system, but most countries have no legislation. According to member countries joining our platform, some countries, such as Japan, South Korea, Germany, and the United States, send teams of 20 or 30 experts, but other countries had sent only one person or even a couple to attend our meetings. This situation reflects the fact that the internationalization of Chinese medicine still has a long way to go and its development is extremely imbalanced. These are problems that the internationalization of Chinese medicine is faced with.

Aiming at these three problems, mechanism, system and imbalanced development, I propose three strategies. First, regarding the talent teams, it is very important to adhere to cultural self-confidence and institutional self-confidence and strengthen the training of international talents in Chinese medicine. International talents must have the background of Chinese medicine, become experts of internationalizing Chinese medicine, speak a foreign language and have knowledge of standardization, so we need interdisciplinary talents. Further, how to attract excellent talents to work on this platform and contribute to internationalization and standardization requires the evaluation and assessment of professional talents and the standards of the promotion system. International standardization is not as attractive as the National Natural Science Foundation. However, it is indeed very important for the formulation of international standards for Chinese medicine. Just as was pointed out by Mr. Yan, it is important to have a feeling for our Chinese people's scientific and cultural beliefs and confidence in institutions and policies.

Second, the mechanism and system of innovation is very important. The topic of today's forum is also innovation. Therefore, we must have the mechanism and system of innovation on the international platform of Chinese medicine. We must optimize the combination of resources in the top design, have the synergy and organize efficient operating and incentive mechanisms. This is also a strategy.

Third, we must support the development of Chinese medicine overseas, which means overseas organizations, associations of Chinese medicine or some schools and institutions. In the process of supporting overseas development, the spread of the culture of Chinese medicine can play a very important role in the recognition and understanding of traditional Chinese medicine. I had no idea of this before, but after formulating international standards of Chinese medicine, I realized that the spread of the culture of Chinese medicine could greatly drive the international development of Chinese medicine. Like railroad tracks, if international trains drive to the world, the tracks must be laid first. In addition, the legal status of Chinese medicine in the international arena is also very important. One is cultural communication and the other is legislation and a legal status for Chinese medicine. If no breakthroughs are made, we cannot become officially recognized. For the Chinese program and standards "going global", cultural exchanges and communication are mainly civilian, but legislation should be driven by the government.

Moreover, we also did some research in Shanghai on how to support the development of Chinese medicine overseas. I once gave advice to some ministers to build a foundation for supporting the development of Chinese medicine overseas. Later, when Director Wang paid a visit, I talked about this idea. Now that foundation has been established and has begun to operate this year for supporting countries and groups who have a weak foundation but favor Chinese medicine and have taken part in the activities of its internationalization for many years. Likewise, we hope that more enterprises can join the internationalization and standardization platform of Chinese medicine. Thank you.

Yan Haifeng (Dean, Professor and Doctoral Supervisor of the Business School of East China University of Science and Technology)

I am doing business research and have less contact with this industry. I have learned a lot. As a layman, I would like to share some of my points.

First, one of my perceptions, we talk about Chinese medicine, but from the perspective of studying enterprises, the Chinese medical science and Chinese medicine are two different things in the process of internationalization. Chinese medical science provides services, but Chinese medicine is cargo. They had better be clearly distinguished. Due to scientism and culture in Western countries, everything must be clearly divided with a boundary and a definition. This is not good for "going global".

The second perception, the problem of the Chinese medicine industry, lies neither in enterprises, nor is it a matter of a business model, or even a technical issue. It is a problem of the entire industry. I think the strategic should be more clear. If an industry's positioning is unclear, its direction of development is usually quite blurry.

The third perception, there are few large enterprises in this industry, as they are generally small and medium-sized. It means that this industry is not mature and its degree of industrial concentration is not high. If competing internationally, this industry will face many difficulties because its opponent is Western medicine.

The fourth perception, internationalization needs a strong financial guarantee. Without a certain degree of industrial concentration, it is difficult to achieve this goal. If the whole industry does not work together, it will cost a lot of money. Medicine has high costs all over the world, with a high degree of concentration. If the industrial concentration is not high, there may be problems.

The fifth perception, I would like to talk about a few small suggestions from the perspective of the basic path and mode of enterprise internationalization. First, there are three barriers to the internationalization of an enterprise, namely the market, which needs money and has competition, then the institutional barrier and the cultural barrier. Let's set aside for the moment the national economic interests; in my opinion, the fact that an enterprise makes profits is very important. It cannot be sustainable without making profits. An industry must have profits. Even if it fails to achieve it now, there must be profit-making in the future, otherwise, it is meaningless for us to go global. Institutional constraints and cultural constraints, or institutional barriers and cultural barriers, are higher for the Chinese medicine industry than for other general products and services because it has cultural characteristics different from other countries. It is closely related to human life and health, so the regulations of all countries must be strict. That is why it is different from general cargoes, articles and services. These two factors must be taken seriously into consideration in the process of the internationalization of enterprises in the Chinese medicine industry. The two dimensions can be divided into four categories.

The first category is countries with a close cultural connection to China and low regulatory barriers, which can be given priority if the market is not highlighted now. The second category is those with low regulatory barriers but a remote cultural distance, like Africa, which can be considered because it is less difficult. The third category is countries with high regulatory barriers but a close cultural distance, such as Japan and South Korea, which can also be considered. Singapore has high regulatory barriers because it is relatively developed, but its cultural distance is close. The last category is those with high regulatory barriers and a remote cultural distance. Although they might be meaningful, from the perspective of profitability and sustainable development, the reality must be considered. This is the first suggestion. At this point, you cannot get in if the institutional barriers are high because you do not have enough legitimacy. It is also difficult if the cultural distance is remote with a low degree of acceptance because medicine is different from anything else.

Then, the entry mode. From our perspective, there are two entry modes for this industry, partnership or doing it yourself by sole proprietorship and direct investment. Because of high cultural barriers and some institutional barriers, it is important for enterprises to enter in the form of a joint venture. Also, the so-called breakthrough in point. Acupuncture is actually a good breakthrough. You must be able to achieve a breakthrough at a certain point. In this case, it will be fruitful after accumulation to a certain extent, such as Compound Danshen Dripping Pills. It will have an explosive effect in the end. We need to make preparations for the long term. There should be such a point eventually.

Third, the internationalization of Chinese medicine. Mr. Liu Baoyan also mentioned this. Acupuncture can drive Chinese medical science and Chinese medicine. It is the feature of this industry. An important point for the Chinese medicine industry is localization, which is necessary for entering any market to break through institutional and cultural barriers.

There is another suggestion, talent training is needed. We do not have enough talents. One of my relatives began to learn about Chinese medicine, but he ended up giving up. There must be many overseas students wanting to learn Chinese medicine, and we should have many talents.

The last suggestion is that we can learn from the channel of the Confucius Institute. It must be elevated to an important national strategy and a joint action of the industry truly reflecting China's original intellectual property rights and national characteristics under the Belt and Road Initiative. If it is elevated to a national strategy,we can adopt the practice of establishing the Confucius Institute all over the world. The Confucius Institute has been criticized for not being specialized , but Chinese medicine is at least one specialization and can benefit local people. In this way, the speed of internationalization would be faster.

Xiong Dajing (Professor and Doctoral Supervisor of Chengdu University of TCM)

First of all, I would like to thank the six entrepreneurs and leaders for their efforts and support regarding the internationalization of Chinese medicine. Mr. Pei from Tasly, I cannot agree with him more. It is very frustrating to apply for a new Chinese medicine.

For example, I had an approval file from the National Medical Products Administration for clinical trials of drugs in 2005, which "agrees with the clinical trial for this product" and "limits the clinical application of this product to no more than seven days". The applicant conducted Phase II and Phase III clinical trials according to the pre-clinical requirements of the National Medical Products Administration, but finally, they were rejected. Why? There were several ridiculous reasons. I wondered if it was the decision of a layman. His reasons were that "there is no design for stratification and classification based on the types of perennial and seasonal allergens" and "there is no adequate consideration to different allergens and different degrees of contact allergens, which has a significant impact on the severity of clinical signs and symptoms. The choice of the control drug was unreasonable. The course of treatment prescribed in the original standard of the control drug Xinqin Granules was 20 days, while the clinical trial only took 7 days".

As is known to us, the 21st century is a century of allergic diseases. Many diseases are related to allergies. Most diseases of respiratory tracts are related to allergic reactions, especially for children. Also because of the severe air pollution, the incidence of respiratory diseases, especially allergic rhinitis, is increasing. I have been engaged in the clinical practice of traditional Chinese medicine for 48 years. I have a deep understanding of Chinese medicine treatment for allergic rhinitis. Decades of clinical experience tell us that Chinese medicine is effective for curing allergic rhinitis and has an obvious curative effect on improving clinical symptoms. It is characterized by short duration, low cost and no side effects. It is a project worthy of clinical application. We have used this Chinese medicine to treat allergic rhinitis for more than 30 years, trained 5 doctors and 8 masters and published more than 10 papers. I have a doctoral student who studied this medicine and after graduation, the student joined the postdoctoral program of Professor Liu Baoyan. It is a traditional Chinese medicine with obvious clinical effects but without toxic side effects. And now we are still using this prescription clinically, it works very well, and patients give very good feedback.

I don't understand: for this new Chinese medicine that has been clinically applied for many years with definite curative effects, why are Chinese medicine practitioners required to do research on perennial and seasonal stratification and classification. This poses a very big problem for Chinese medicine practitioners. The following reasons are even more ridiculous. "There is no design for stratification and classification based on the types of perennial and seasonal allergens" and "there is no adequate consideration about different allergens and different degrees of contact allergens, which has a significant impact on the severity of clinical signs and symptoms". I consulted many Western medical experts. They answered that currently, no country in the world could do research in such a manner. No clinical hospital could distinguish between inhaling 1 pollen, 2 pollens, 10 pollens and 100 pollens. This research is impossible to carry out and quantify.

The second problem is that we have a misunderstanding of new Chinese medicine research: the symptoms of Chinese medicine must be linked to the diseases of Western medicine. Otherwise, the application for research will not be approved. Chinese medicinal cures by syndrome differentiation instead of diseases. I have a suggestion: can Chinese medicine study the symptoms only, without studying the diseases? For example, for allergic rhinitis, I only study the symptoms of allergic rhinitis, sneezing, runny nose, itchy nose, but without studying the disease. There are also drugs studying symptoms only in Western medicine. For example, ephedrine does not treat diseases but relieves symptoms, and painkillers only relieve pain. Chinese medicine can also follow this path. In the future, can the new drug research on Chinese medicine not be linked to Western medicine? For example, to treat a cough you have to combine bronchitis or pneumonia; in fact, it may be caused by other reasons. It is unnecessary to clarify whether it is bronchitis or asthma. It is just a symptom. I take this medicine, and then I will not cough and sneeze. New drug research must follow the laws of Chinese medicine. This is the first suggestion.

The second suggestion is that Chinese medicine cannot be judged according to the standards of Western medicine. As mentioned by an expert just now, some old Chinese medicine practitioners have decades of experience with lifelong efforts at practicing it. If the standards of Western medicine are followed, it is very likely that Chinese medicine will disappear in the future.

The third suggestion is whether catalogues of Chinese medicine can become our intellectual property rights, including catalogues of specialties and prescriptions. For example, Yupingfeng Granule famous in China was renamed Weiyi Granule by the Japanese, and Tongtian Oral Liquid was renamed Tiaoding Granule in Japan. If we have our catalogue and intellectual property rights, this situation would never occur again.

Qi Luguang (Professor and Doctoral Supervisor of Chengdu University of TCM)

I would like to talk about my understanding of the internationalization of Chinese medicine. The first issue is the international attractiveness. Since the Reform and Opening-up, I have been serving as a teacher of foreign students and teaching students and Western medicine teachers from all over the world for decades. I have taken students to check sick berths, hold clinics and teach them. The miracle of Chinese medicine allows them to feel the profoundness of Chinese medicine. They fall in love with this medical science. After returning to their home countries, they become physicians of Chinese medicine.

The second issue is the international influence. In the past two decades, I have had academic exchanges with well-known universities such as Harvard University, the University of Wisconsin, the University of Cambridge and King's

College and some in Germany. I had worked at Nanyang Technological University in Singapore and been invited to give lectures in Germany and Thailand. German experts of Western medicine came to Chengdu to discuss clinical treatment on many occasions. Finally, they decided to invite me and the Vice President of the German Medical Association and the President of the Association of Chinese Medicine to write the *Treatment for Diabetes by Chinese Medicine* . I wrote in Chinese and they translated it into German and English. This was the first monograph written jointly by Chinese and foreign medical experts. After publication, the book was popular in German and Singaporean medical circles. The *Treatment for Diabetes by Chinese Medicine* is currently the first book recommended on the official website of the German Chinese Society of Medicine. This book has been collected by 45 network platforms in 18 countries in Europe, America and Oceania, and 13 foreign libraries. It is also the textbook for the Master's Programs in Chinese medicine at University of Munich and two universities in Austria. This book is used to educate a large number of students of Western medicine abroad.

This book is a best-seller currently published in English and will be published in Chinese. After the publication of this book, we conducted the research project entitled "China-ASEAN Technology Exchange, Demonstration, Promotion and Application of Chinese Medicine for the Prevention and Treatment of Diabetes", which was a training class with the support from Ministry of Foreign Affairs, the Ministry of Education and the National Administration on Traditional Chinese Medicine. We enrolled leaders of ministries of health and students in many ASEAN countries and taught them by lectures and clinical practice. Finally, the China-ASEAN Education and Training Center settled in Chengdu University of TCM. What did we think of this training class? Well, there are some tensions between China and the Philippines at that time. We requested to launch this project. It was unexpected that the Ministry of Education, the Ministry of Foreign Affairs and the Ministry of Science and Technology would give us the greatest support. Leaders of the ministries of health and their students and many very good practitioners of Western medicine came to learn from us. At that time, it was only a small project, but as a result, the China-ASEAN Education and Training Center was established in our university and constantly attracted students from ASEAN countries, who keep in contact with us. Therefore, with the joint efforts of leaders, teachers and students of our universities, there are endless foreign students and we have many branches, too. (In November 2010, led by Professor Qi Luguang, head of the research team, the training class of "China-ASEAN Technology Exchange, Demonstration, Promotion and Application of Chinese Medicine for the Prevention and Treatment of Diabetes" was taught in Chengdu University of TCM with the support from Ministry of Science and Technology and the Ministry of Foreign Affairs. Xu Jie, Director of the Department of International Cooperation of the Ministry of Science and Technology, He Xiangqi, Head of the Regional Cooperation Division of the Department of Asian Affairs of the Ministry of Foreign Affairs, and Hu Gang, Deputy Head of the International Cooperation Division of the Department of Science and Technology of Sichuan Province attended the opening ceremony. Twenty-seven experts of Chinese and Western medicines from six ASEAN countries, including Indonesia, Singapore, Vietnam, Thailand, Malaysia and Brunei, participated in the training session. Professor Qi Luguang, the leader of this research project, taught them knowledge and techniques of the prevention of diabetes by means of Chinese medicine. He made a great contribution to medical technology exchanges and cooperation, to the international promotion of Chinese medicine and to enhancing the friendship between China and the ASEAN countries.)

The culture and ideas of Chinese medicine are being spread throughout the world, but without a carrier. American culture can be spread to China by Coca-Cola and McDonald's. However, Chinese culture lacks carriers. In my opinion, Chinese medicine going global lacks drugs as the carrier.

I have been engaged in clinical work for a long period of time. We should build our brand well. Our university (Chengdu University of TCM), founded 60 years ago, had 164 national research projects and 348 provincial-level projects that won two second prizes in the National Award for Progress in Science and Technology, 42 ministerial and provincial awards and 63 third prizes. We had the research funds of more than 80 million yuan, but only about ten preparations were transferred, the Shenkang Injection, the Sinusitis Oral Liquid and the Yiqing Capsule. In my thirties, I participated in the development of the Yiqing Capsule (Grade A Achievement Award of the Ministry of Health). All of them were good products with annual sales of over 100 million yuan and were transferred in the 1970s. Our research capabilities have improved day by day over several decades. Our research funds are increasing. But no research results can be transformed and transferred. The main reason is that the research period is too long with too many uncertainties. Therefore, factories are reluctant to invest in new drug research. There are many achievements in research institutes. I have obtained many award-winning achievements in recent years, but they cannot be transformed into finished products. This is an absolute waste. Why am I jumping into my speech today? I must emphasize this point. I hope that our country can open a green channel for prescriptions of old Chinese medicine practitioners that have worked for more than 40 years and are clinically effective and scientifically capable. I have been in the clinic for over 40 years. How many patients have I cured? Why is it possible that I have been asked to give lectures at Harvard University? Because I was studying the treatment of diabetes and the professor of the Diabetes Center at Harvard University came to the clinic with me. Originally, he planned to stay for a week and finally he followed me for half a year. During this period, he witnessed many cases that shocked him. For example, I once cured gangrene caused by diabetes. He said that he had patients with similar conditions. The result was amputation, hands were cut off, the left hand, the right hand, and then the right leg. He said that the patient was yelling every day when he changed medicine.

Chinese medicine is exceptionally great. There are still many good things in need of government support. Thank you.